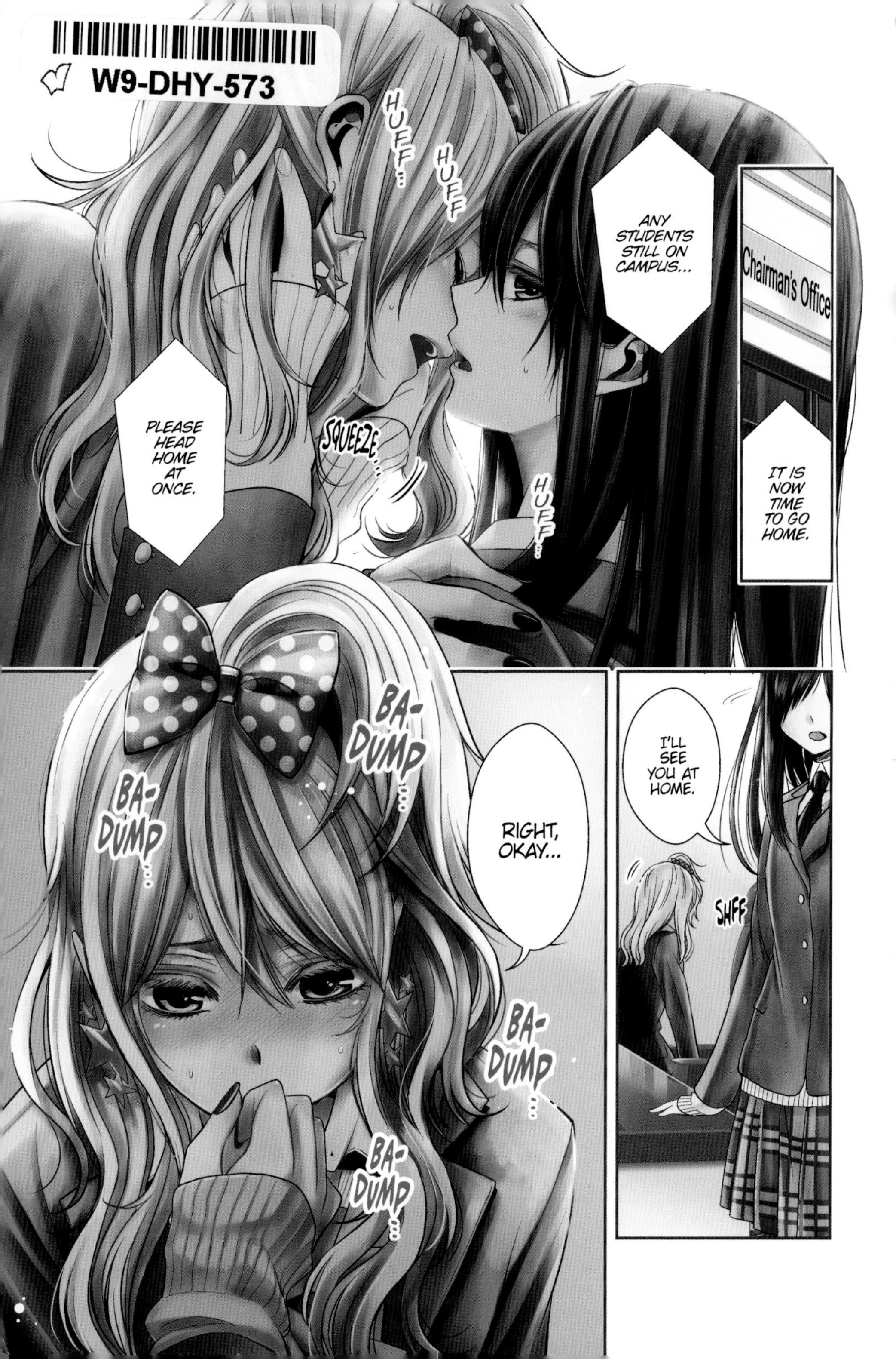
Chairman's Office
ANY STUDENTS STILL ON CAMPUS...
IT IS NOW TIME TO GO HOME.
HUFF...
HUFF
PLEASE HEAD HOME AT ONCE.
SQUEEZE...
HUFF...
I'LL SEE YOU AT HOME.
SHFF
RIGHT, OKAY...
BA-DUMP...
BA-DUMP...
BA-DUMP...
BA-DUMP...

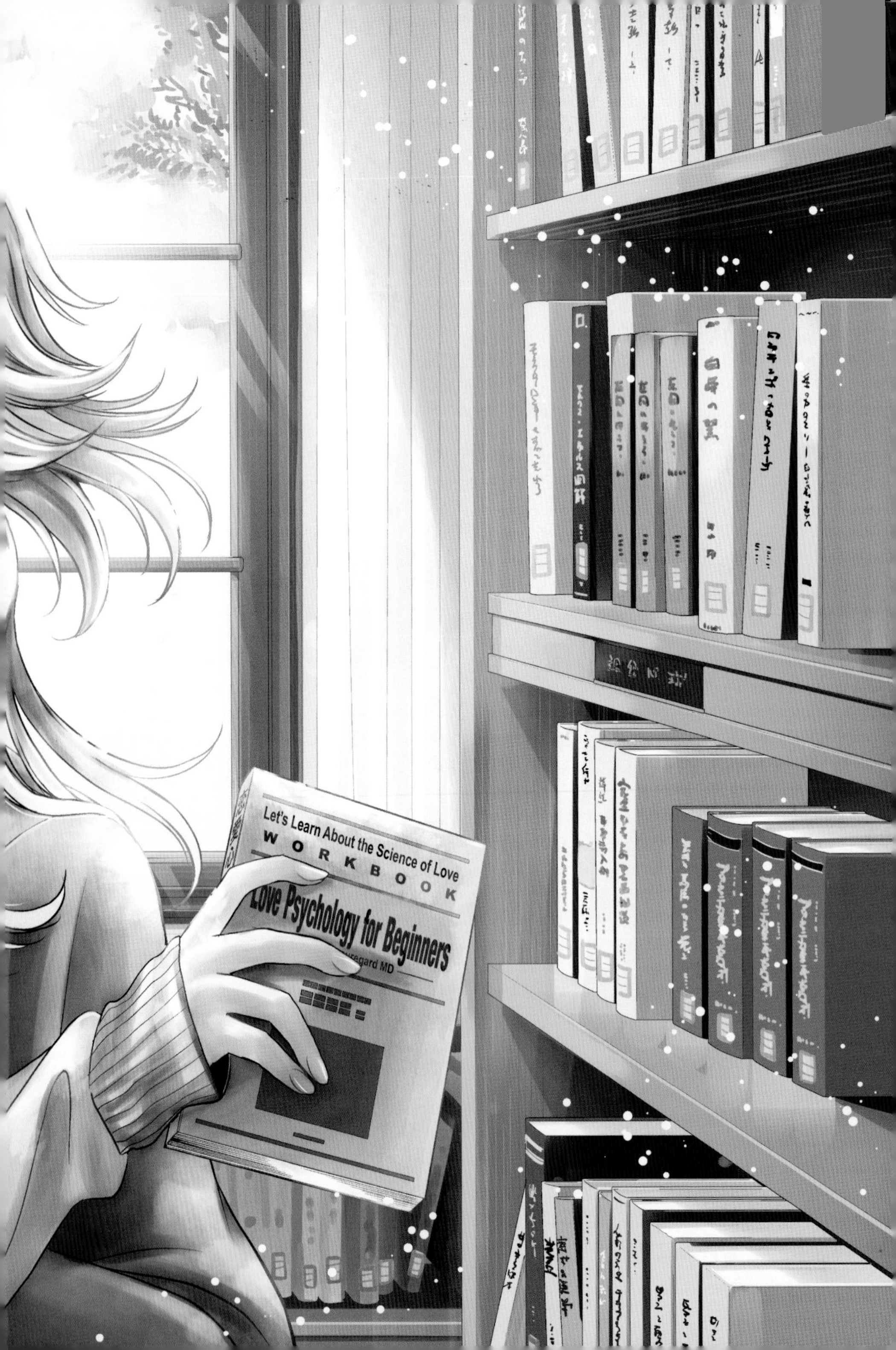
Let's Learn About the Science of Love
WORKBOOK
Love Psychology for Beginners

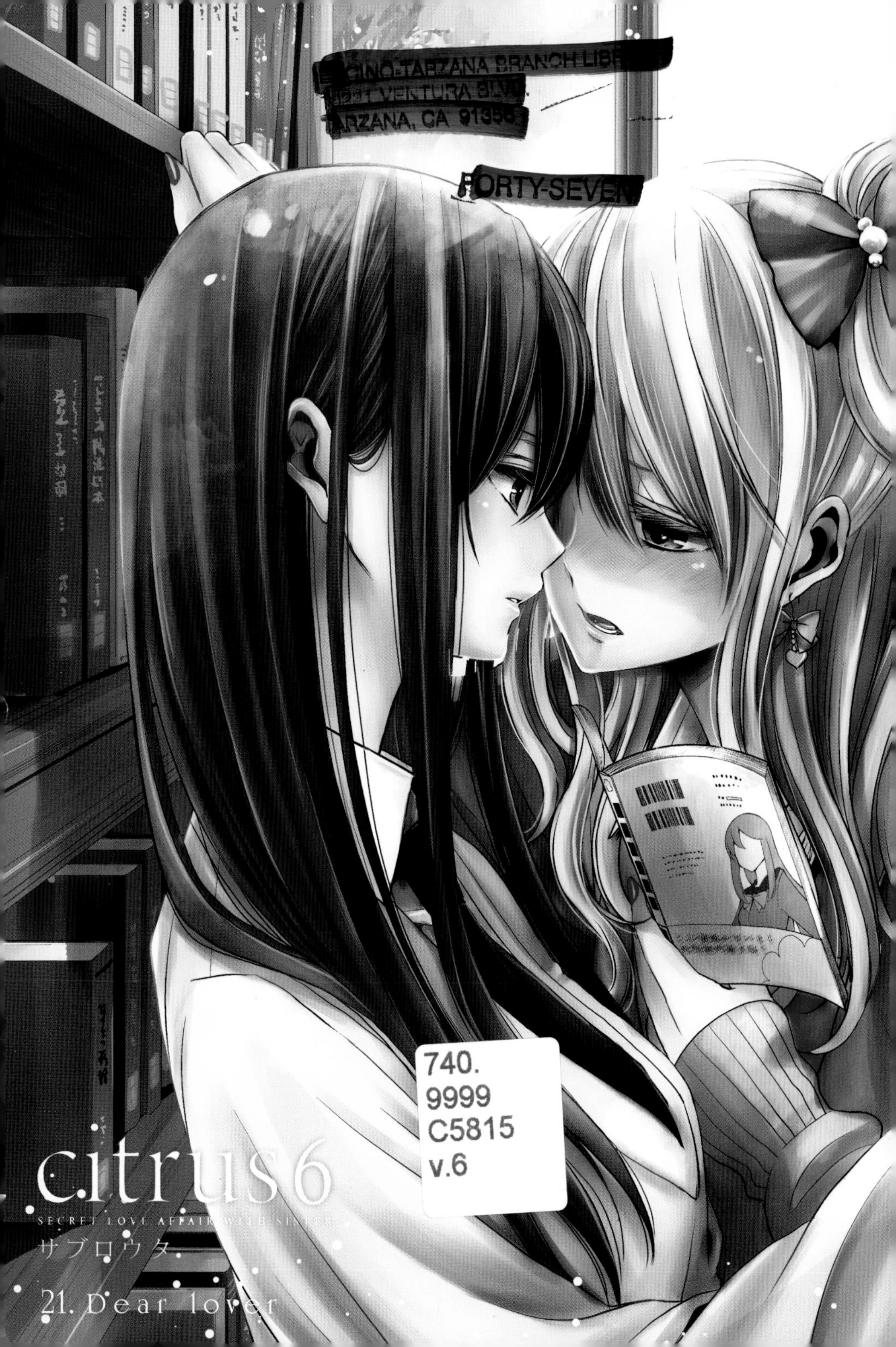
citrus6
SECRET LOVE AFFAIR WITH SISTER
サブロウタ
21. Dear lover

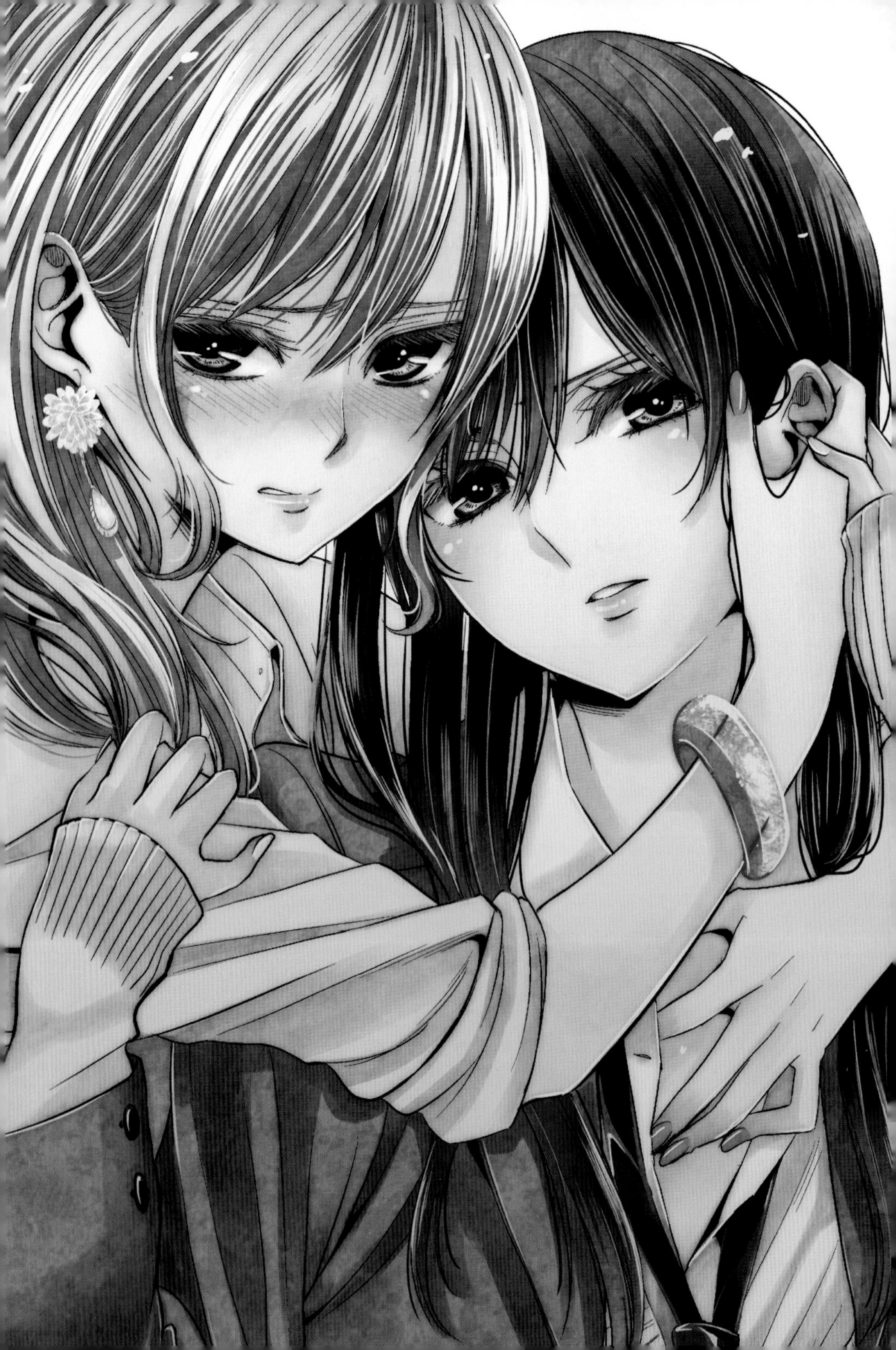

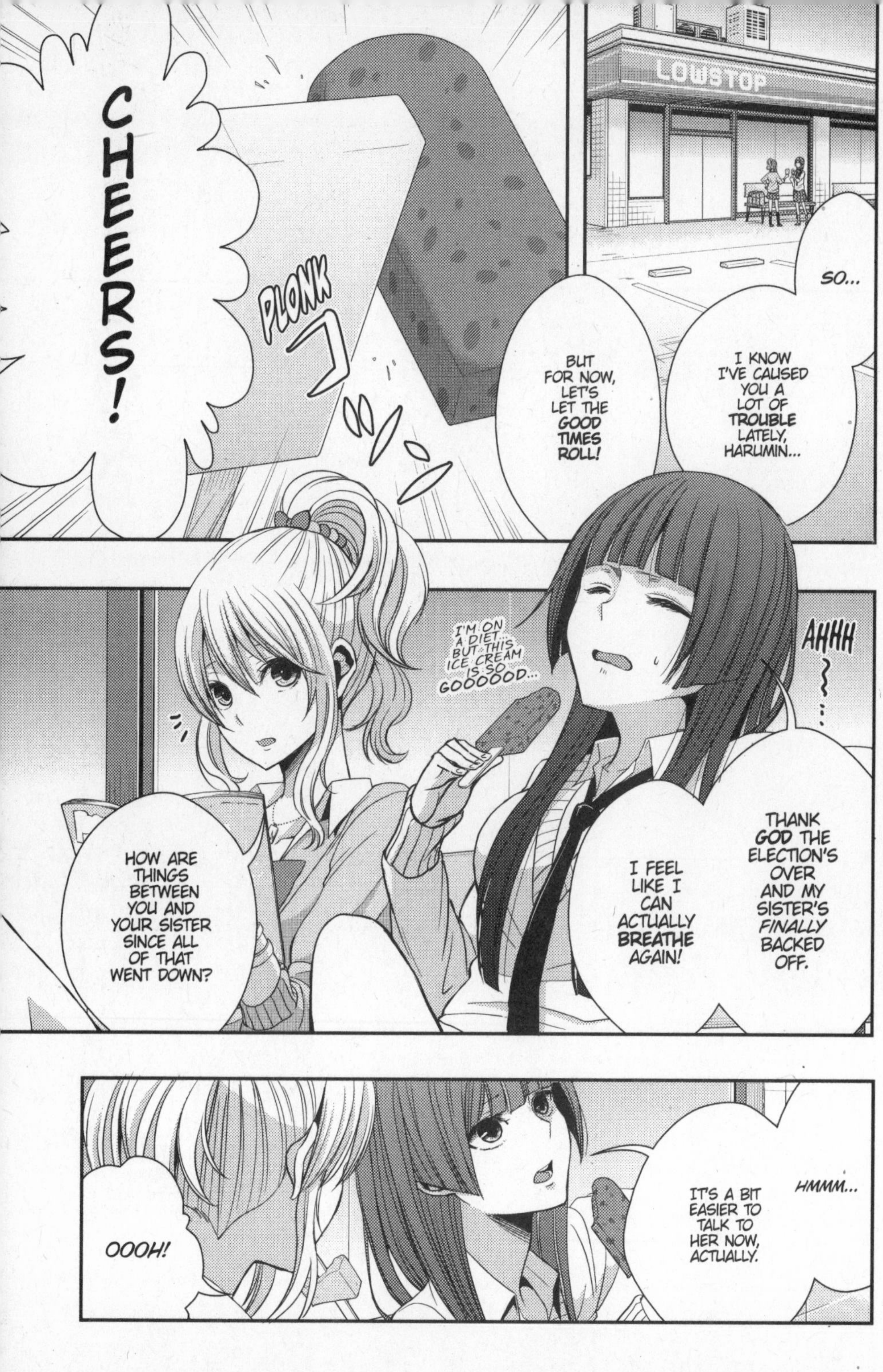
LOWSTOP
SO...
I KNOW I'VE CAUSED YOU A LOT OF TROUBLE LATELY, HARUMIN...
BUT FOR NOW, LET'S LET THE GOOD TIMES ROLL!
CHEERS!
PLONK
AHHH~...
THANK GOD THE ELECTION'S OVER AND MY SISTER'S FINALLY BACKED OFF.
I FEEL LIKE I CAN ACTUALLY BREATHE AGAIN!
I'M ON A DIET... BUT THIS ICE CREAM IS SO GOOOOOD...
HOW ARE THINGS BETWEEN YOU AND YOUR SISTER SINCE ALL OF THAT WENT DOWN?
HMMM...
IT'S A BIT EASIER TO TALK TO HER NOW, ACTUALLY.
OOOH!

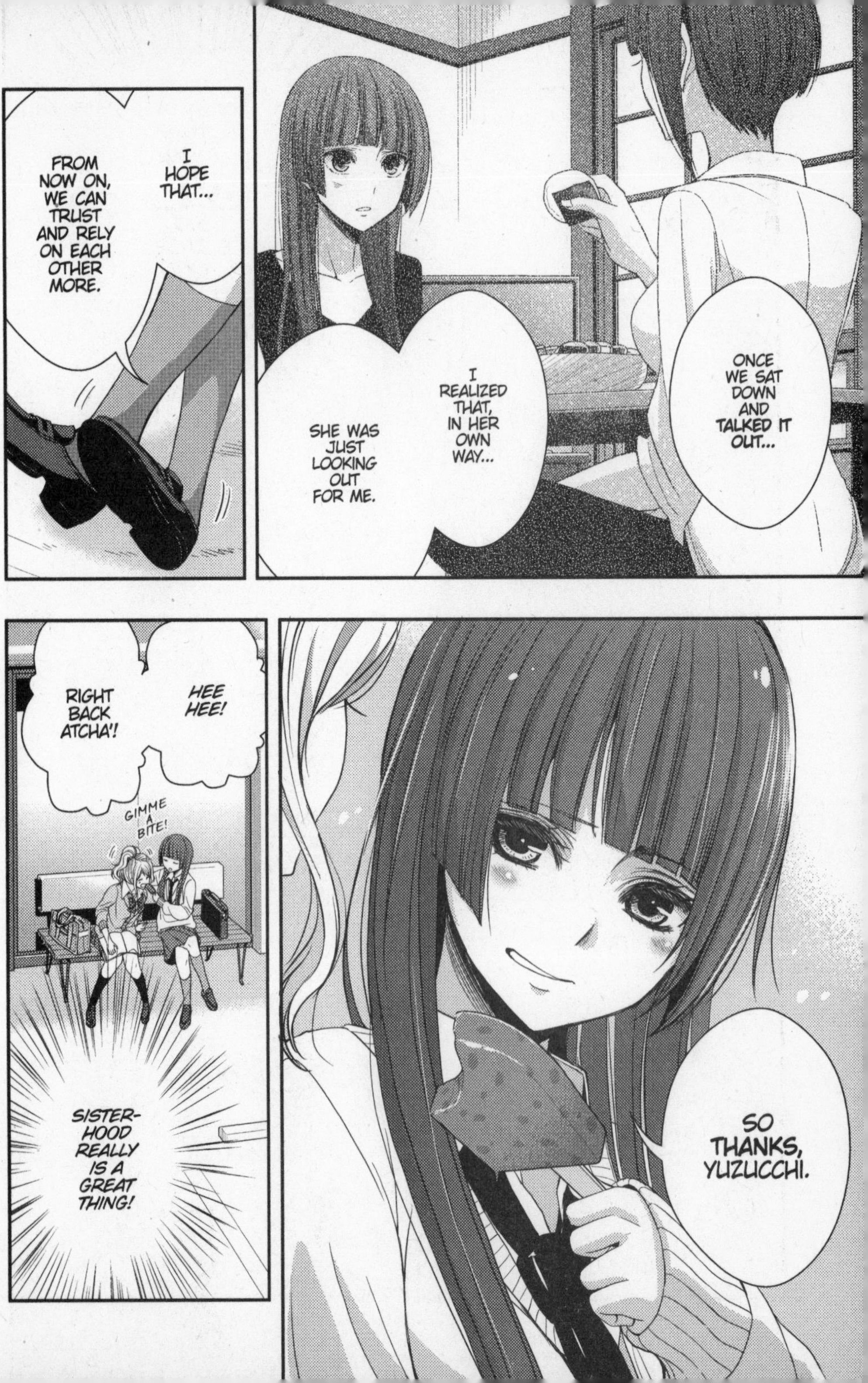
ONCE WE SAT DOWN AND TALKED IT OUT...
I REALIZED THAT, IN HER OWN WAY...
SHE WAS JUST LOOKING OUT FOR ME.
I HOPE THAT...
FROM NOW ON, WE CAN TRUST AND RELY ON EACH OTHER MORE.
SO THANKS, YUZUCCHI.
HEE HEE!
RIGHT BACK ATCHA'!
GIMME A BITE!
SISTER-HOOD REALLY IS A GREAT THING!

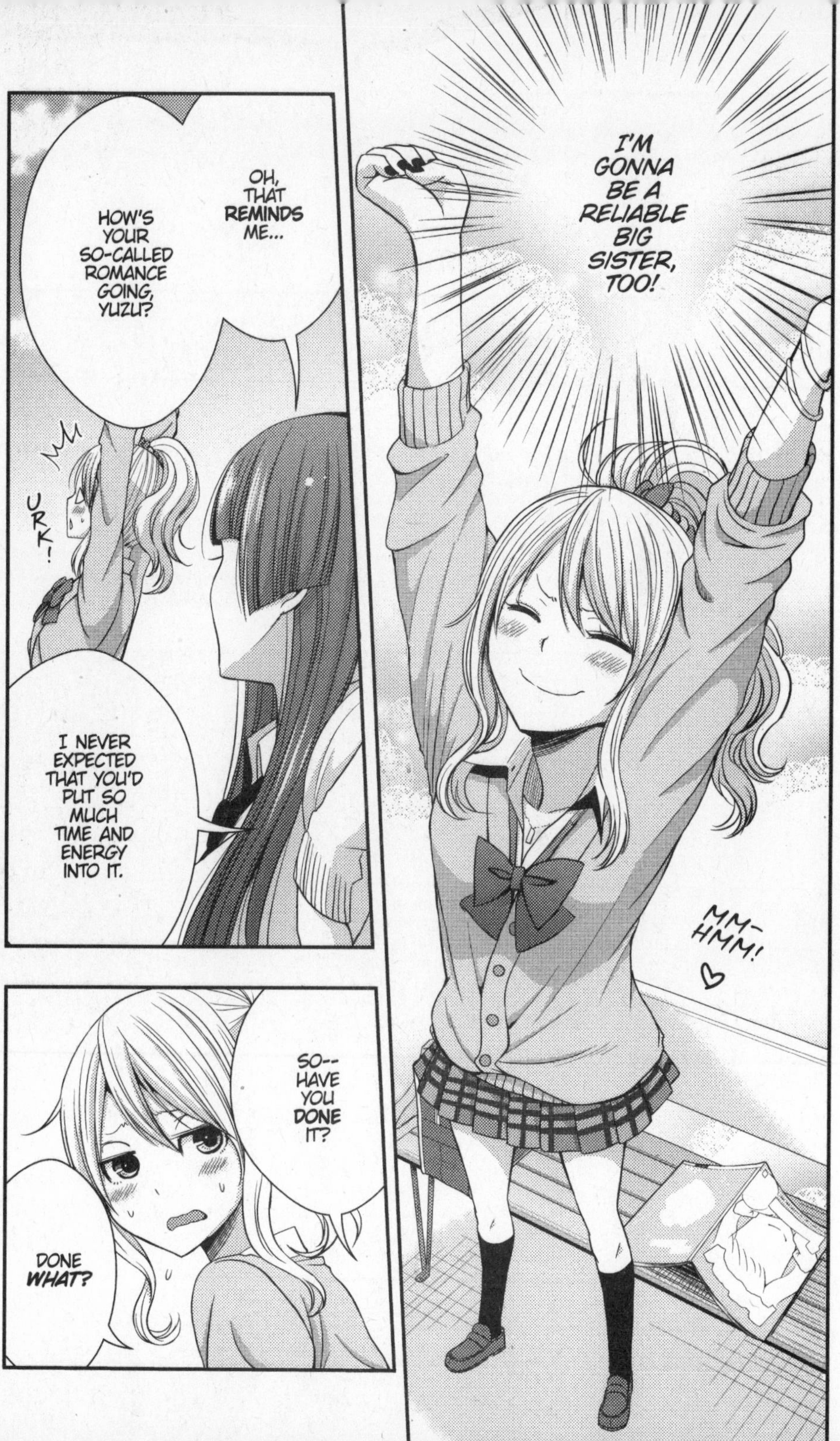
I'M GONNA BE A RELIABLE BIG SISTER, TOO!
MM-HMM!
OH, THAT REMINDS ME...
HOW'S YOUR SO-CALLED ROMANCE GOING, YUZU?
URK!
I NEVER EXPECTED THAT YOU'D PUT SO MUCH TIME AND ENERGY INTO IT.
SO-- HAVE YOU DONE IT?
DONE WHAT?

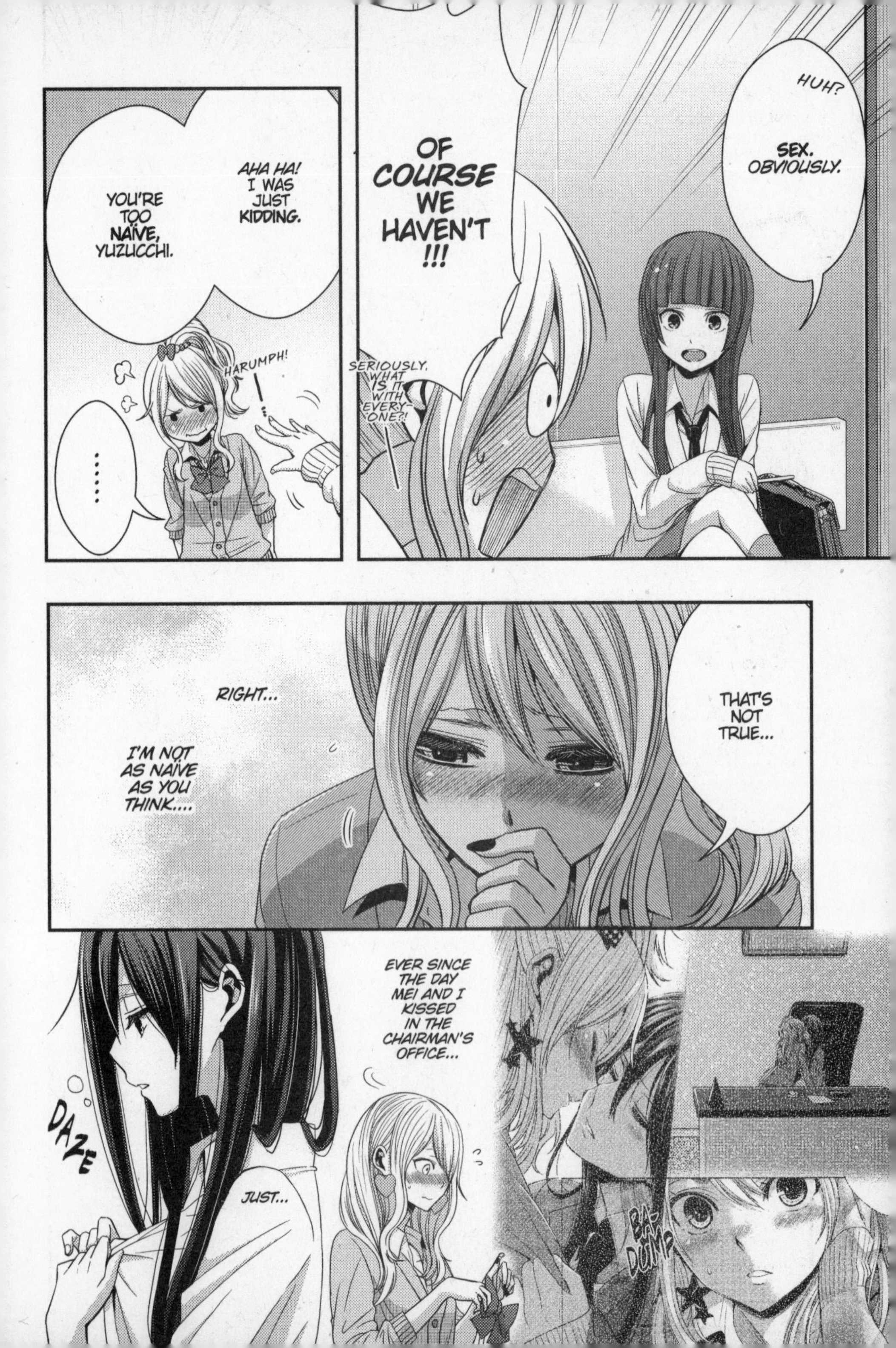
HUH?
SEX. OBVIOUSLY.
OF COURSE WE HAVEN'T !!!
SERIOUSLY, WHAT IS IT WITH EVERYONE?!
AHA HA! I WAS JUST KIDDING.
YOU'RE TOO NAÏVE, YUZUCCHI.
HARUMPH!
......
THAT'S NOT TRUE...
RIGHT...
I'M NOT AS NAÏVE AS YOU THINK....
EVER SINCE THE DAY MEI AND I KISSED IN THE CHAIRMAN'S OFFICE...
BA-BUMP
DAZE
JUST...

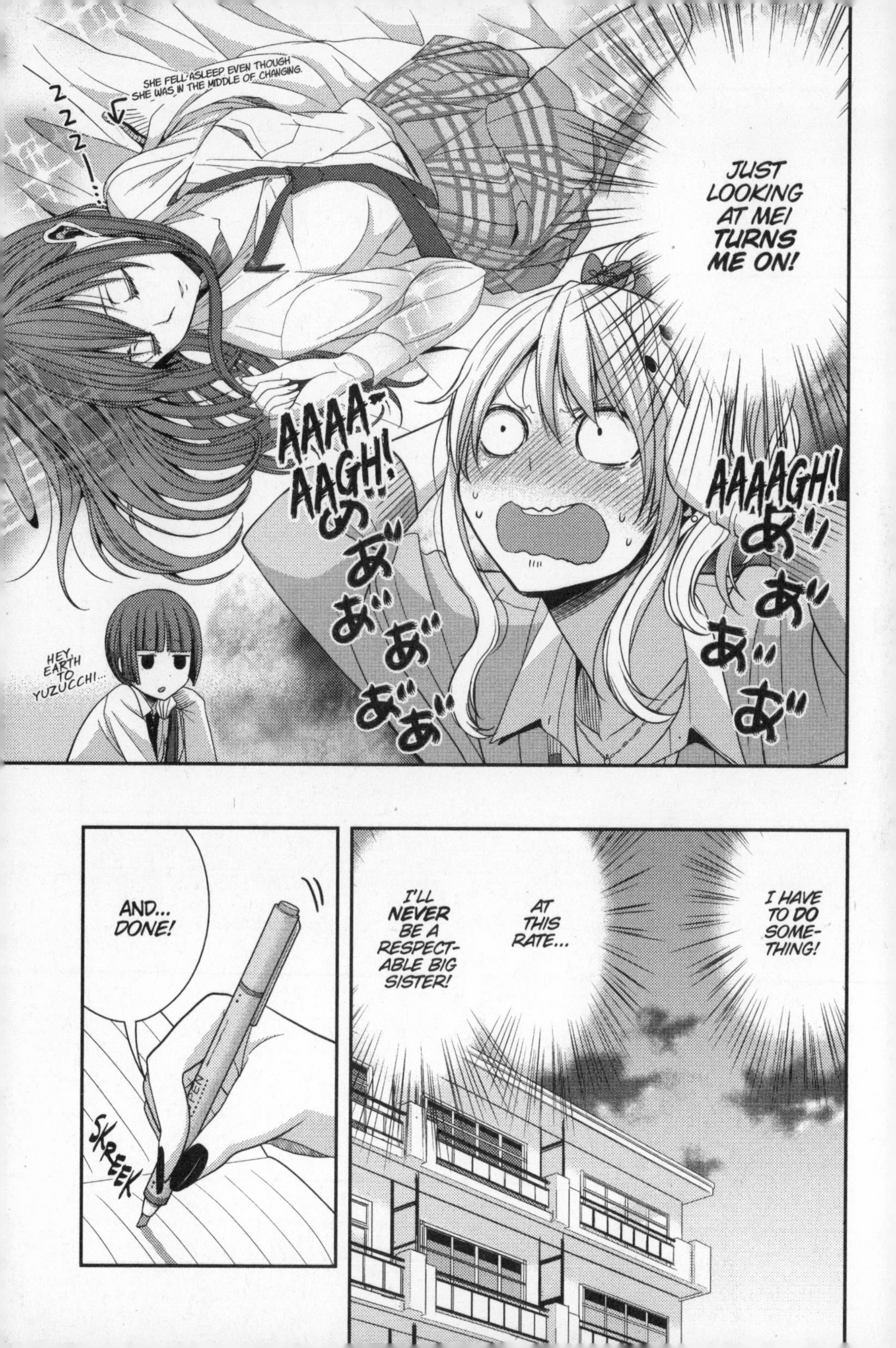
JUST LOOKING AT MEI TURNS ME ON!
AAAAGH!
SHE FELL ASLEEP EVEN THOUGH SHE WAS IN THE MIDDLE OF CHANGING.
Zzz...!
AAAA-AAGH!!
HEY, EARTH TO YUZUCCHI...
I HAVE TO DO SOME-THING!
AT THIS RATE...
I'LL NEVER BE A RESPECTABLE BIG SISTER!
AND... DONE!
SKREEK

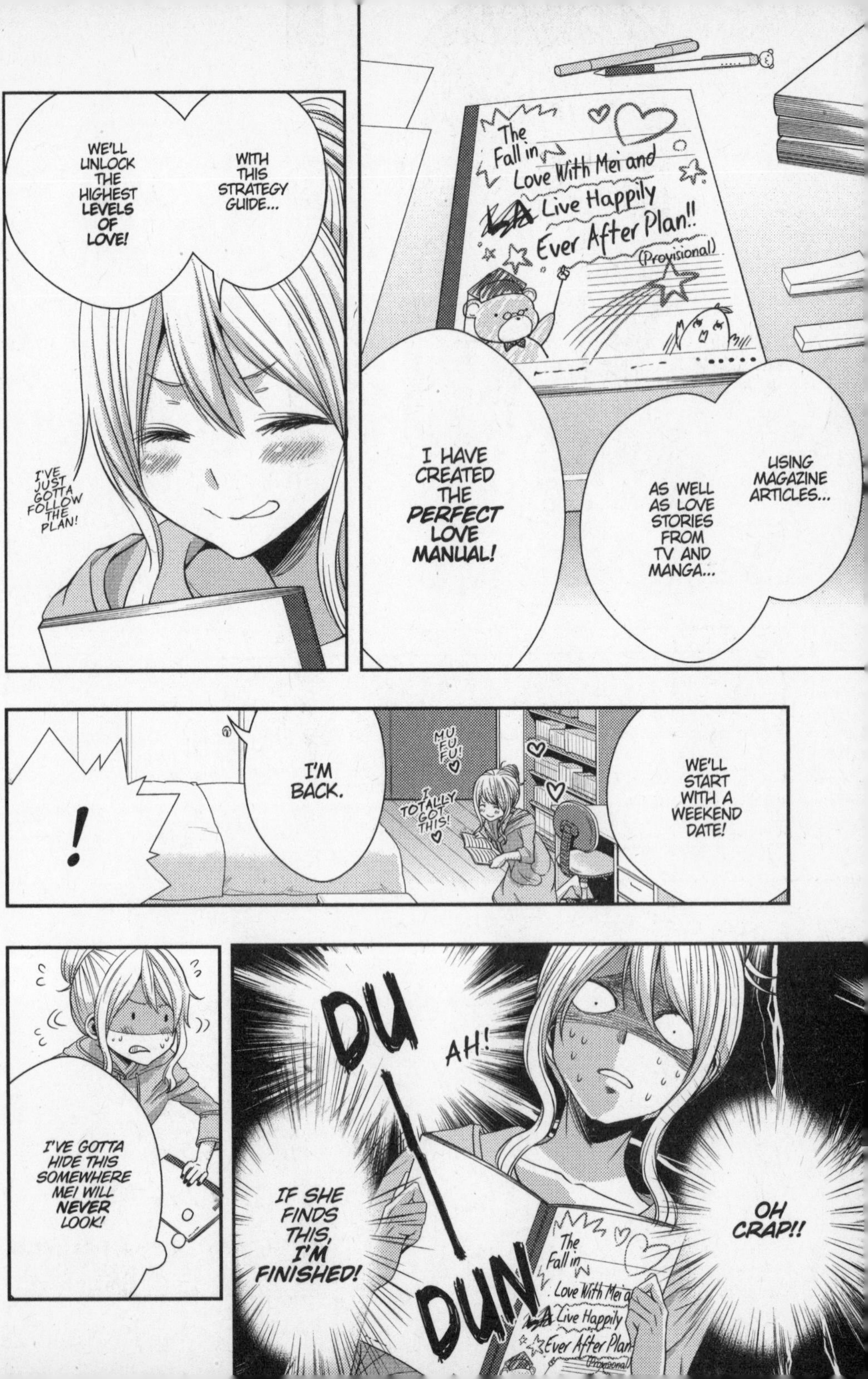
The Fall in Love With Mei and Live Happily Ever After Plan!! (Provisional)
USING MAGAZINE ARTICLES...
AS WELL AS LOVE STORIES FROM TV AND MANGA...
I HAVE CREATED THE PERFECT LOVE MANUAL!
WITH THIS STRATEGY GUIDE...
WE'LL UNLOCK THE HIGHEST LEVELS OF LOVE!
I'VE JUST GOTTA FOLLOW THE PLAN!
WE'LL START WITH A WEEKEND DATE!
MU FU FU!
I TOTALLY GOT THIS!
I'M BACK.
!
OH CRAP!!
AH!
DU DUN
IF SHE FINDS THIS, I'M FINISHED!
The Fall in Love With Mei a Live Happily Ever After Plan
I'VE GOTTA HIDE THIS SOMEWHERE MEI WILL NEVER LOOK!

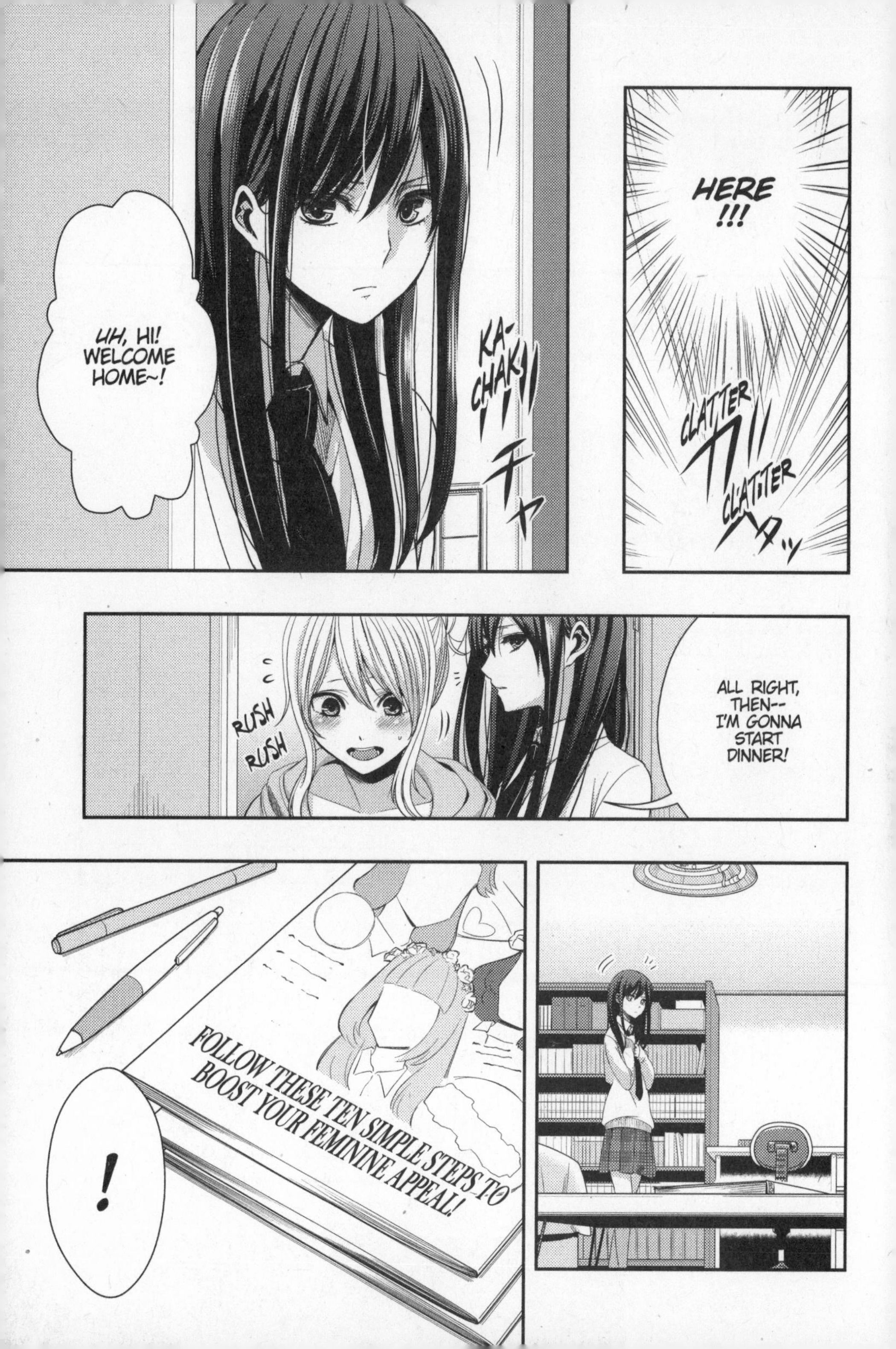
HERE !!!
CLATTER
カ
CLATTER
タッ
KA-CHAK
チャ
UH, HI! WELCOME HOME~!
ALL RIGHT, THEN-- I'M GONNA START DINNER!
RUSH
RUSH
FOLLOW THESE TEN SIMPLE STEPS TO BOOST YOUR FEMININE APPEAL!
!

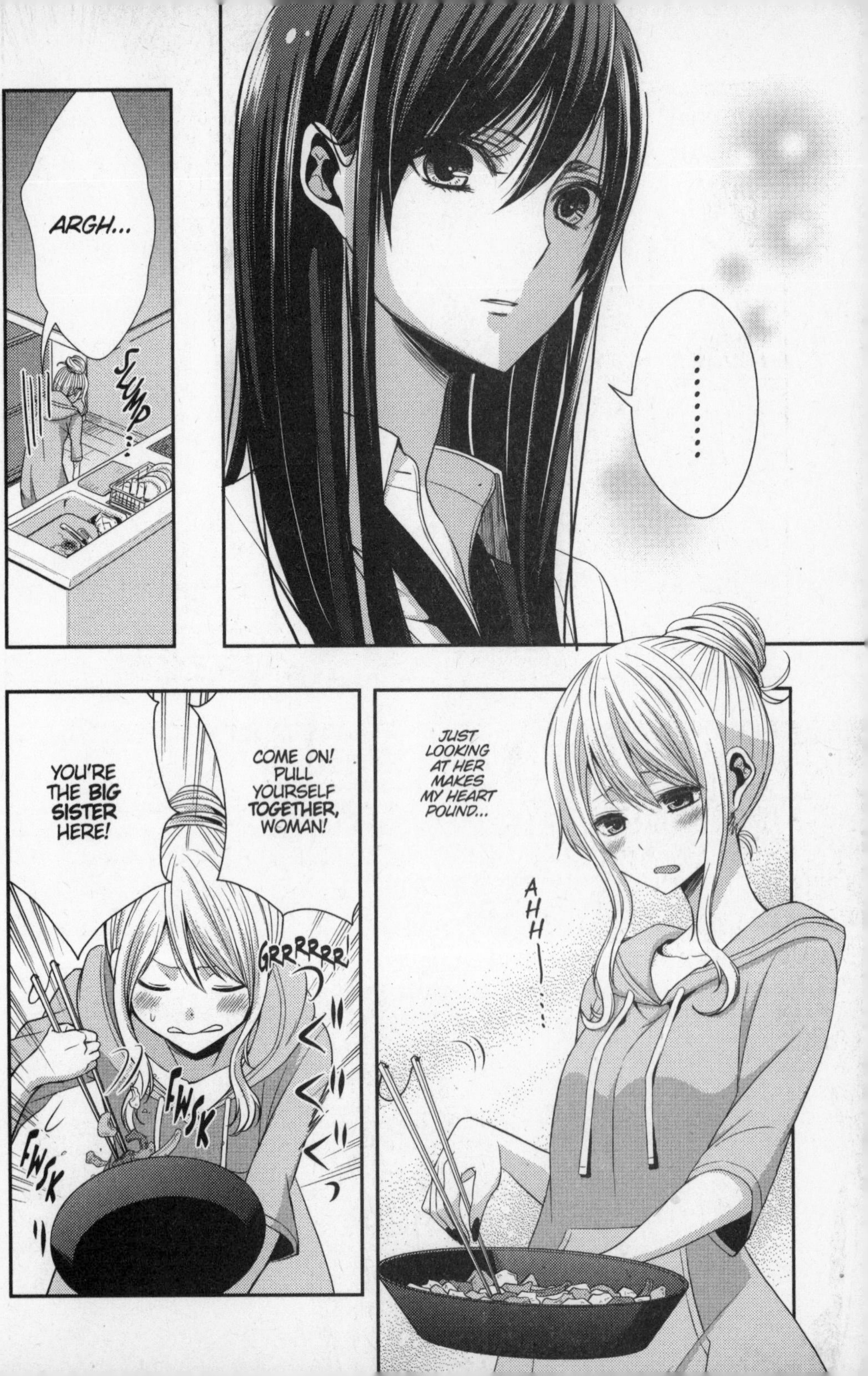
......
ARGH...
SLUMP...
JUST LOOKING AT HER MAKES MY HEART POUND...
AHH!...
COME ON! PULL YOURSELF TOGETHER, WOMAN!
YOU'RE THE BIG SISTER HERE!
GRRRRRR!
FWSK
FWSK

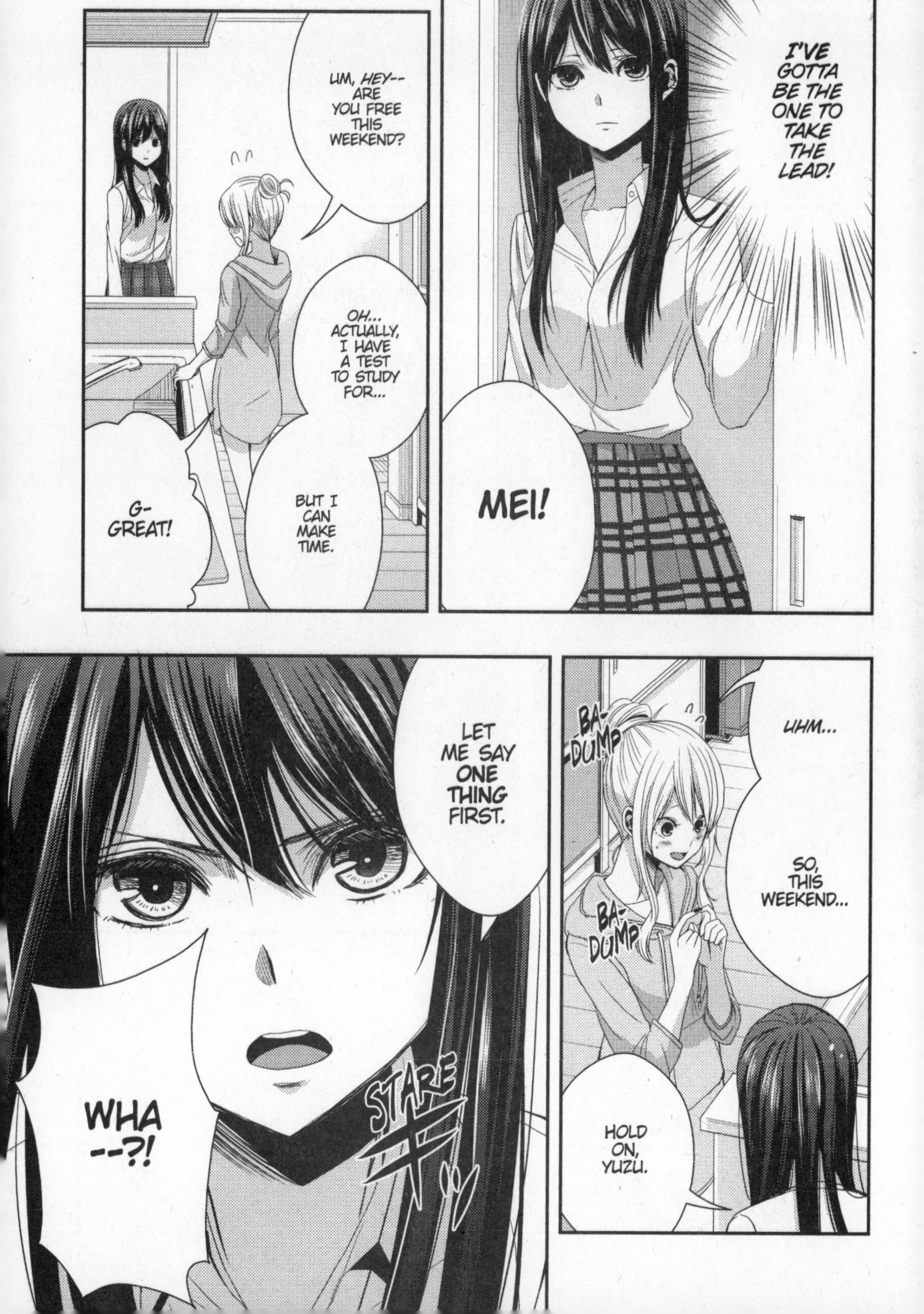
I'VE GOTTA BE THE ONE TO TAKE THE LEAD!
MEI!
UM, HEY-- ARE YOU FREE THIS WEEKEND?
OH... ACTUALLY, I HAVE A TEST TO STUDY FOR...
BUT I CAN MAKE TIME.
G-GREAT!
UHM...
BA-DUMP
SO, THIS WEEKEND...
BA-DUMP
HOLD ON, YUZU.
LET ME SAY ONE THING FIRST.
STARE
WHA--?!

OW!

DINNER'S BURNING.

SZZZZZ...

AAAAAAGH!

SWF

GULP...

SPSSH

THAT WASN'T LIKE YOU AT ALL.

ARE YOU NOT FEELING WELL?

SPSSH

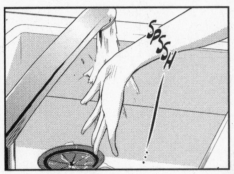

SHOVE

I-I-I-I-I'M FINE!!

I'M JUST HUNGRY! I'LL BE FINE ONCE I EAT!

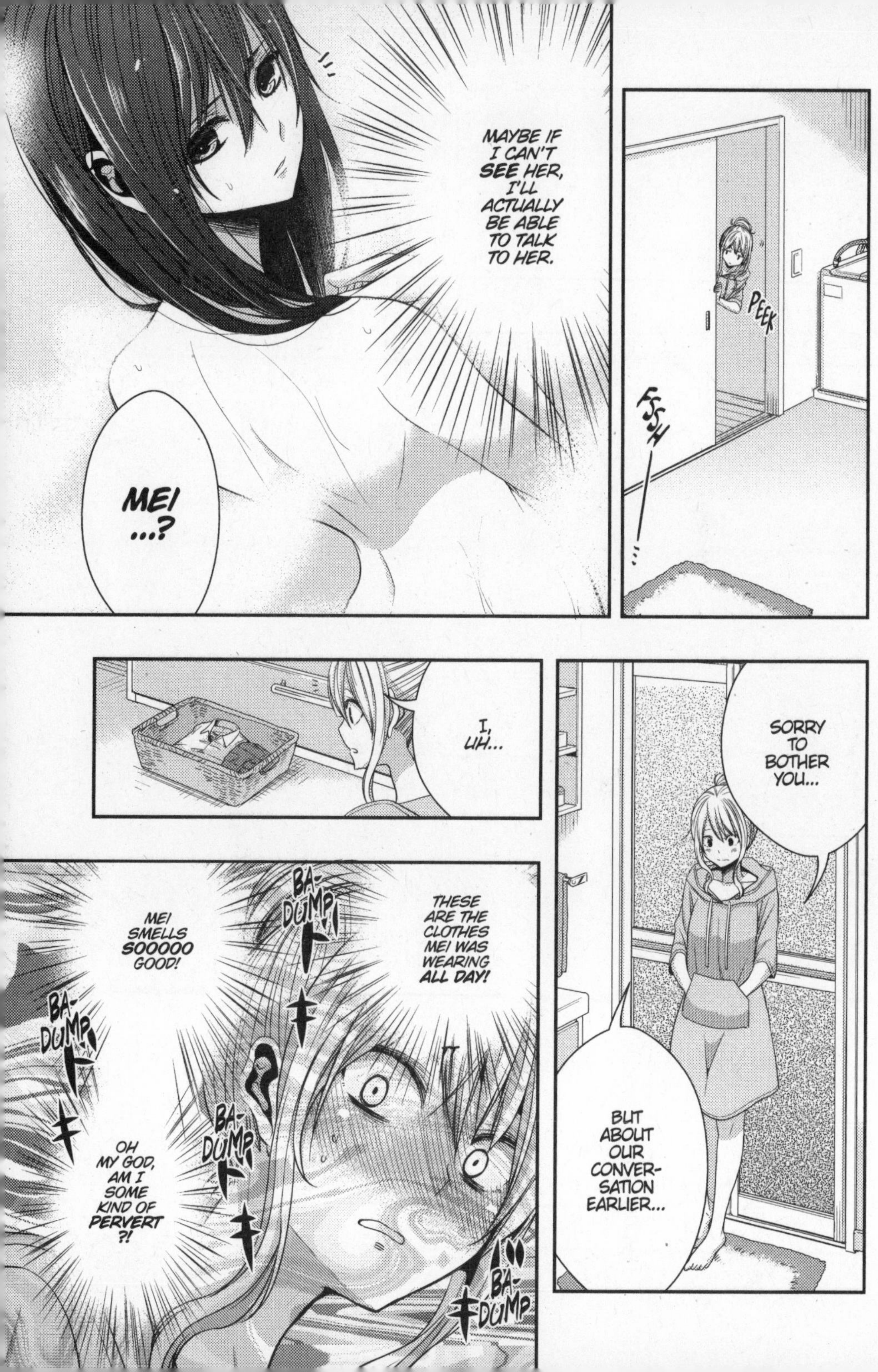
PEEK
FSSH...
MAYBE IF I CAN'T SEE HER, I'LL ACTUALLY BE ABLE TO TALK TO HER.
MEI ...?
SORRY TO BOTHER YOU...
BUT ABOUT OUR CONVER-SATION EARLIER...
I, UH...
BA-DUMP
THESE ARE THE CLOTHES MEI WAS WEARING ALL DAY!
MEI SMELLS SOOOOO GOOD!
BA-DUMP
BA-DUMP
OH MY GOD, AM I SOME KIND OF PERVERT ?!
BA-DUMP

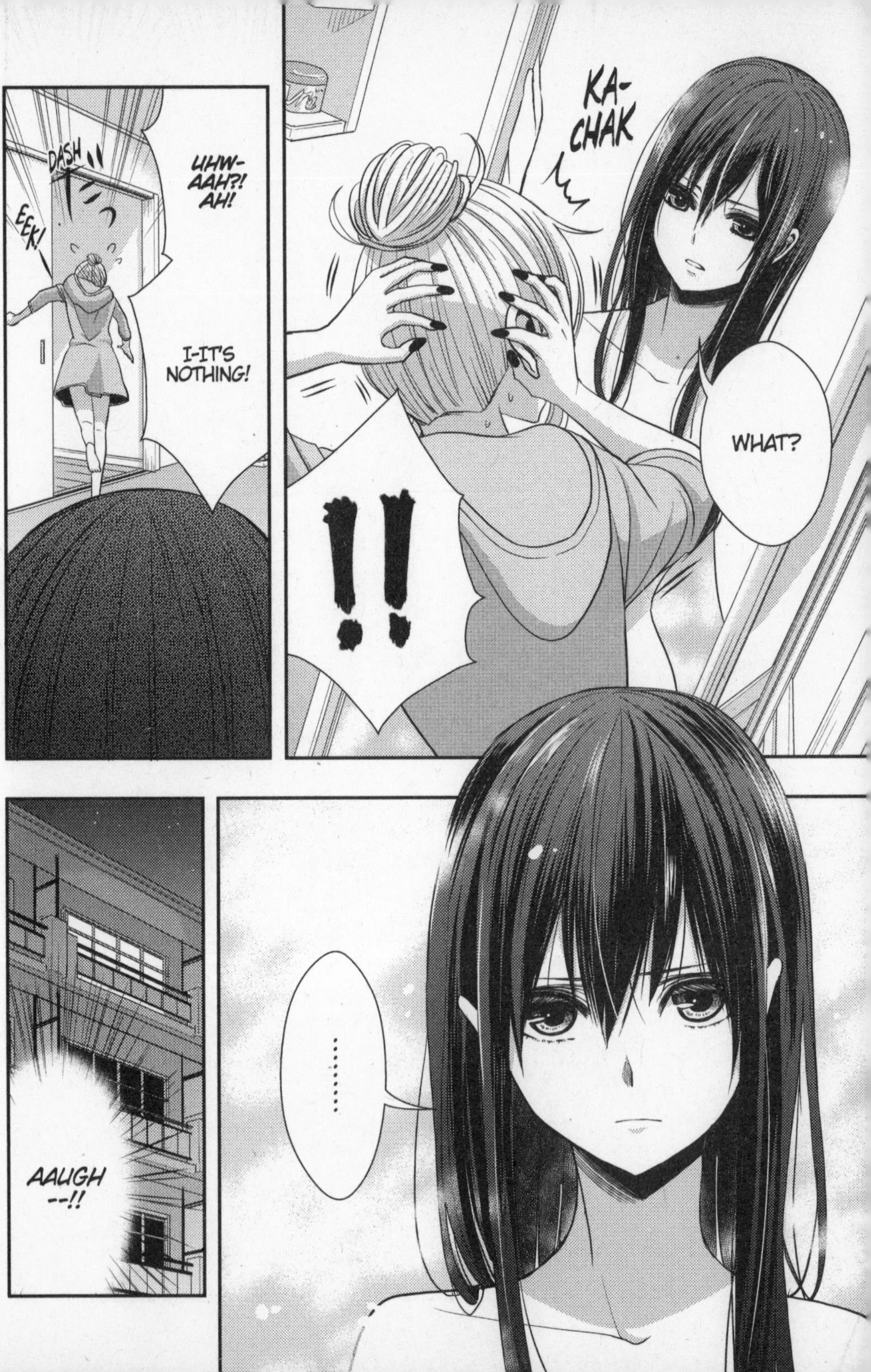
KA-CHAK
WHAT?
!!
DASH
EEK!
UHW-AAH?! AH!
I-IT'S NOTHING!
......
AAUGH--!!

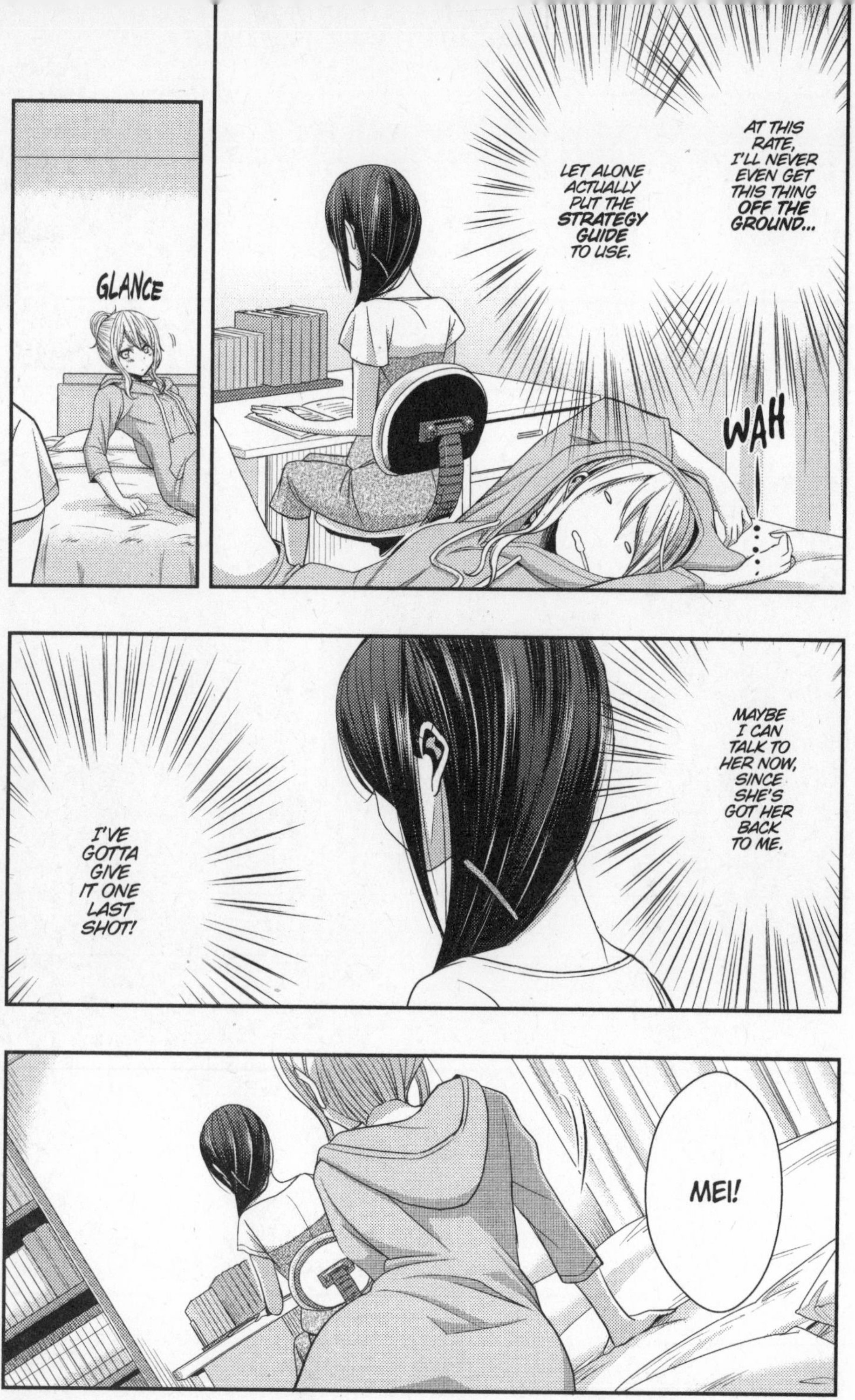
AT THIS RATE, I'LL NEVER EVEN GET THIS THING OFF THE GROUND...
LET ALONE ACTUALLY PUT THE STRATEGY GUIDE TO USE.
WAH
GLANCE
MAYBE I CAN TALK TO HER NOW, SINCE SHE'S GOT HER BACK TO ME.
I'VE GOTTA GIVE IT ONE LAST SHOT!
MEI!

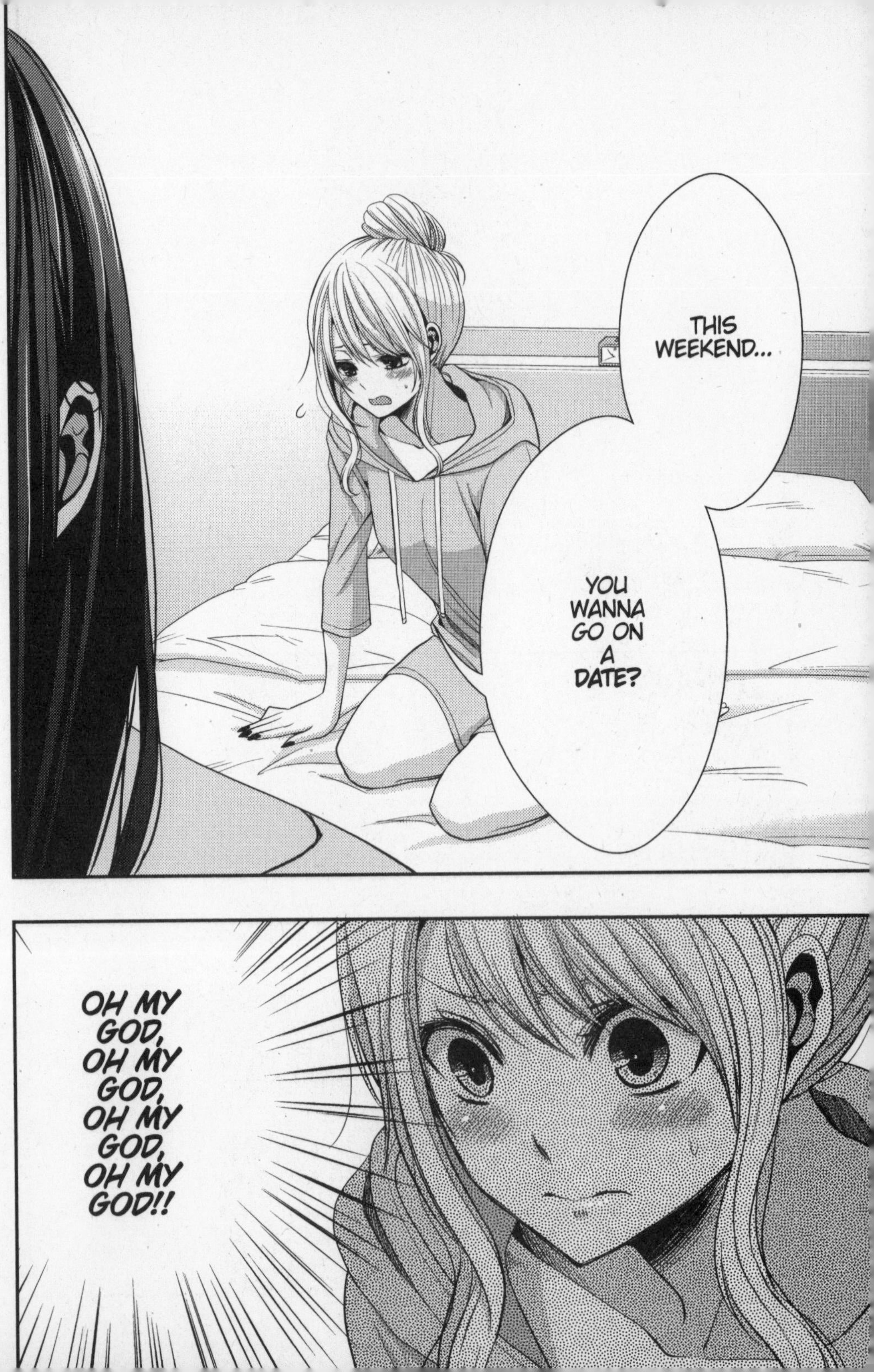
THIS WEEKEND...
YOU WANNA GO ON A DATE?
OH MY GOD, OH MY GOD, OH MY GOD, OH MY GOD!!

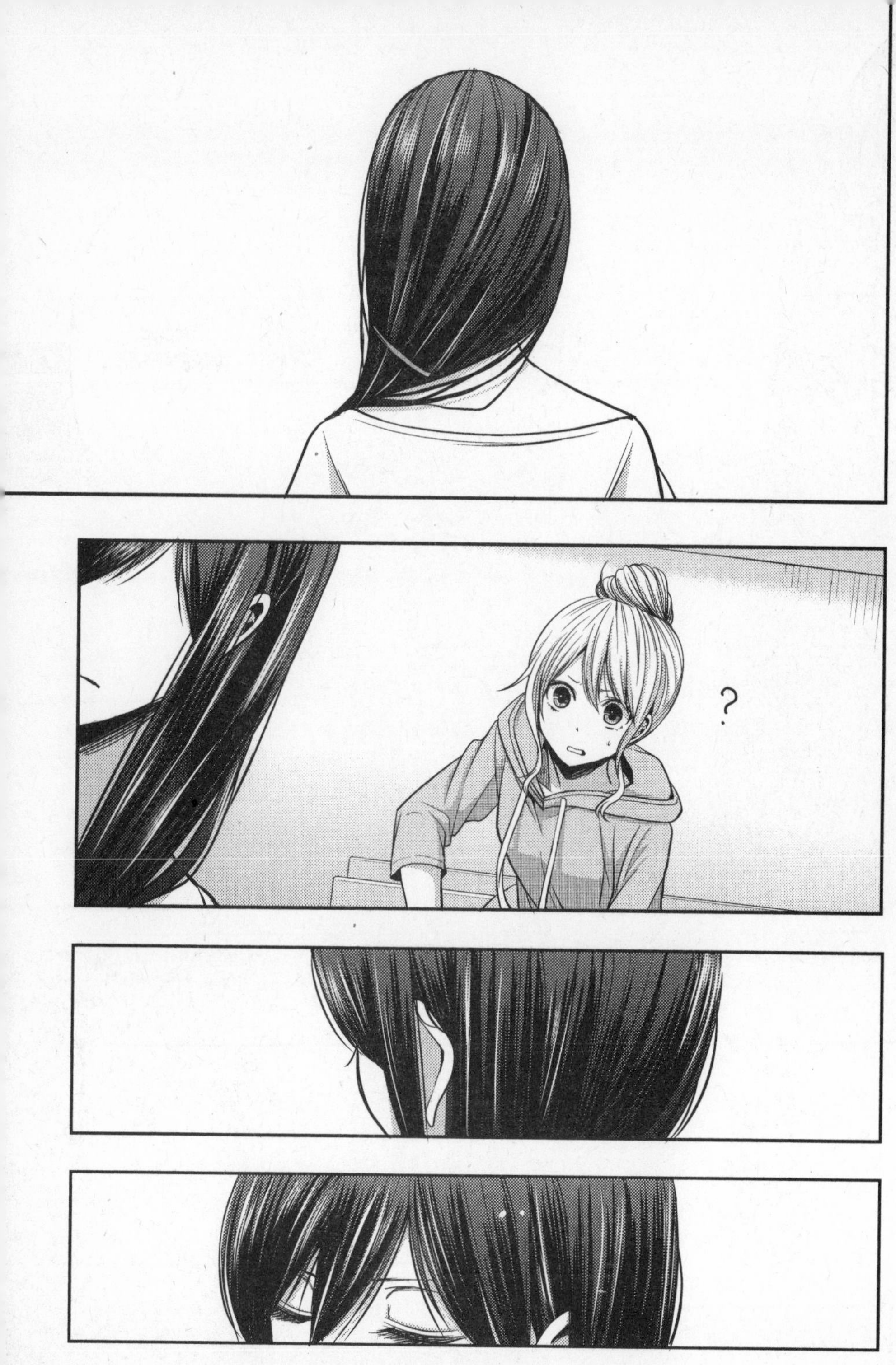
?

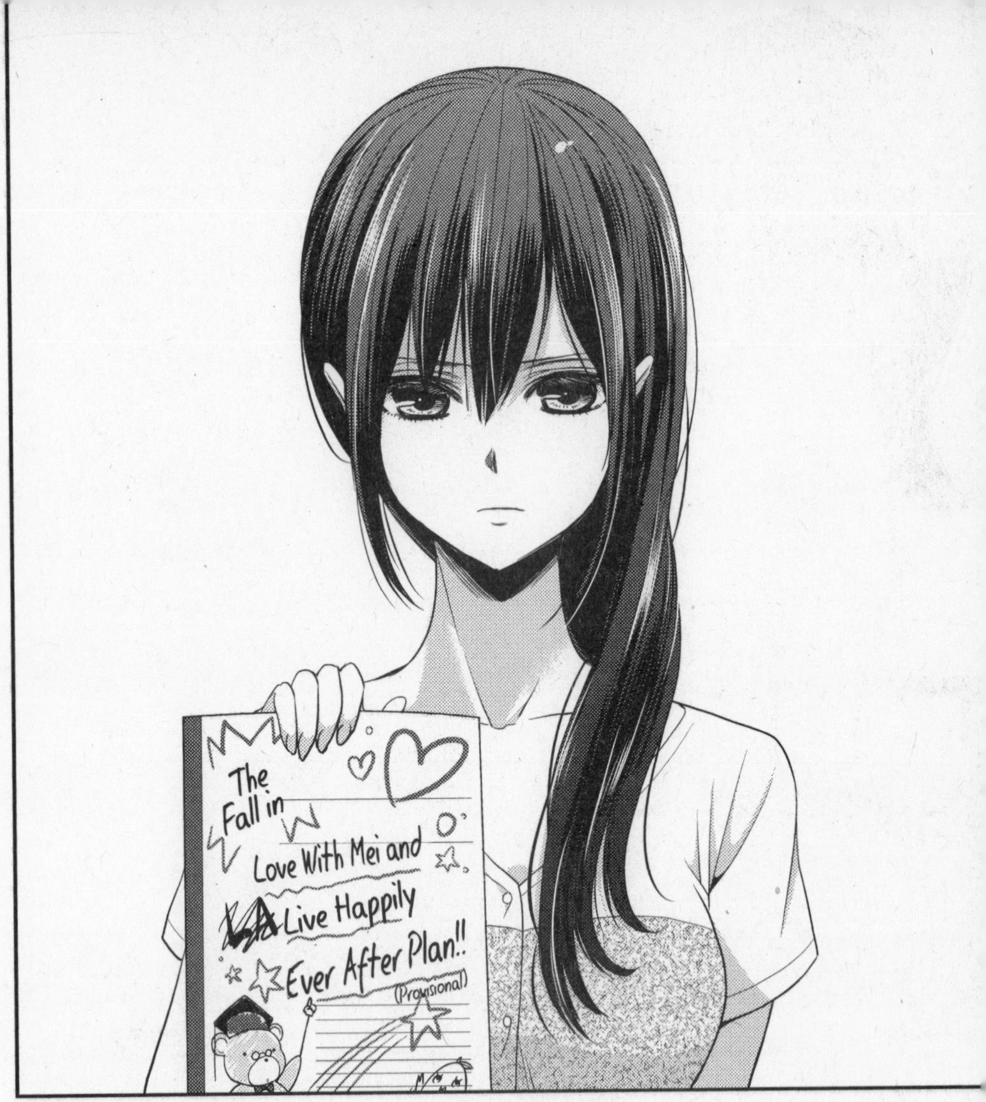
The
Fall in
Love With Mei and
Live Happily
Ever After Plan!!
(Provisional)
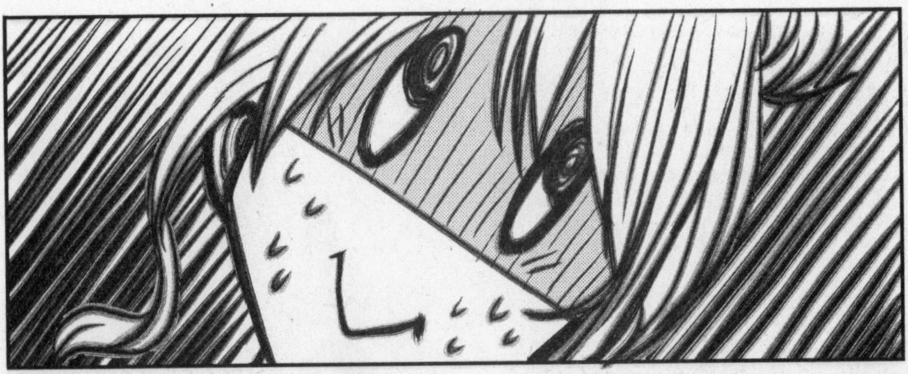

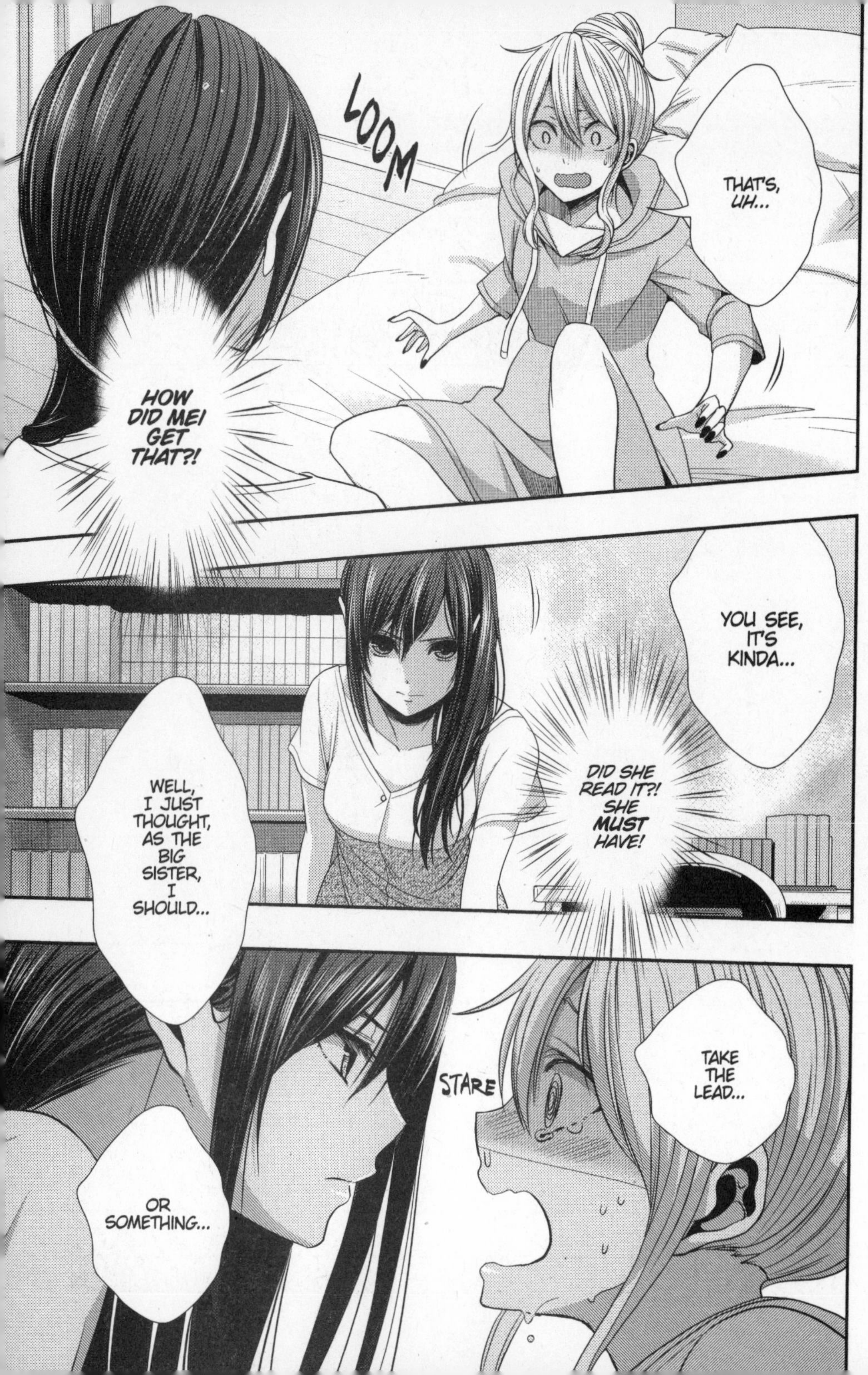
LOOM
THAT'S, UH...
HOW DID MEI GET THAT?!
YOU SEE, IT'S KINDA...
DID SHE READ IT?! SHE MUST HAVE!
WELL, I JUST THOUGHT, AS THE BIG SISTER, I SHOULD...
TAKE THE LEAD...
STARE
OR SOMETHING...

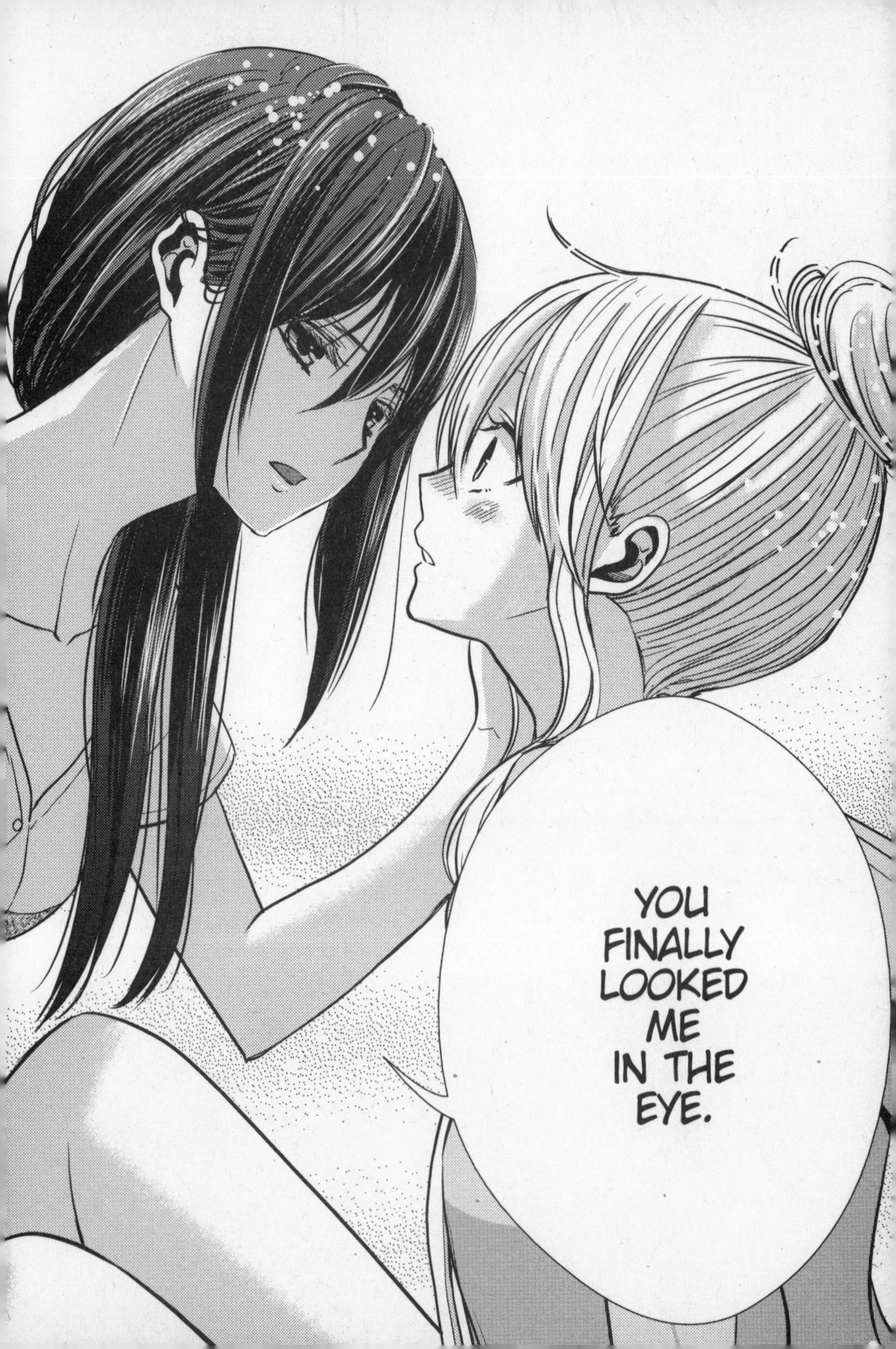
YOU FINALLY LOOKED ME IN THE EYE.

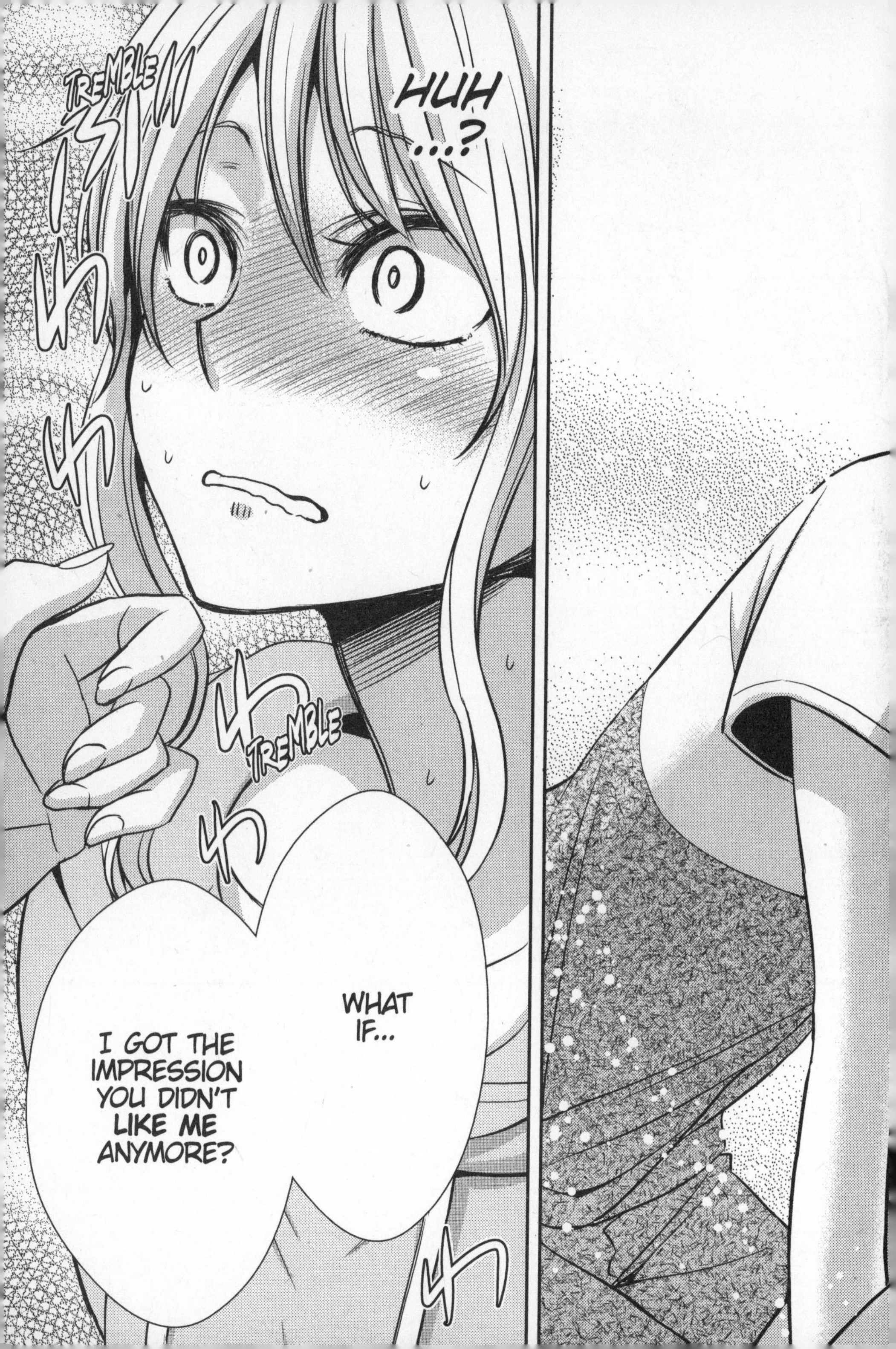
HUH ...?
TREMBLE
TREMBLE
WHAT IF...
I GOT THE IMPRESSION YOU DIDN'T LIKE ME ANYMORE?

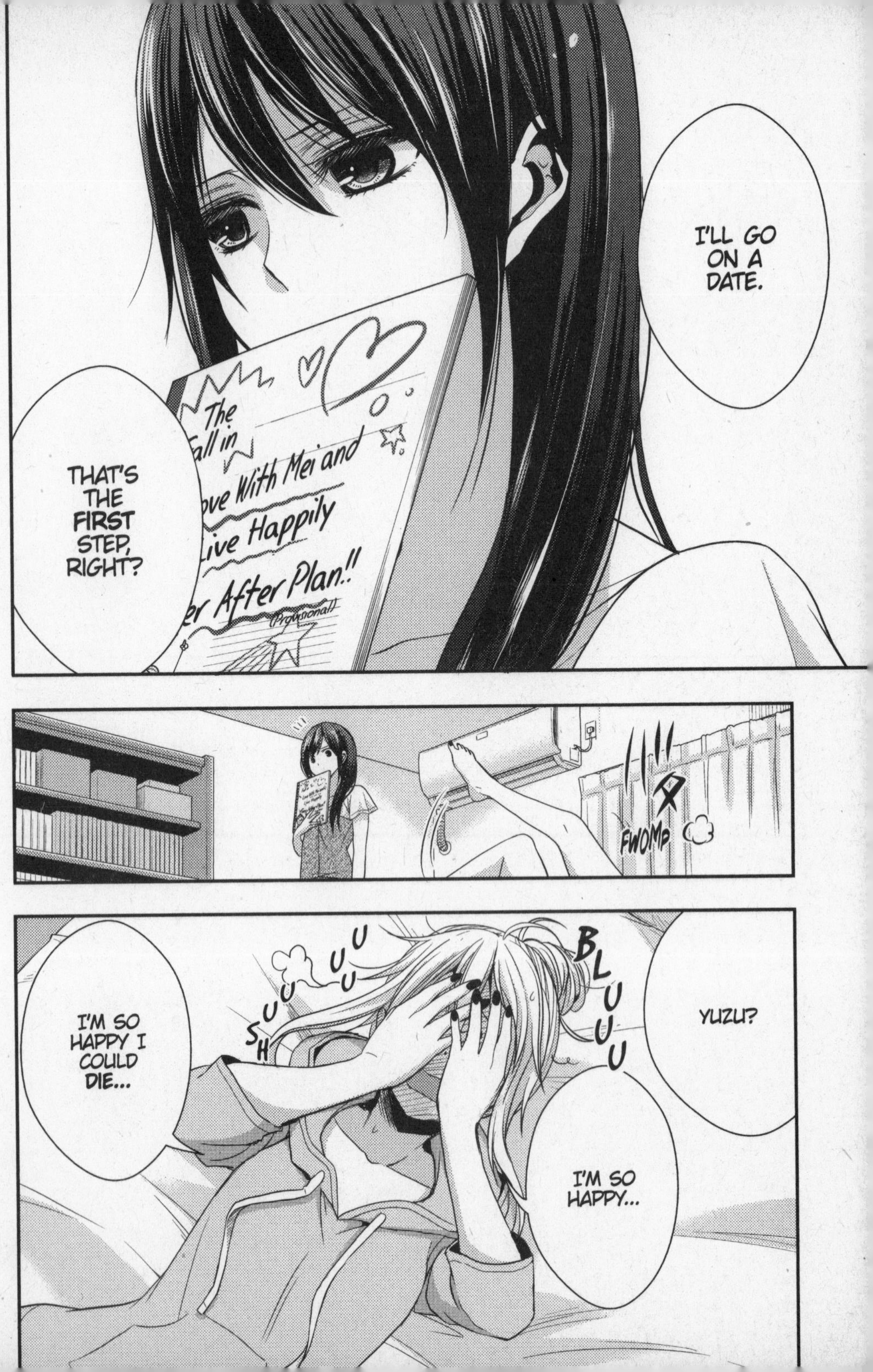
I'LL GO ON A DATE.
The Fall in
ove With Mei and
Live Happily
er After Plan!!
(Provisional)
THAT'S THE FIRST STEP, RIGHT?
FWOMP
YUZU?
BLUUUU
I'M SO HAPPY...
SHUUUUU
I'M SO HAPPY I COULD DIE...

citrus
【シトラス】

SECRET LOVE AFFAIR WITH SISTER

citrus

SABUROUTA PRESENTS SECRET LOVE AFFAIR WITH SISTER

6

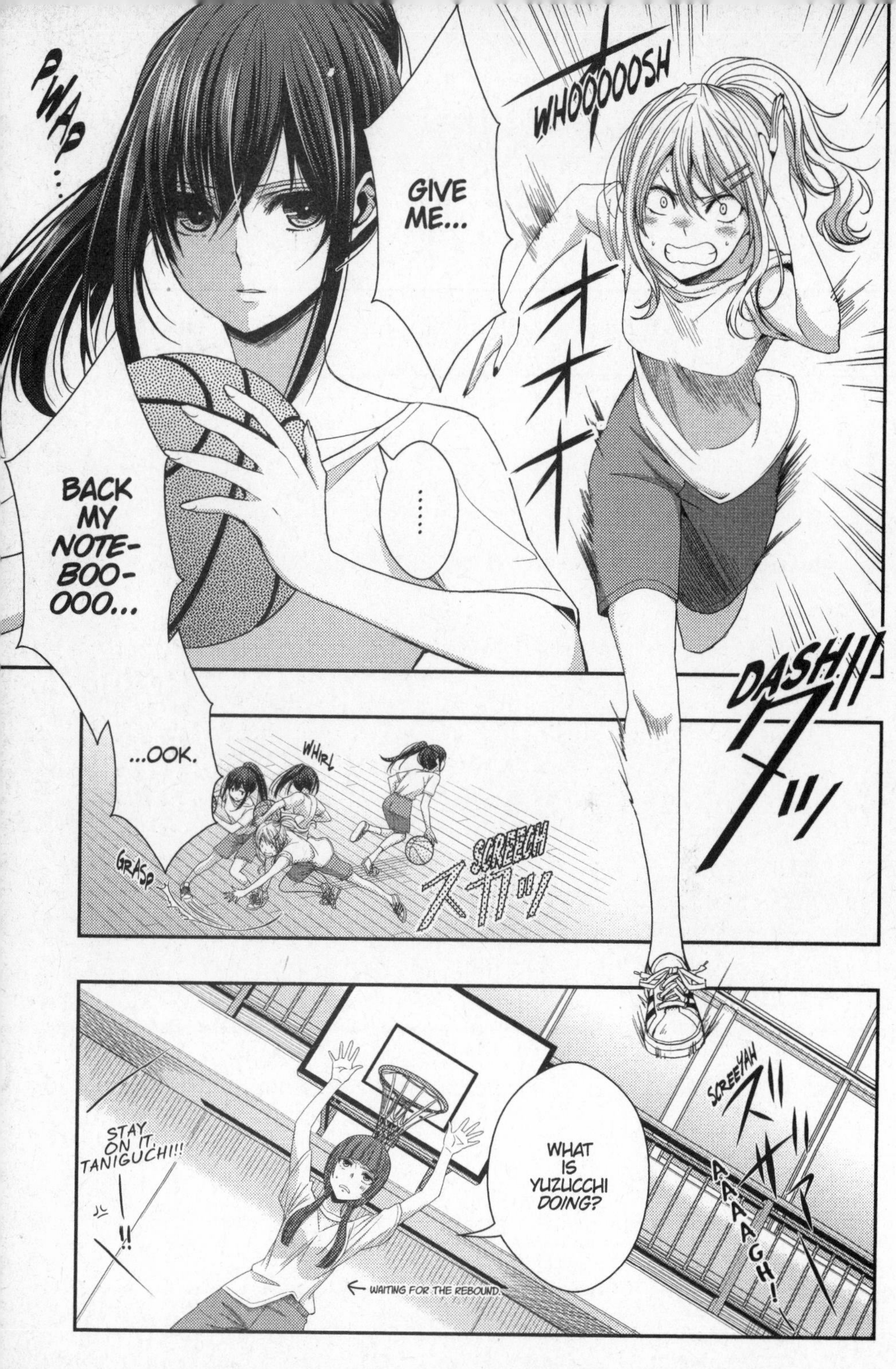
WHOOOOOSH
GIVE ME...
......
BACK MY NOTE-BOOO-OOO...
PWAP...
DASH!!
...OOK.
WHIRL
SCREECH
GRASP
SCREEYAH
AAAAGH!
WHAT IS YUZUCCHI DOING?
STAY ON IT, TANIGUCHI!!!
!!
← WAITING FOR THE REBOUND.

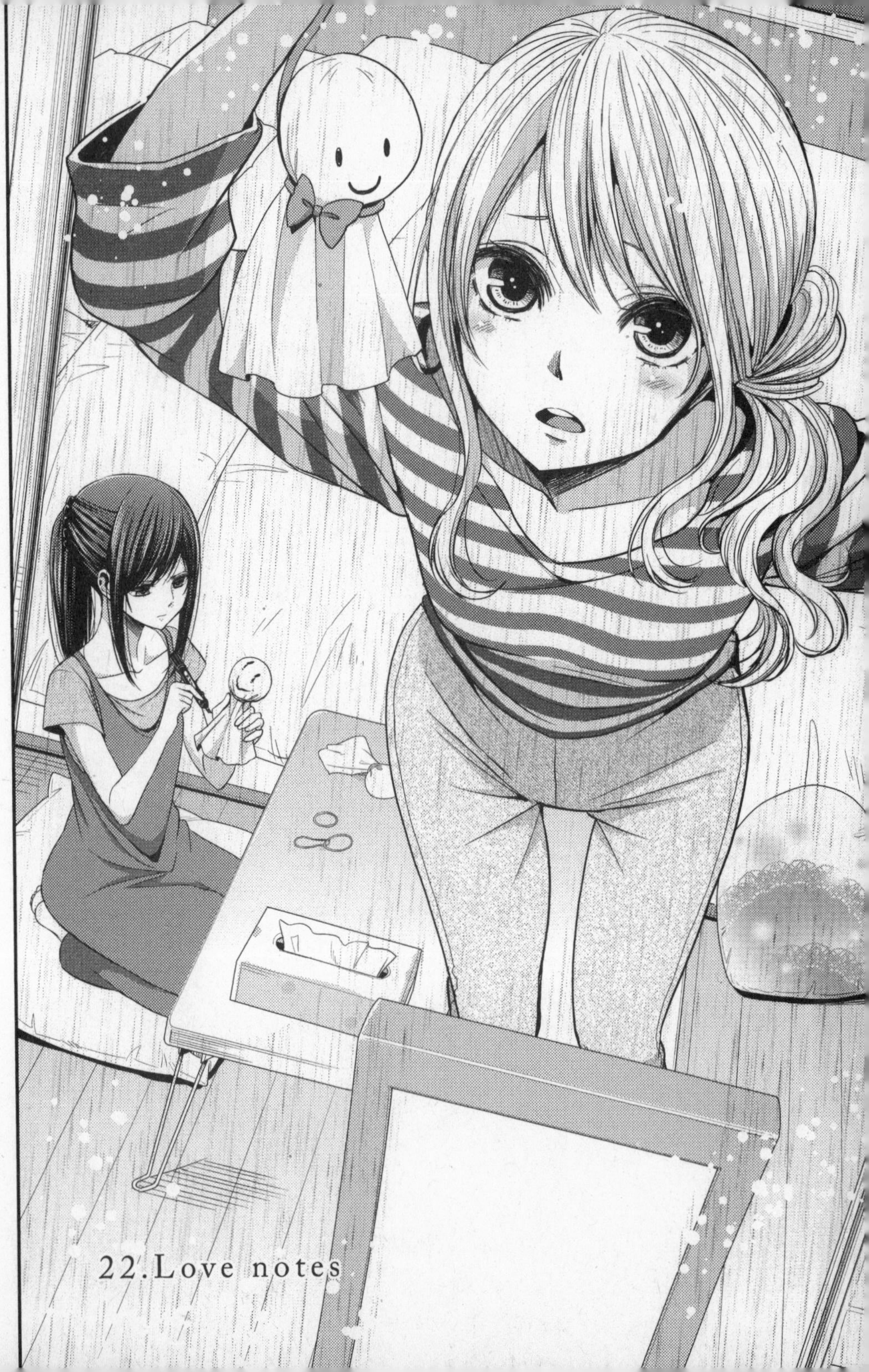

22. Love notes

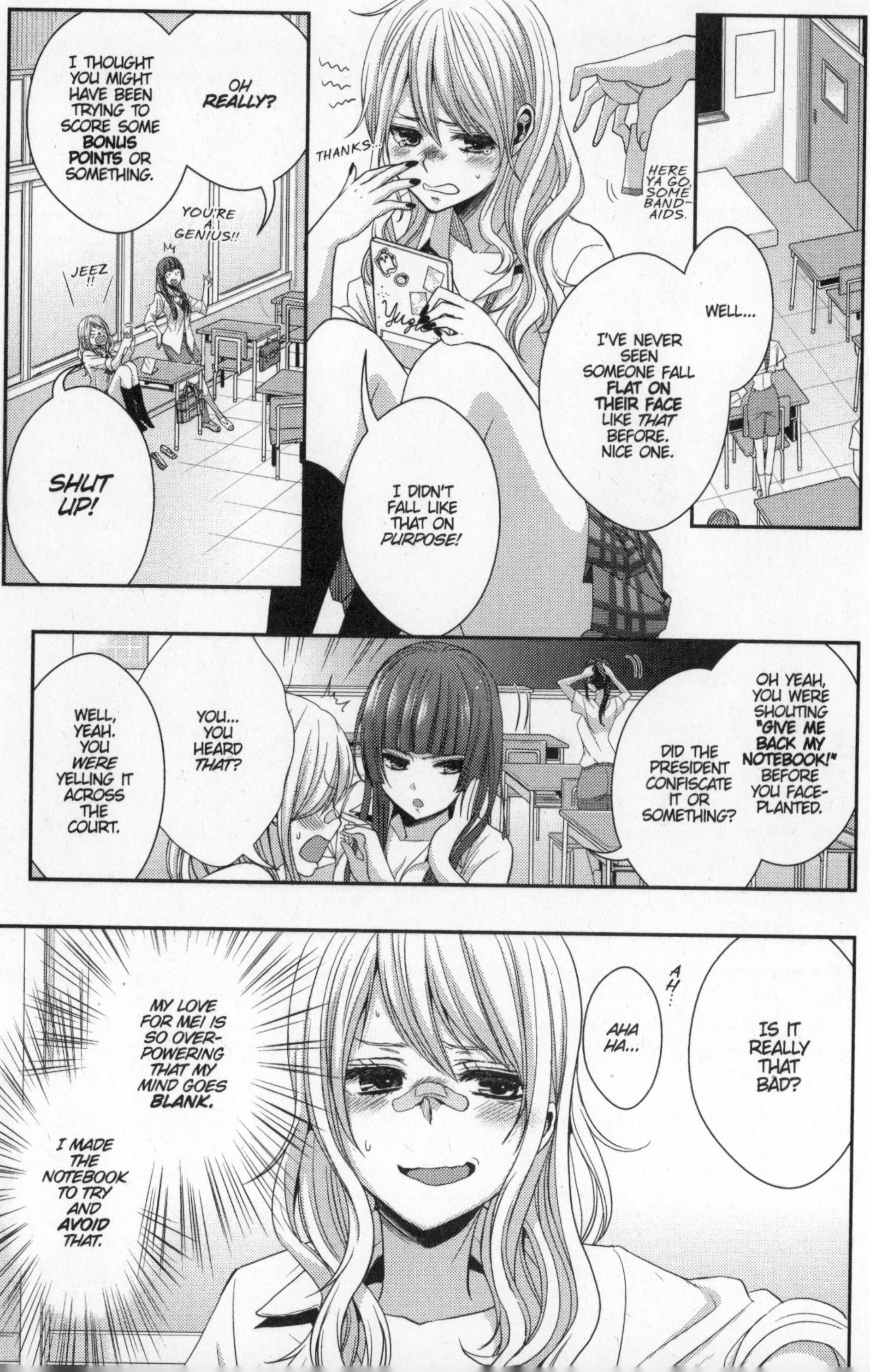
HERE YA GO, SOME BAND-AIDS.
THANKS...
WELL...
I'VE NEVER SEEN SOMEONE FALL **FLAT ON THEIR FACE** LIKE *THAT* BEFORE. NICE ONE.
I DIDN'T FALL LIKE THAT ON *PURPOSE!*
I THOUGHT YOU MIGHT HAVE BEEN TRYING TO SCORE SOME **BONUS POINTS** OR SOMETHING.
OH **REALLY?**
YOU'RE A GENIUS!!
JEEZ!!
SHUT UP!
OH YEAH, YOU WERE SHOUTING **"GIVE ME BACK MY NOTEBOOK!"** BEFORE YOU FACE-PLANTED.
DID THE PRESIDENT CONFISCATE IT OR SOMETHING?
YOU... YOU *HEARD* THAT?
WELL, YEAH. YOU *WERE* YELLING IT ACROSS THE COURT.
IS IT REALLY THAT BAD?
AH...
AHA HA...
MY LOVE FOR MEI IS SO OVER-POWERING THAT MY MIND GOES **BLANK.**
I MADE THE NOTEBOOK TO TRY AND **AVOID** THAT.

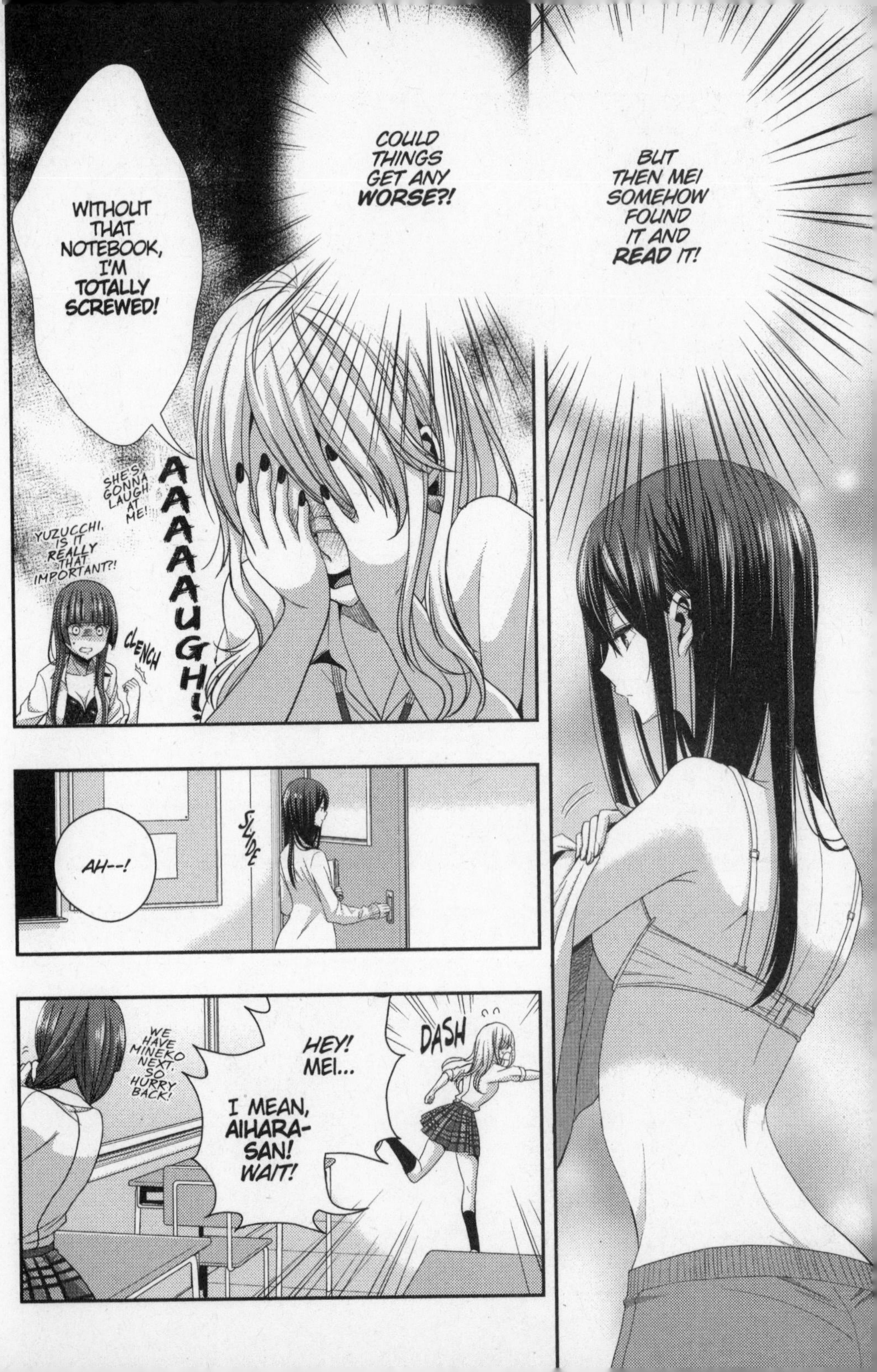
BUT THEN MEI SOMEHOW FOUND IT AND READ IT!
COULD THINGS GET ANY WORSE?!
WITHOUT THAT NOTEBOOK, I'M TOTALLY SCREWED!
AAAAAAAUGH!
SHE'S GONNA LAUGH AT ME!
YUZUCCHI, IS IT REALLY THAT IMPORTANT?!
CLENCH
SLIDE
AH--!
DASH
HEY! MEI...
I MEAN, AIHARA-SAN! WAIT!
WE HAVE MINEKO NEXT, SO HURRY BACK!

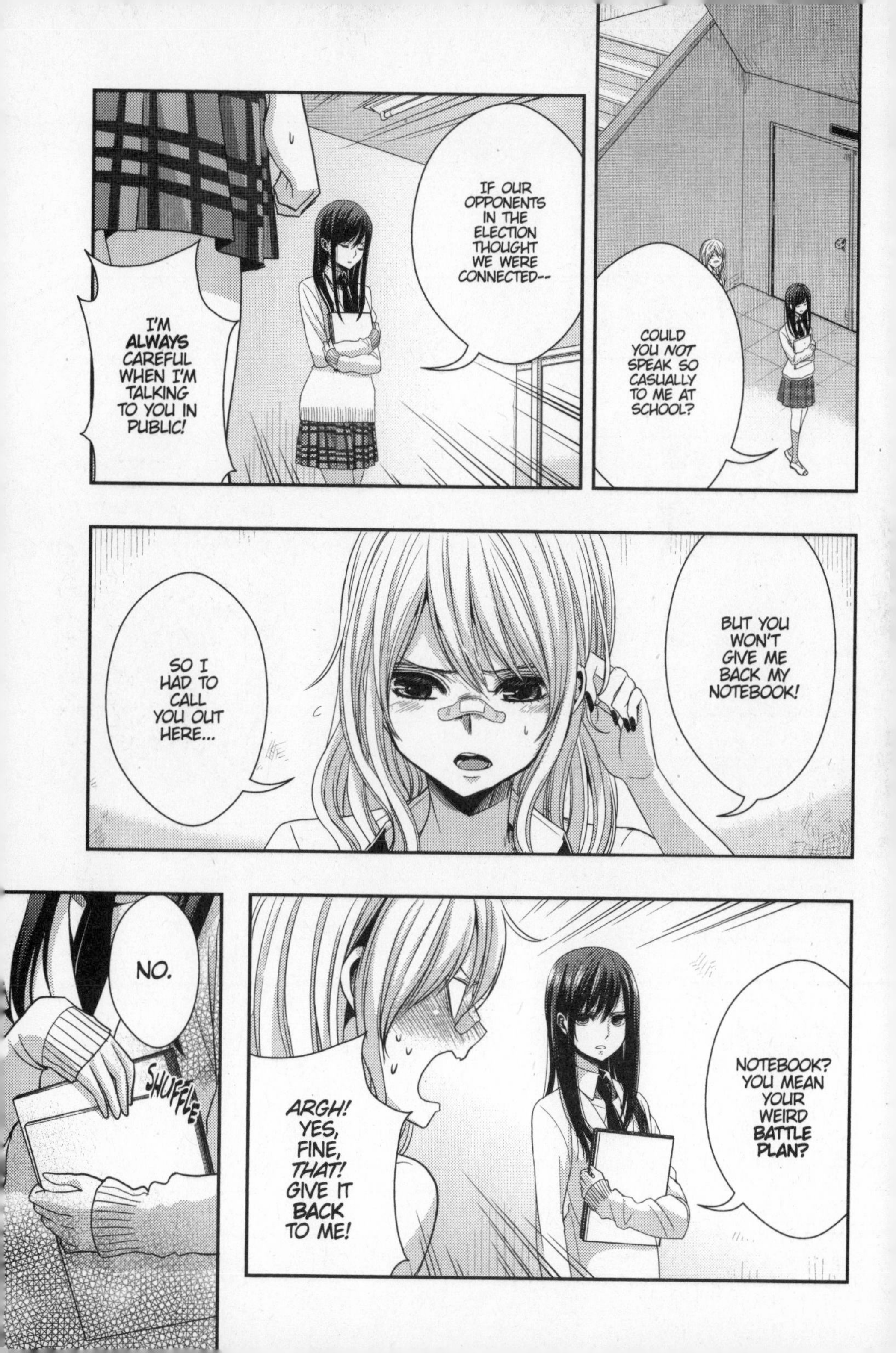
COULD YOU *NOT* SPEAK SO CASUALLY TO ME AT SCHOOL?
IF OUR OPPONENTS IN THE ELECTION THOUGHT WE WERE CONNECTED--
I'M **ALWAYS** CAREFUL WHEN I'M TALKING TO YOU IN PUBLIC!
BUT YOU WON'T GIVE ME BACK MY NOTEBOOK!
SO I HAD TO CALL YOU OUT HERE...
NOTEBOOK? YOU MEAN YOUR WEIRD **BATTLE PLAN?**
ARGH! YES, FINE, THAT! GIVE IT BACK TO ME!
NO.
SHUFFLE

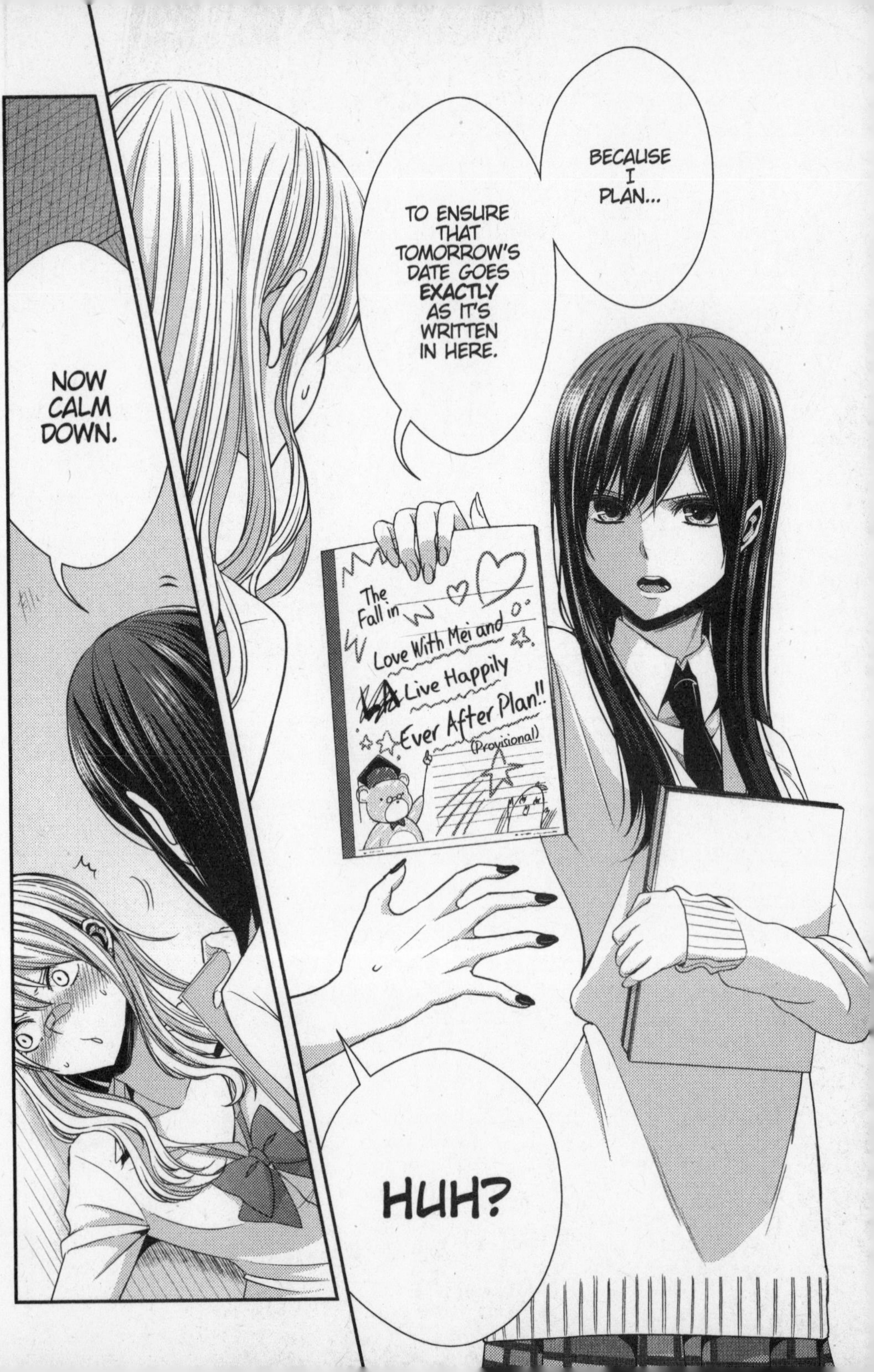
BECAUSE I PLAN...
TO ENSURE THAT TOMORROW'S DATE GOES **EXACTLY** AS IT'S WRITTEN IN HERE.
The Fall in Love With Mei and Live Happily Ever After Plan!!
(Provisional)
HUH?
NOW CALM DOWN.

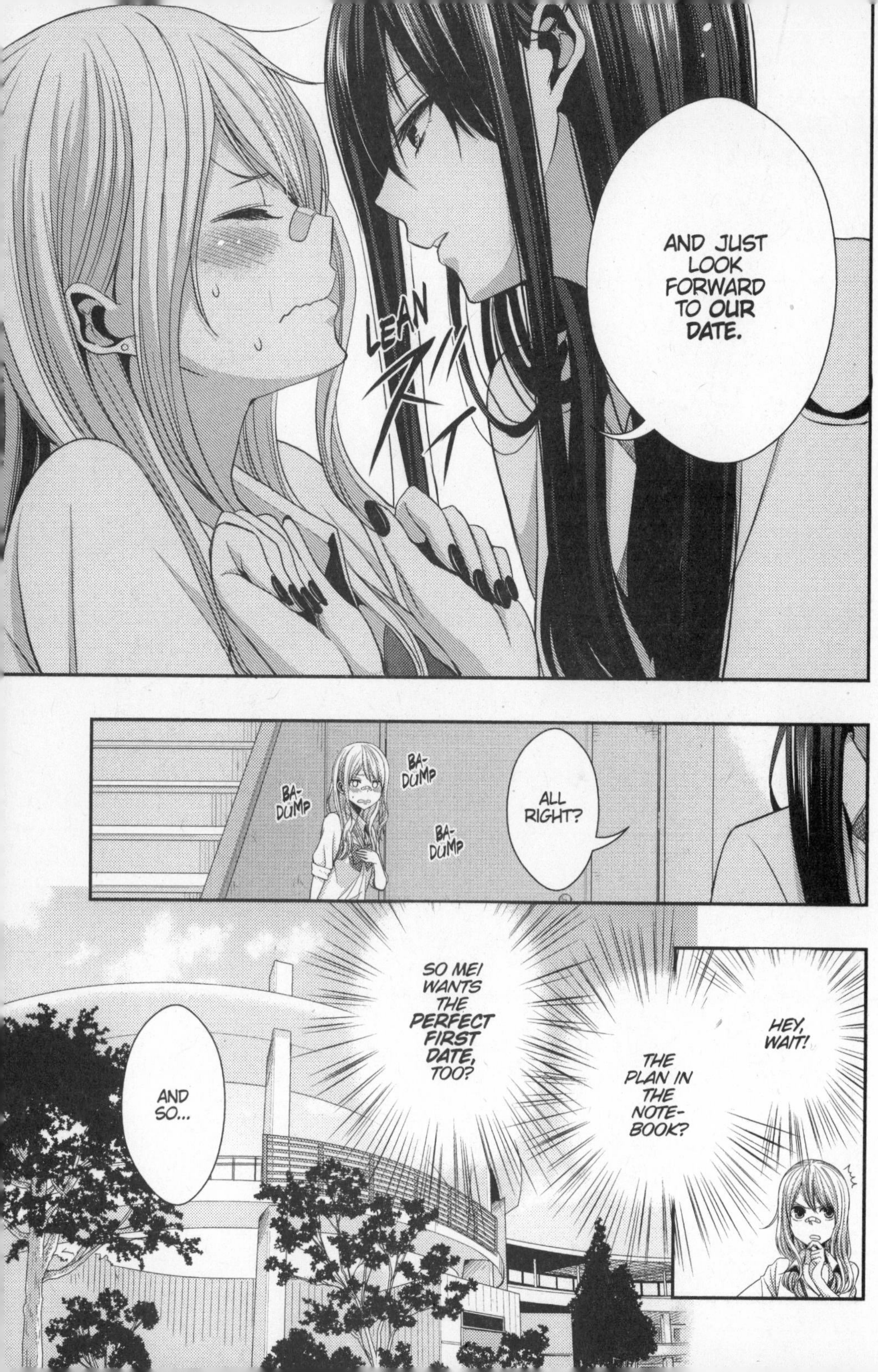
AND JUST LOOK FORWARD TO OUR DATE.
LEAN
ALL RIGHT?
BA-DUMP
BA-DUMP
BA-DUMP
HEY, WAIT!
THE PLAN IN THE NOTE-BOOK?
SO MEI WANTS THE PERFECT FIRST DATE, TOO?
AND SO...

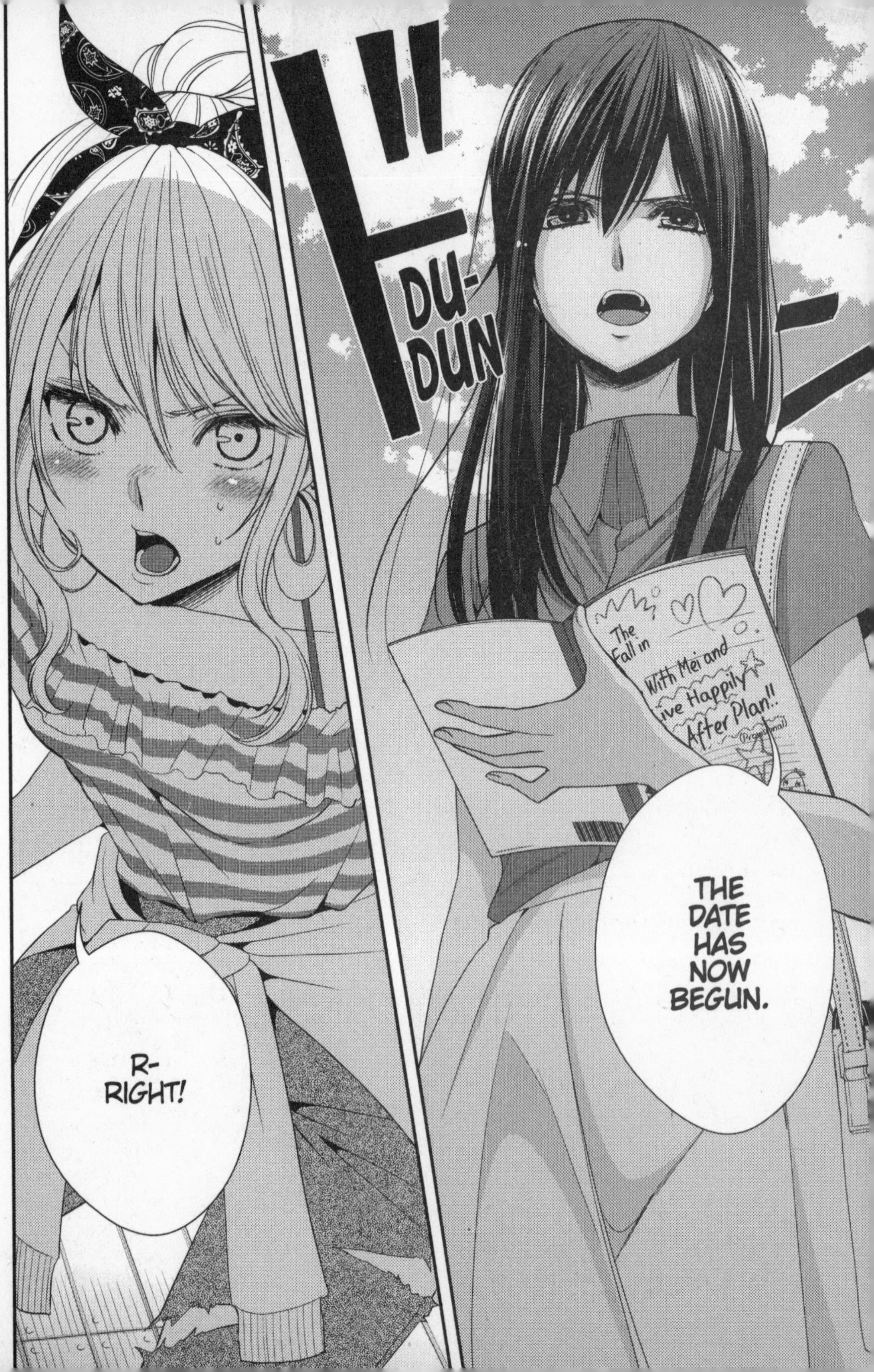
DU-DUN
The
Fall in
With Mei and
ive Happily
After Plan!!
THE DATE HAS NOW BEGUN.
R-RIGHT!

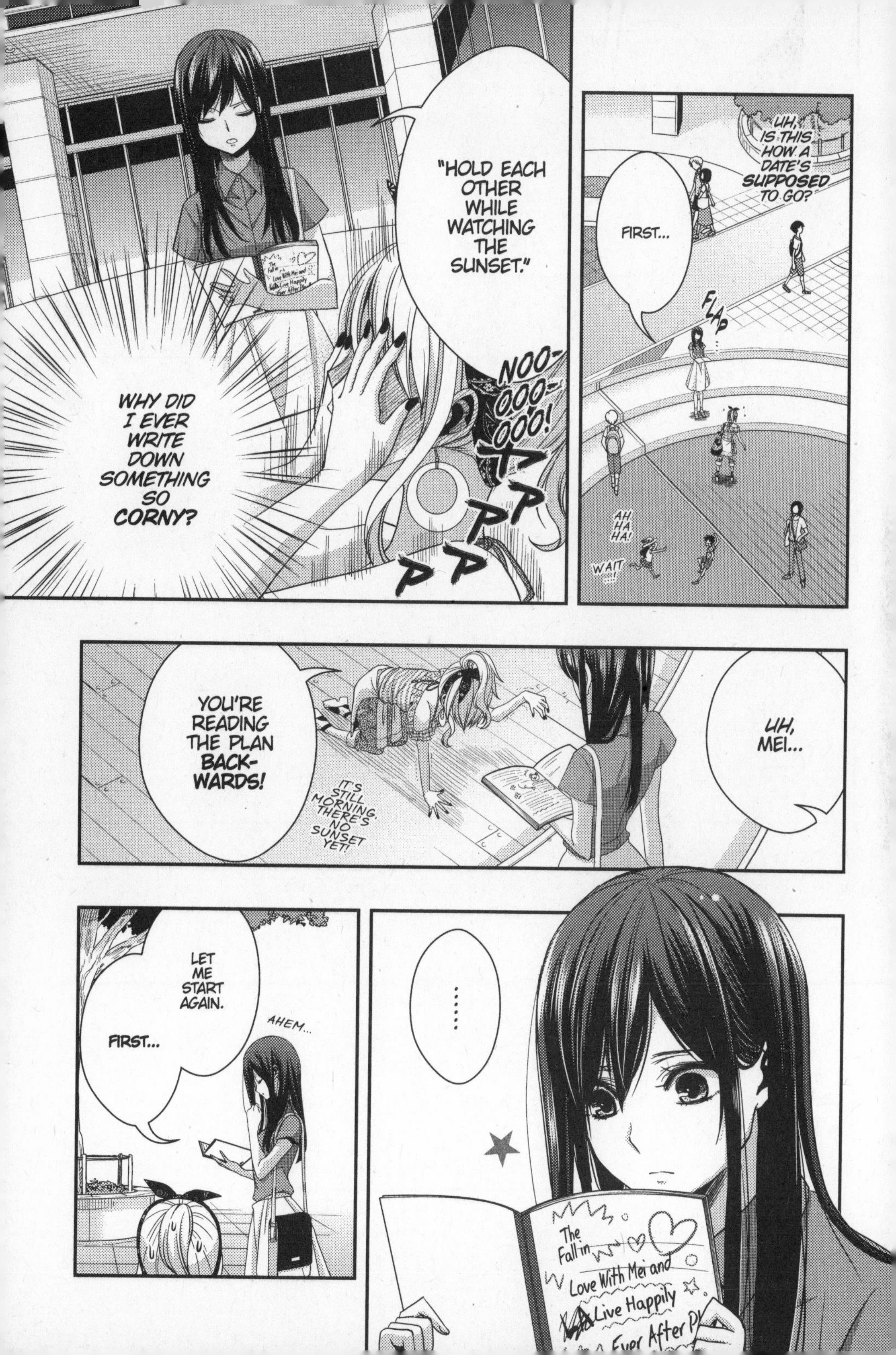
UH, IS THIS HOW A DATE'S SUPPOSED TO GO?
FIRST...
FLAP
AH HA HA!
WAIT...
"HOLD EACH OTHER WHILE WATCHING THE SUNSET."
NOO-OOO-OOO!
WHY DID I EVER WRITE DOWN SOMETHING SO CORNY?
UH, MEI...
YOU'RE READING THE PLAN BACKWARDS!
IT'S STILL MORNING. THERE'S NO SUNSET YET!
......
The Fall in Love With Mei and Live Happily Ever After P
LET ME START AGAIN.
AHEM...
FIRST...

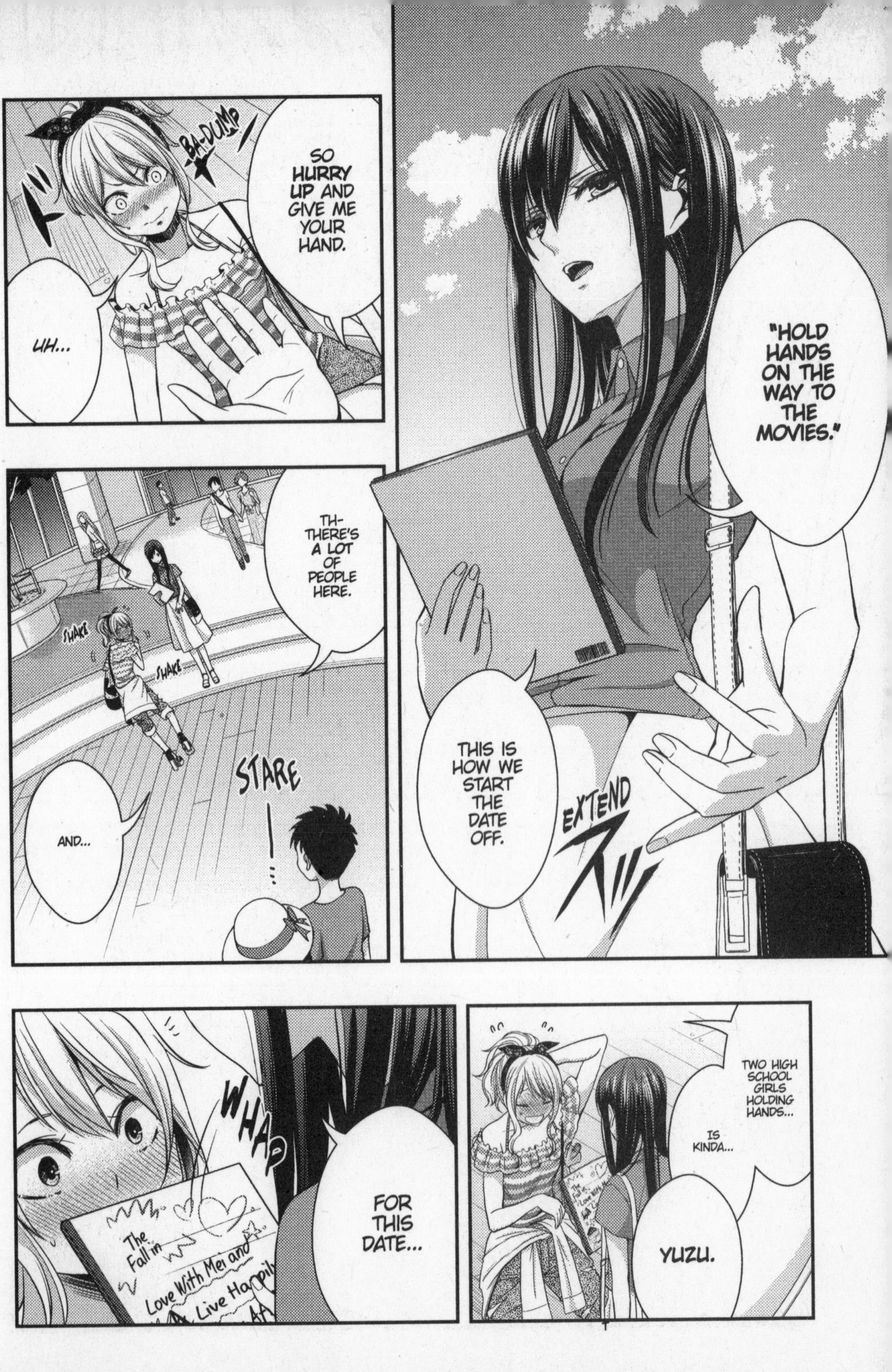

"HOLD HANDS ON THE WAY TO THE MOVIES."
THIS IS HOW WE START THE DATE OFF.
EXTEND
SO HURRY UP AND GIVE ME YOUR HAND.
BA-DUMP
UH...
TH-THERE'S A LOT OF PEOPLE HERE.
SHAKE
SHAKE
STARE
AND...
TWO HIGH SCHOOL GIRLS HOLDING HANDS...
IS KINDA...
YUZU.
WHAP
FOR THIS DATE...
The
Fall in
Love With Mei and

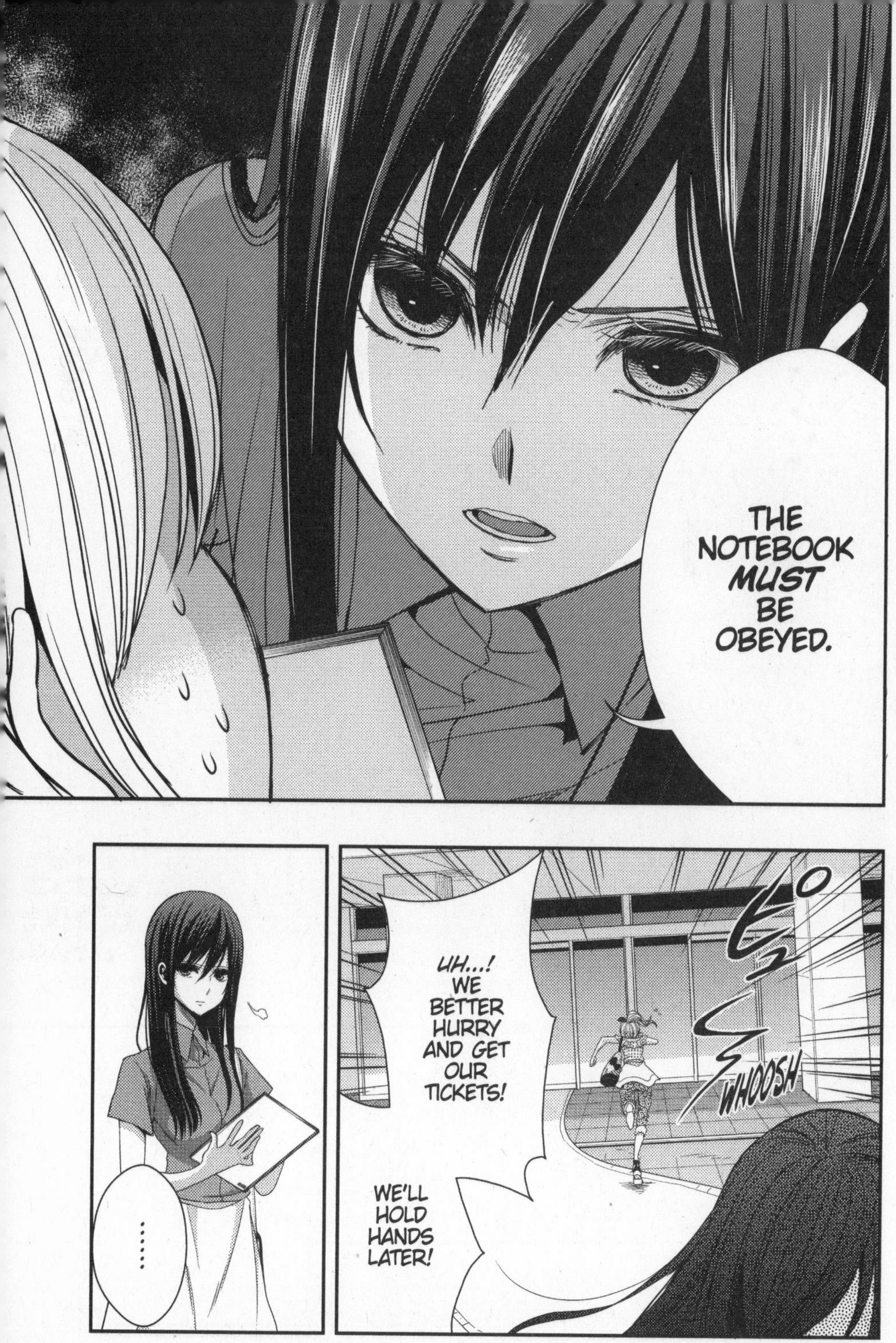
THE NOTEBOOK MUST BE OBEYED.
UH...! WE BETTER HURRY AND GET OUR TICKETS!
WHOOSH
WE'LL HOLD HANDS LATER!
......

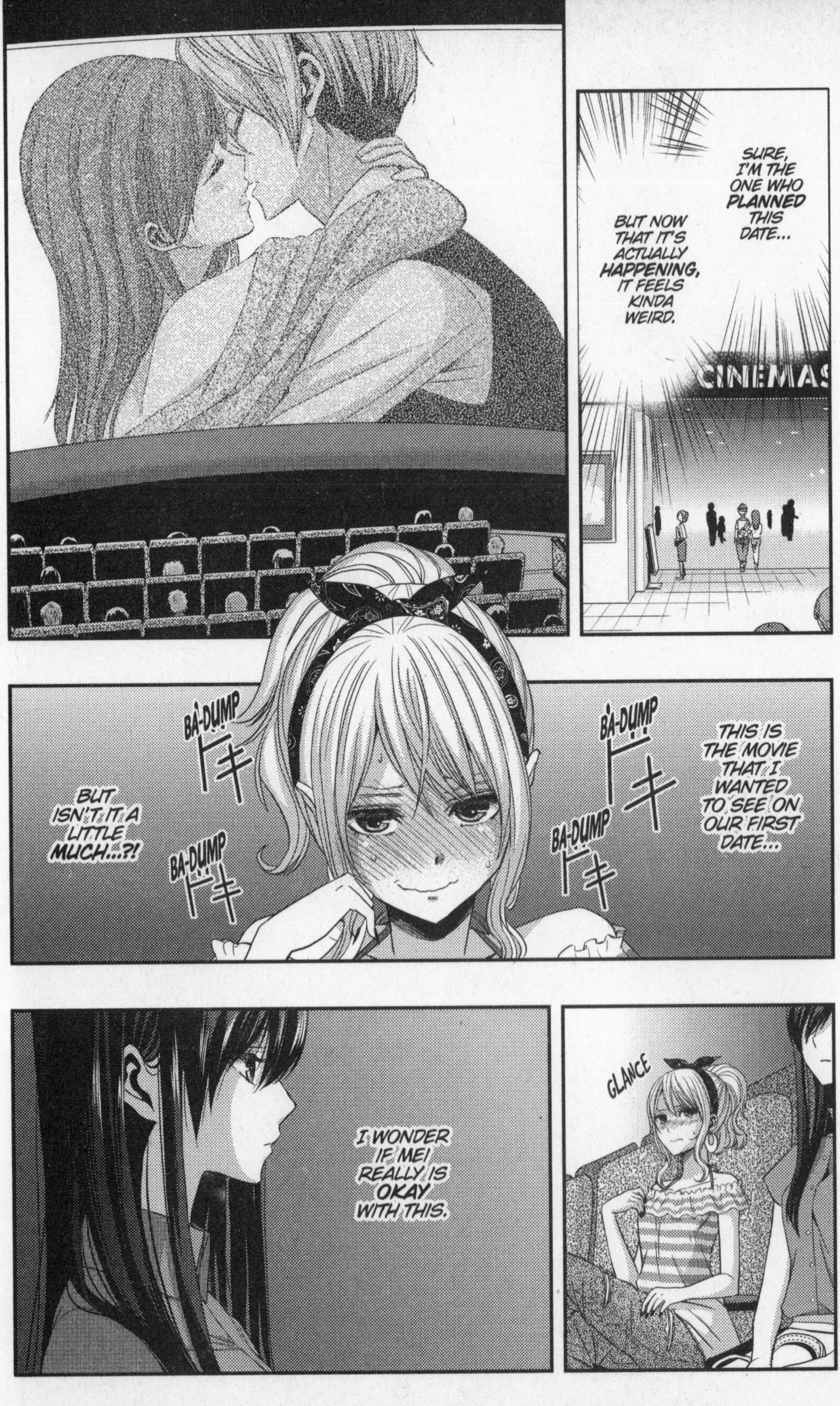
SURE, I'M THE ONE WHO PLANNED THIS DATE...
BUT NOW THAT IT'S ACTUALLY HAPPENING, IT FEELS KINDA WEIRD.
CINEMAS
THIS IS THE MOVIE THAT I WANTED TO SEE ON OUR FIRST DATE...
BA-DUMP ドキ
BA-DUMP ドキ
BA-DUMP ドキ
BA-DUMP ドキ
BUT ISN'T IT A LITTLE MUCH...?!
GLANCE
I WONDER IF MEI REALLY IS OKAY WITH THIS.

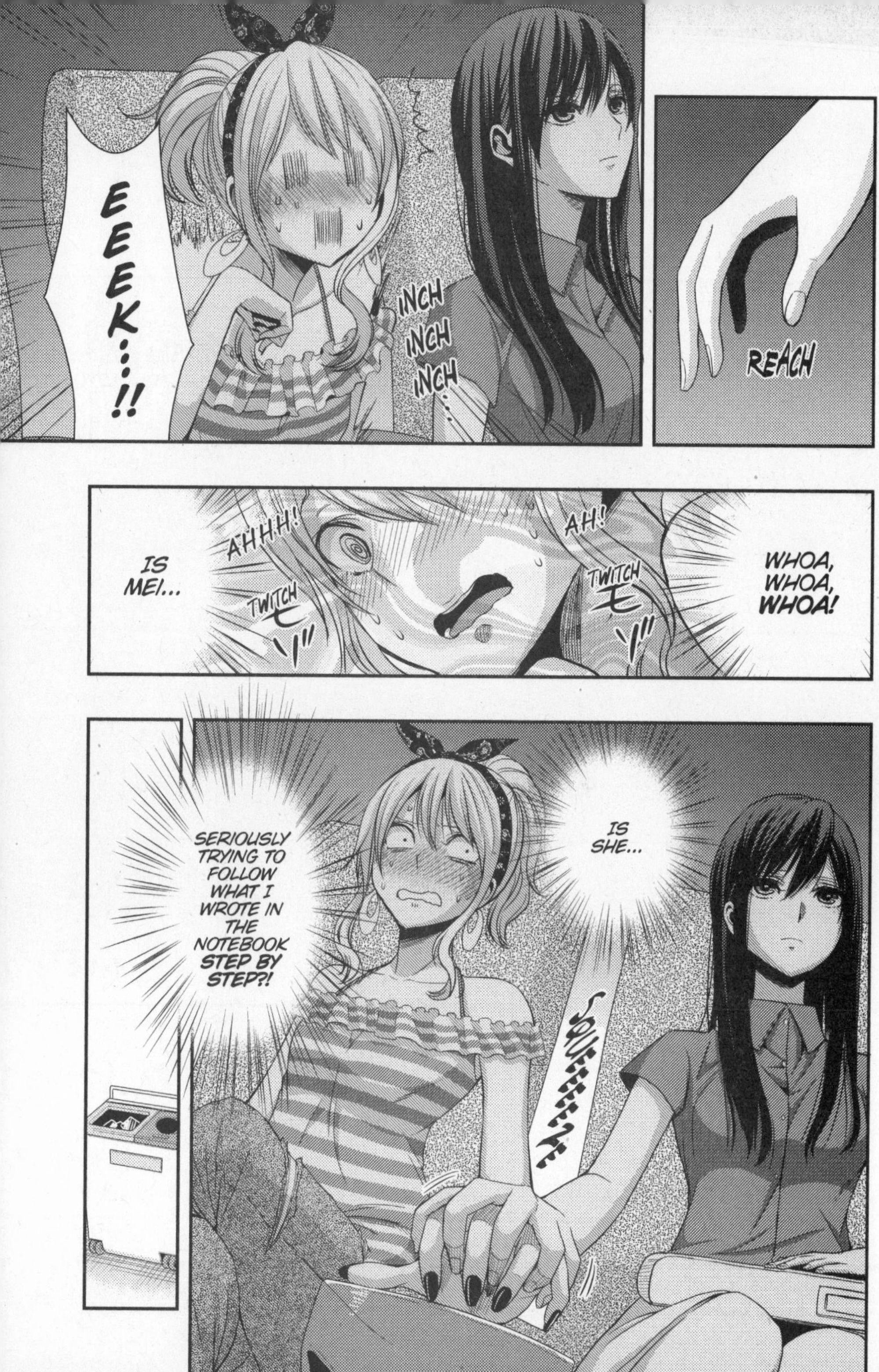
REACH
INCH
INCH
INCH
EEEK...!!
WHOA, WHOA, WHOA!
AH!
TWITCH
TWITCH
AHHH!
IS MEI...
IS SHE...
SQUEEEEEZE
SERIOUSLY TRYING TO FOLLOW WHAT I WROTE IN THE NOTEBOOK STEP BY STEP?!

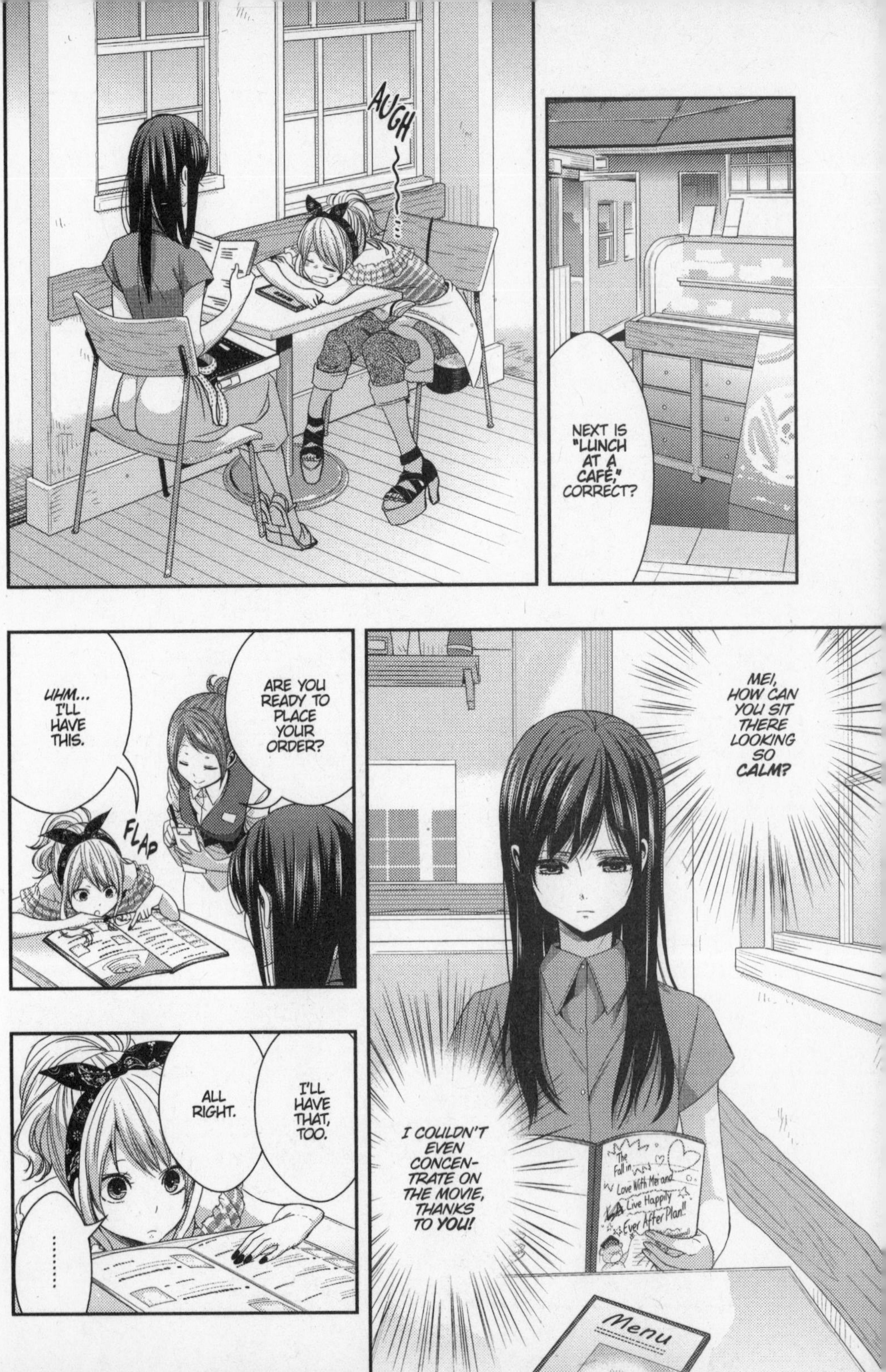
NEXT IS "LUNCH AT A CAFÉ," CORRECT?
AUGH~~~
MEI, HOW CAN YOU SIT THERE LOOKING SO CALM?
I COULDN'T EVEN CONCENTRATE ON THE MOVIE, THANKS TO YOU!
The Fall in Love With Mei and Live Happily Ever After Plan!!
Menu
ARE YOU READY TO PLACE YOUR ORDER?
UHM... I'LL HAVE THIS.
FLAP
I'LL HAVE THAT, TOO.
ALL RIGHT.
......

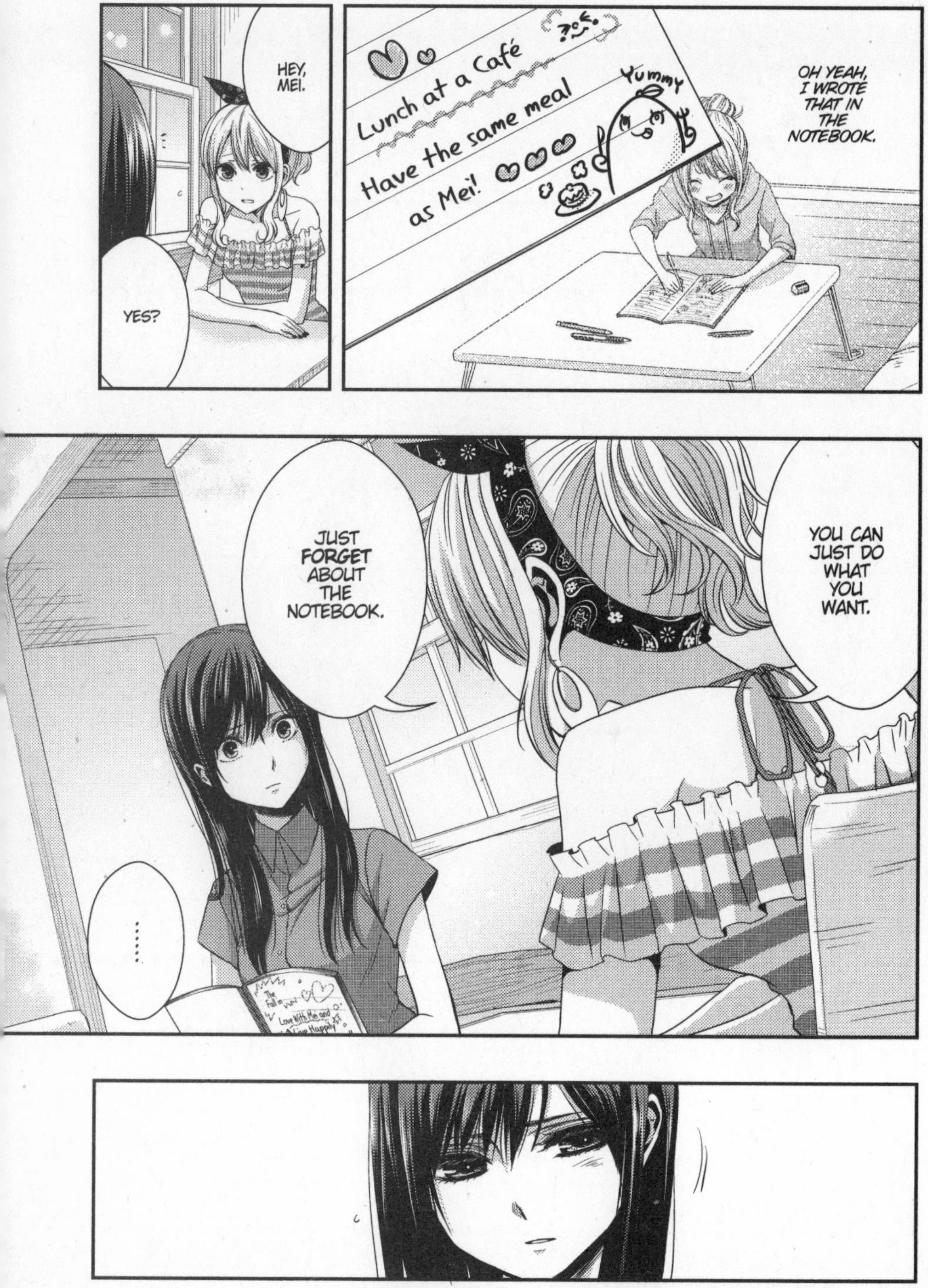
Lunch at a Café
Have the same meal as Mei!
Yummy
OH YEAH, I WROTE THAT IN THE NOTEBOOK.
HEY, MEI.
YES?
YOU CAN JUST DO WHAT YOU WANT.
JUST FORGET ABOUT THE NOTEBOOK.
......

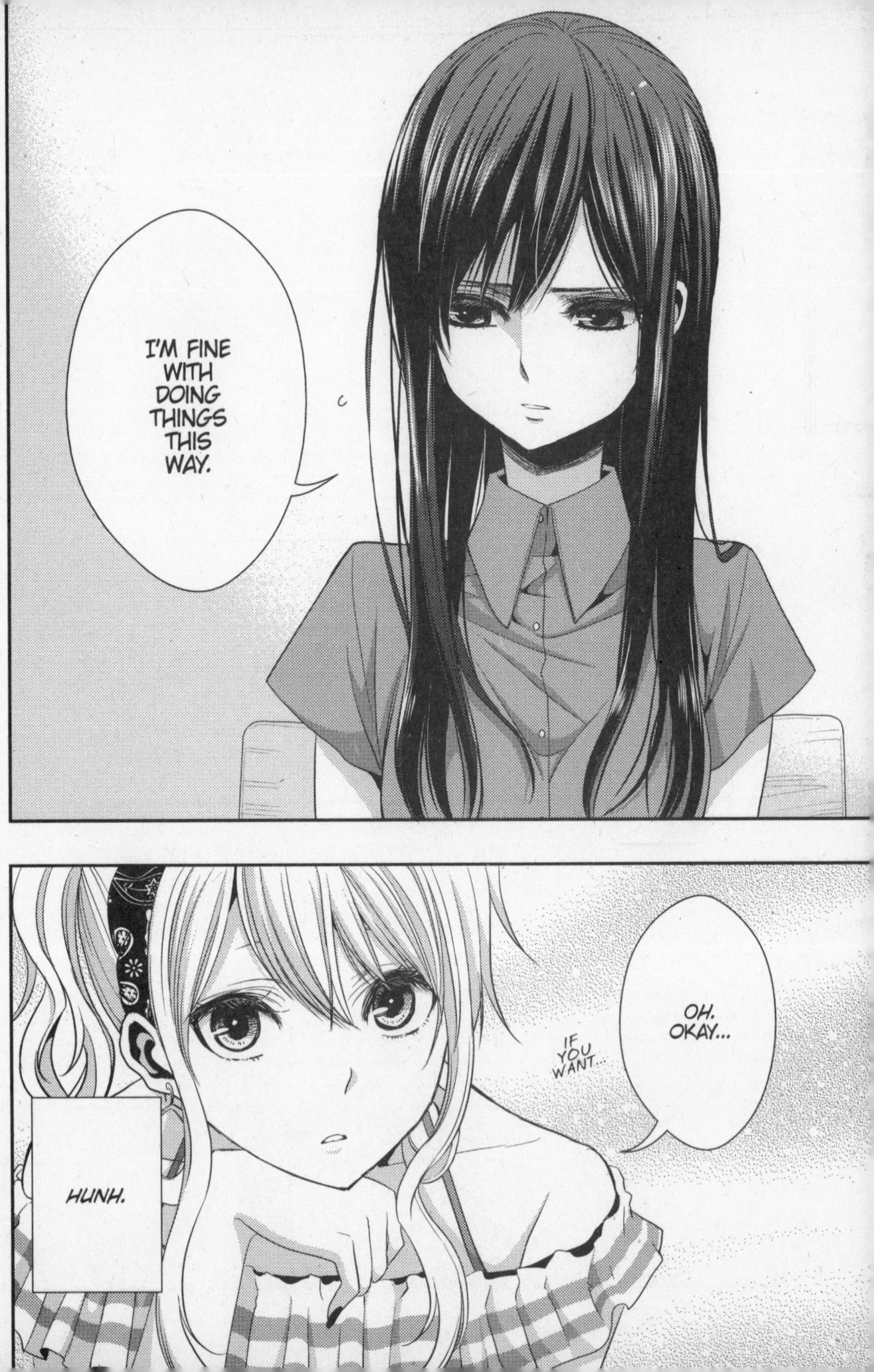
I'M FINE WITH DOING THINGS THIS WAY.
OH. OKAY...
IF YOU WANT...
HUNH.

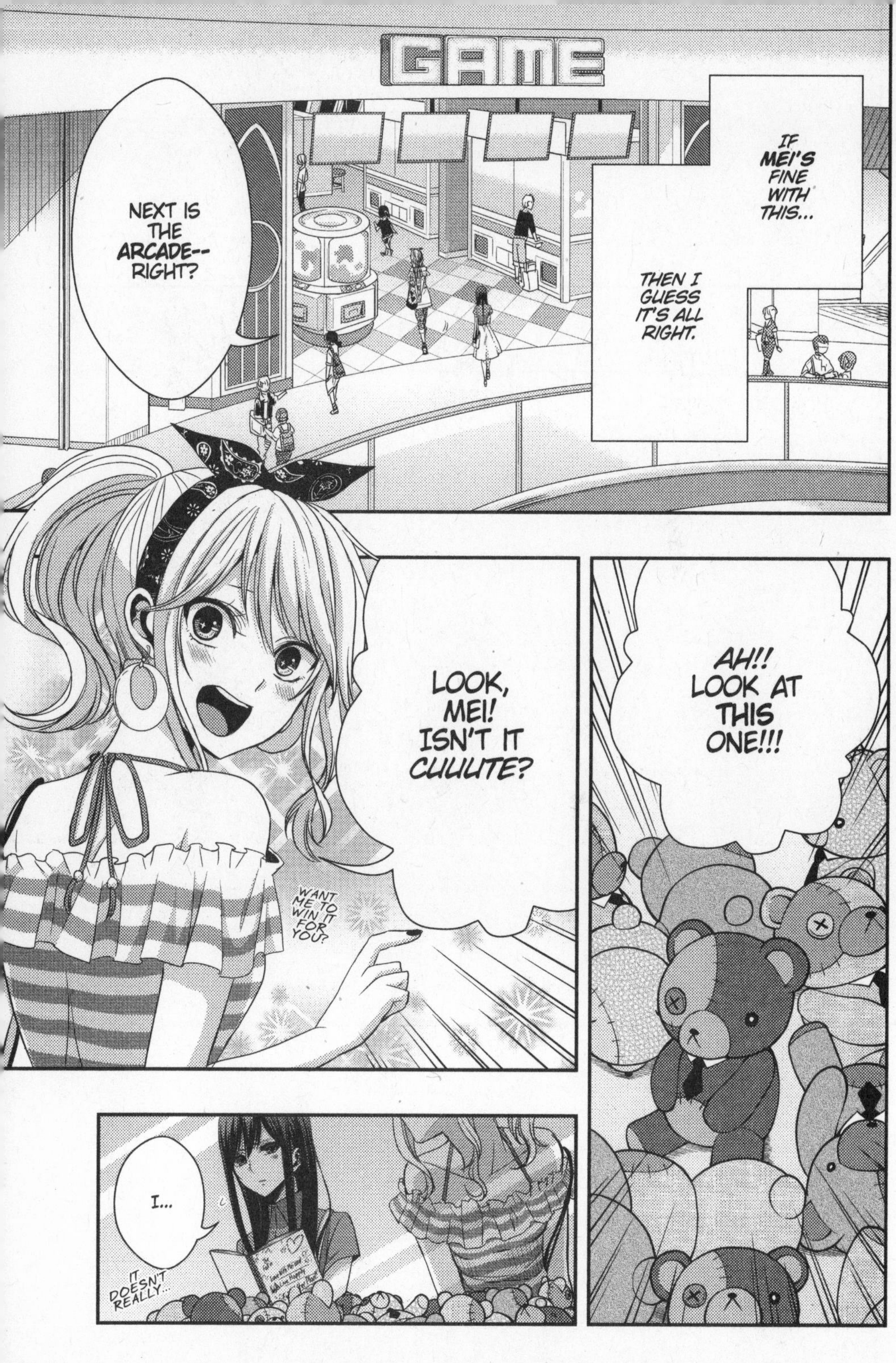
GAME
IF MEI'S FINE WITH THIS...
THEN I GUESS IT'S ALL RIGHT.
NEXT IS THE ARCADE-- RIGHT?
AH!! LOOK AT THIS ONE!!!
LOOK, MEI! ISN'T IT CUUUTE?
WANT ME TO WIN IT FOR YOU?
I...
IT DOESN'T REALLY...

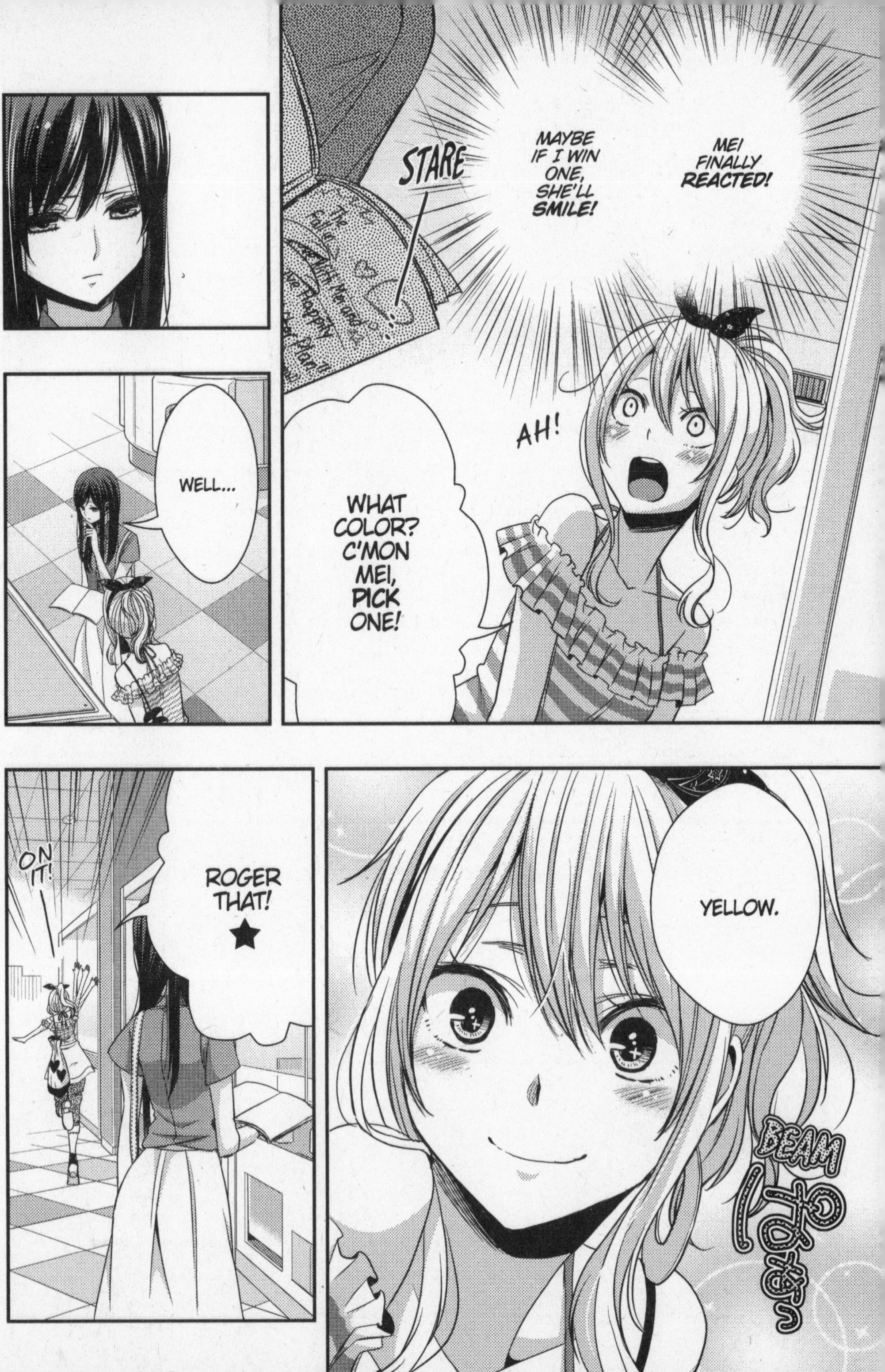
MEI FINALLY REACTED!
MAYBE IF I WIN ONE, SHE'LL SMILE!
STARE
AH!
WHAT COLOR? C'MON MEI, PICK ONE!
WELL...
YELLOW.
BEAM
ROGER THAT! ★
ON IT!

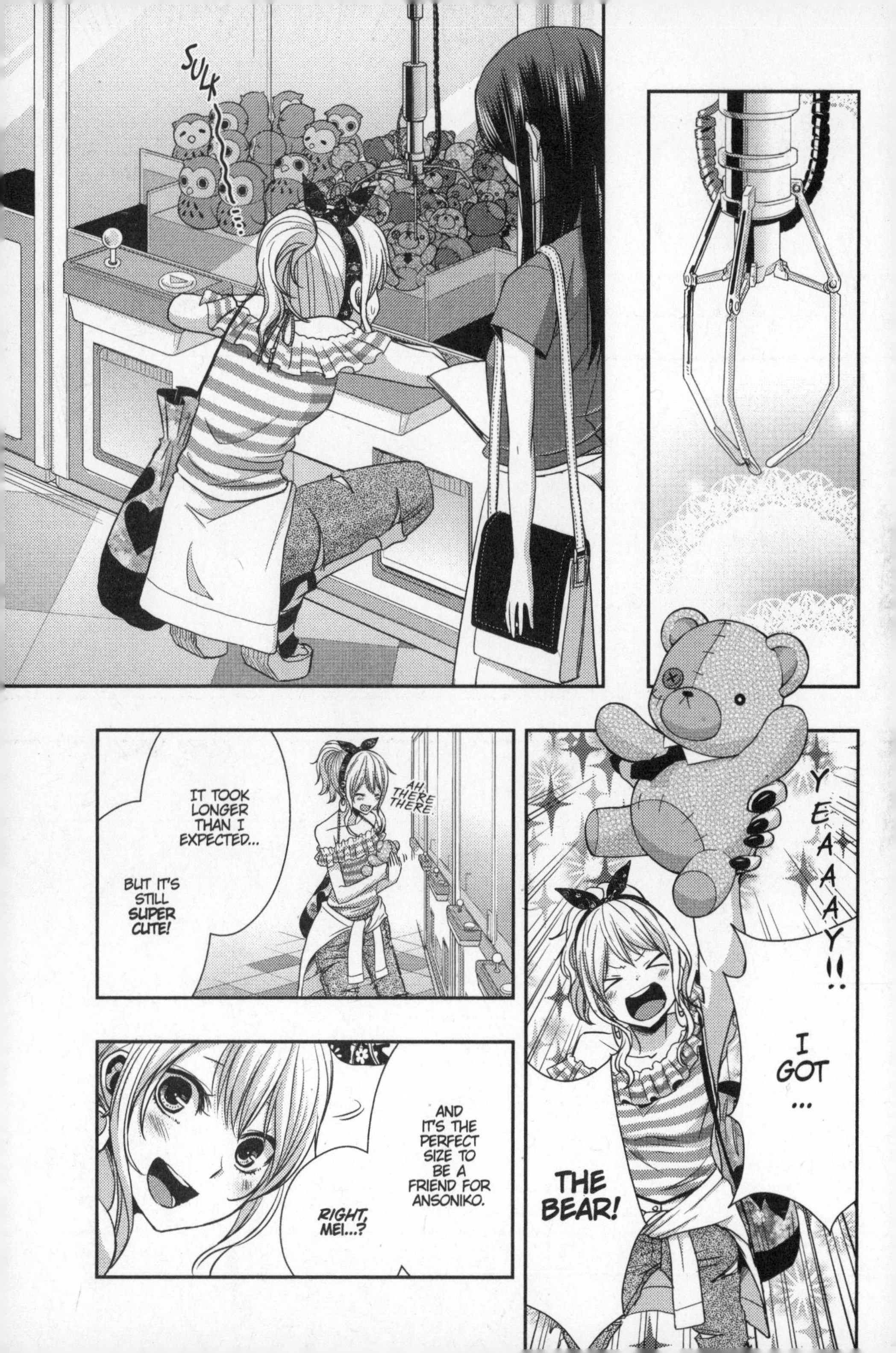
SULK
YEAAAAY!!
I GOT...
THE BEAR!
AH, THERE THERE.
IT TOOK LONGER THAN I EXPECTED...
BUT IT'S STILL SUPER CUTE!
AND IT'S THE PERFECT SIZE TO BE A FRIEND FOR ANSONIKO.
RIGHT, MEI...?

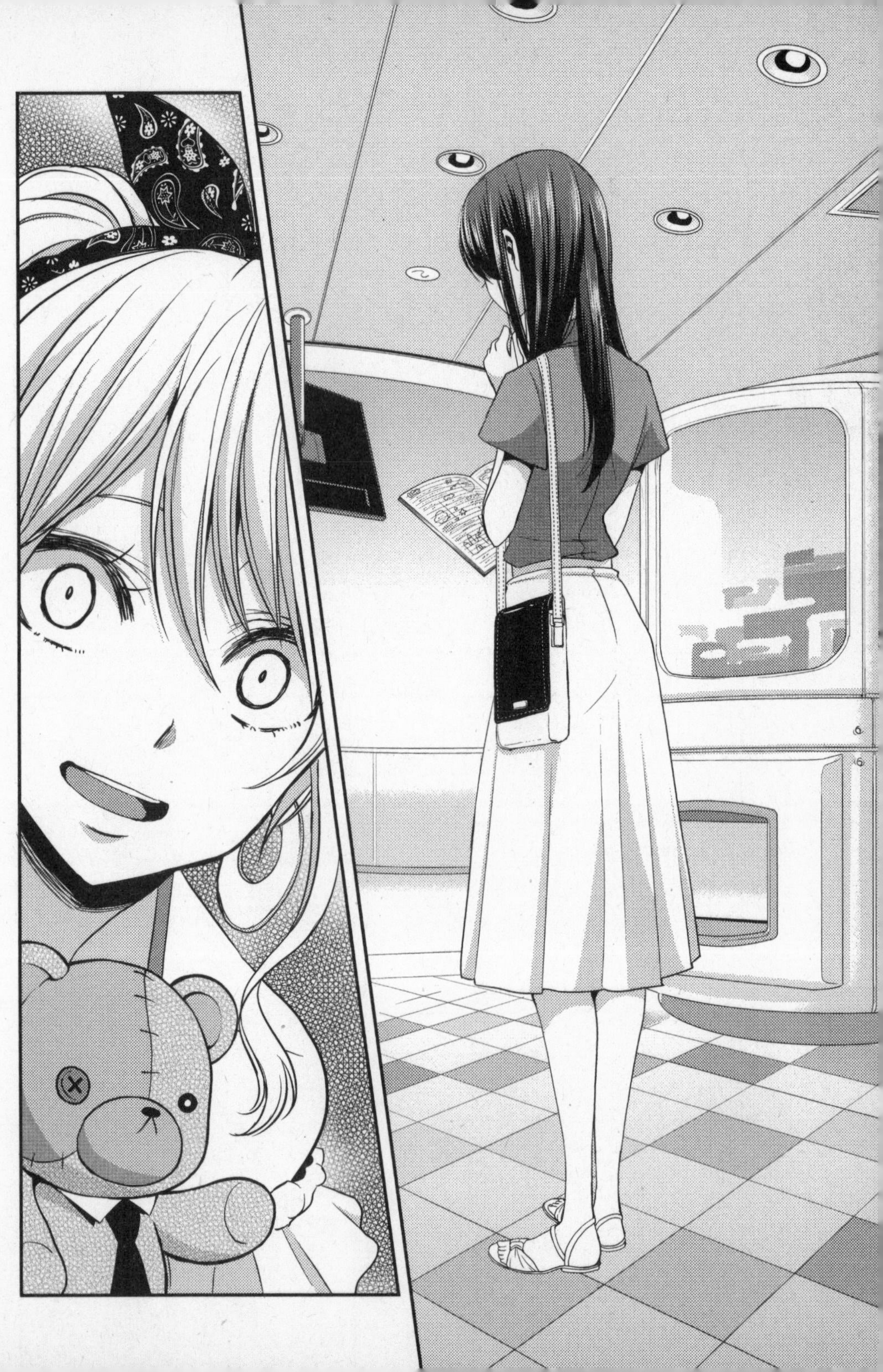

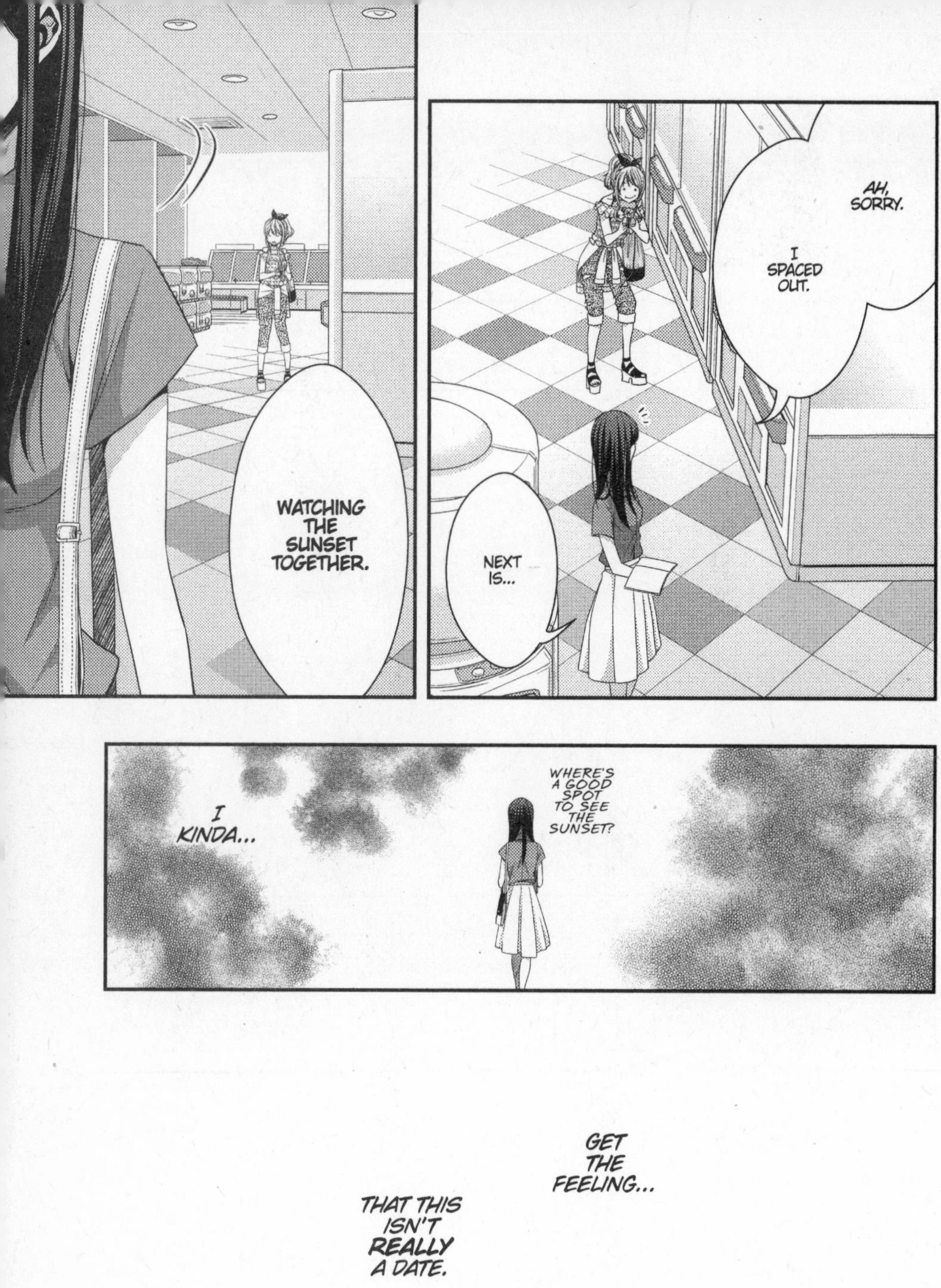
AH, SORRY.
I SPACED OUT.
NEXT IS...
WATCHING THE SUNSET TOGETHER.
WHERE'S A GOOD SPOT TO SEE THE SUNSET?
I KINDA...
GET THE FEELING...
THAT THIS ISN'T REALLY A DATE.

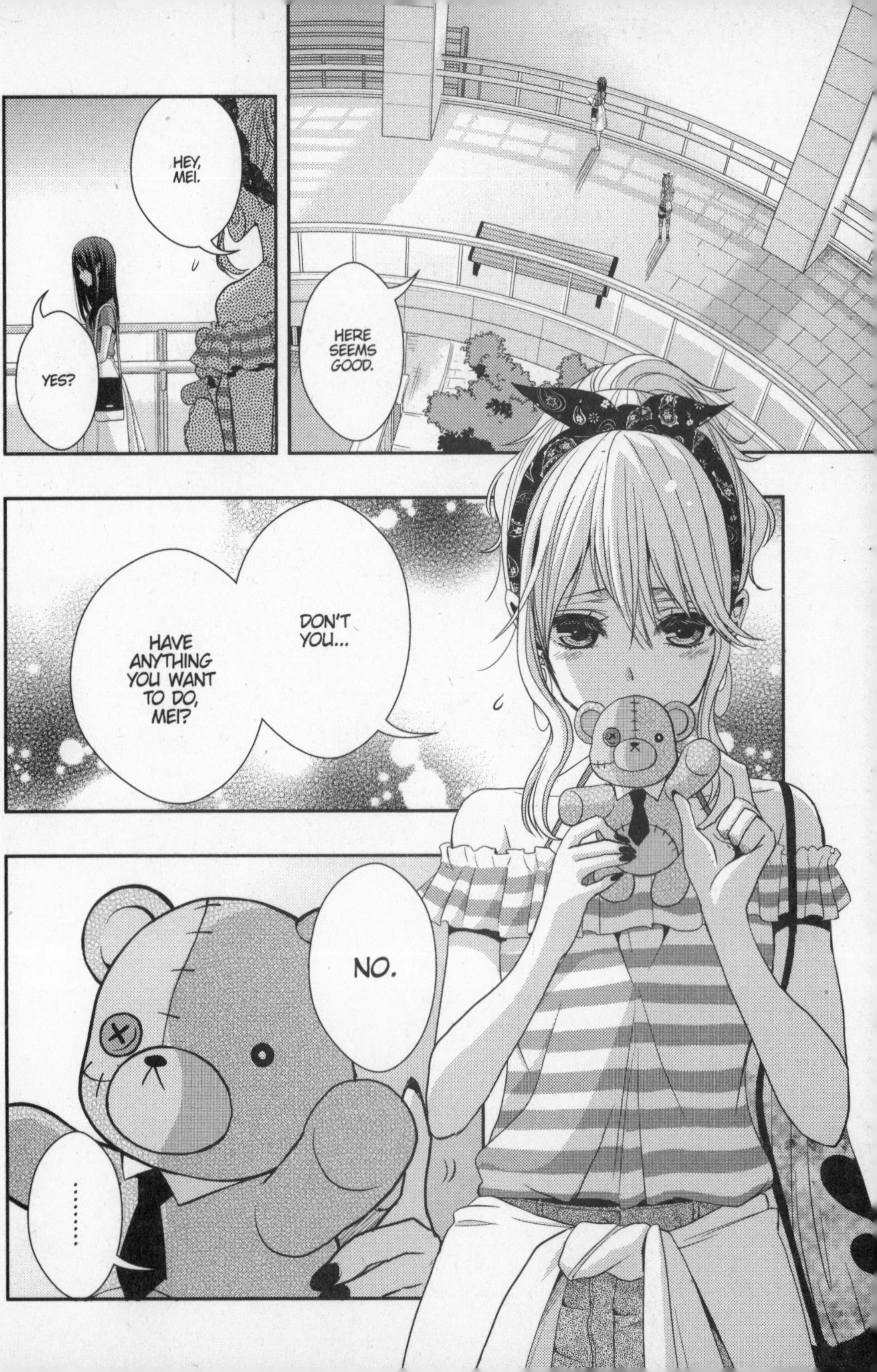
HERE SEEMS GOOD.
HEY, MEI.
YES?
DON'T YOU...
HAVE ANYTHING YOU WANT TO DO, MEI?
NO.
......

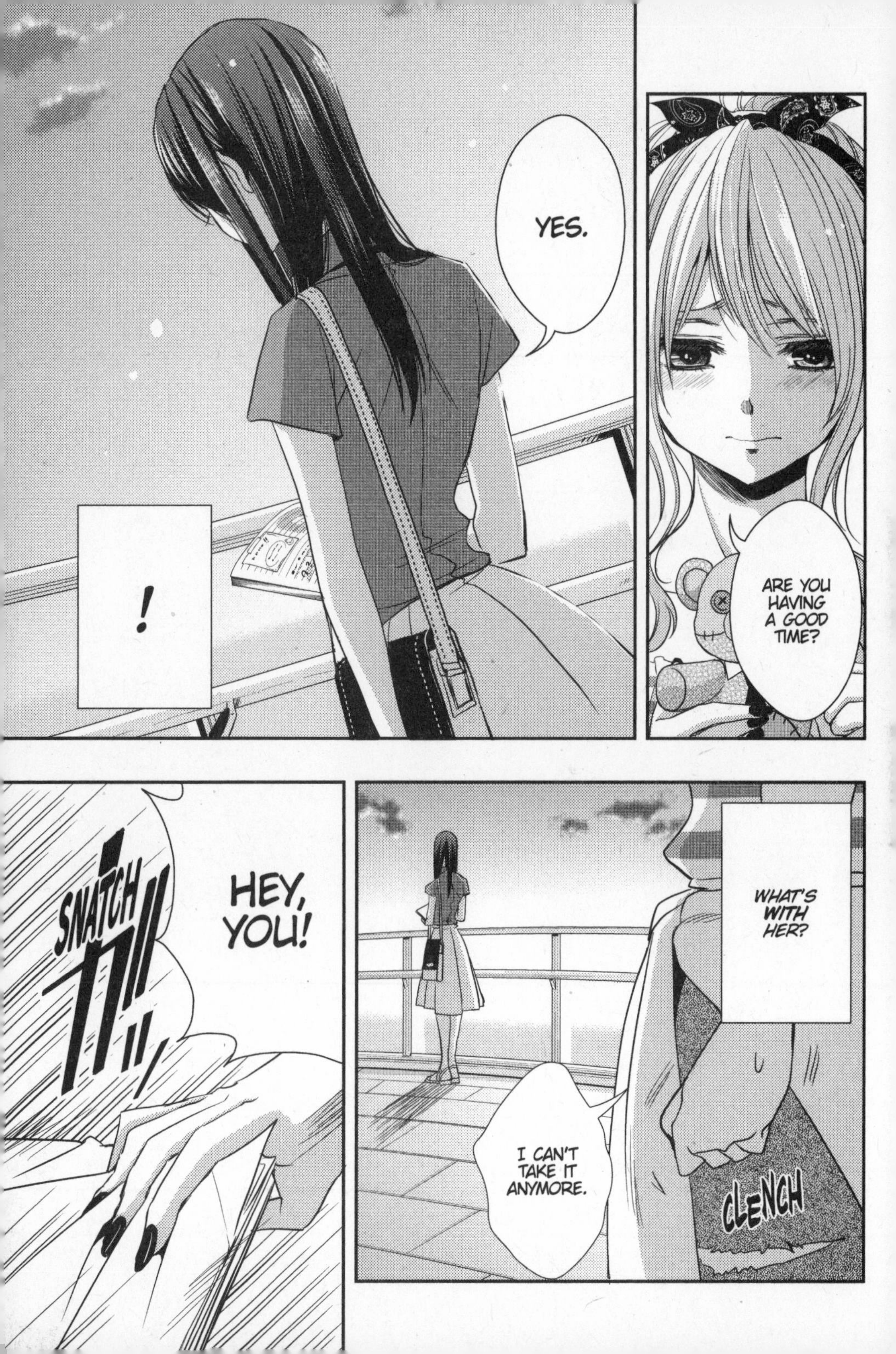
ARE YOU HAVING A GOOD TIME?
YES.
!
WHAT'S WITH HER?
I CAN'T TAKE IT ANYMORE.
CLENCH
HEY, YOU!
SNATCH

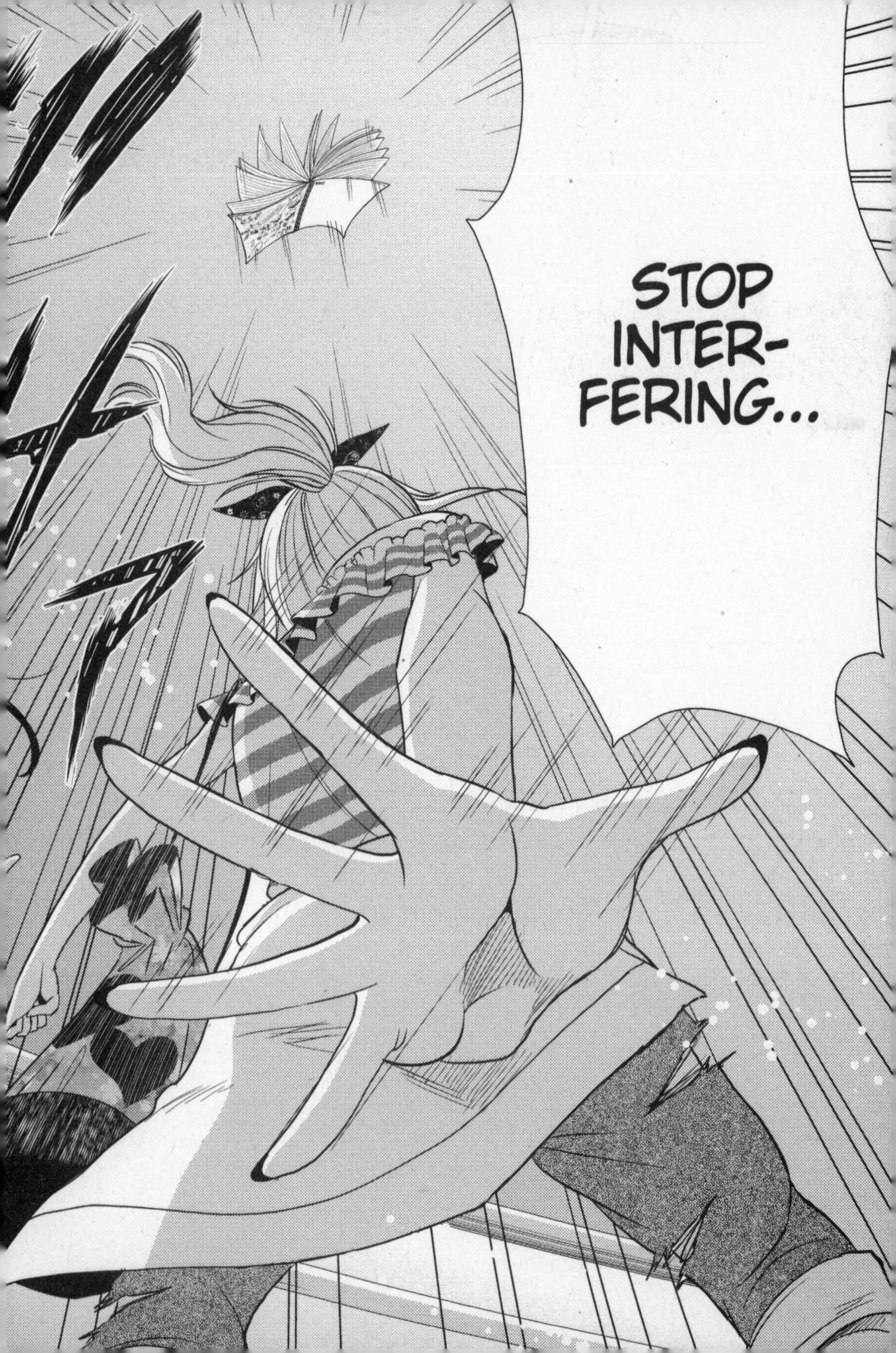
STOP INTER-FERING...

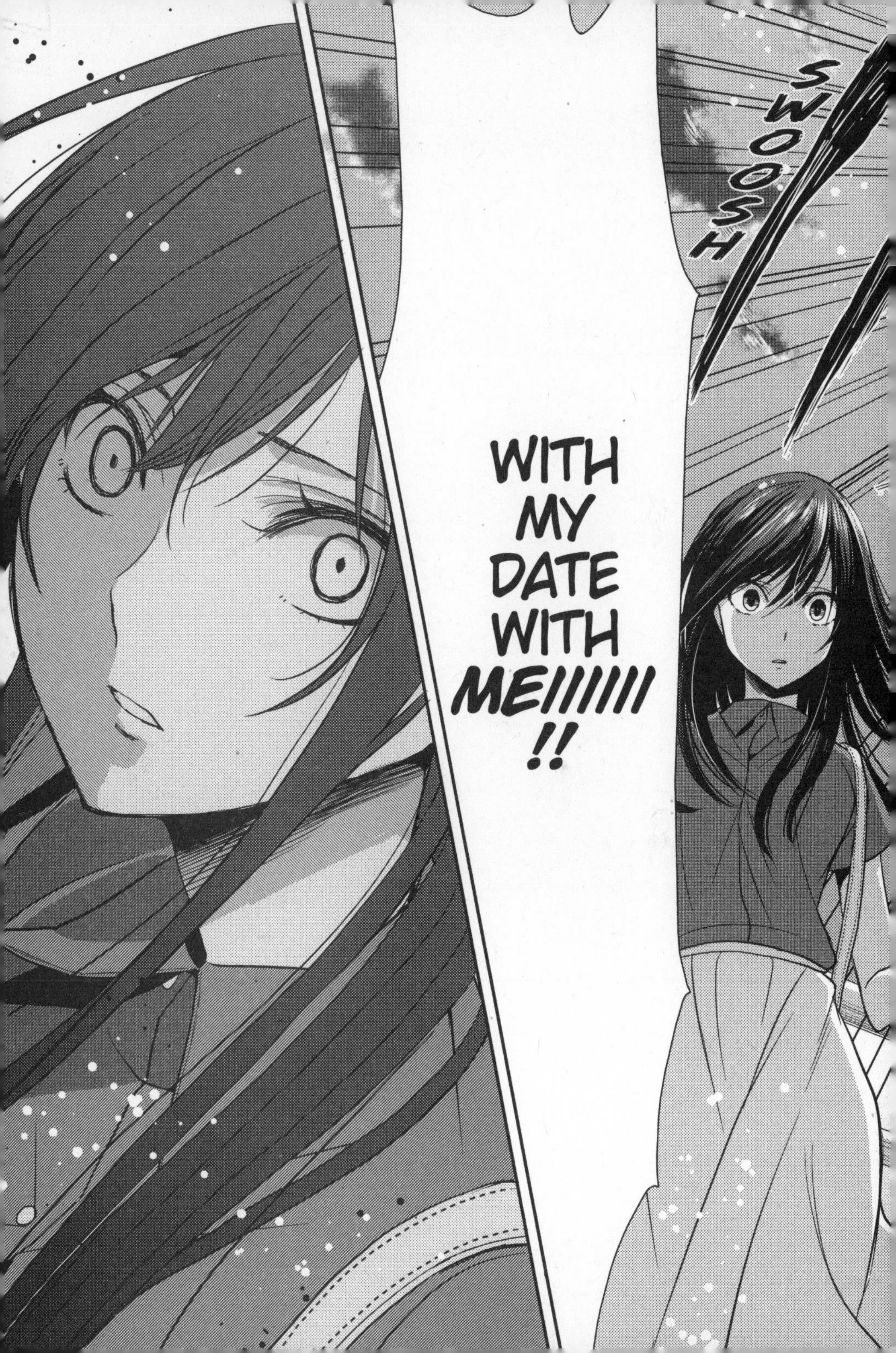

SWOOSH
WITH MY DATE WITH ME!!!!!!
!!

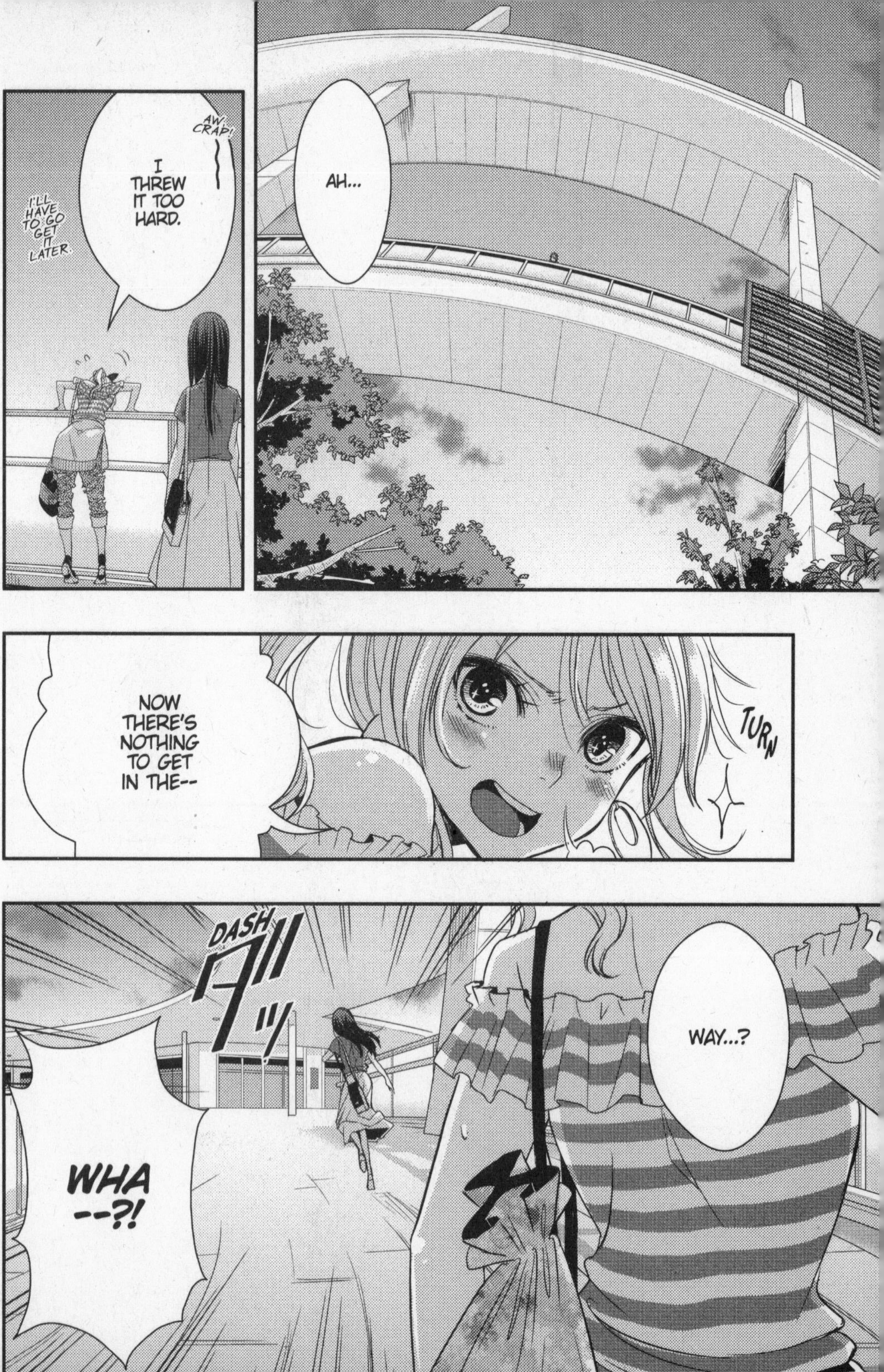
AH...
I THREW IT TOO HARD.
AW CRAP!
I'LL HAVE TO GO GET IT LATER.
NOW THERE'S NOTHING TO GET IN THE--
TURN
WAY...?
DASH
WHA--?!

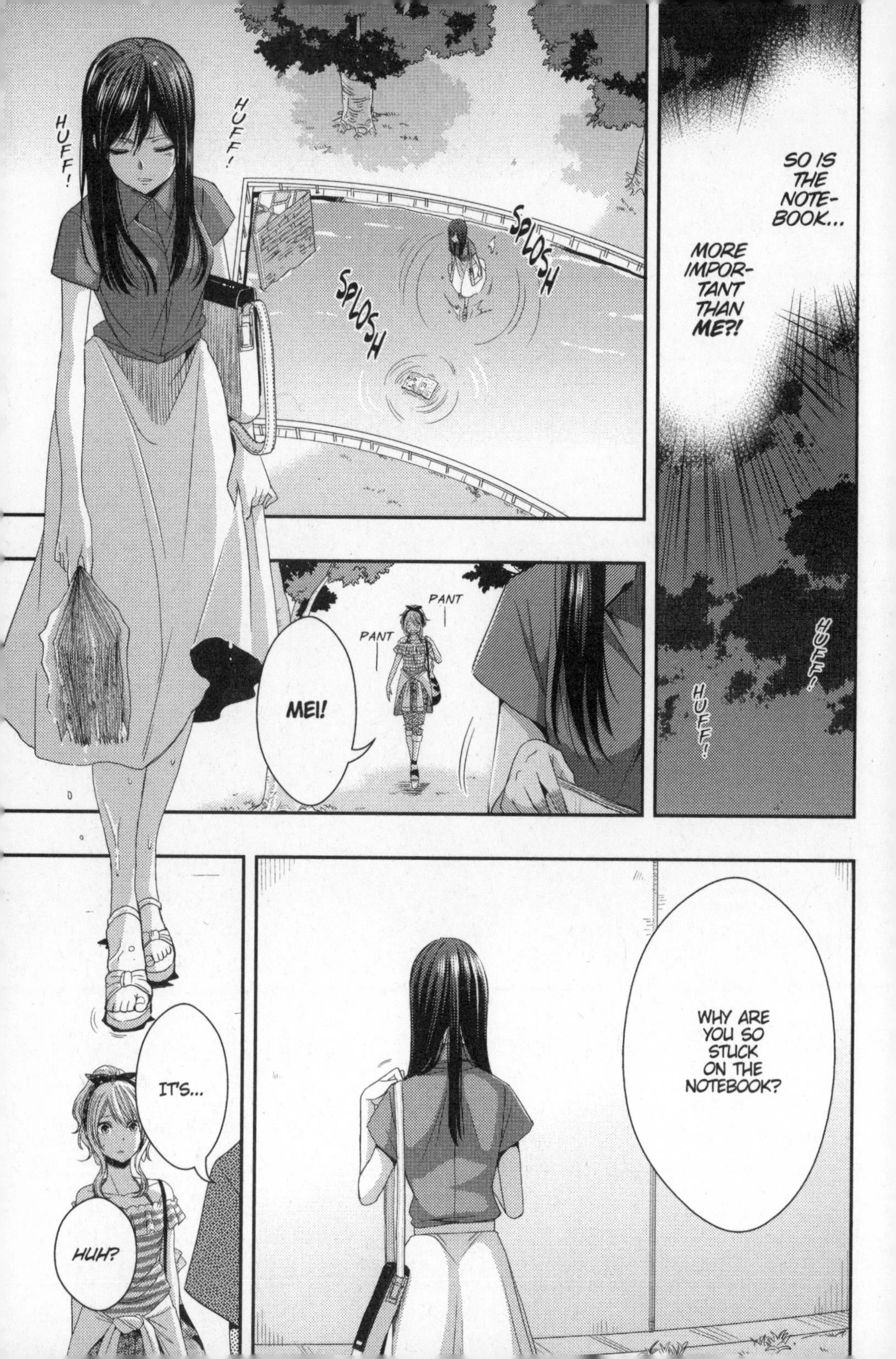
SO IS THE NOTE-BOOK...
MORE IMPORTANT THAN ME?!
HUFF!
HUFF!
SPLOSH
SPLOSH
HUFF!
HUFF!
PANT
PANT
MEI!
WHY ARE YOU SO STUCK ON THE NOTEBOOK?
IT'S...
HUH?

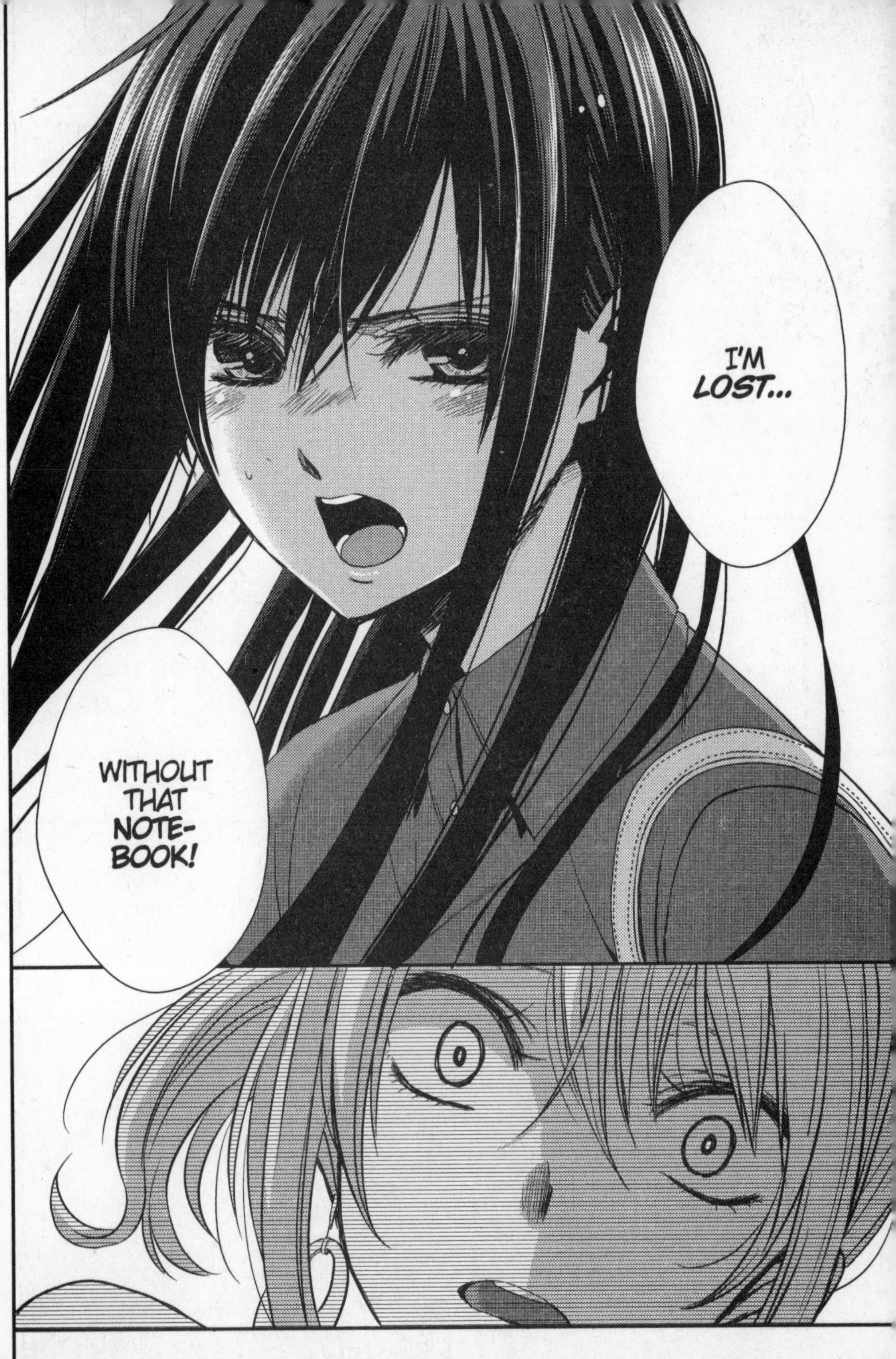
I'M LOST...
WITHOUT THAT NOTE-BOOK!

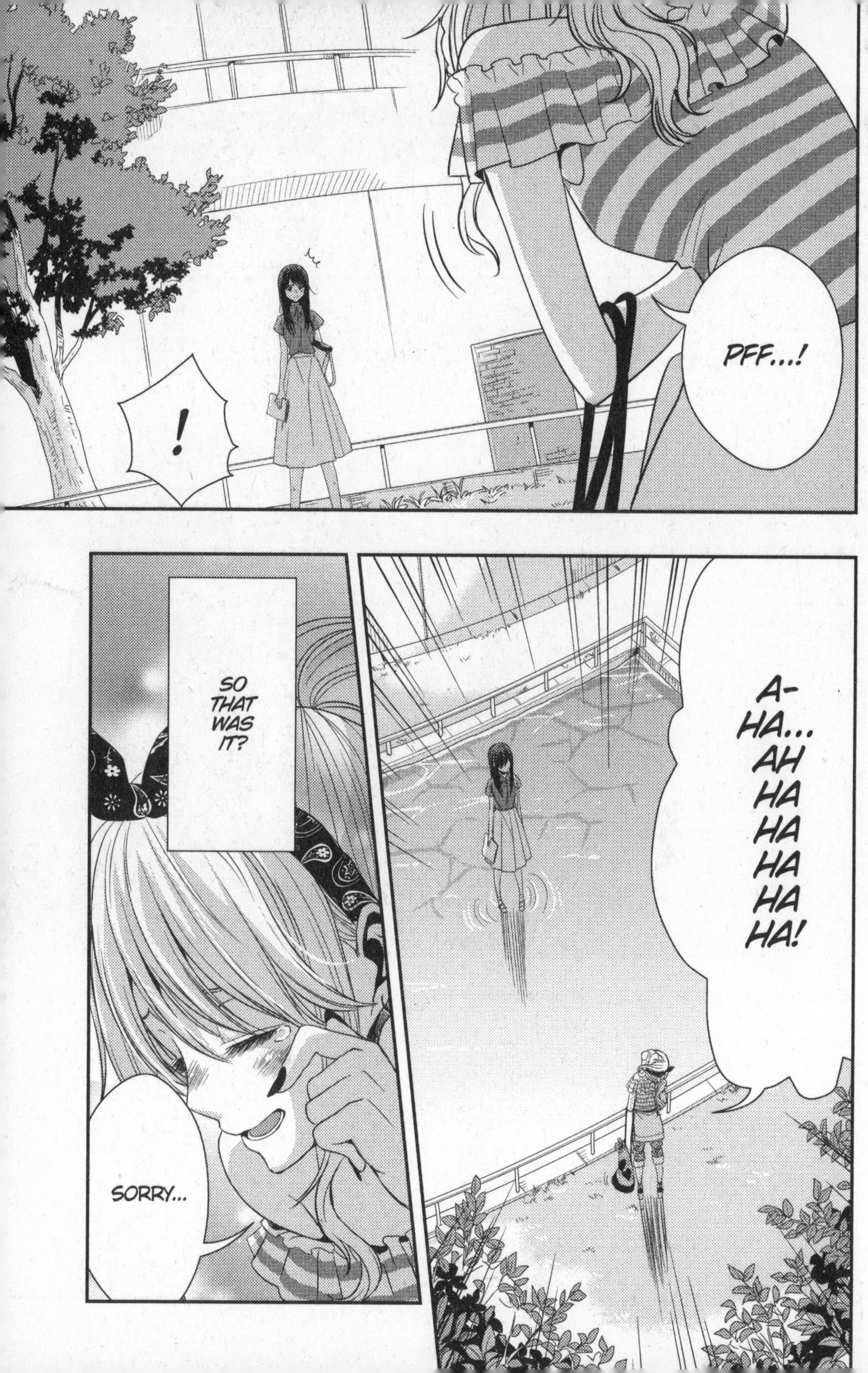
PFF...!
!
A-HA... AH HA HA HA HA HA!
SO THAT WAS IT?
SORRY...

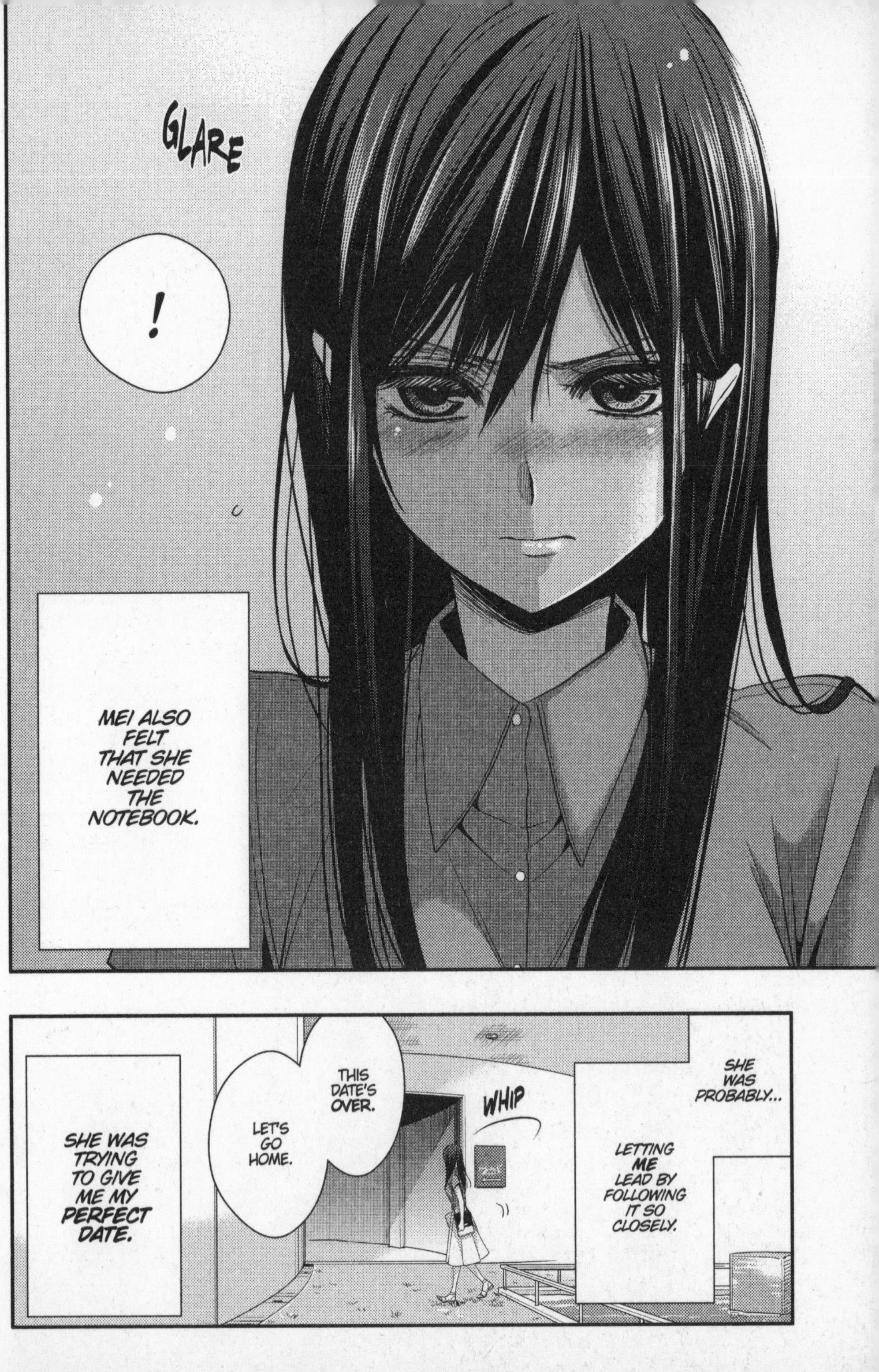
GLARE
!
MEI ALSO FELT THAT SHE NEEDED THE NOTEBOOK.
SHE WAS PROBABLY...
LETTING ME LEAD BY FOLLOWING IT SO CLOSELY.
WHIP
THIS DATE'S OVER.
LET'S GO HOME.
SHE WAS TRYING TO GIVE ME MY PERFECT DATE.

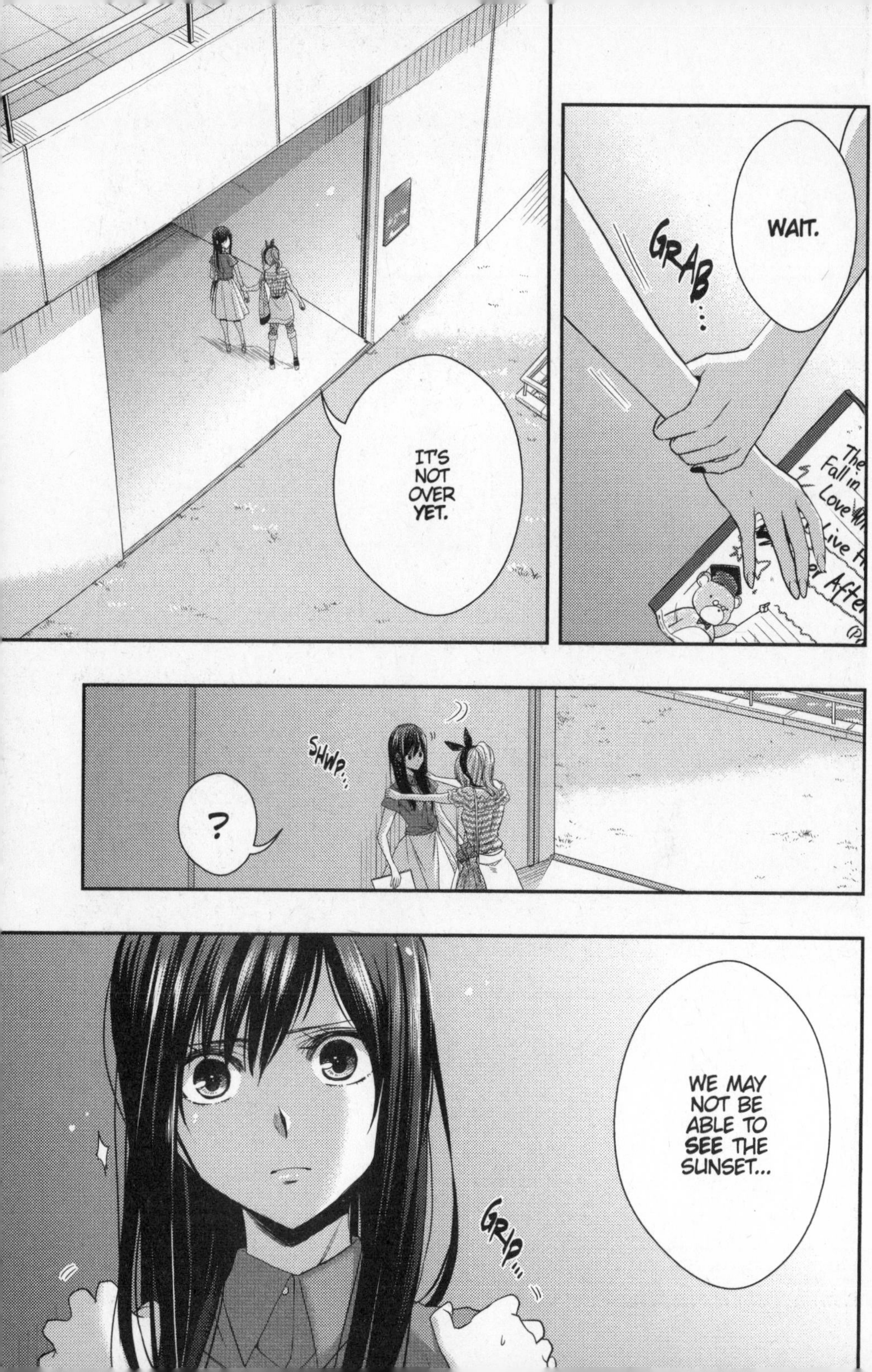
WAIT.
GRAB...
The
Fall in
Love
Live
IT'S NOT OVER YET.
SHWP..
?
WE MAY NOT BE ABLE TO SEE THE SUNSET...
GRIP...

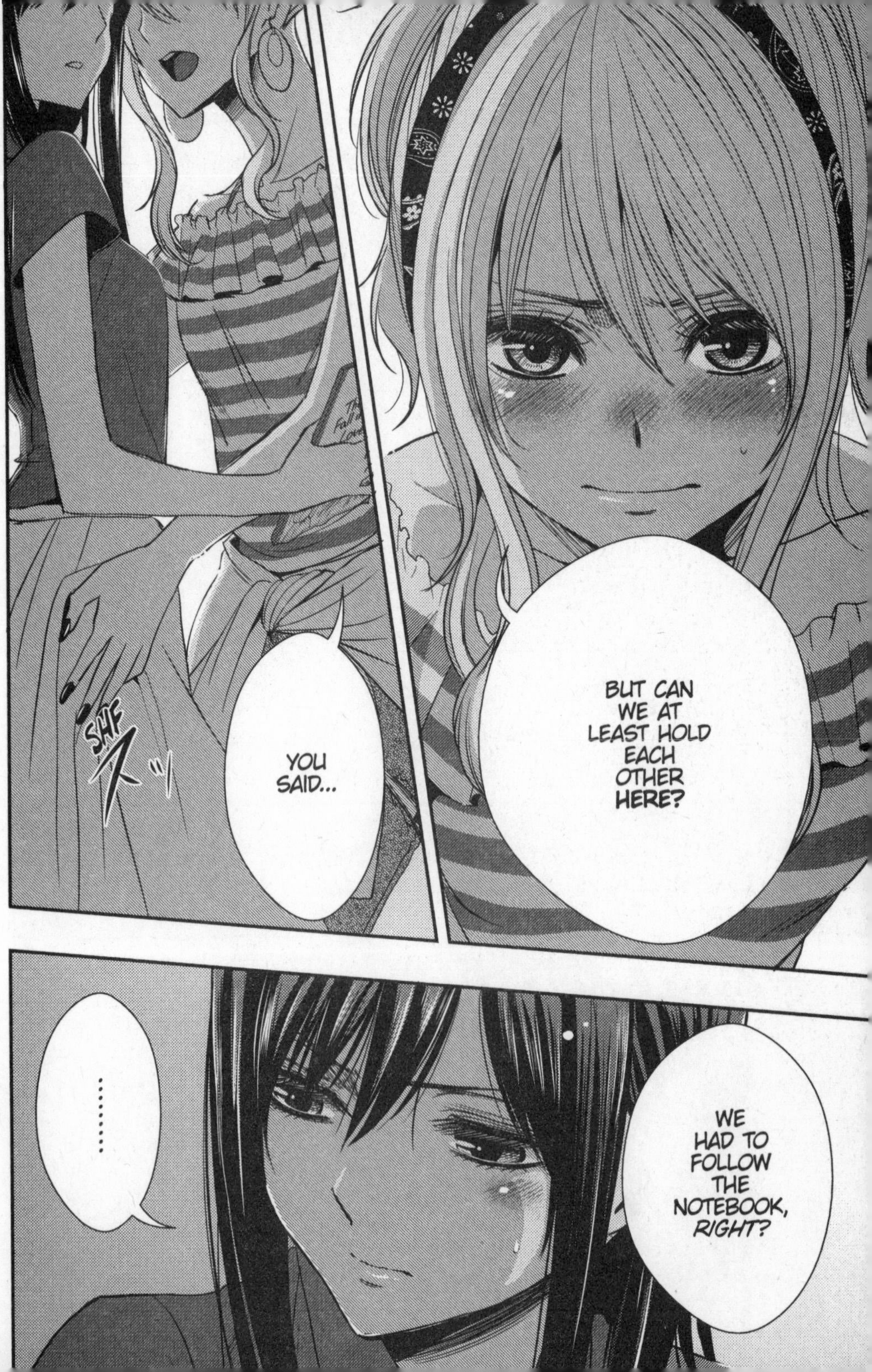
BUT CAN WE AT LEAST HOLD EACH OTHER HERE?
YOU SAID...
SHF
WE HAD TO FOLLOW THE NOTEBOOK, *RIGHT?*
......

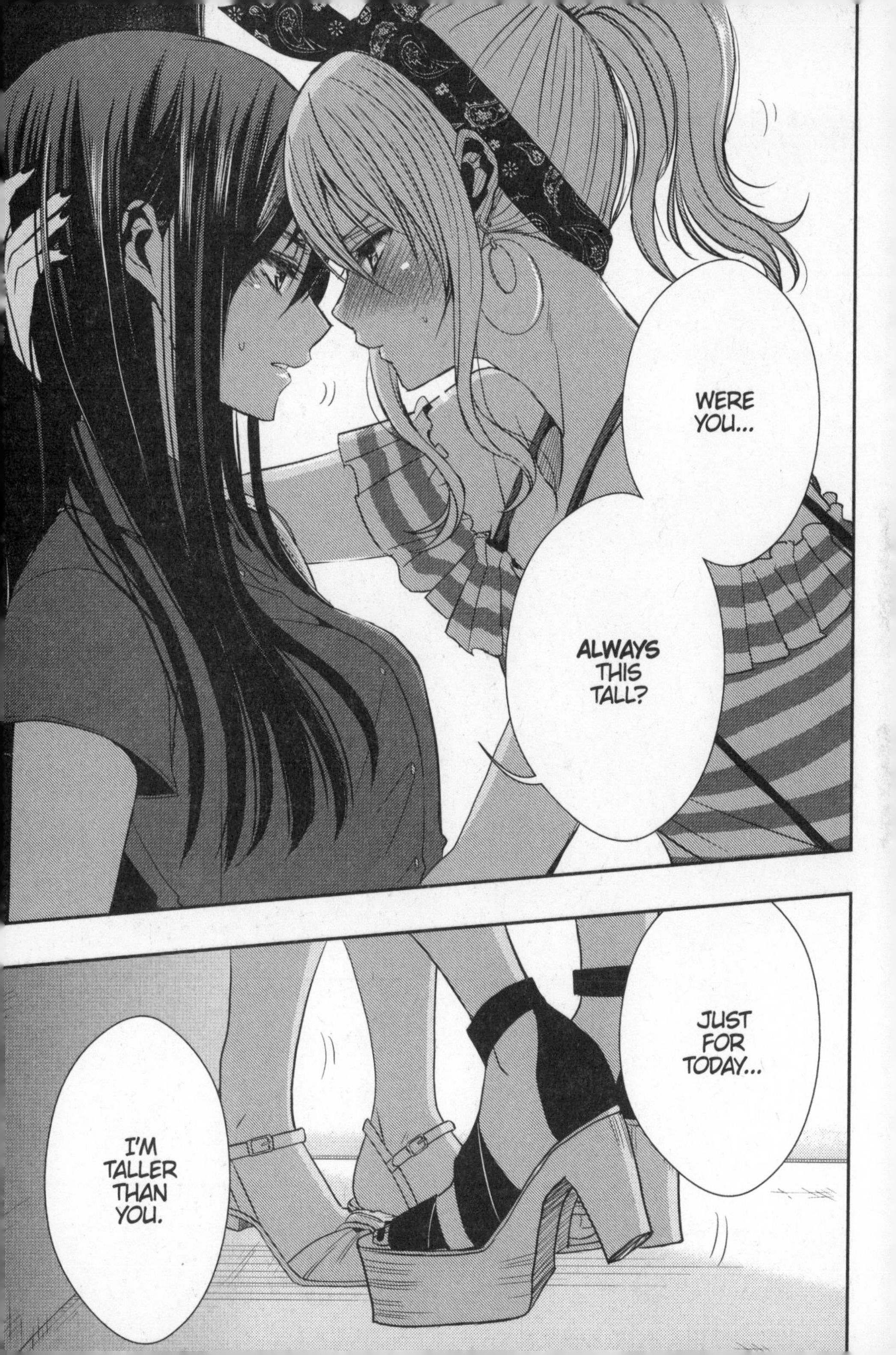
WERE YOU...
ALWAYS THIS TALL?
JUST FOR TODAY...
I'M TALLER THAN YOU.

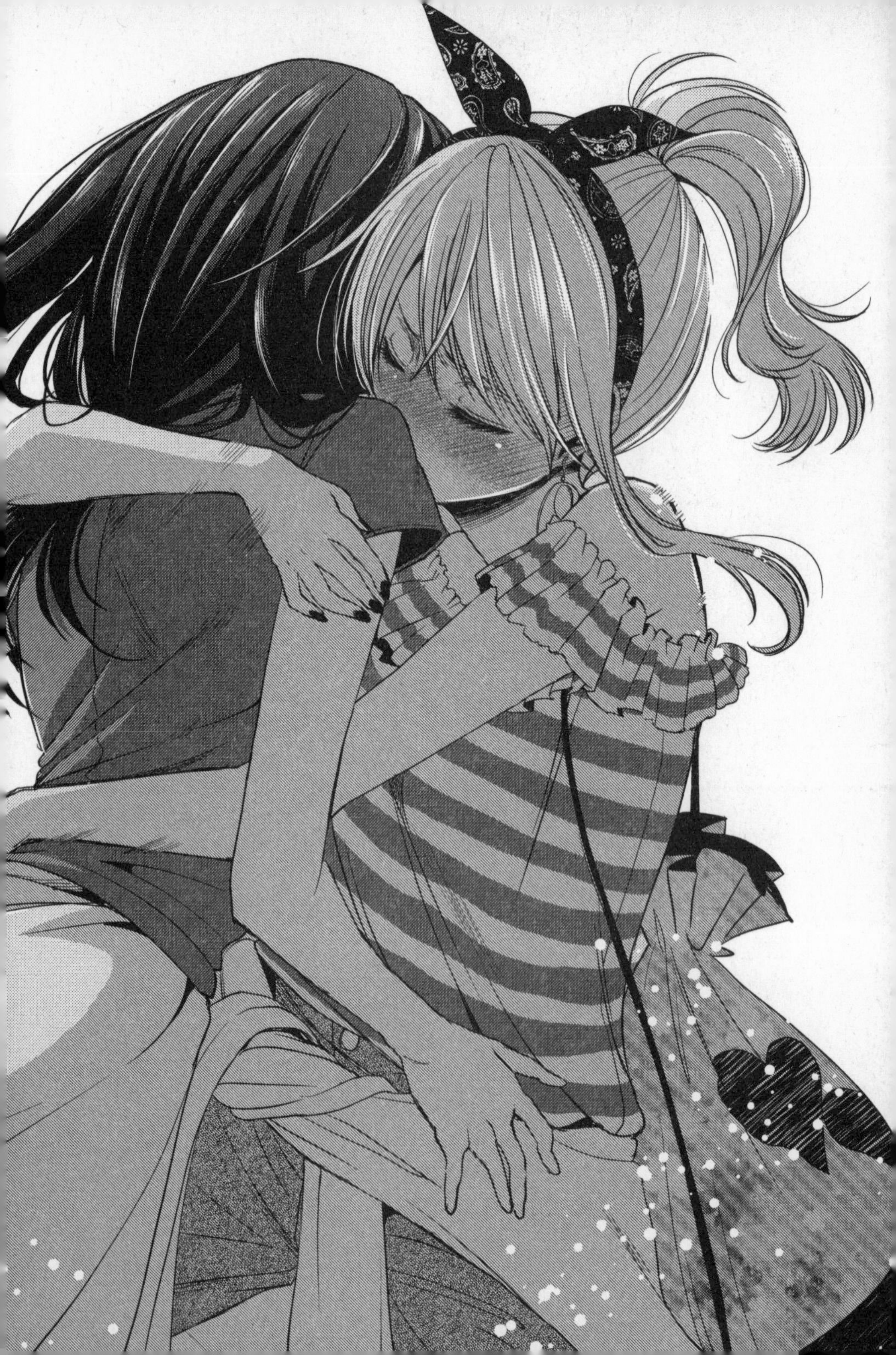

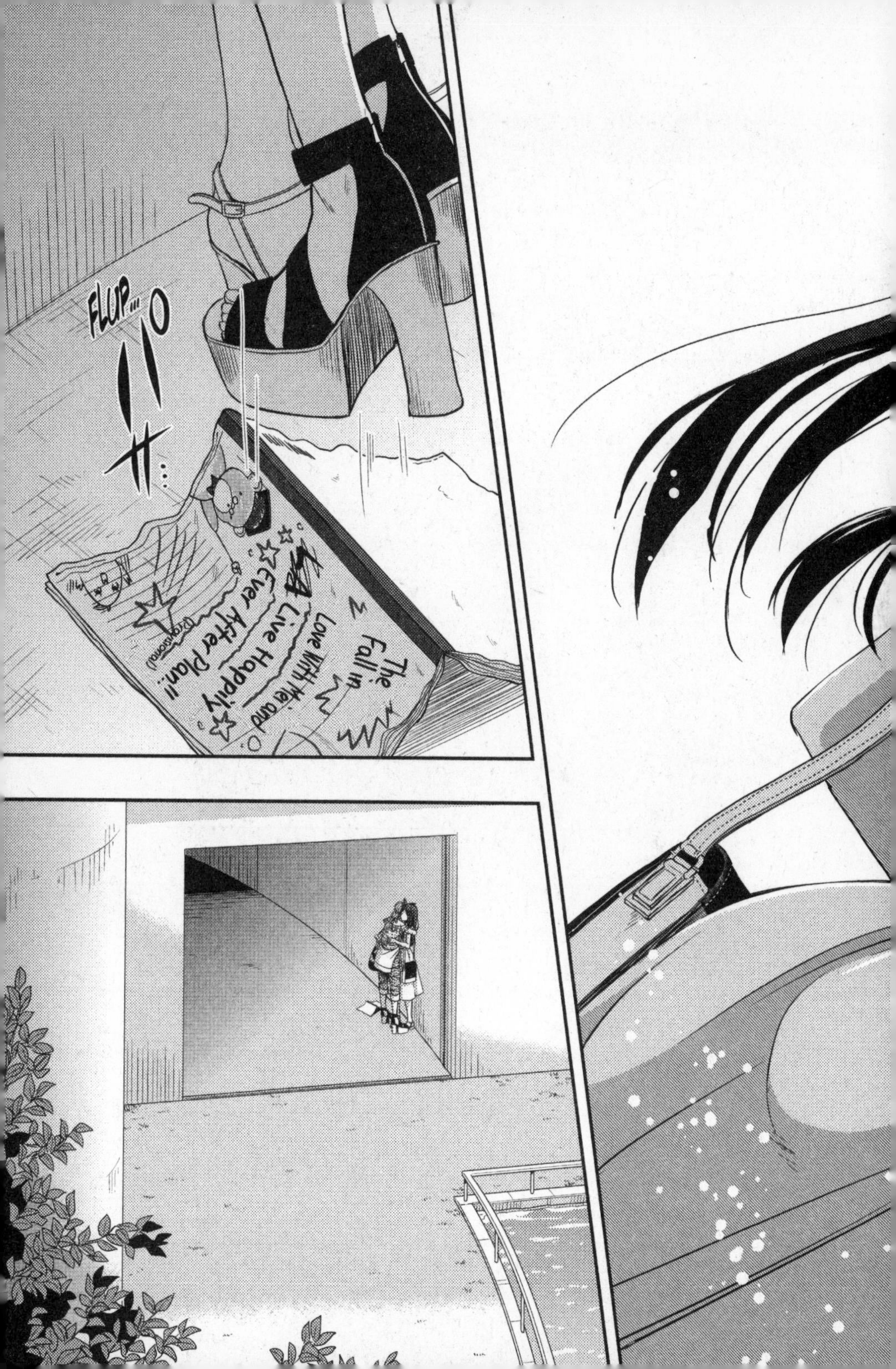
FLUP...
!!
The Fall in Love With Me and Live Happily Ever After Plan!!
(provisional)

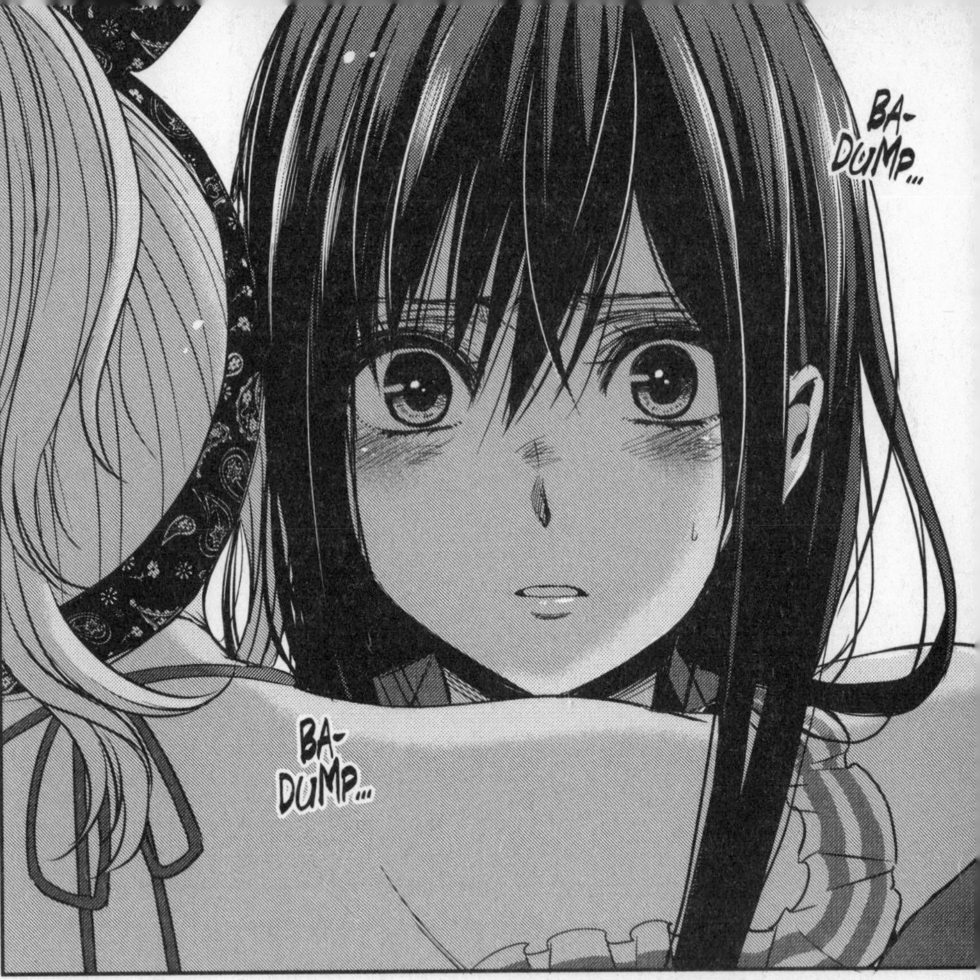
BA-DUMP...
BA-DUMP...

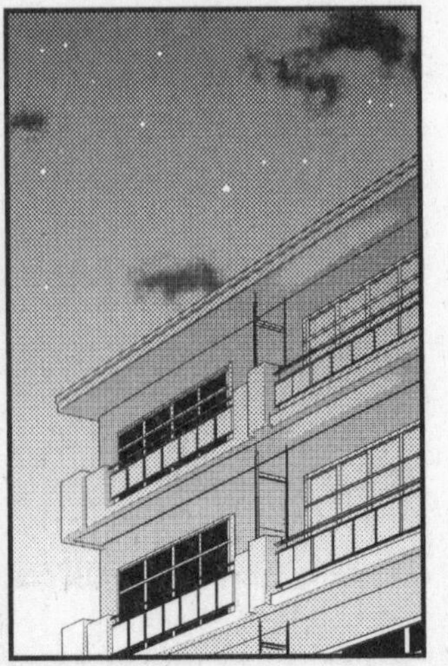

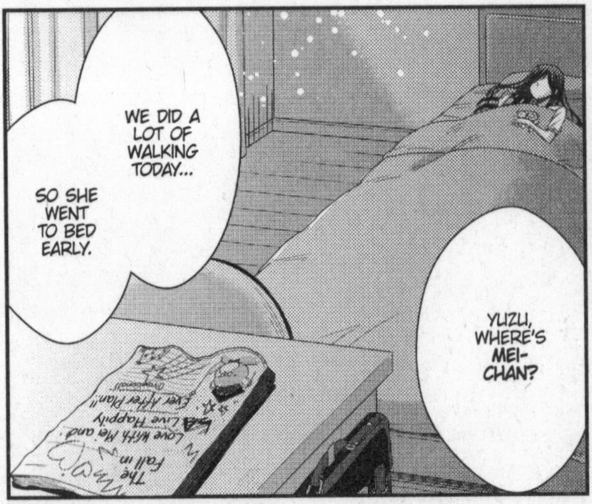
YUZU, WHERE'S MEI-CHAN?
WE DID A LOT OF WALKING TODAY...
SO SHE WENT TO BED EARLY.

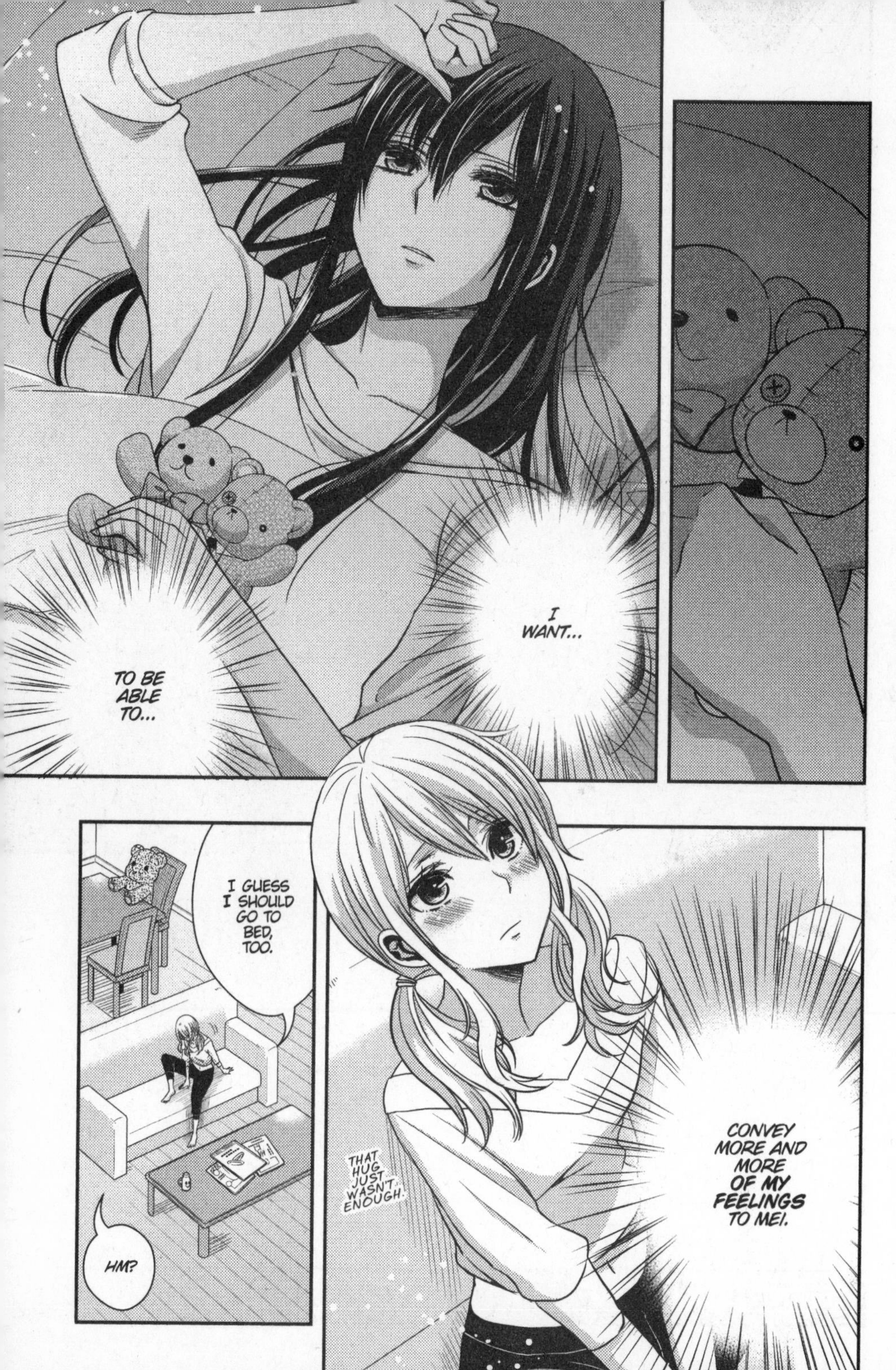
I WANT...
TO BE ABLE TO...
CONVEY MORE AND MORE OF MY FEELINGS TO MEI.
THAT HUG JUST WASN'T ENOUGH.
I GUESS I SHOULD GO TO BED, TOO.
HM?

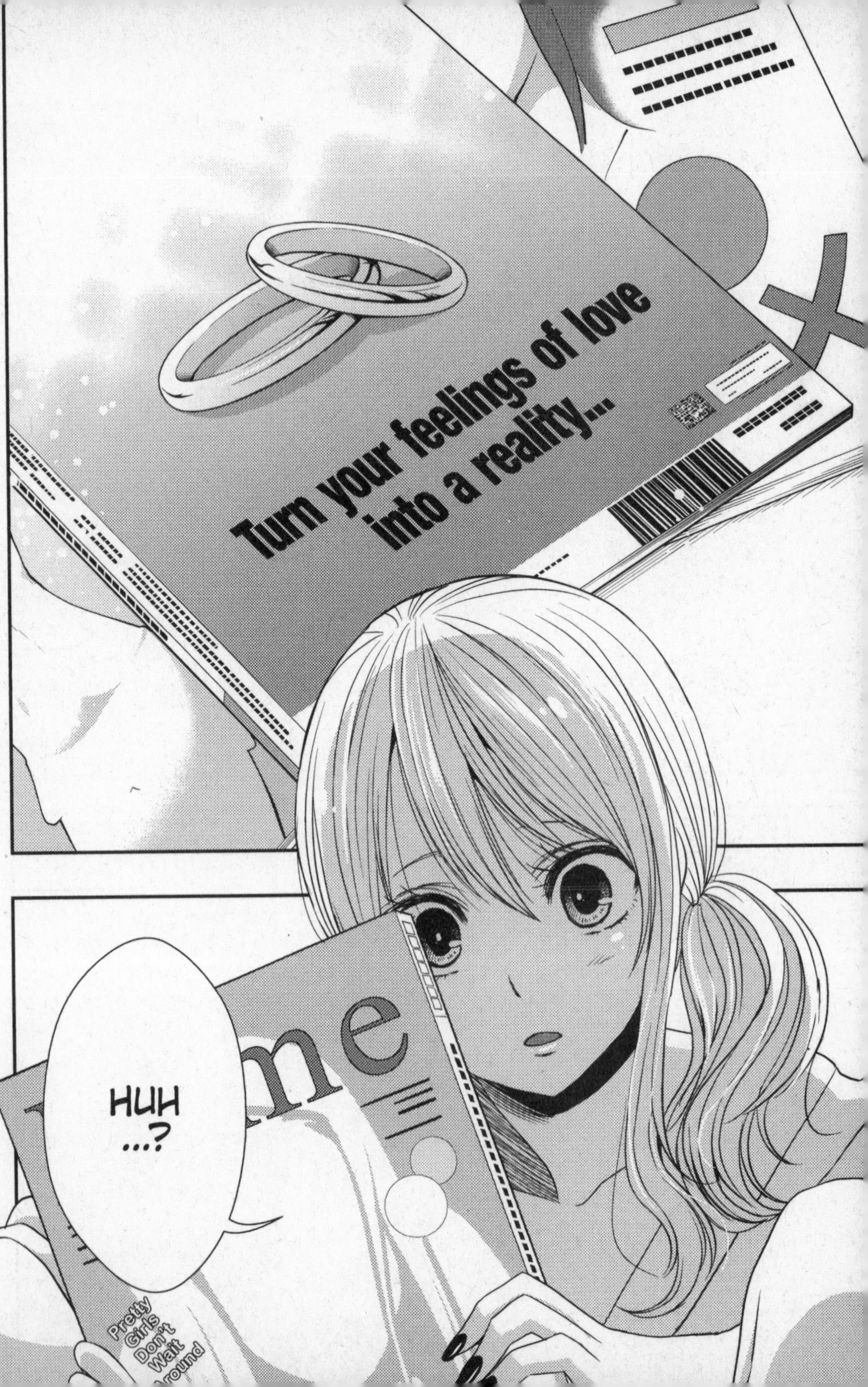
Turn your feelings of love into a reality...
me
HUH ...?
Pretty Girls Don't Wait Around

citrus
SECRET LOVE AFFAIR WITH SISTER

citrus

SABUROUTA PRESENTS SECRET LOVE AFFAIR WITH SISTER

6

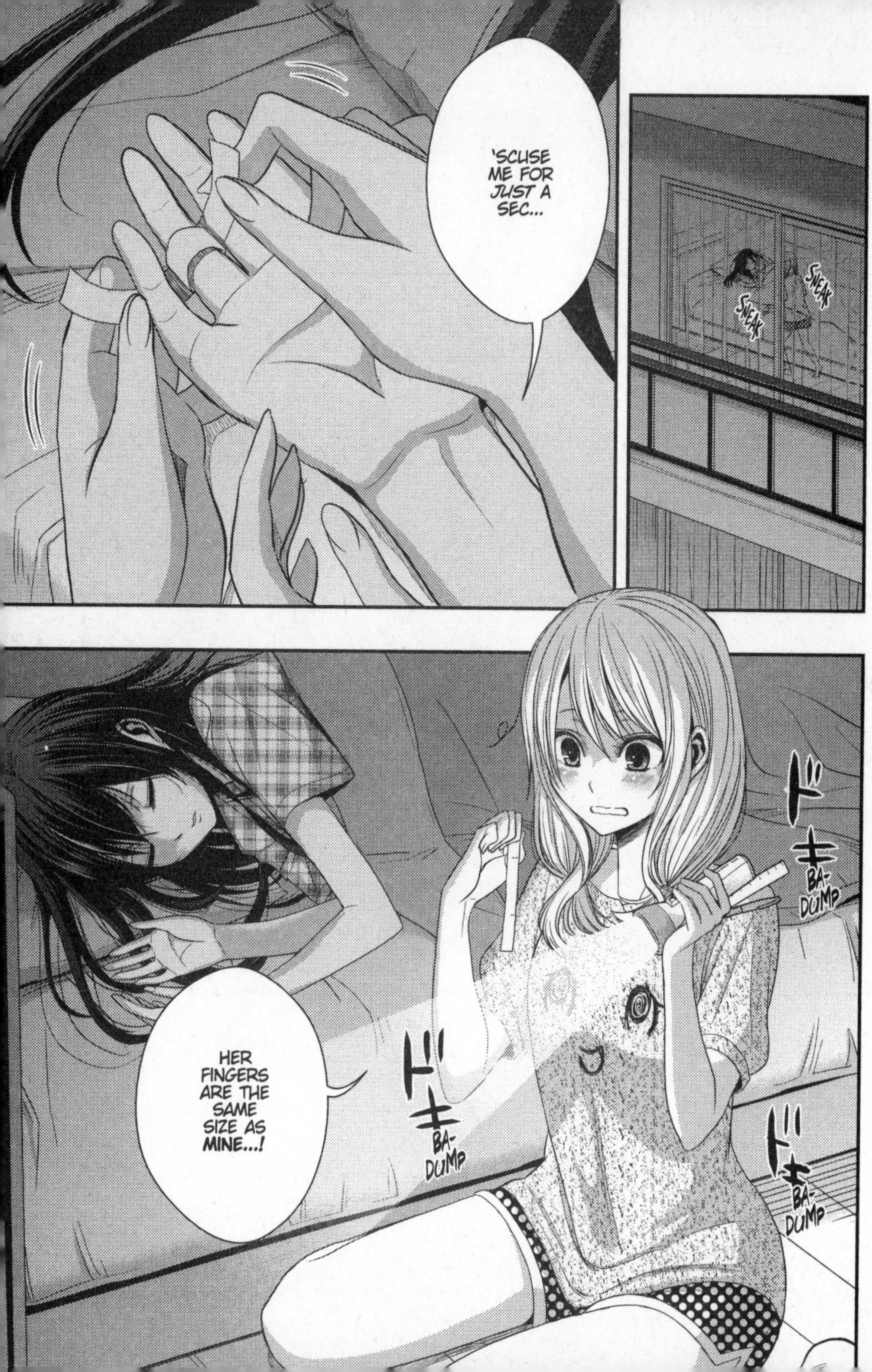
SNEAK
SNEAK
'SCUSE ME FOR JUST A SEC...
ドキ
BA-DUMP
ドキ
BA-DUMP
ドキ
BA-DUMP
HER FINGERS ARE THE SAME SIZE AS MINE...!

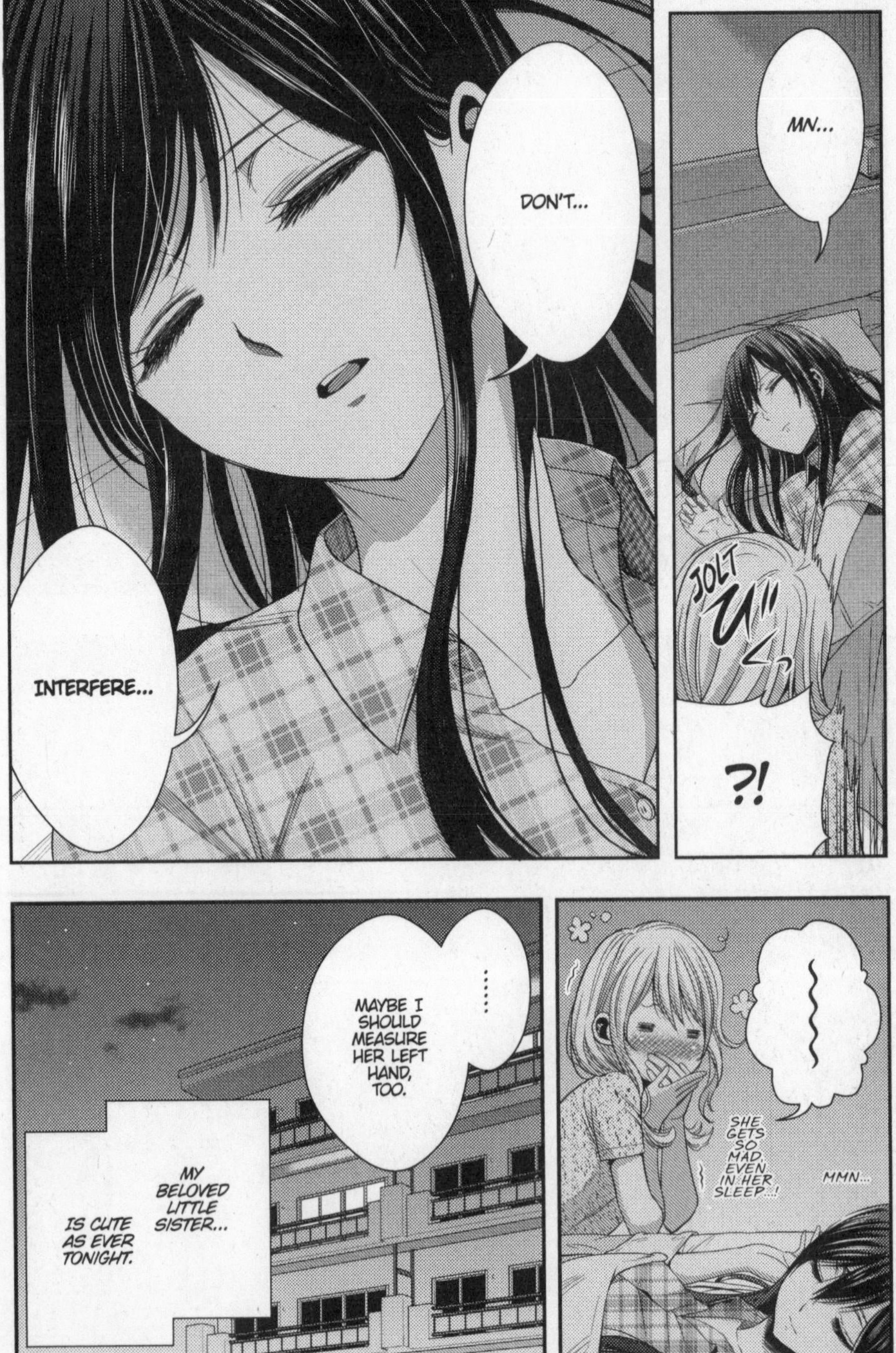
MN...
JOLT
?!
DON'T...
INTERFERE...
SHE GETS SO MAD, EVEN IN HER SLEEP...!
MMN...
......
MAYBE I SHOULD MEASURE HER LEFT HAND, TOO.
MY BELOVED LITTLE SISTER...
IS CUTE AS EVER TONIGHT.

23.the way I love

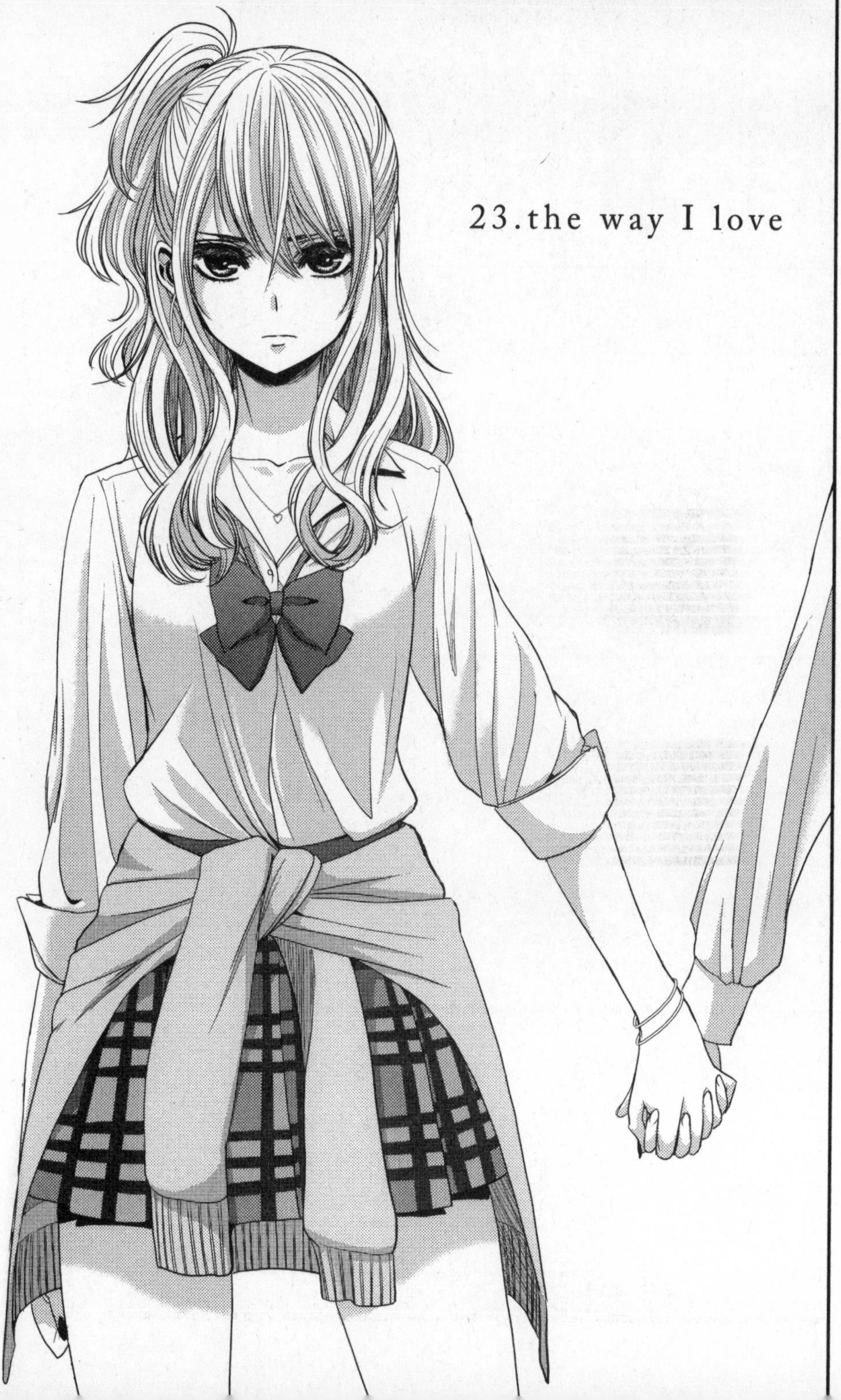

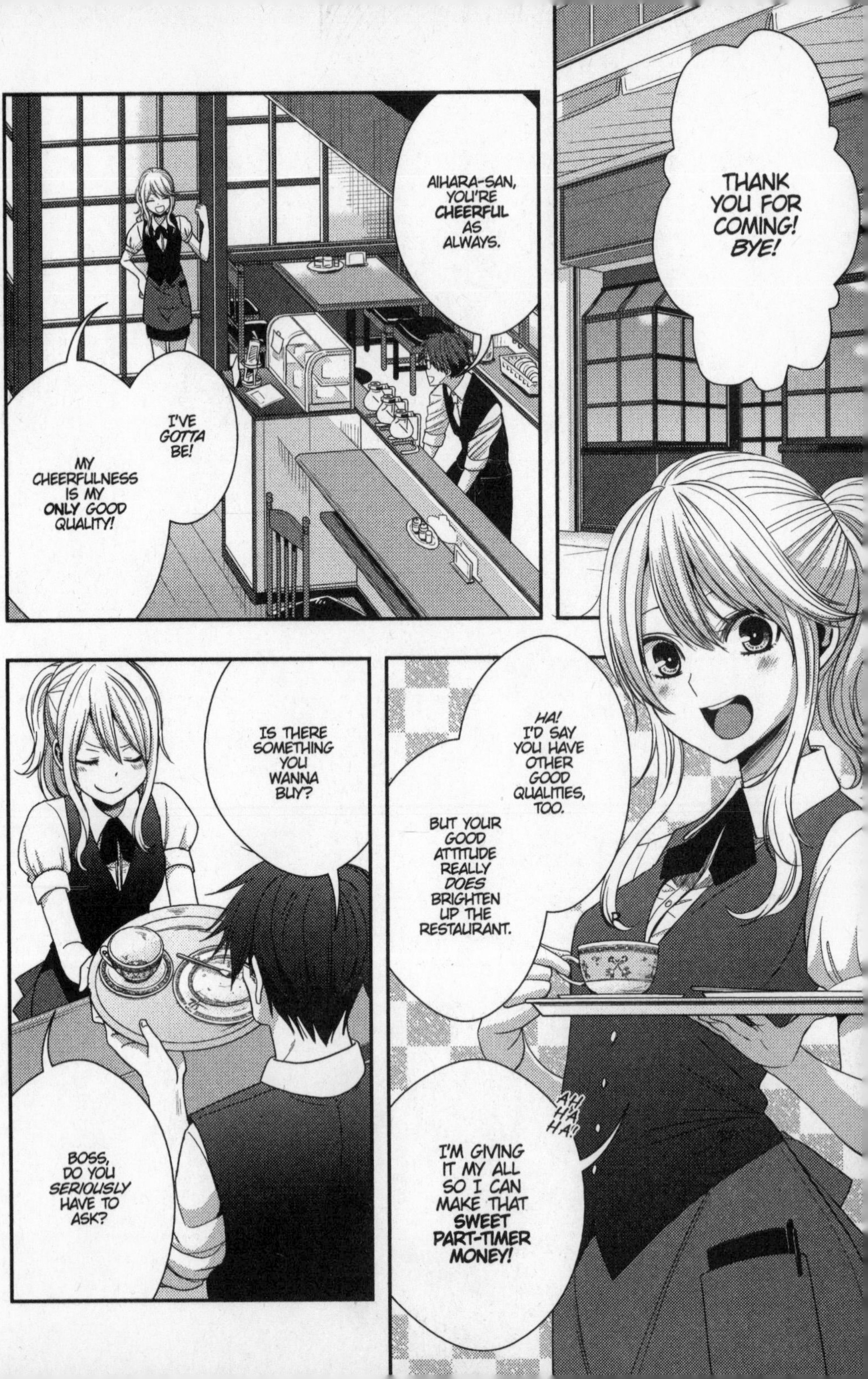
THANK YOU FOR COMING! BYE!
AIHARA-SAN, YOU'RE CHEERFUL AS ALWAYS.
I'VE GOTTA BE!
MY CHEERFULNESS IS MY ONLY GOOD QUALITY!
HA! I'D SAY YOU HAVE OTHER GOOD QUALITIES, TOO.
BUT YOUR GOOD ATTITUDE REALLY DOES BRIGHTEN UP THE RESTAURANT.
AH HA HA!
I'M GIVING IT MY ALL SO I CAN MAKE THAT SWEET PART-TIMER MONEY!
IS THERE SOMETHING YOU WANNA BUY?
BOSS, DO YOU SERIOUSLY HAVE TO ASK?

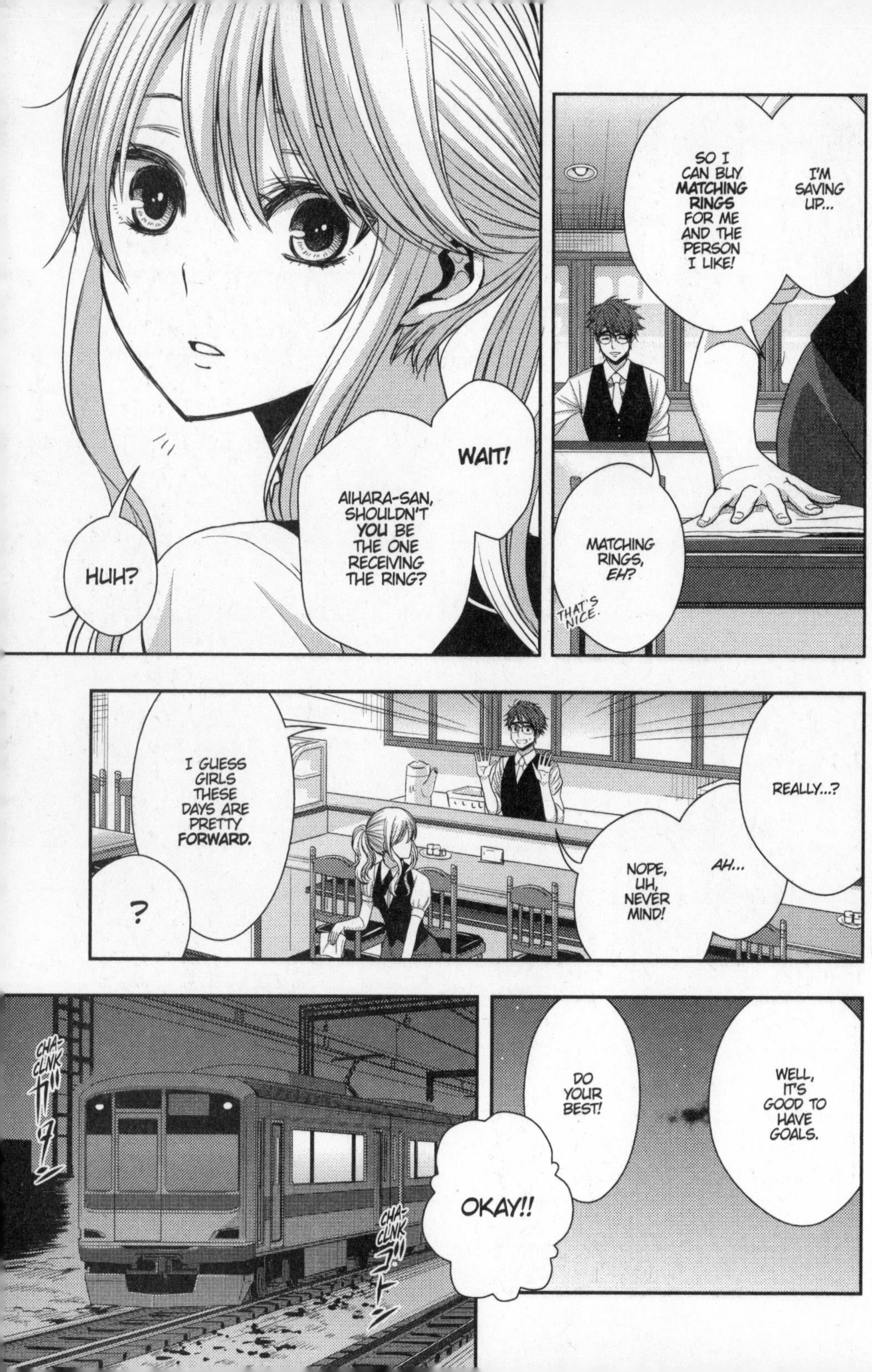
I'M SAVING UP...
SO I CAN BUY MATCHING RINGS FOR ME AND THE PERSON I LIKE!
MATCHING RINGS, EH?
THAT'S NICE.
WAIT!
AIHARA-SAN, SHOULDN'T YOU BE THE ONE RECEIVING THE RING?
HUH?
REALLY...?
AH...
NOPE, UH, NEVER MIND!
I GUESS GIRLS THESE DAYS ARE PRETTY FORWARD.
?
WELL, IT'S GOOD TO HAVE GOALS.
DO YOUR BEST!
OKAY!!
CHA-CLINK
CHA-CLINK

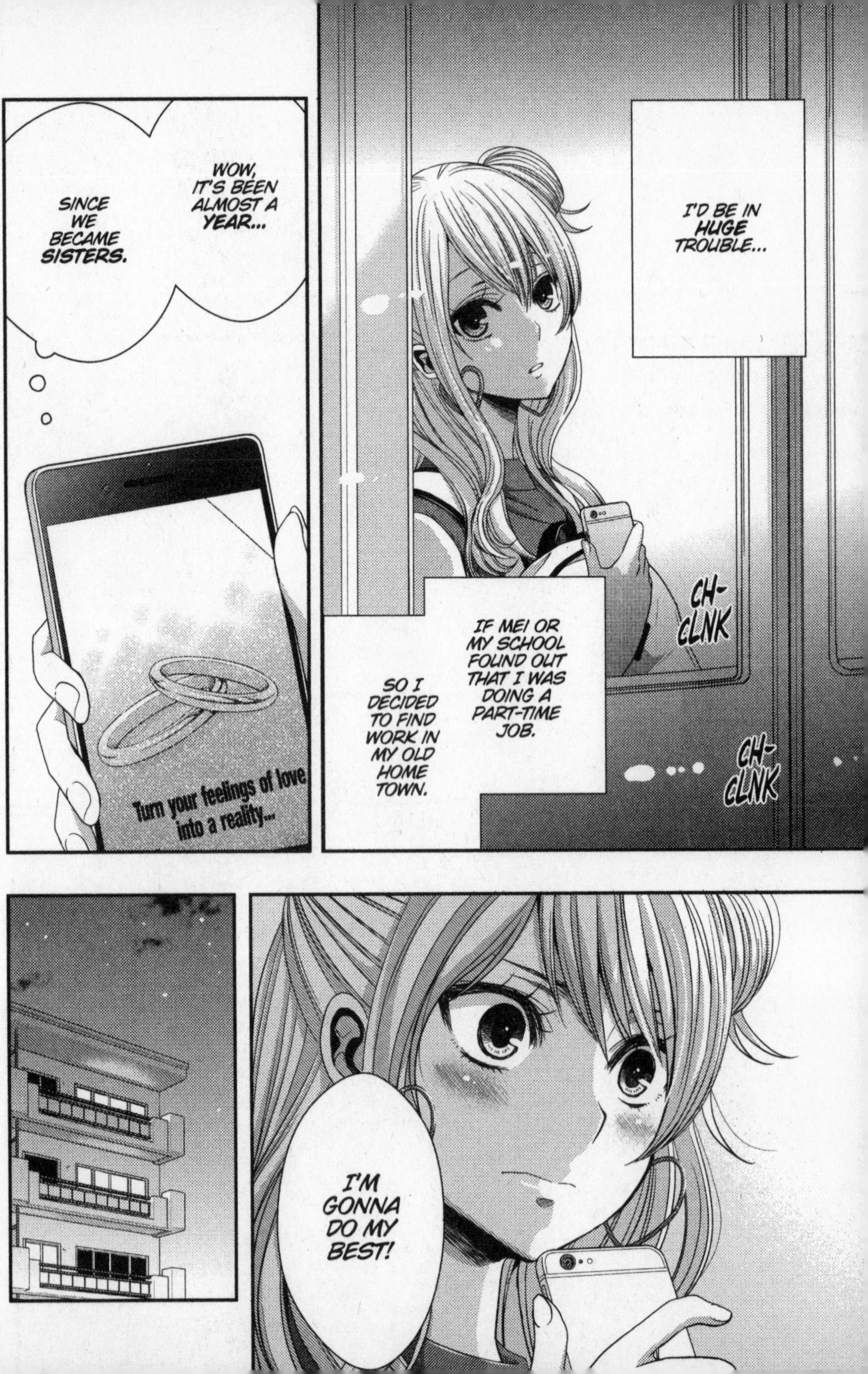
I'D BE IN HUGE TROUBLE...
CH-CLNK
IF MEI OR MY SCHOOL FOUND OUT THAT I WAS DOING A PART-TIME JOB.
SO I DECIDED TO FIND WORK IN MY OLD HOME TOWN.
CH-CLNK
WOW, IT'S BEEN ALMOST A YEAR...
SINCE WE BECAME SISTERS.
Turn your feelings of love into a reality...
I'M GONNA DO MY BEST!

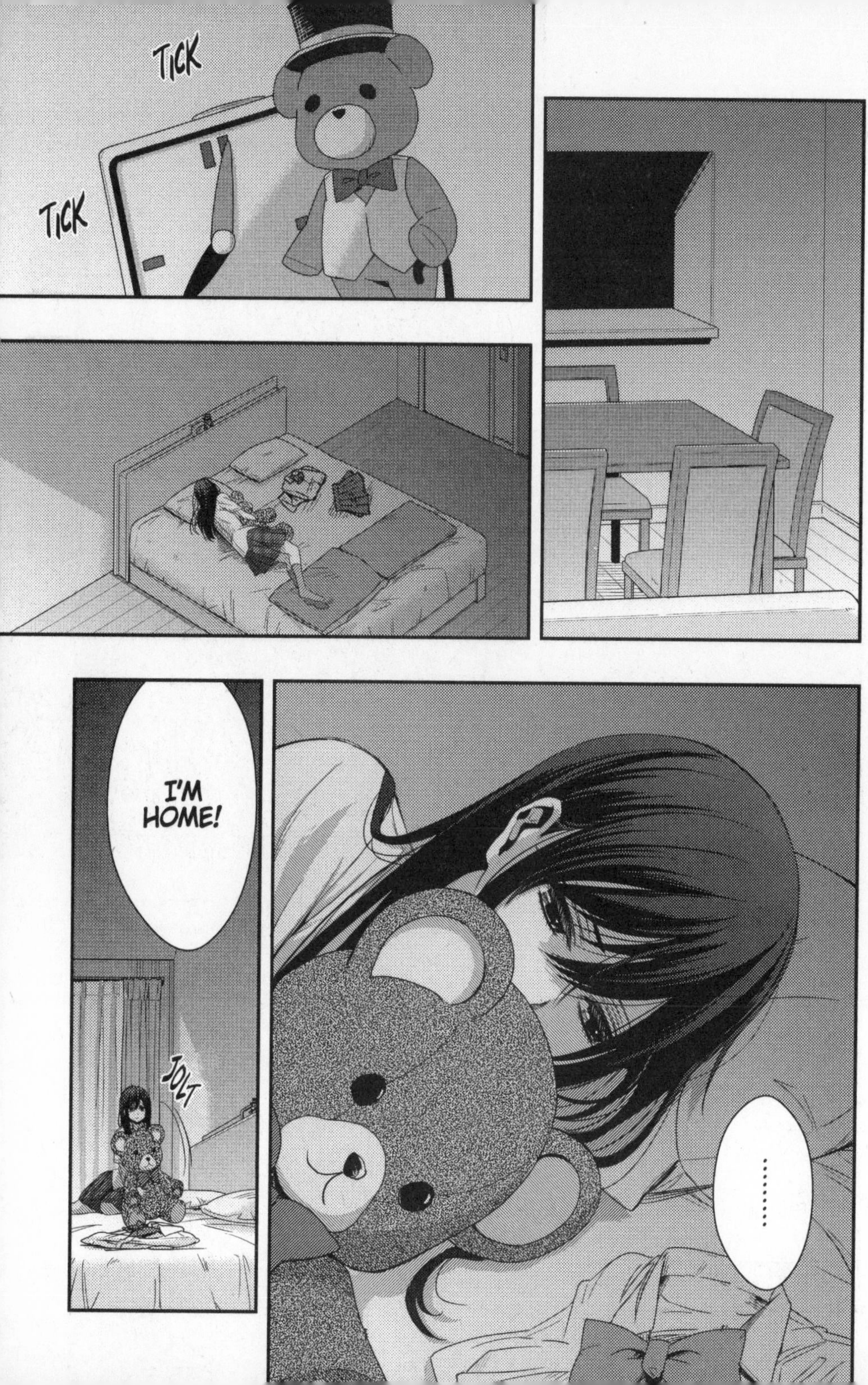
TICK
TICK
......
I'M HOME!
JOLT

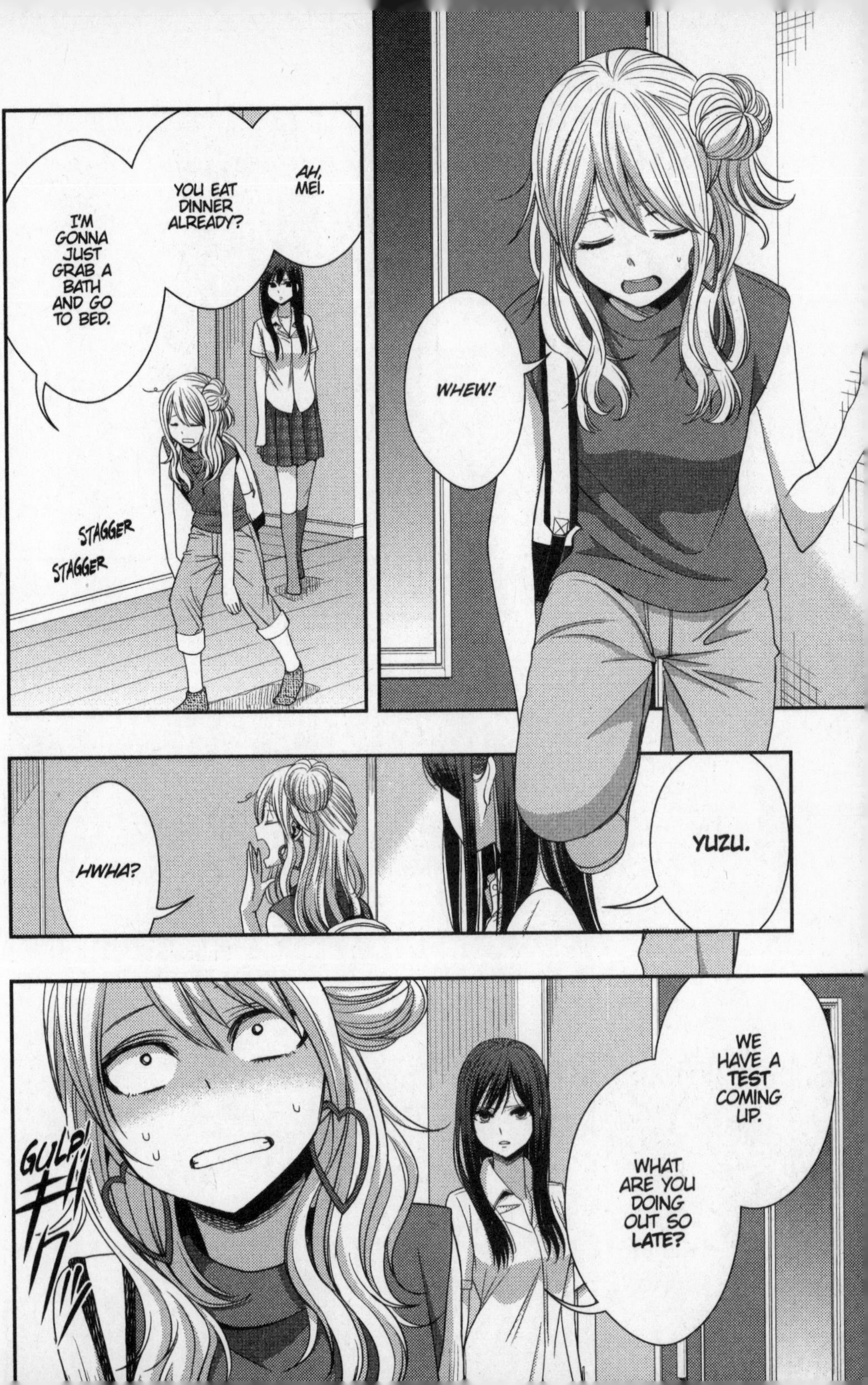
WHEW!
AH, MEI.
YOU EAT DINNER ALREADY?
I'M GONNA JUST GRAB A BATH AND GO TO BED.
STAGGER
STAGGER
YUZU.
HWHA?
WE HAVE A TEST COMING UP.
WHAT ARE YOU DOING OUT SO LATE?
GULP!

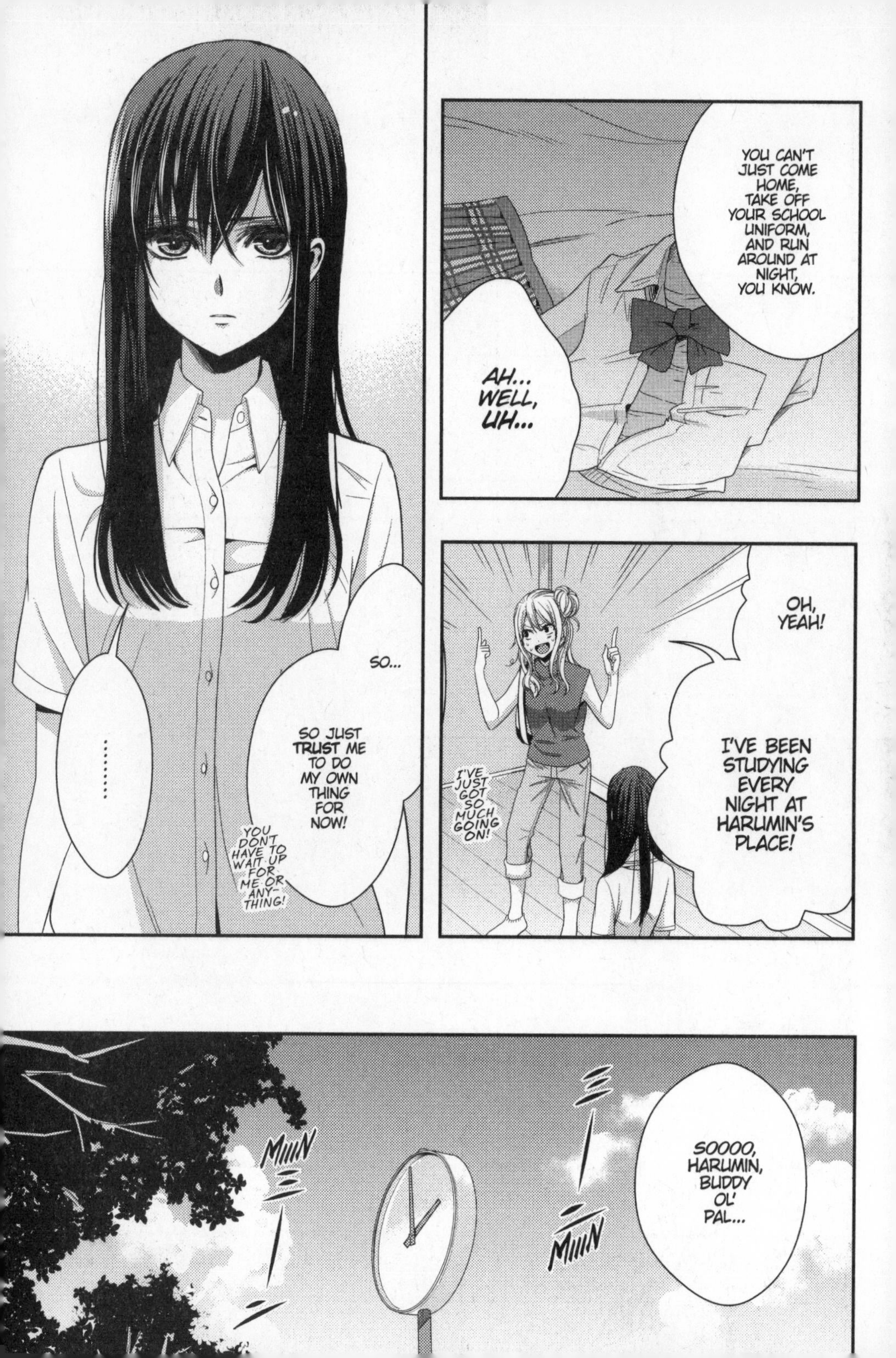
YOU CAN'T JUST COME HOME, TAKE OFF YOUR SCHOOL UNIFORM, AND RUN AROUND AT NIGHT, YOU KNOW.
AH... WELL, UH...
OH, YEAH!
I'VE BEEN STUDYING EVERY NIGHT AT HARUMIN'S PLACE!
I'VE JUST GOT SO MUCH GOING ON!
SO...
SO JUST TRUST ME TO DO MY OWN THING FOR NOW!
YOU DON'T HAVE TO WAIT UP FOR ME OR ANYTHING!
......
SOOOO, HARUMIN, BUDDY OL' PAL...
MIIIN
MIIIN

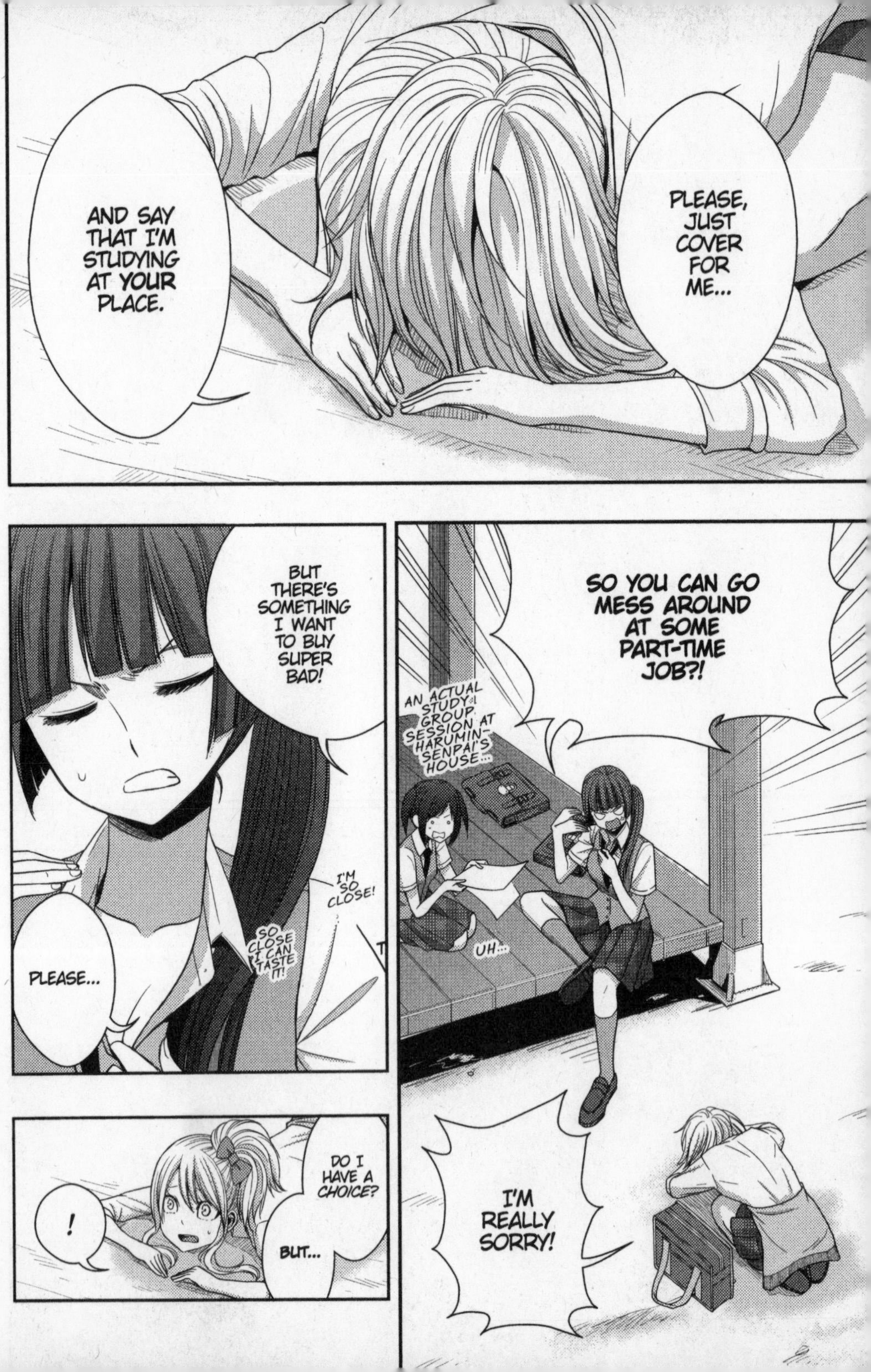
PLEASE, JUST COVER FOR ME...
AND SAY THAT I'M STUDYING AT YOUR PLACE.
SO YOU CAN GO MESS AROUND AT SOME PART-TIME JOB?!
AN ACTUAL STUDY GROUP SESSION AT HARUMIN-SENPAI'S HOUSE...
UH...
I'M REALLY SORRY!
BUT THERE'S SOMETHING I WANT TO BUY SUPER BAD!
I'M SO CLOSE!
SO CLOSE I CAN TASTE IT!
PLEASE...
DO I HAVE A CHOICE?
BUT...
!

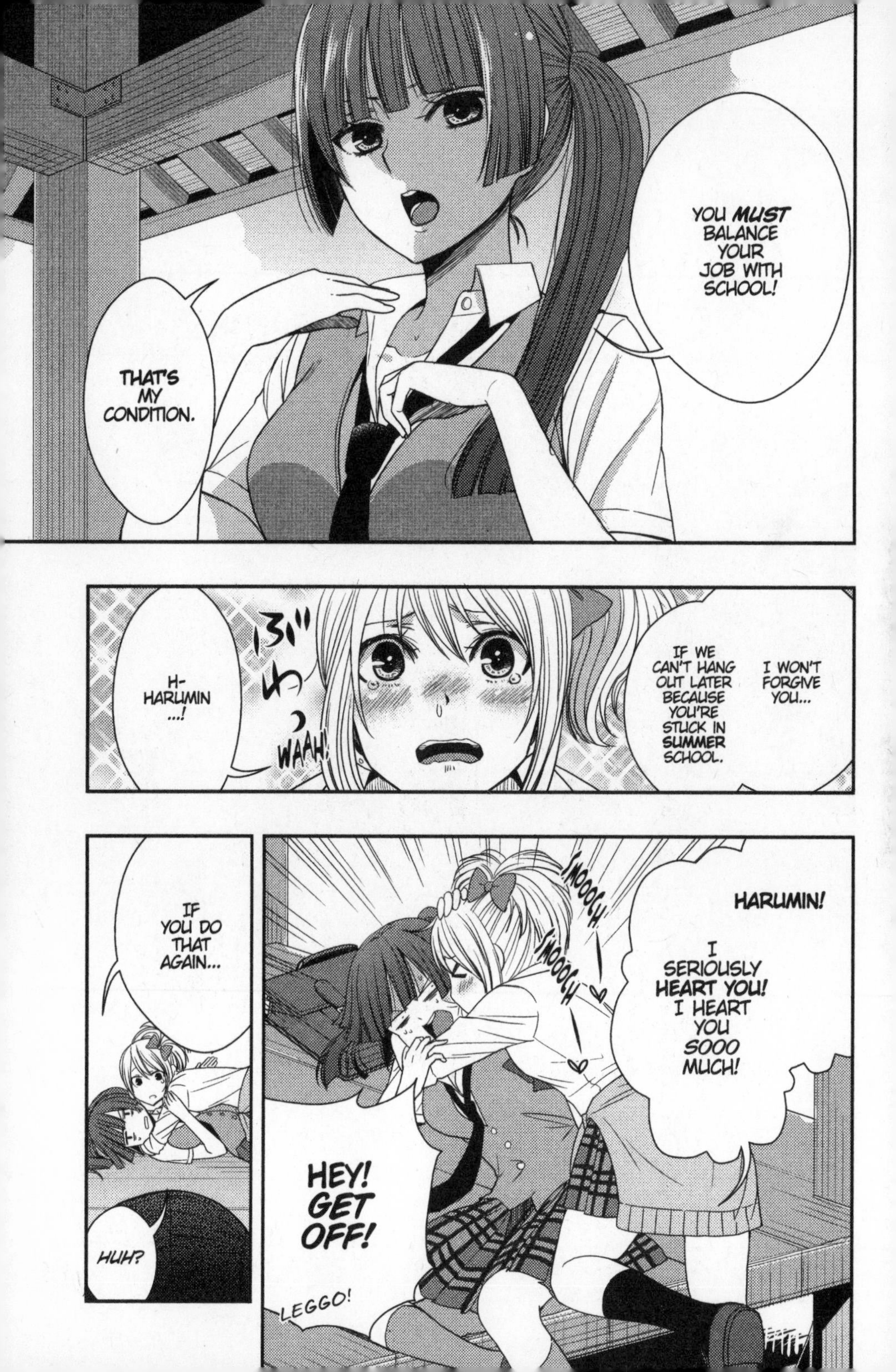
YOU MUST BALANCE YOUR JOB WITH SCHOOL!
THAT'S MY CONDITION.
I WON'T FORGIVE YOU...
IF WE CAN'T HANG OUT LATER BECAUSE YOU'RE STUCK IN SUMMER SCHOOL.
WAAH!
H-HARUMIN...!
HARUMIN!
I SERIOUSLY HEART YOU! I HEART YOU SOOO MUCH!
SMOOCH
SMOOCH
HEY! GET OFF!
LEGGO!
IF YOU DO THAT AGAIN...
HUH?

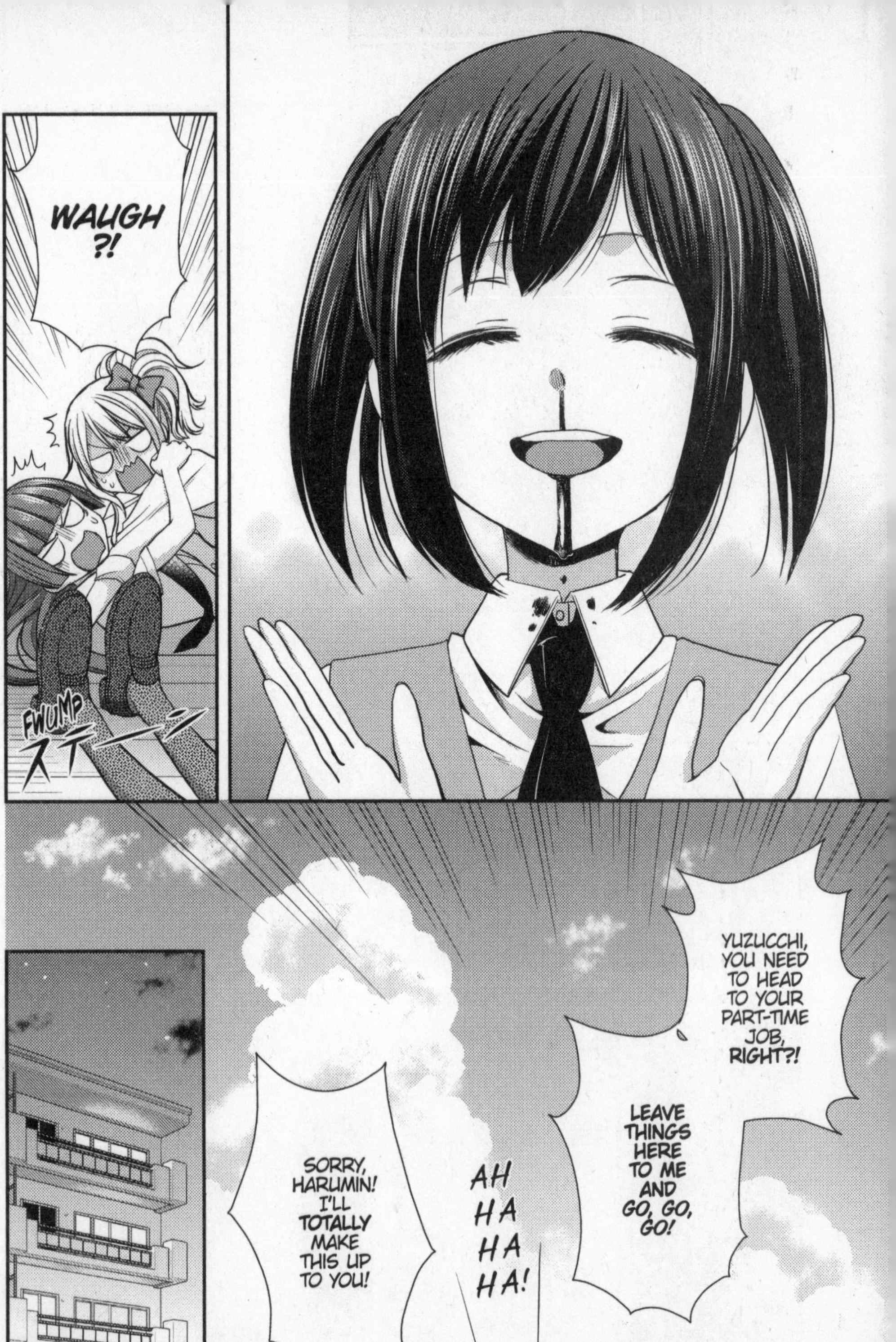
WAUGH ?!
FWUMP
スー
YUZUCCHI, YOU NEED TO HEAD TO YOUR PART-TIME JOB, RIGHT?!
LEAVE THINGS HERE TO ME AND GO, GO, GO!
AH HA HA HA!
SORRY, HARUMIN! I'LL TOTALLY MAKE THIS UP TO YOU!

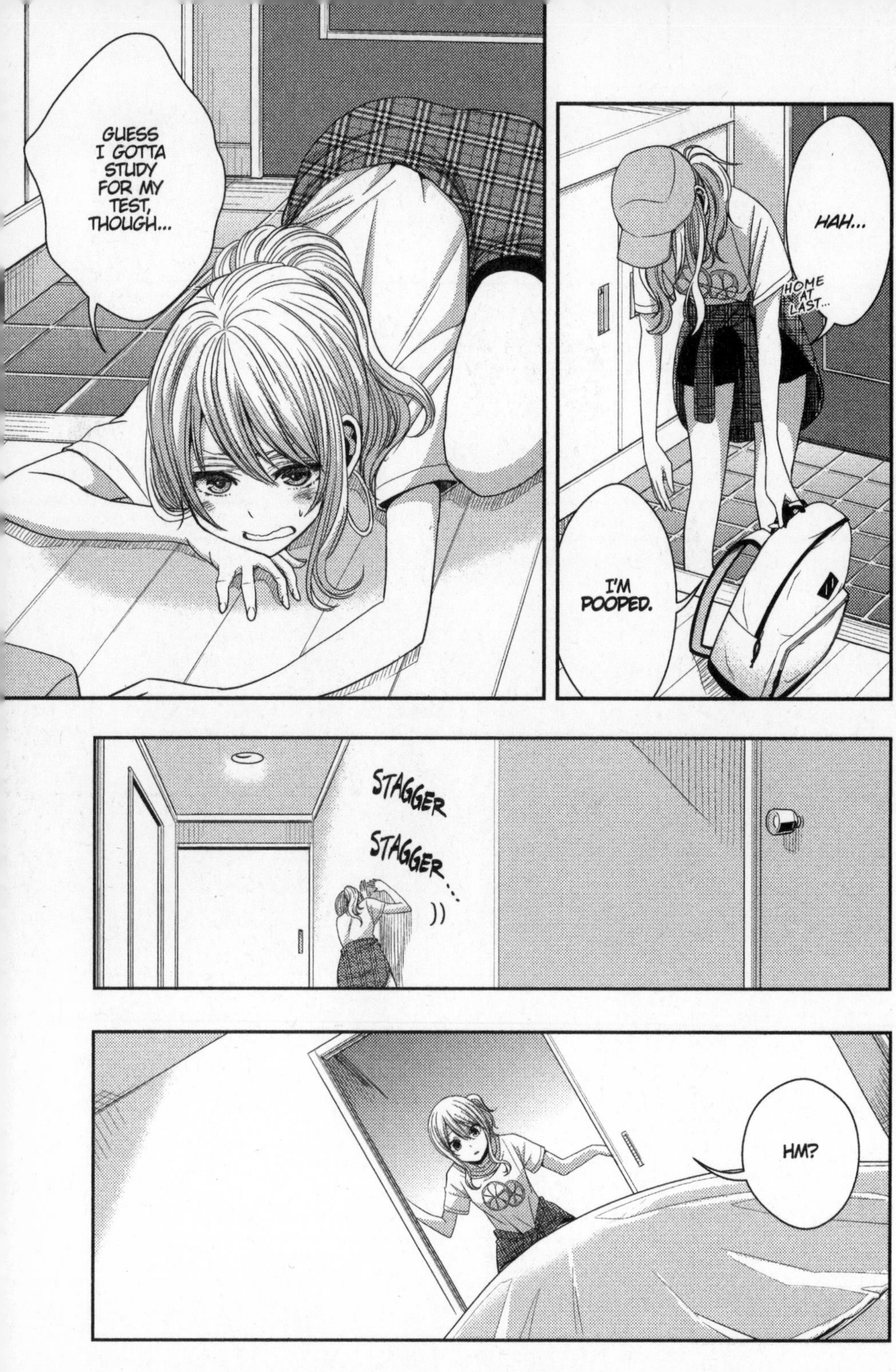
HAH...
HOME AT LAST...
I'M POOPED.
GUESS I GOTTA STUDY FOR MY TEST, THOUGH...
STAGGER
STAGGER...
HM?

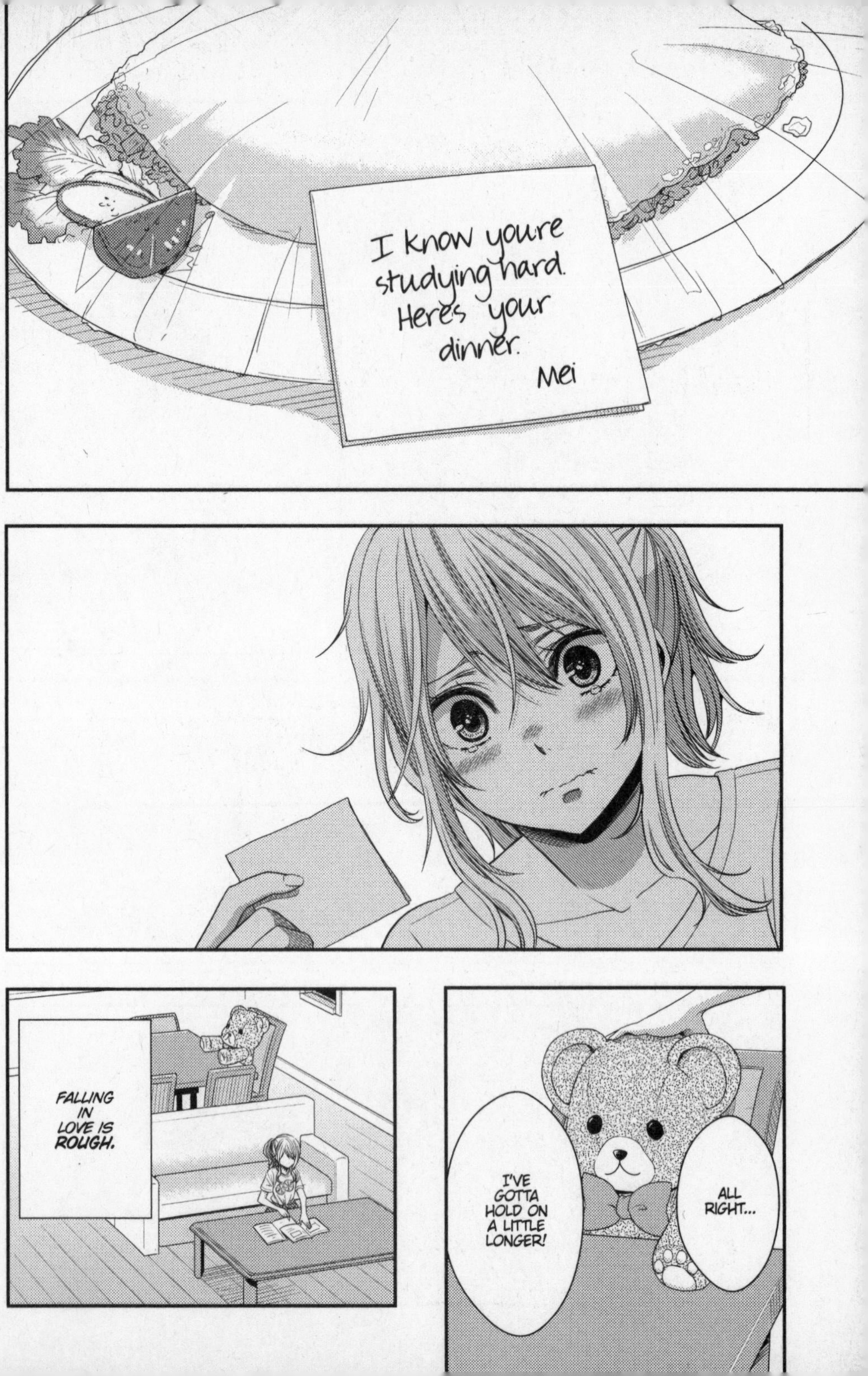
I know you're studying hard. Here's your dinner. Mei
ALL RIGHT...
I'VE GOTTA HOLD ON A LITTLE LONGER!
FALLING IN LOVE IS ROUGH.

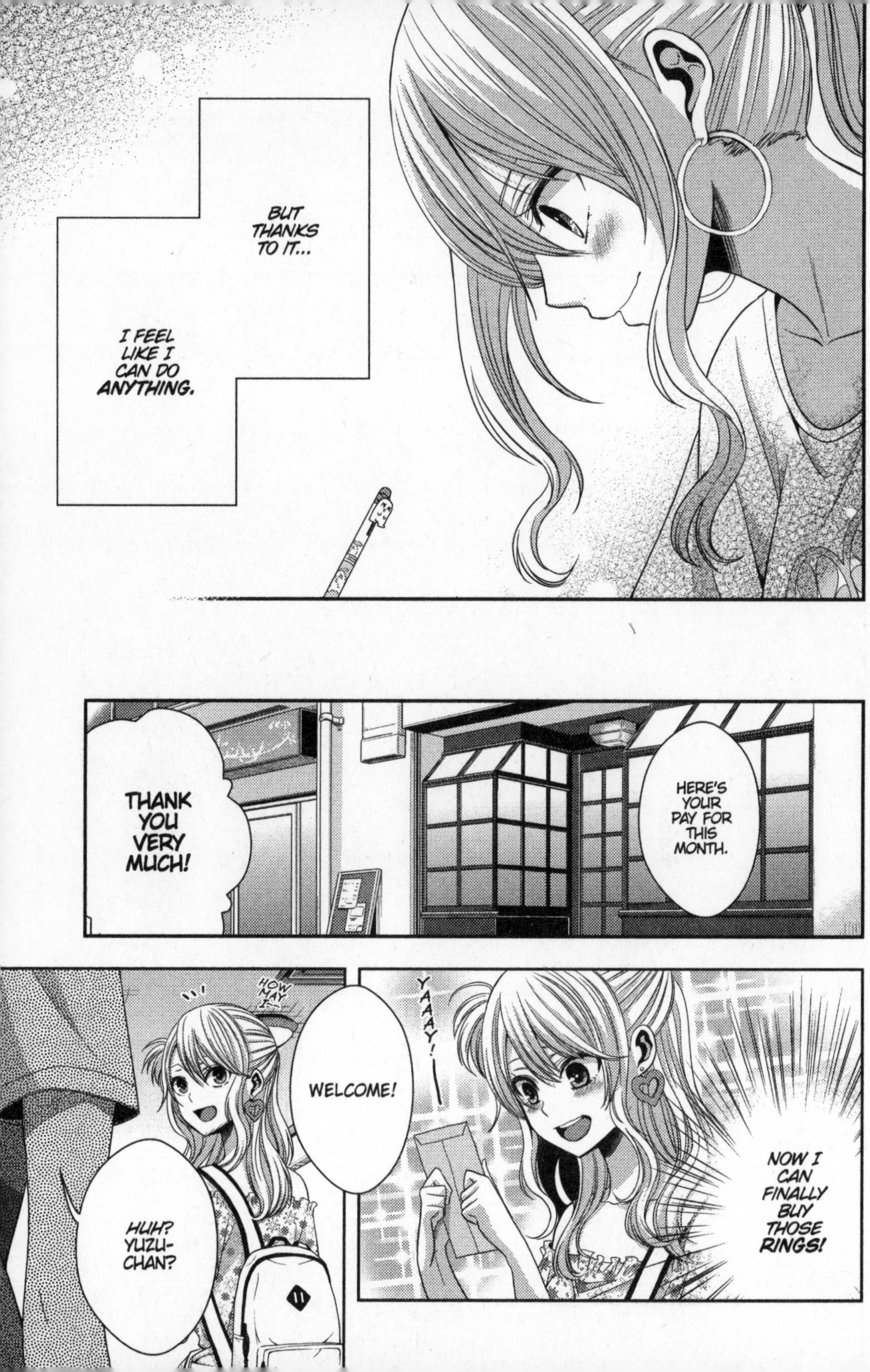
BUT THANKS TO IT...
I FEEL LIKE I CAN DO ANYTHING.
HERE'S YOUR PAY FOR THIS MONTH.
THANK YOU VERY MUCH!
YAAAY!
NOW I CAN FINALLY BUY THOSE RINGS!
HOW MAY I—
WELCOME!
HUH? YUZU-CHAN?

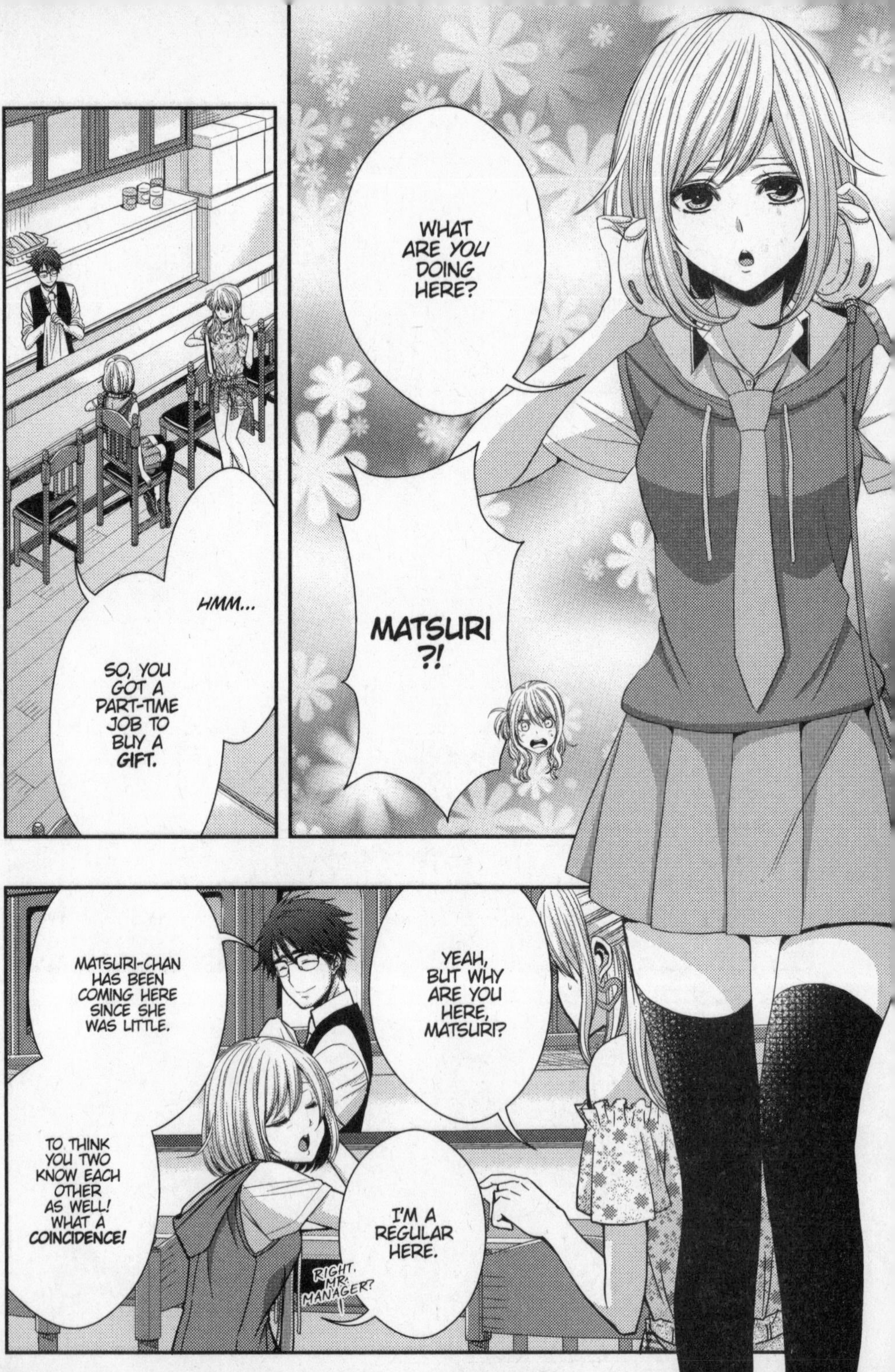
WHAT ARE YOU DOING HERE?
MATSURI ?!
HMM...
SO, YOU GOT A PART-TIME JOB TO BUY A GIFT.
YEAH, BUT WHY ARE YOU HERE, MATSURI?
I'M A REGULAR HERE.
RIGHT, MR. MANAGER?
MATSURI-CHAN HAS BEEN COMING HERE SINCE SHE WAS LITTLE.
TO THINK YOU TWO KNOW EACH OTHER AS WELL! WHAT A COINCIDENCE!

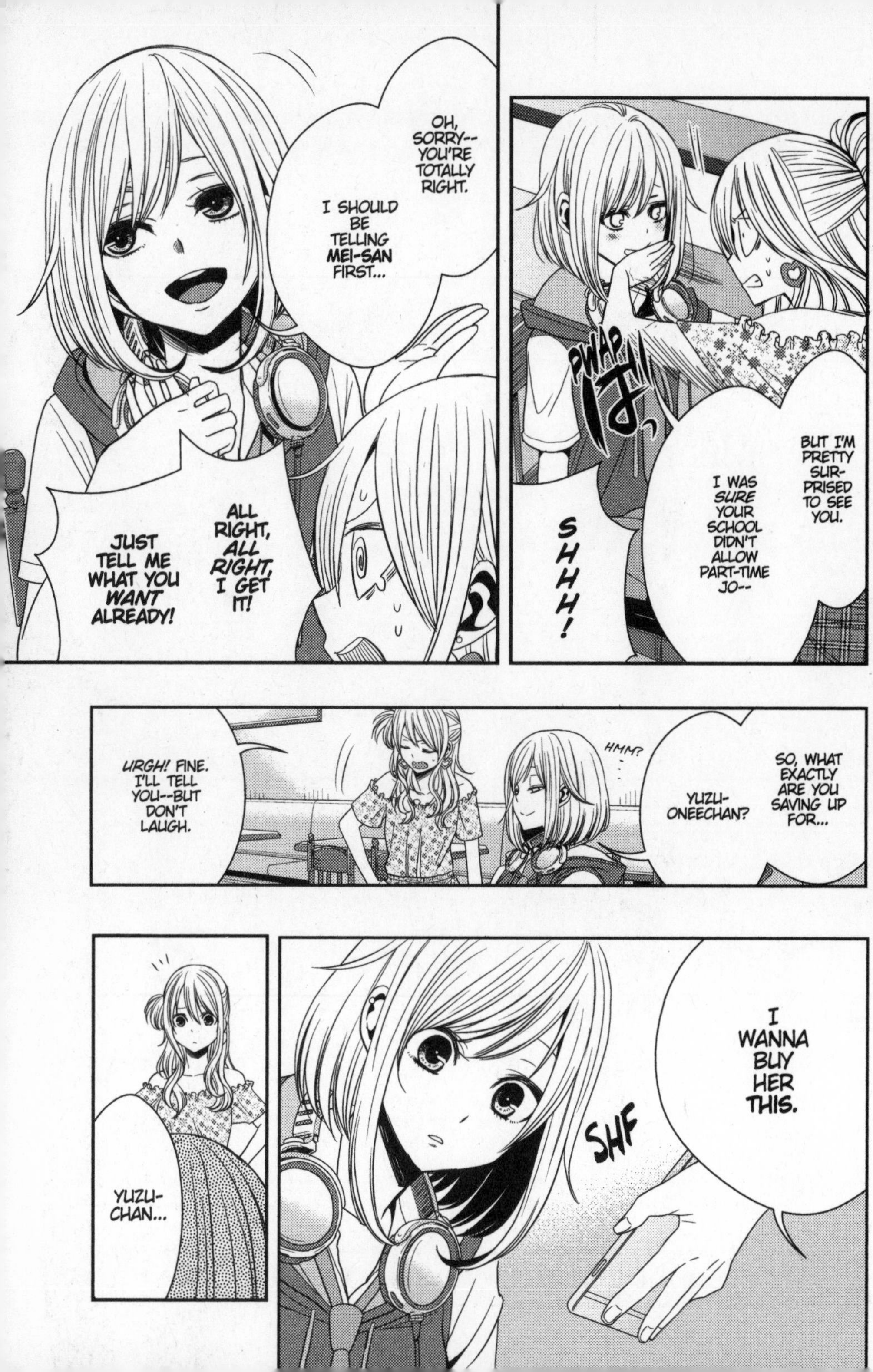
PWAP
BUT I'M PRETTY SURPRISED TO SEE YOU.
I WAS SURE YOUR SCHOOL DIDN'T ALLOW PART-TIME JO--
SHHHH!
OH, SORRY-- YOU'RE TOTALLY RIGHT.
I SHOULD BE TELLING MEI-SAN FIRST...
ALL RIGHT, ALL RIGHT, I GET IT!
JUST TELL ME WHAT YOU WANT ALREADY!
SO, WHAT EXACTLY ARE YOU SAVING UP FOR...
YUZU-ONEECHAN?
HMM?
URGH! FINE. I'LL TELL YOU--BUT DON'T LAUGH.
I WANNA BUY HER THIS.
SHF
YUZU-CHAN...

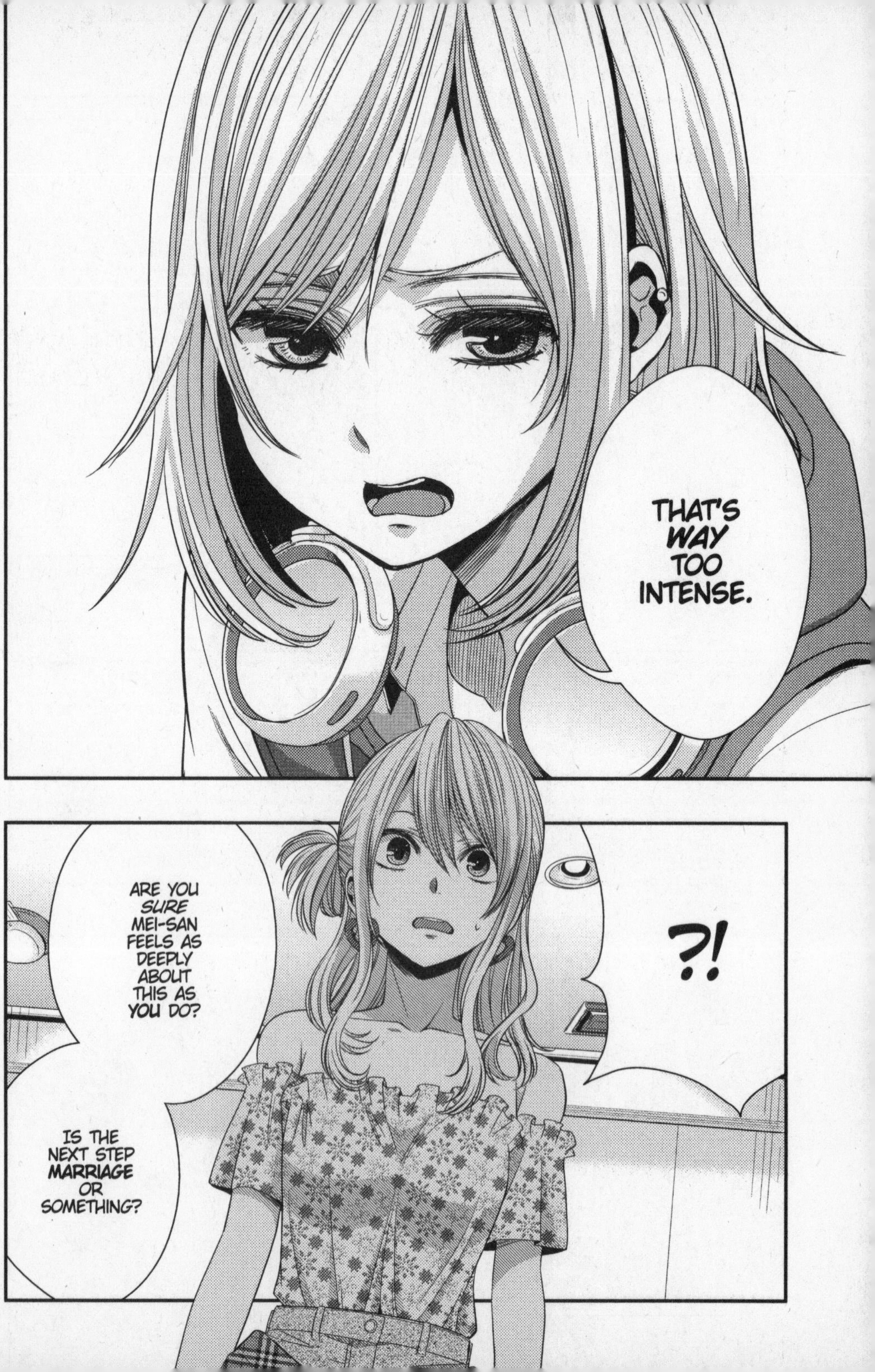
THAT'S WAY TOO INTENSE.
?!
ARE YOU SURE MEI-SAN FEELS AS DEEPLY ABOUT THIS AS YOU DO?
IS THE NEXT STEP MARRIAGE OR SOMETHING?

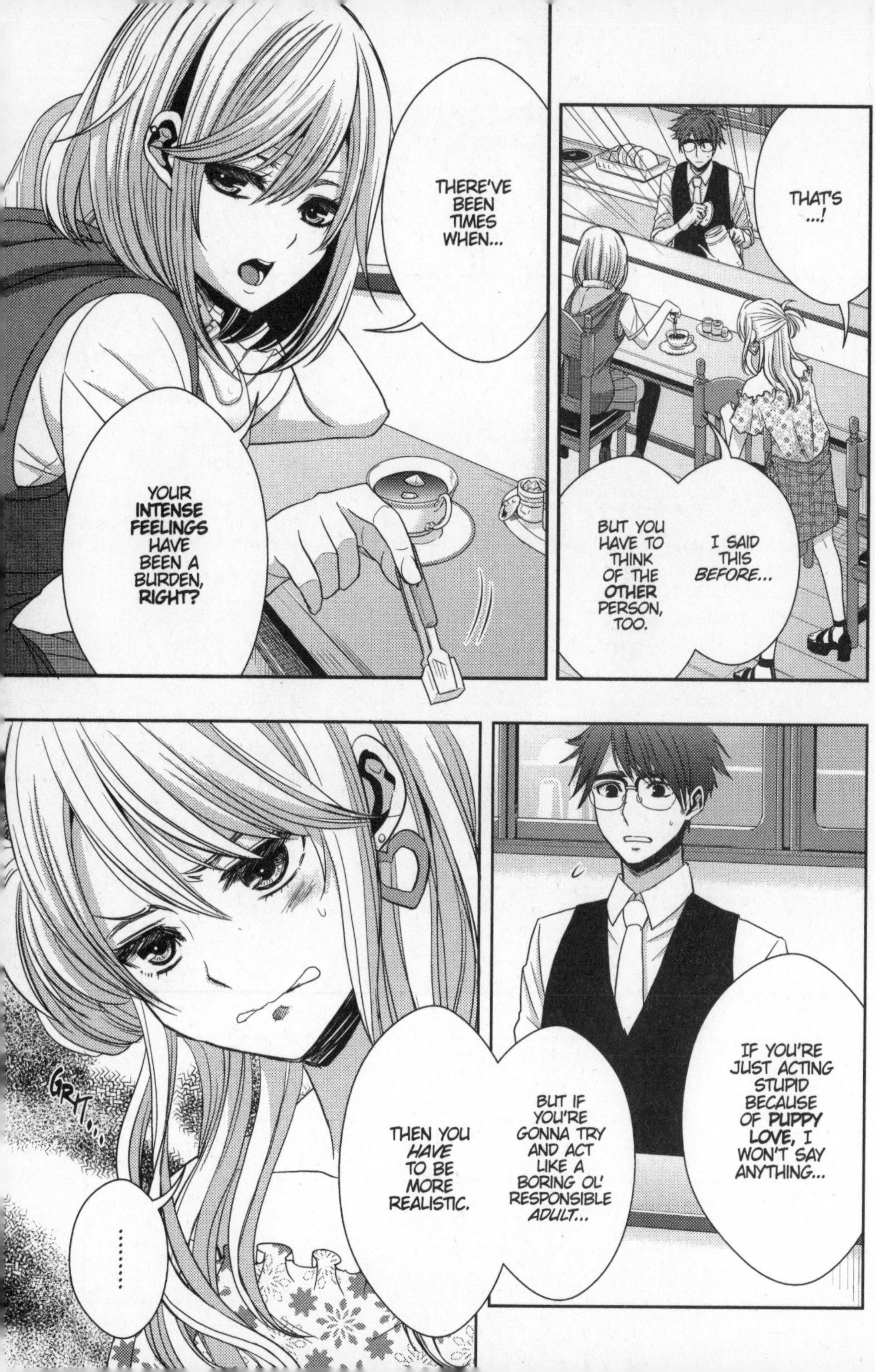
THAT'S ...!
I SAID THIS *BEFORE*...
BUT YOU HAVE TO THINK OF THE **OTHER** PERSON, TOO.
THERE'VE BEEN TIMES WHEN...
YOUR **INTENSE FEELINGS** HAVE BEEN A **BURDEN**, RIGHT?
IF YOU'RE JUST ACTING STUPID BECAUSE OF **PUPPY LOVE**, I WON'T SAY ANYTHING...
BUT IF YOU'RE GONNA TRY AND ACT LIKE A BORING OL' RESPONSIBLE *ADULT*...
THEN YOU *HAVE* TO BE MORE REALISTIC.
GRYT...
......

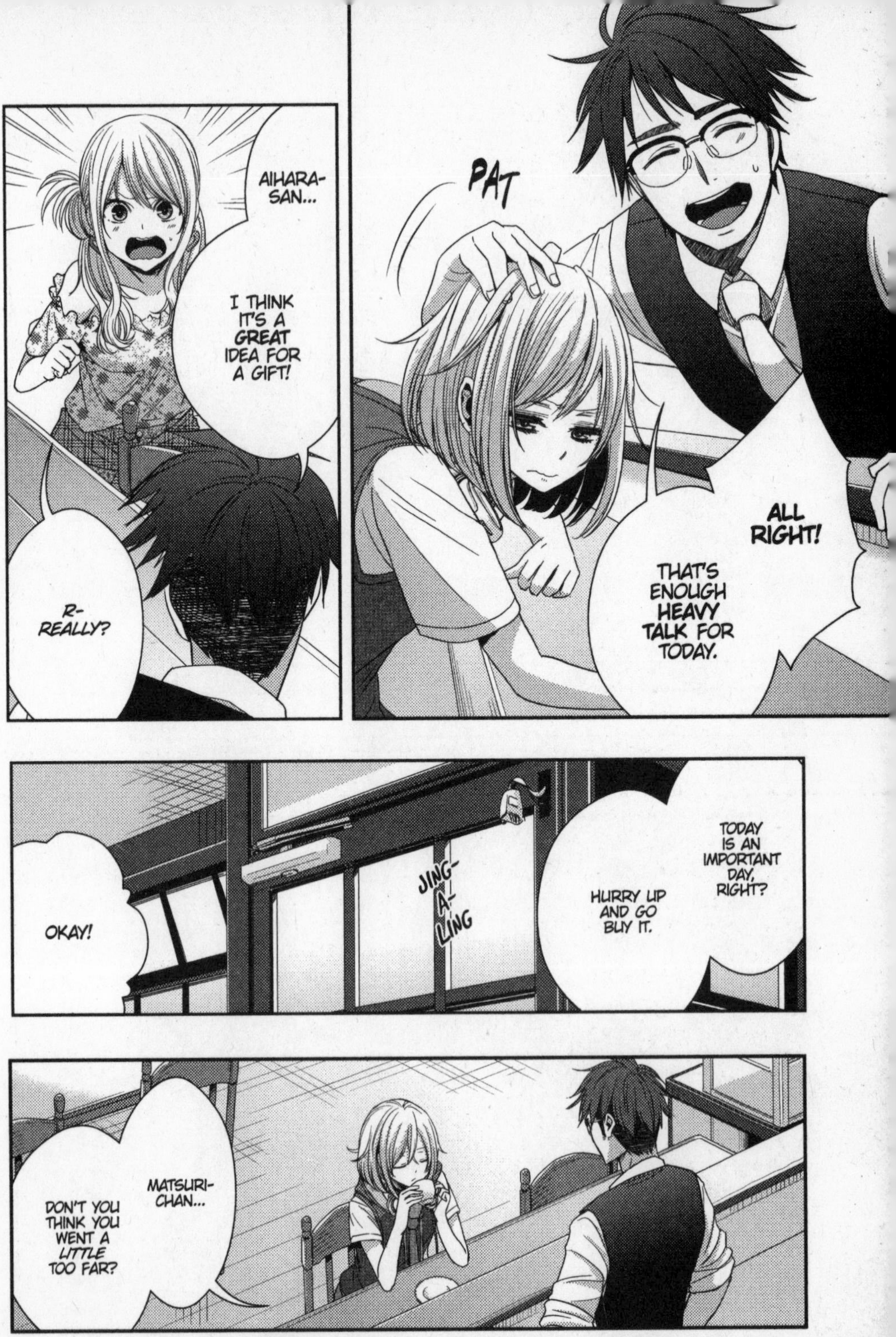
PAT
ALL RIGHT!
THAT'S ENOUGH HEAVY TALK FOR TODAY.
AIHARA-SAN...
I THINK IT'S A GREAT IDEA FOR A GIFT!
R-REALLY?
TODAY IS AN IMPORTANT DAY, RIGHT?
HURRY UP AND GO BUY IT.
JING-A-LING
OKAY!
MATSURI-CHAN...
DON'T YOU THINK YOU WENT A LITTLE TOO FAR?

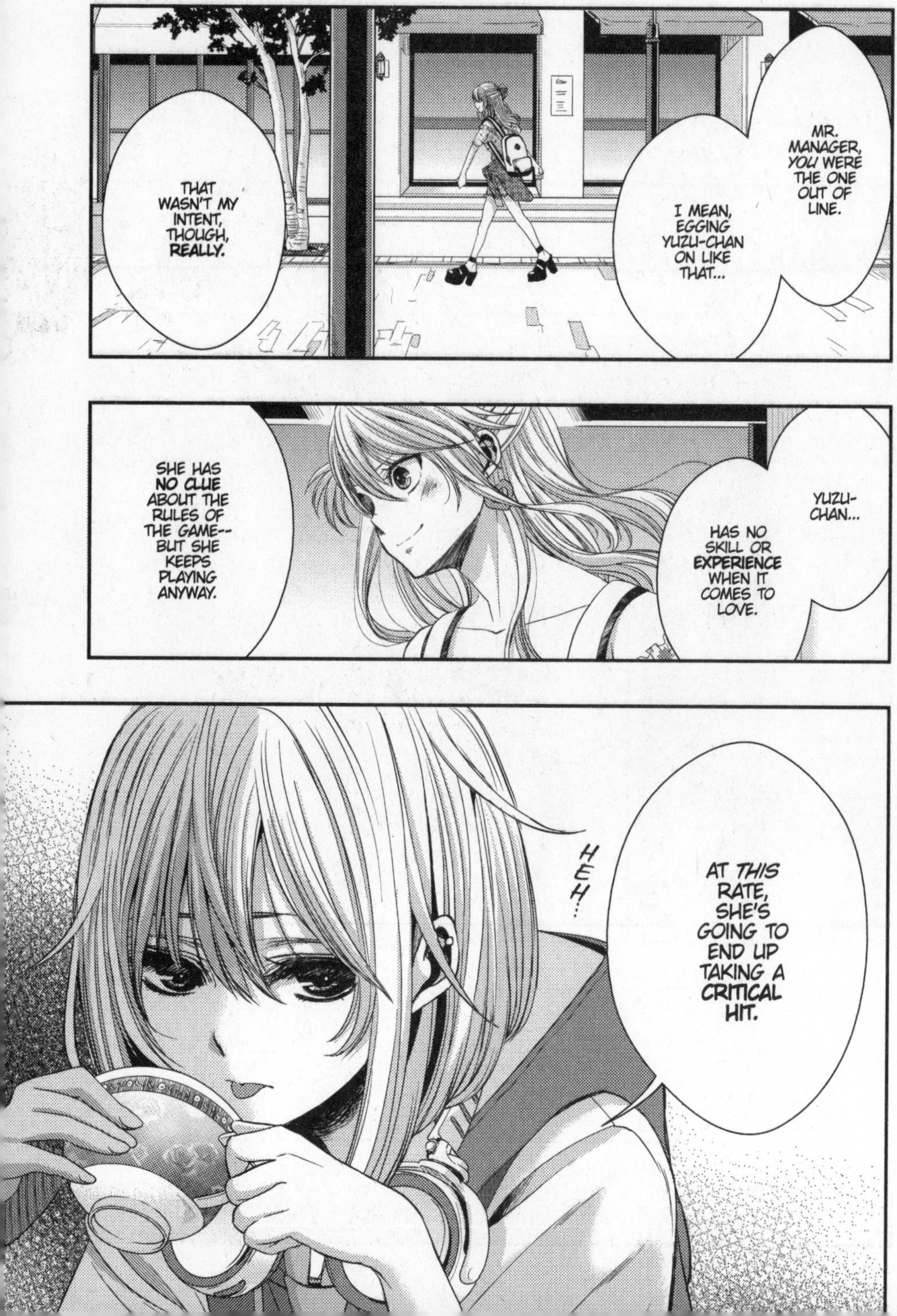
MR. MANAGER, YOU WERE THE ONE OUT OF LINE.
I MEAN, EGGING YUZU-CHAN ON LIKE THAT...
THAT WASN'T MY INTENT, THOUGH, REALLY.
YUZU-CHAN...
HAS NO SKILL OR EXPERIENCE WHEN IT COMES TO LOVE.
SHE HAS NO CLUE ABOUT THE RULES OF THE GAME--BUT SHE KEEPS PLAYING ANYWAY.
AT THIS RATE, SHE'S GOING TO END UP TAKING A CRITICAL HIT.
HEH...

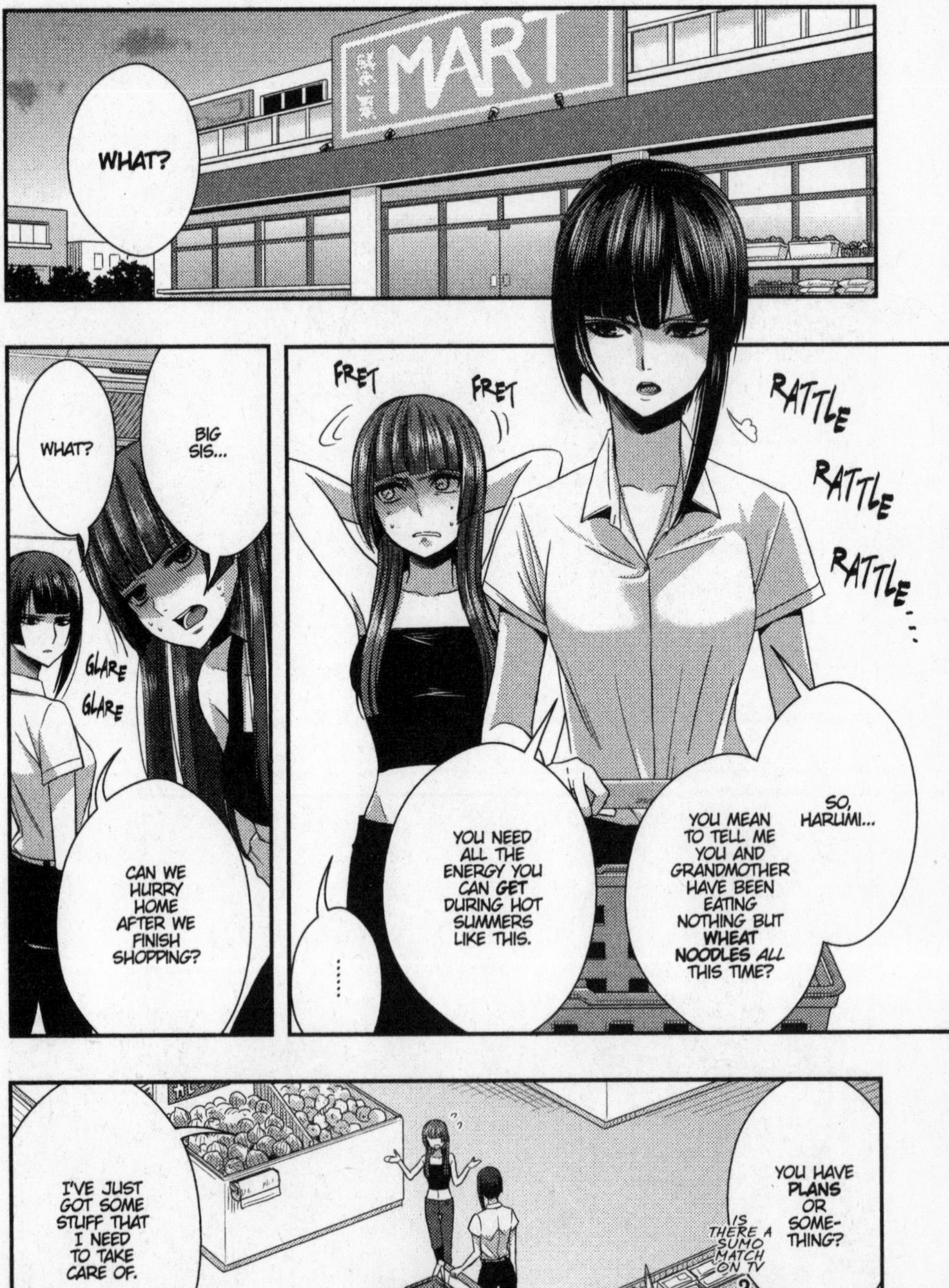
MART
WHAT?
RATTLE RATTLE RATTLE...
FRET FRET
SO, HARUMI...
YOU MEAN TO TELL ME YOU AND GRANDMOTHER HAVE BEEN EATING NOTHING BUT WHEAT NOODLES ALL THIS TIME?
YOU NEED ALL THE ENERGY YOU CAN GET DURING HOT SUMMERS LIKE THIS.
......
BIG SIS...
WHAT?
GLARE GLARE
CAN WE HURRY HOME AFTER WE FINISH SHOPPING?
YOU HAVE PLANS OR SOME-THING?
IS THERE A SUMO MATCH ON TV?
I'VE JUST GOT SOME STUFF THAT I NEED TO TAKE CARE OF.

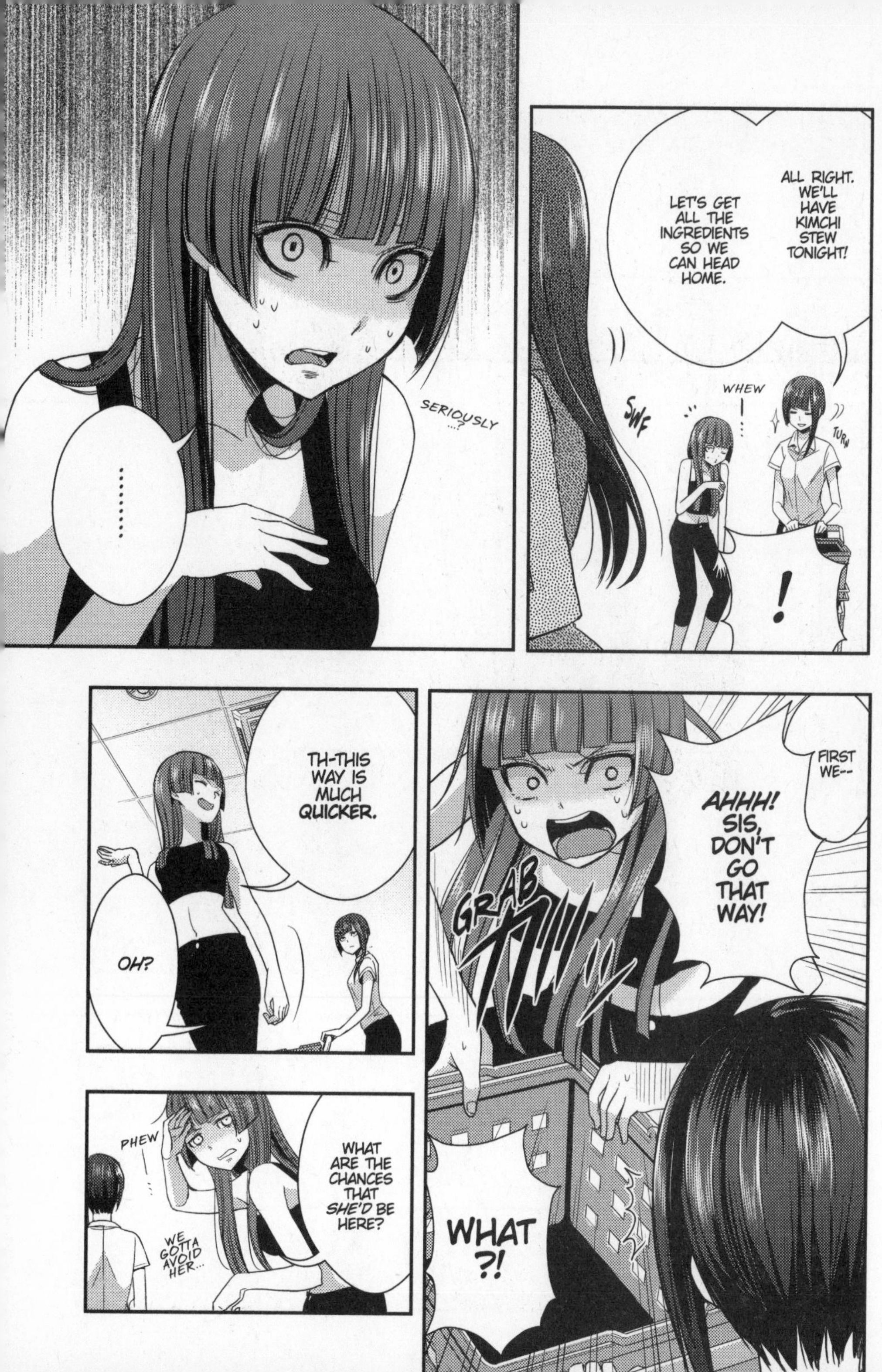
ALL RIGHT. WE'LL HAVE KIMCHI STEW TONIGHT!
LET'S GET ALL THE INGREDIENTS SO WE CAN HEAD HOME.
SWF
WHEW
...!
TURN
!
SERIOUSLY ...?
....
FIRST WE--
AHHH! SIS, DON'T GO THAT WAY!
GRAB
WHAT ?!
TH-THIS WAY IS MUCH QUICKER.
OH?
WHAT ARE THE CHANCES THAT SHE'D BE HERE?
PHEW
...!
WE GOTTA AVOID HER...

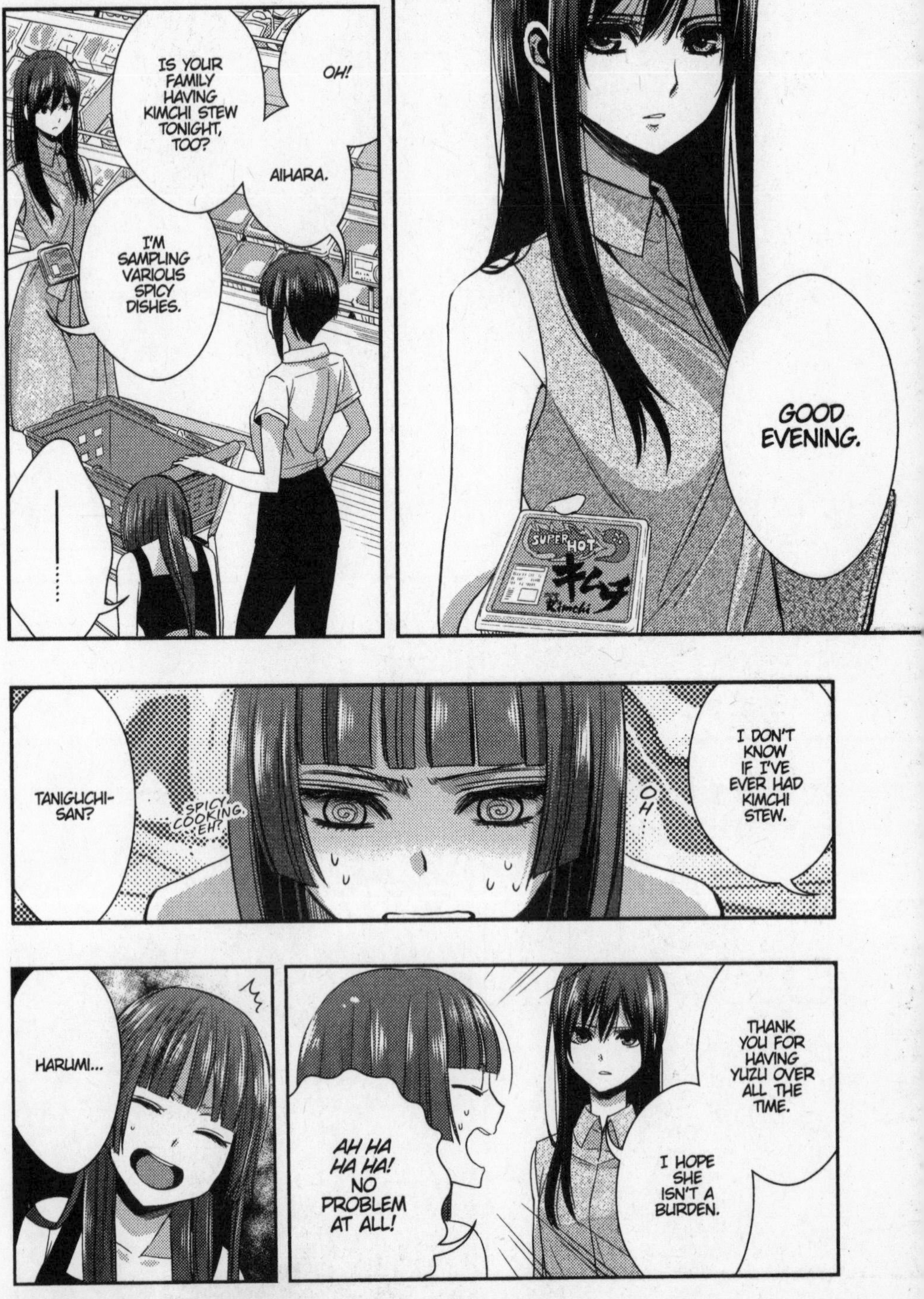
GOOD EVENING.
SUPER HOT
キムチ
Kimchi
OH!
AIHARA.
IS YOUR FAMILY HAVING KIMCHI STEW TONIGHT, TOO?
I'M SAMPLING VARIOUS SPICY DISHES.
......
I DON'T KNOW IF I'VE EVER HAD KIMCHI STEW.
OH
SPICY COOKING, EH?
TANIGUCHI-SAN?
THANK YOU FOR HAVING YUZU OVER ALL THE TIME.
I HOPE SHE ISN'T A BURDEN.
AH HA HA HA! NO PROBLEM AT ALL!
HARUMI...

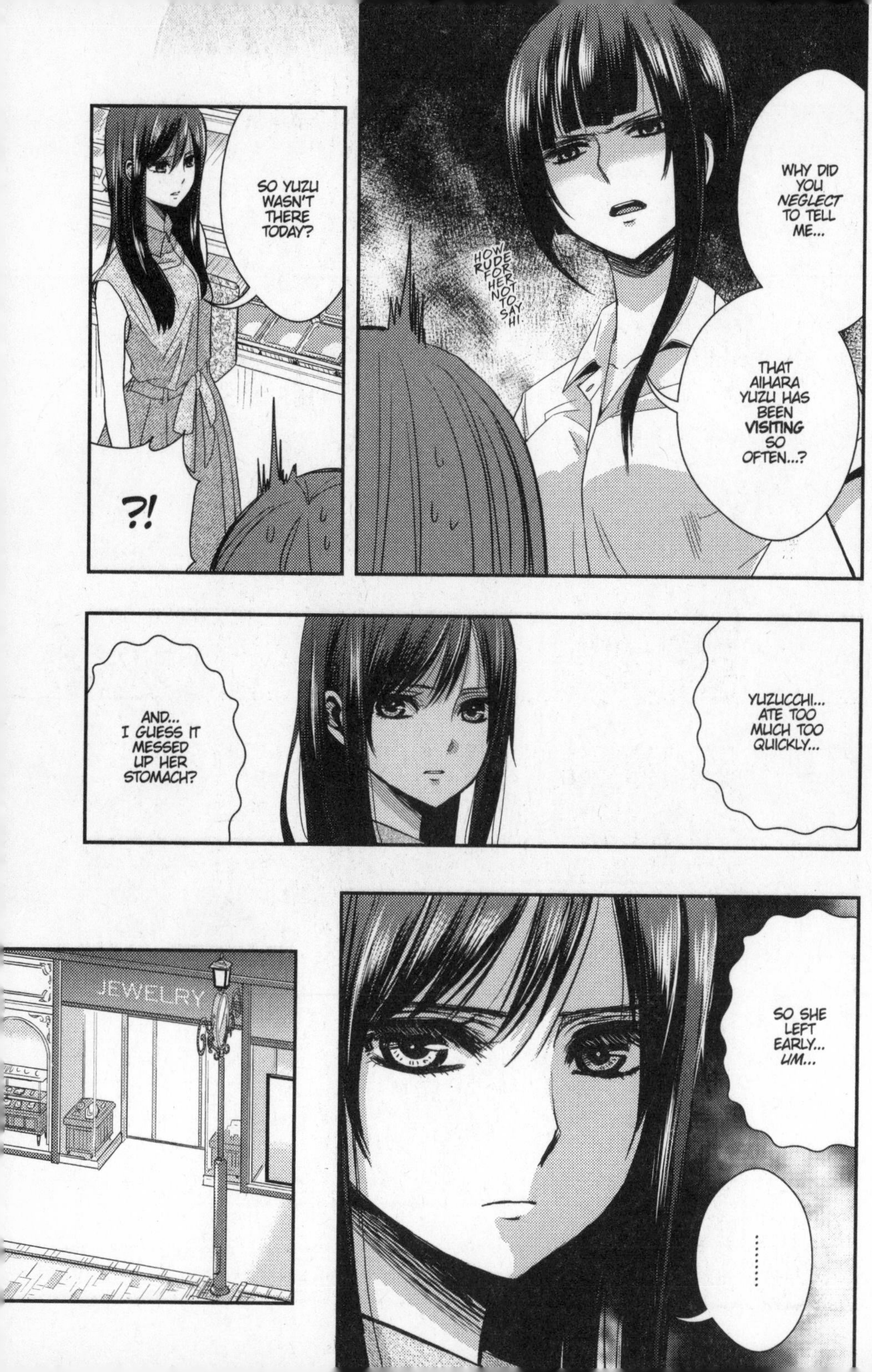
WHY DID YOU *NEGLECT* TO TELL ME...
HOW RUDE FOR HER NOT TO SAY HI.
THAT AIHARA YUZU HAS BEEN **VISITING** SO OFTEN...?
SO YUZU WASN'T THERE TODAY?
?!
YUZUCCHI... ATE TOO MUCH TOO QUICKLY...
AND... I GUESS IT MESSED UP HER STOMACH?
SO SHE LEFT EARLY... *UM*...
......
JEWELRY

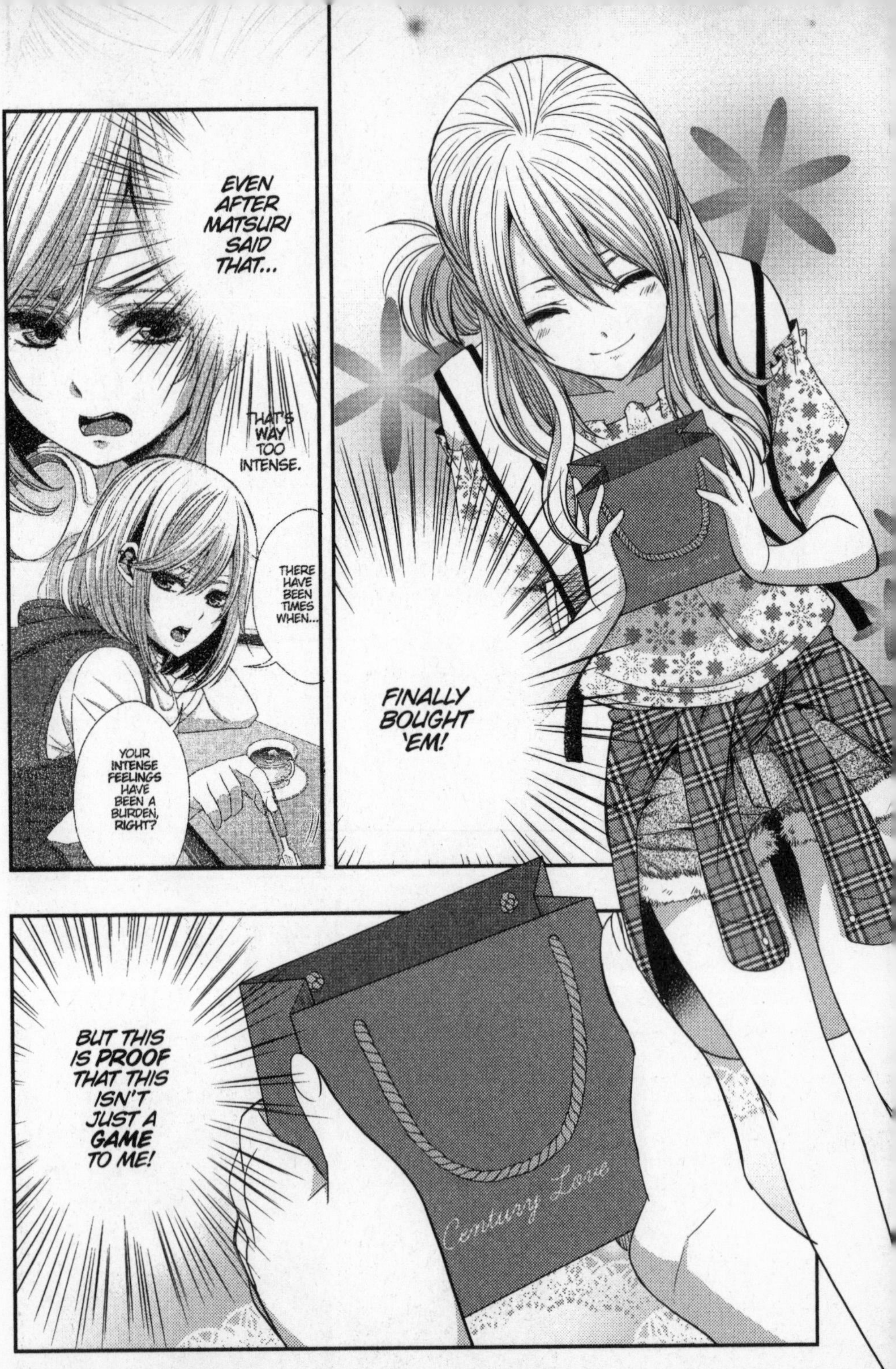
FINALLY BOUGHT 'EM!
EVEN AFTER MATSURI SAID THAT...
THAT'S WAY TOO INTENSE.
THERE HAVE BEEN TIMES WHEN...
YOUR INTENSE FEELINGS HAVE BEEN A BURDEN, RIGHT?
BUT THIS IS PROOF THAT THIS ISN'T JUST A GAME TO ME!
Century Love

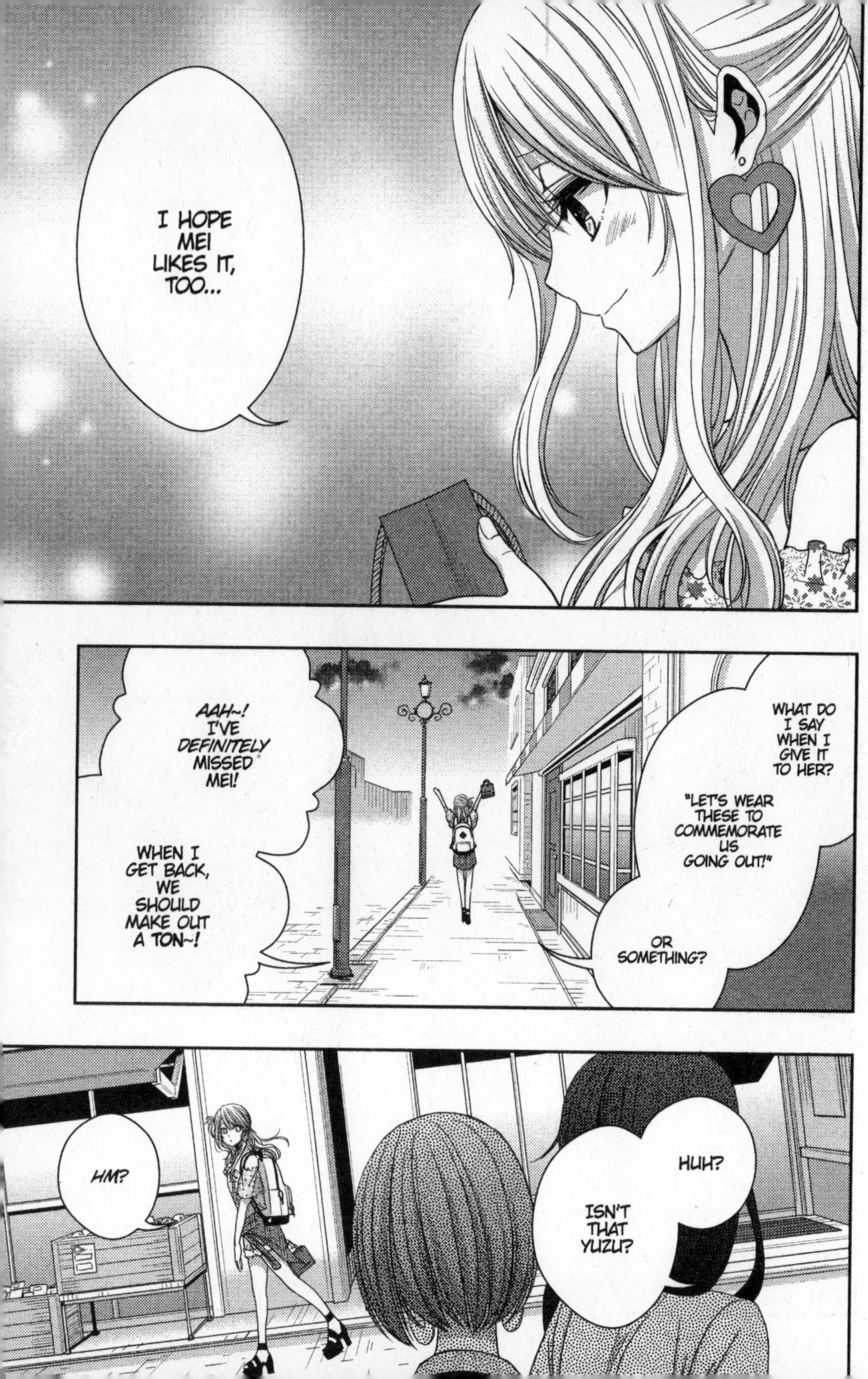
I HOPE MEI LIKES IT, TOO...
WHAT DO I SAY WHEN I GIVE IT TO HER?
"LET'S WEAR THESE TO COMMEMORATE US GOING OUT!"
OR SOMETHING?
AAH~! I'VE DEFINITELY MISSED MEI!
WHEN I GET BACK, WE SHOULD MAKE OUT A TON~!
HUH?
ISN'T THAT YUZU?
HM?

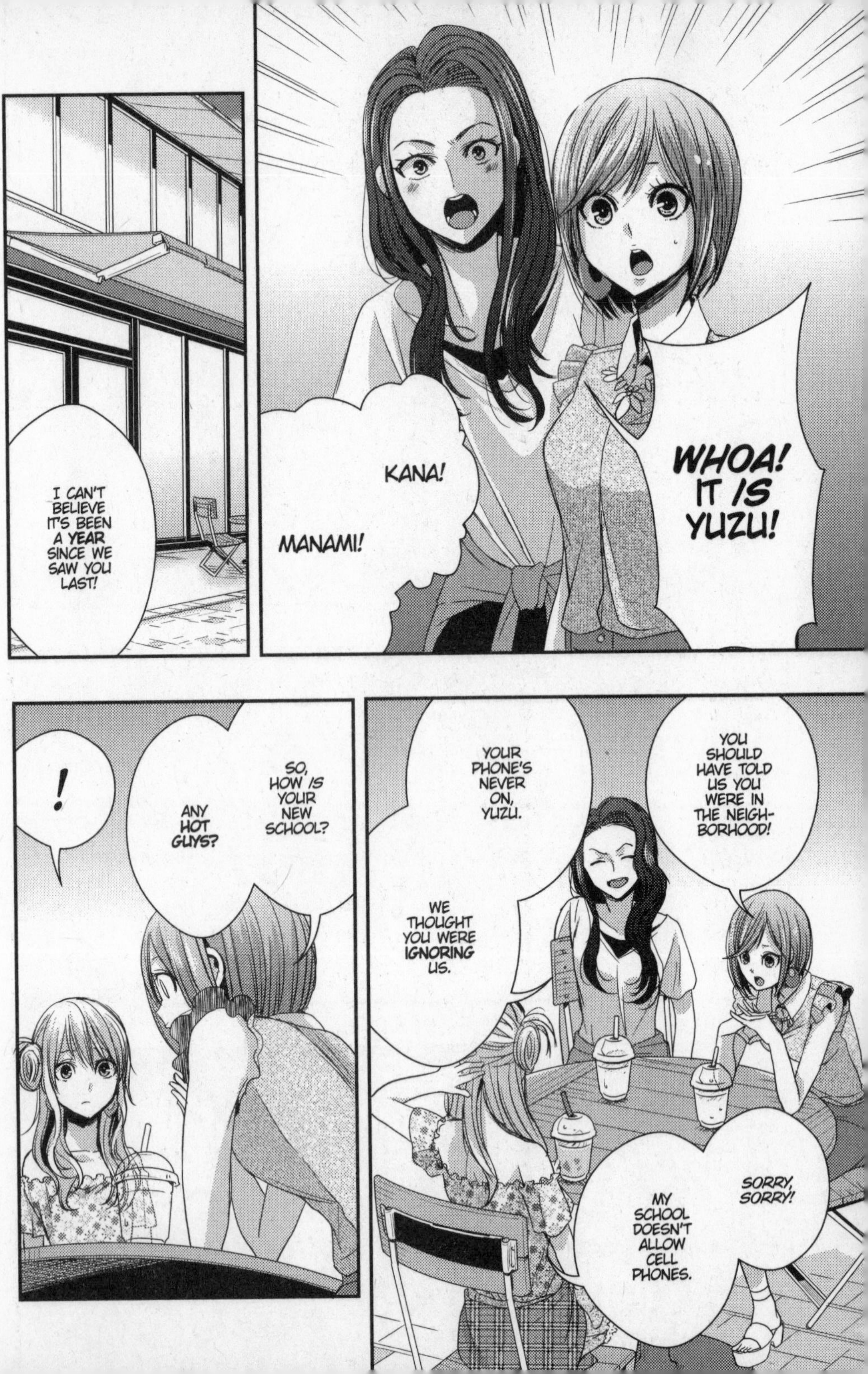
WHOA! IT *IS* YUZU!
KANA!
MANAMI!
I CAN'T BELIEVE IT'S BEEN A YEAR SINCE WE SAW YOU LAST!
YOU SHOULD HAVE TOLD US YOU WERE IN THE NEIGH-BORHOOD!
YOUR PHONE'S NEVER ON, YUZU.
WE THOUGHT YOU WERE IGNORING US.
SORRY, SORRY!
MY SCHOOL DOESN'T ALLOW CELL PHONES.
SO, HOW *IS* YOUR NEW SCHOOL?
ANY HOT GUYS?
!

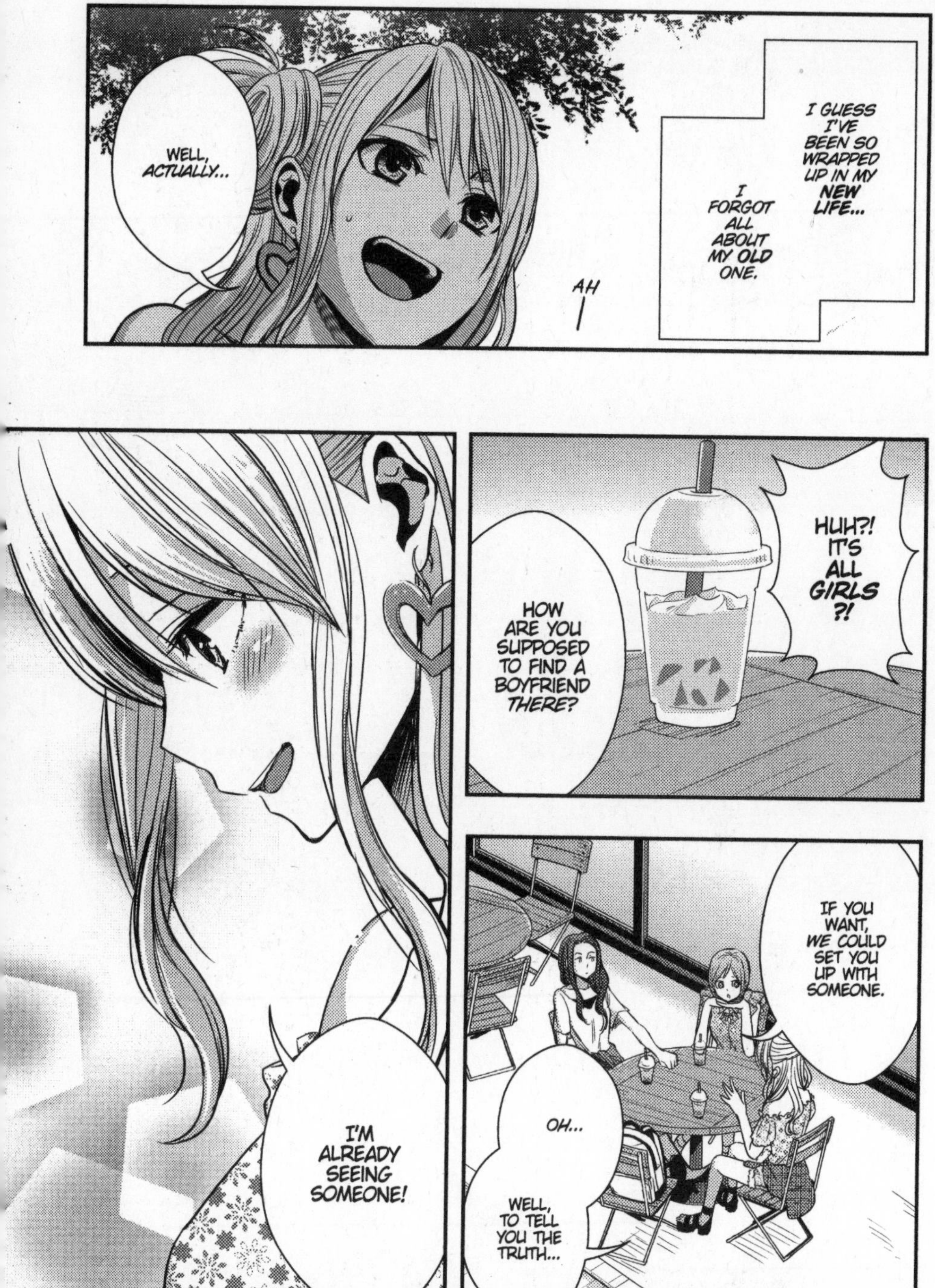
I GUESS I'VE BEEN SO WRAPPED UP IN MY NEW LIFE...
I FORGOT ALL ABOUT MY OLD ONE.
AH
WELL, ACTUALLY...
HUH?! IT'S ALL GIRLS?!
HOW ARE YOU SUPPOSED TO FIND A BOYFRIEND THERE?
IF YOU WANT, WE COULD SET YOU UP WITH SOMEONE.
OH...
WELL, TO TELL YOU THE TRUTH...
I'M ALREADY SEEING SOMEONE!

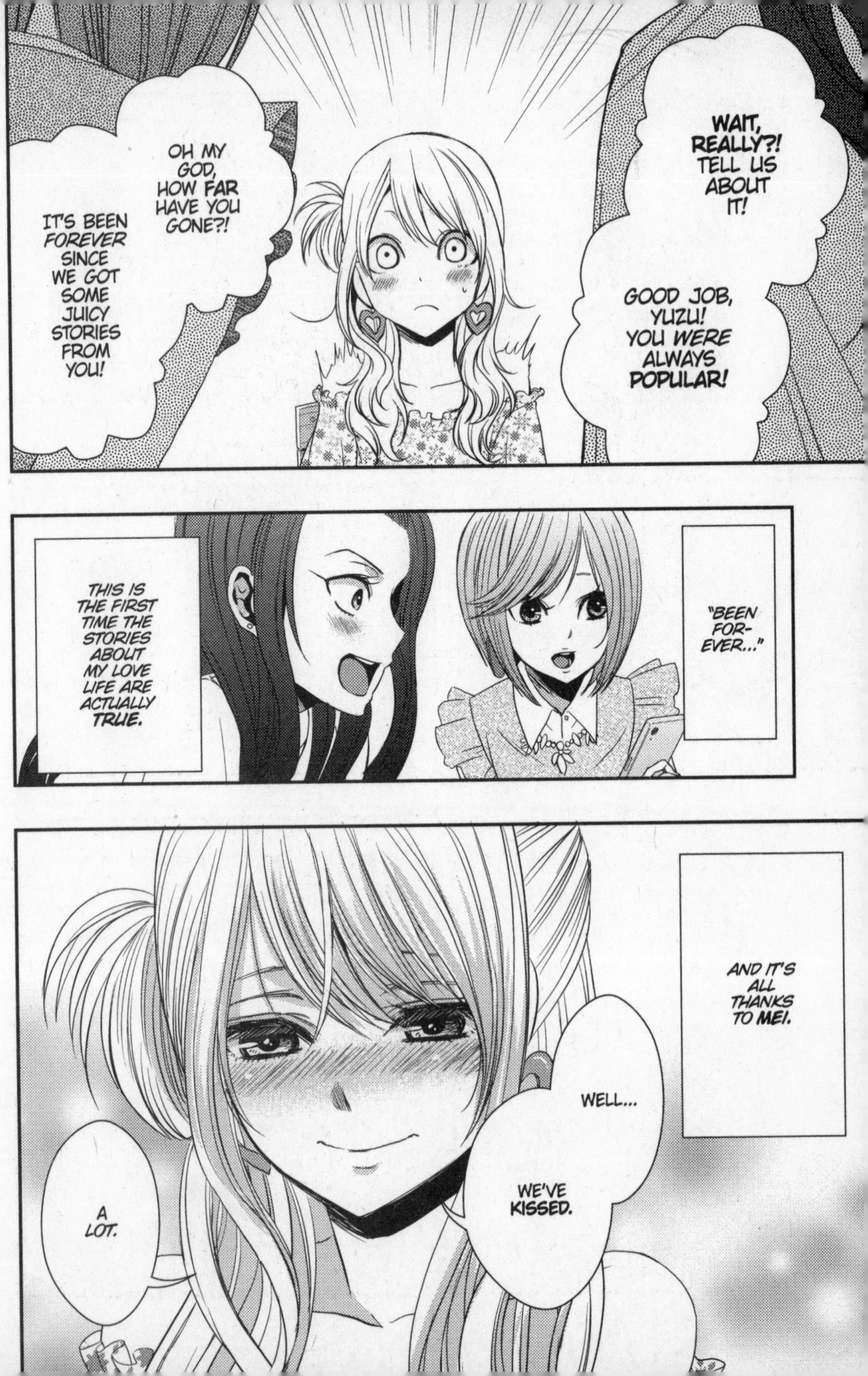
WAIT, REALLY?! TELL US ABOUT IT!
GOOD JOB, YUZU! YOU WERE ALWAYS POPULAR!
OH MY GOD, HOW FAR HAVE YOU GONE?!
IT'S BEEN FOREVER SINCE WE GOT SOME JUICY STORIES FROM YOU!
"BEEN FOR-EVER..."
THIS IS THE FIRST TIME THE STORIES ABOUT MY LOVE LIFE ARE ACTUALLY TRUE.
AND IT'S ALL THANKS TO MEI.
WELL...
WE'VE KISSED.
A LOT.

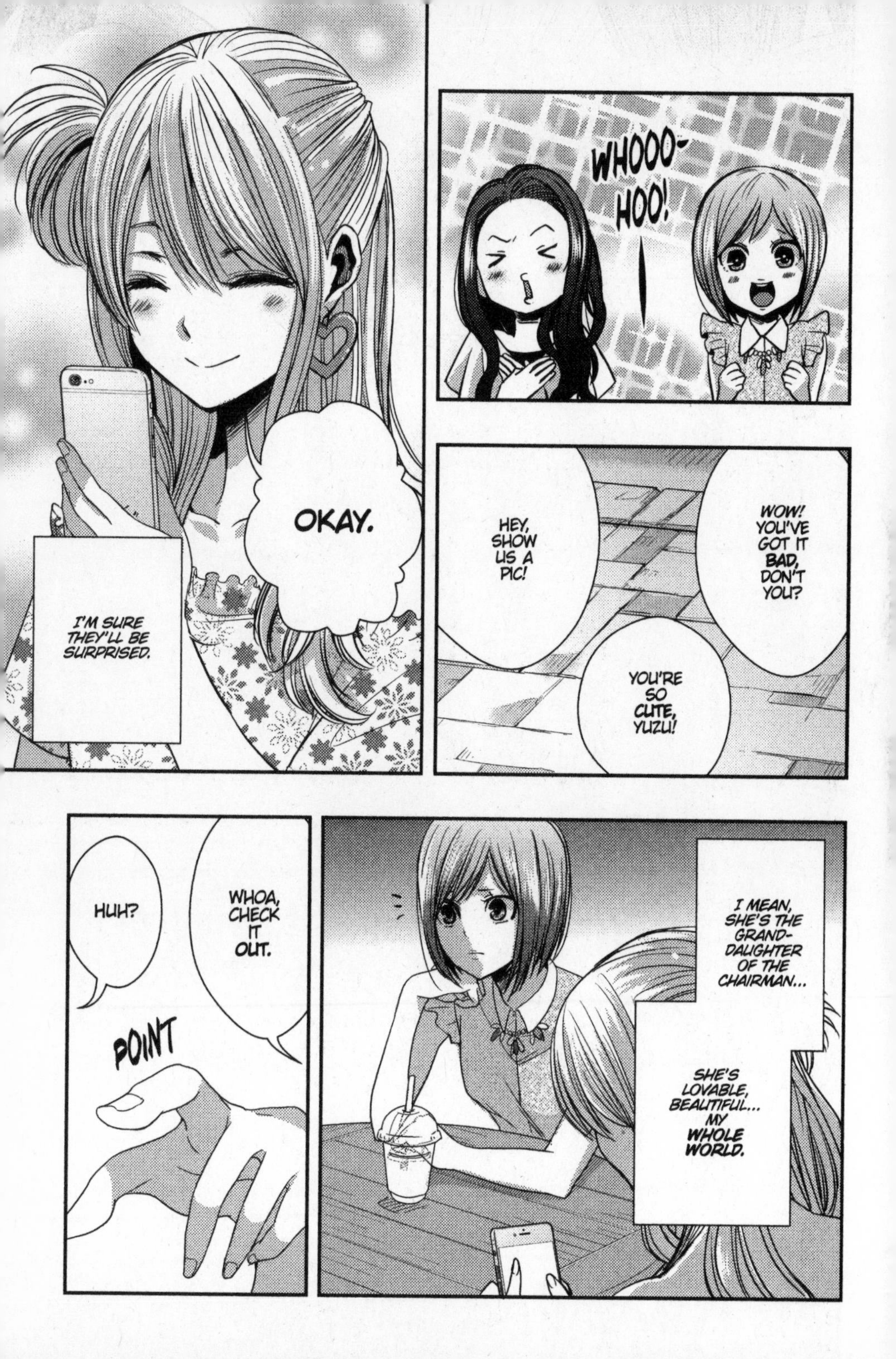
WHOOO-HOO!
WOW! YOU'VE GOT IT BAD, DON'T YOU?
HEY, SHOW US A PIC!
YOU'RE SO CUTE, YUZU!
OKAY.
I'M SURE THEY'LL BE SURPRISED.
I MEAN, SHE'S THE GRAND-DAUGHTER OF THE CHAIRMAN...
SHE'S LOVABLE, BEAUTIFUL... MY WHOLE WORLD.
WHOA, CHECK IT OUT.
HUH?
POINT

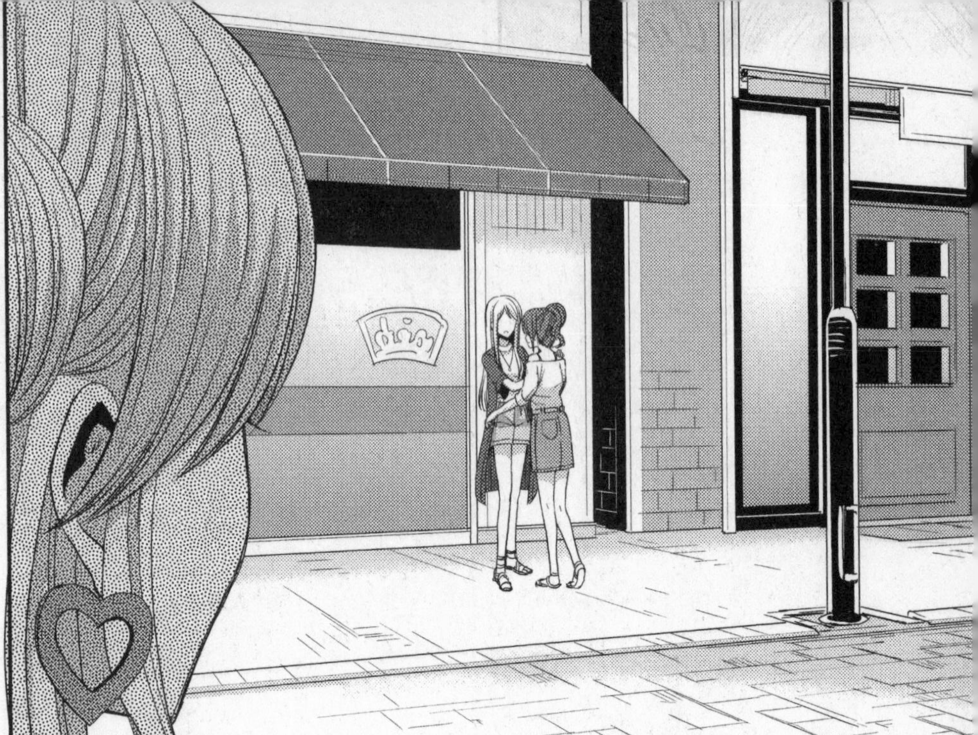
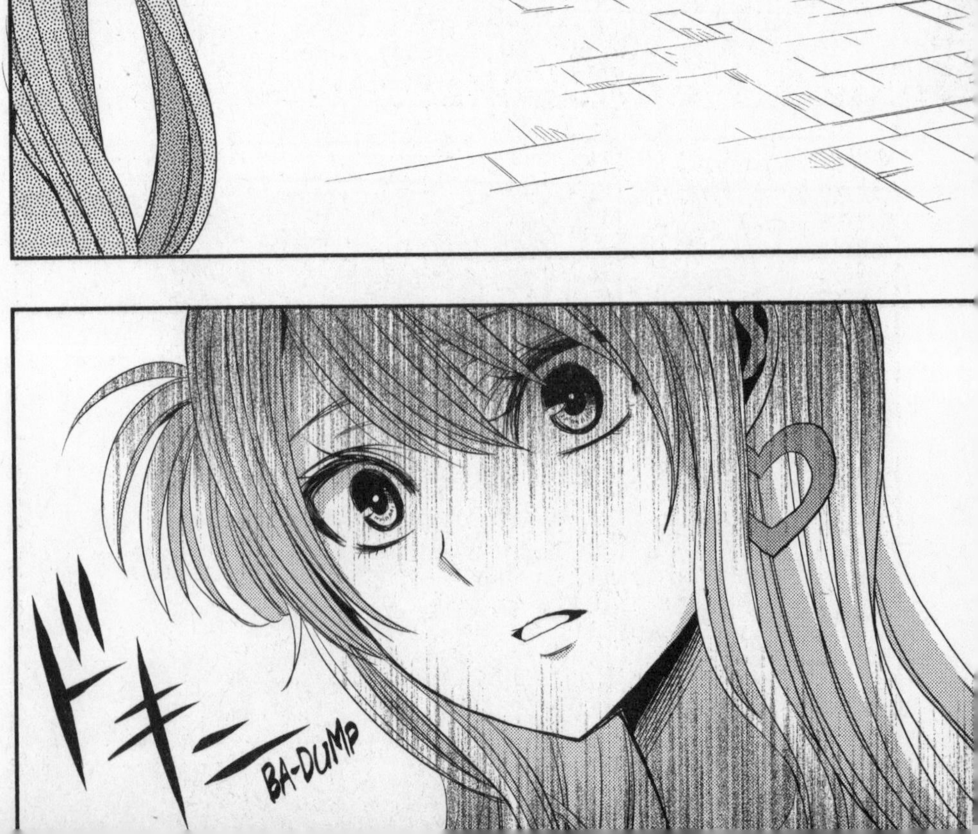
ドキー
BA-DUMP

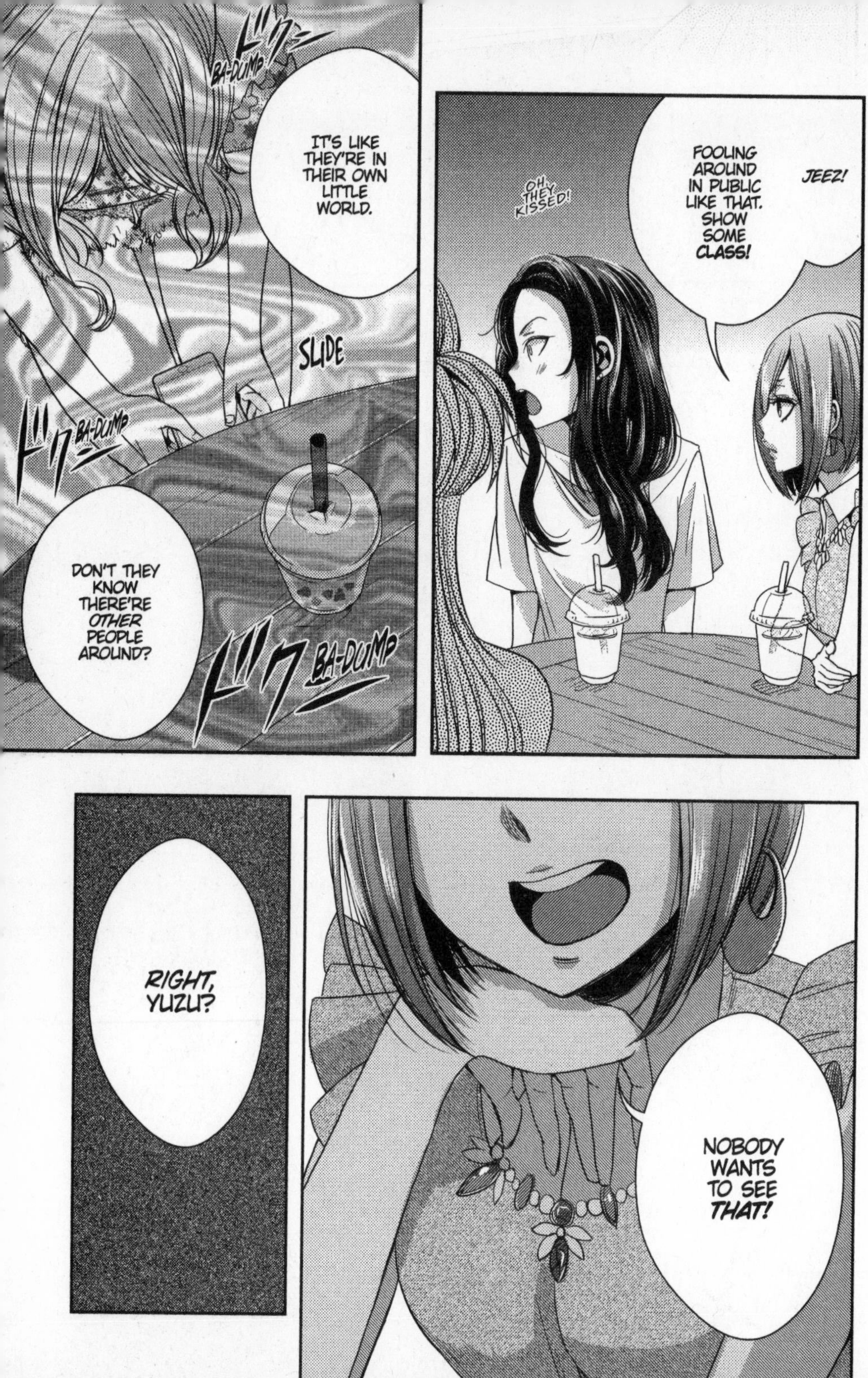
JEEZ!
FOOLING AROUND IN PUBLIC LIKE THAT. SHOW SOME CLASS!
OH, THEY KISSED!
ドクン
BA-DUMP
IT'S LIKE THEY'RE IN THEIR OWN LITTLE WORLD.
SLIDE
ドクン
BA-DUMP
DON'T THEY KNOW THERE'RE OTHER PEOPLE AROUND?
ドクン
BA-DUMP
NOBODY WANTS TO SEE THAT!
RIGHT, YUZU?

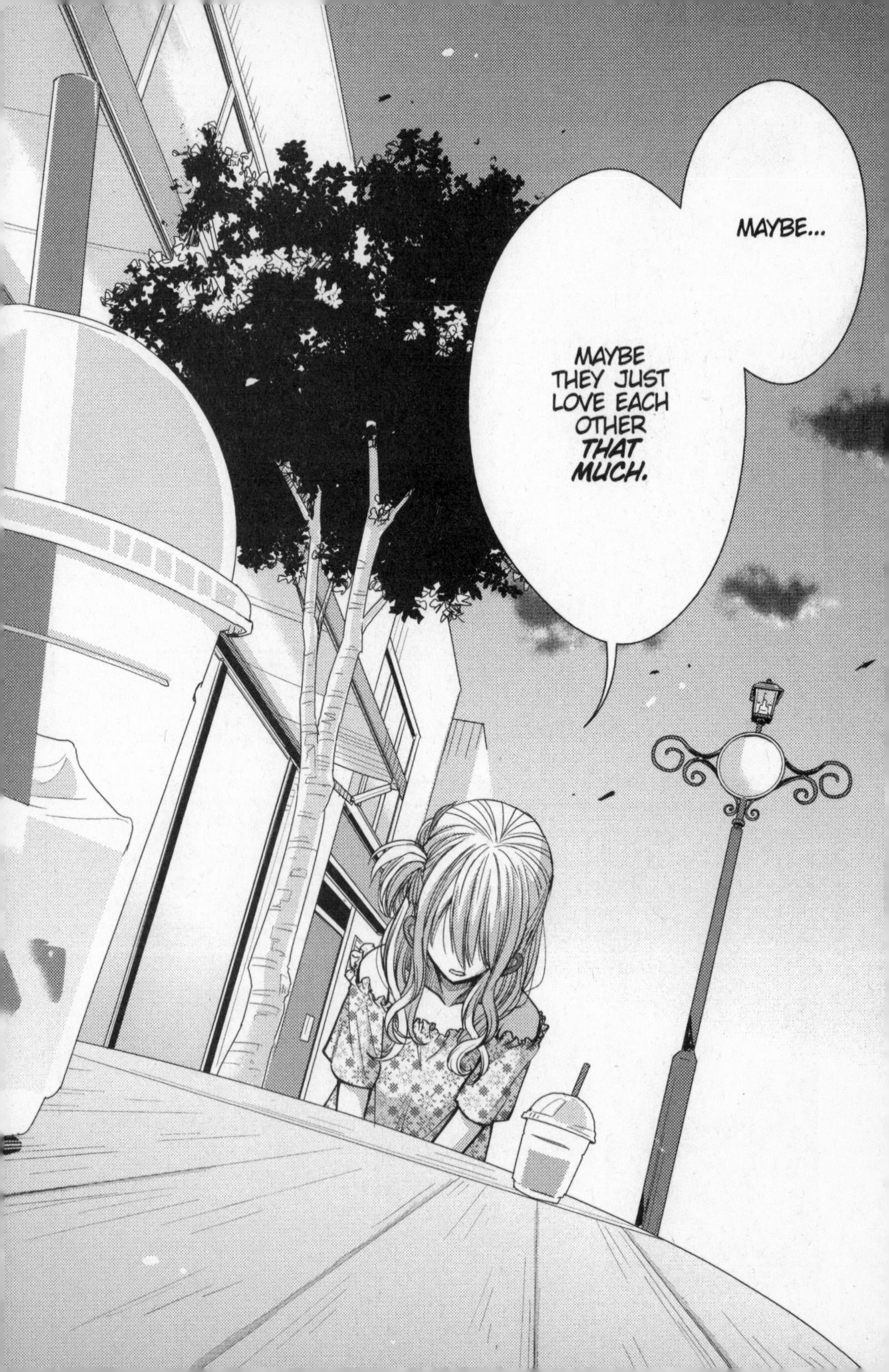
MAYBE...
MAYBE THEY JUST LOVE EACH OTHER *THAT MUCH.*

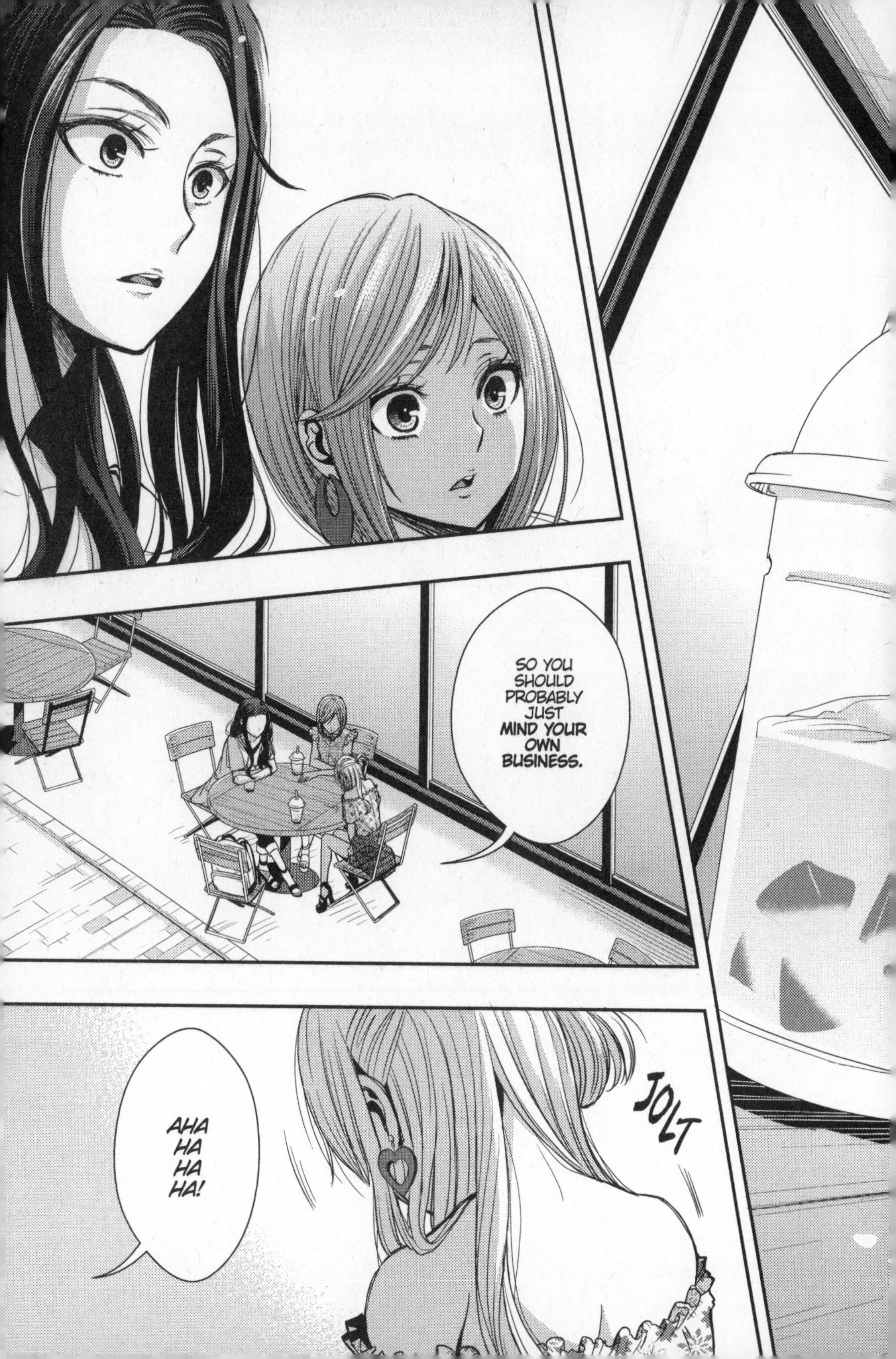
SO YOU SHOULD PROBABLY JUST MIND YOUR OWN BUSINESS.
JOLT
AHA HA HA HA!

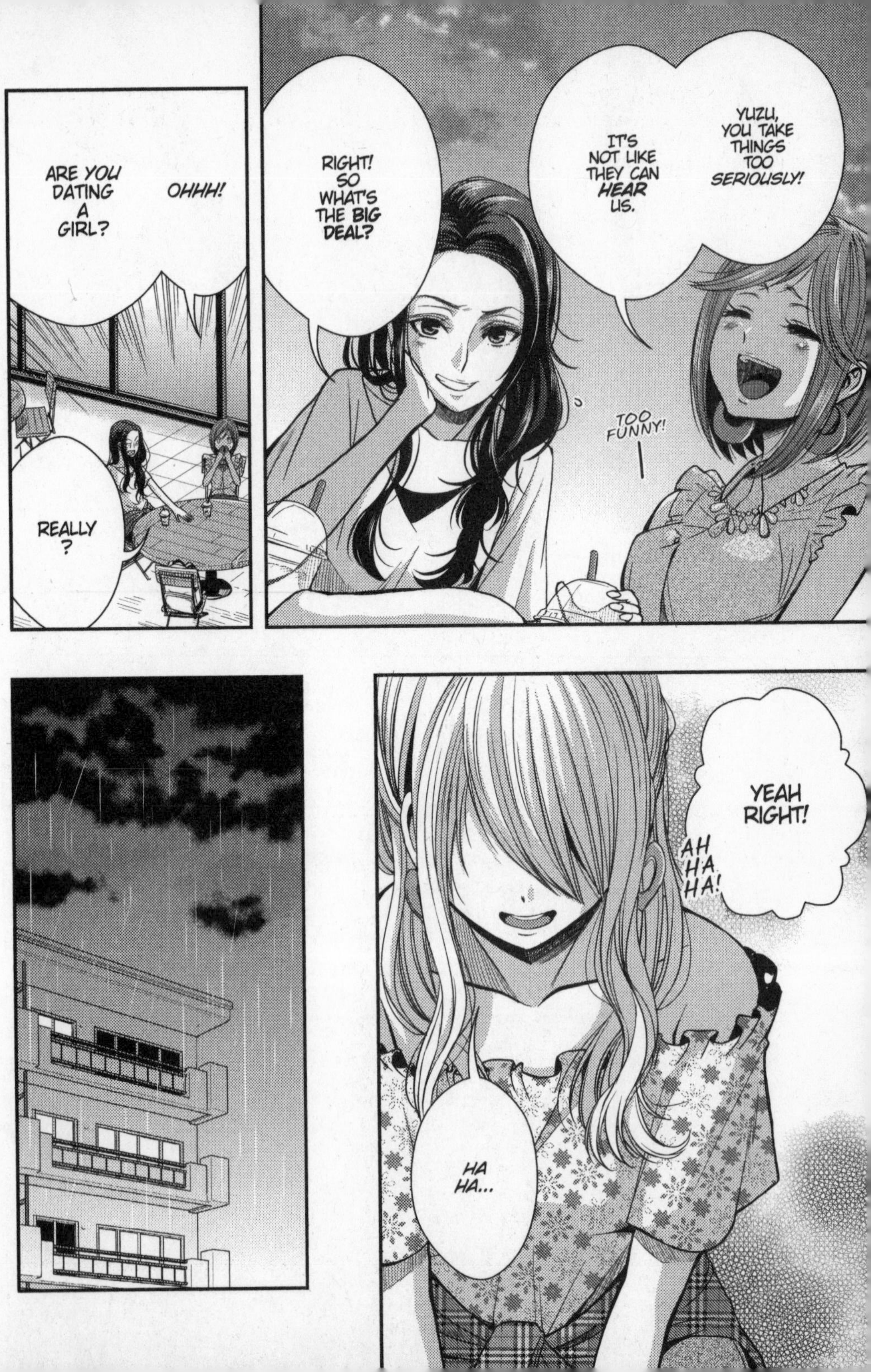
YUZU, YOU TAKE THINGS TOO SERIOUSLY!
IT'S NOT LIKE THEY CAN HEAR US.
TOO FUNNY!
RIGHT! SO WHAT'S THE BIG DEAL?
OHHH!
ARE YOU DATING A GIRL?
REALLY?
YEAH RIGHT!
AH HA HA!
HA HA...

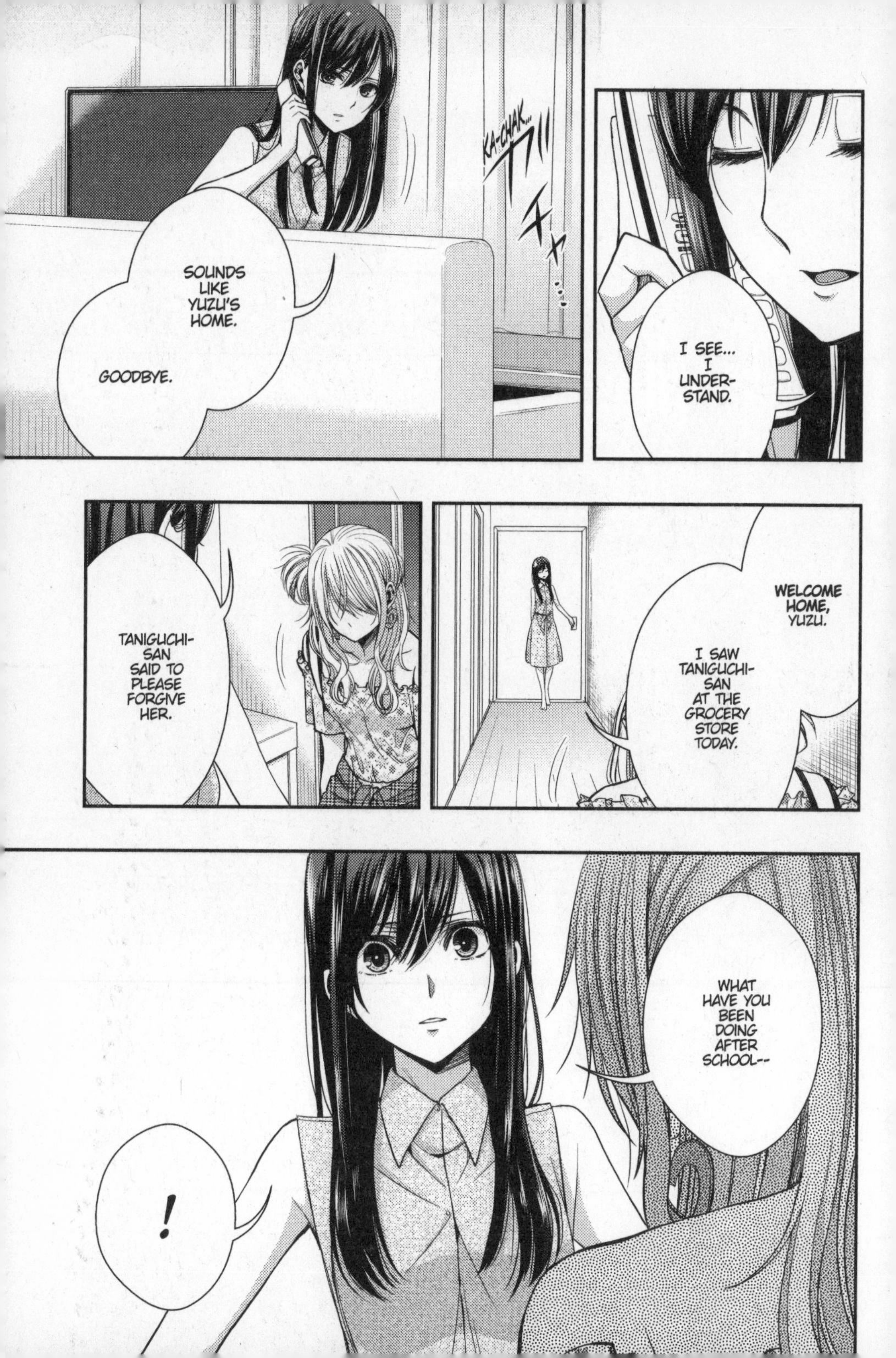
I SEE... I UNDER-STAND.
KA-CHAK...
SOUNDS LIKE YUZU'S HOME.
GOODBYE.
WELCOME HOME, YUZU.
I SAW TANIGUCHI-SAN AT THE GROCERY STORE TODAY.
TANIGUCHI-SAN SAID TO PLEASE FORGIVE HER.
WHAT HAVE YOU BEEN DOING AFTER SCHOOL--
!

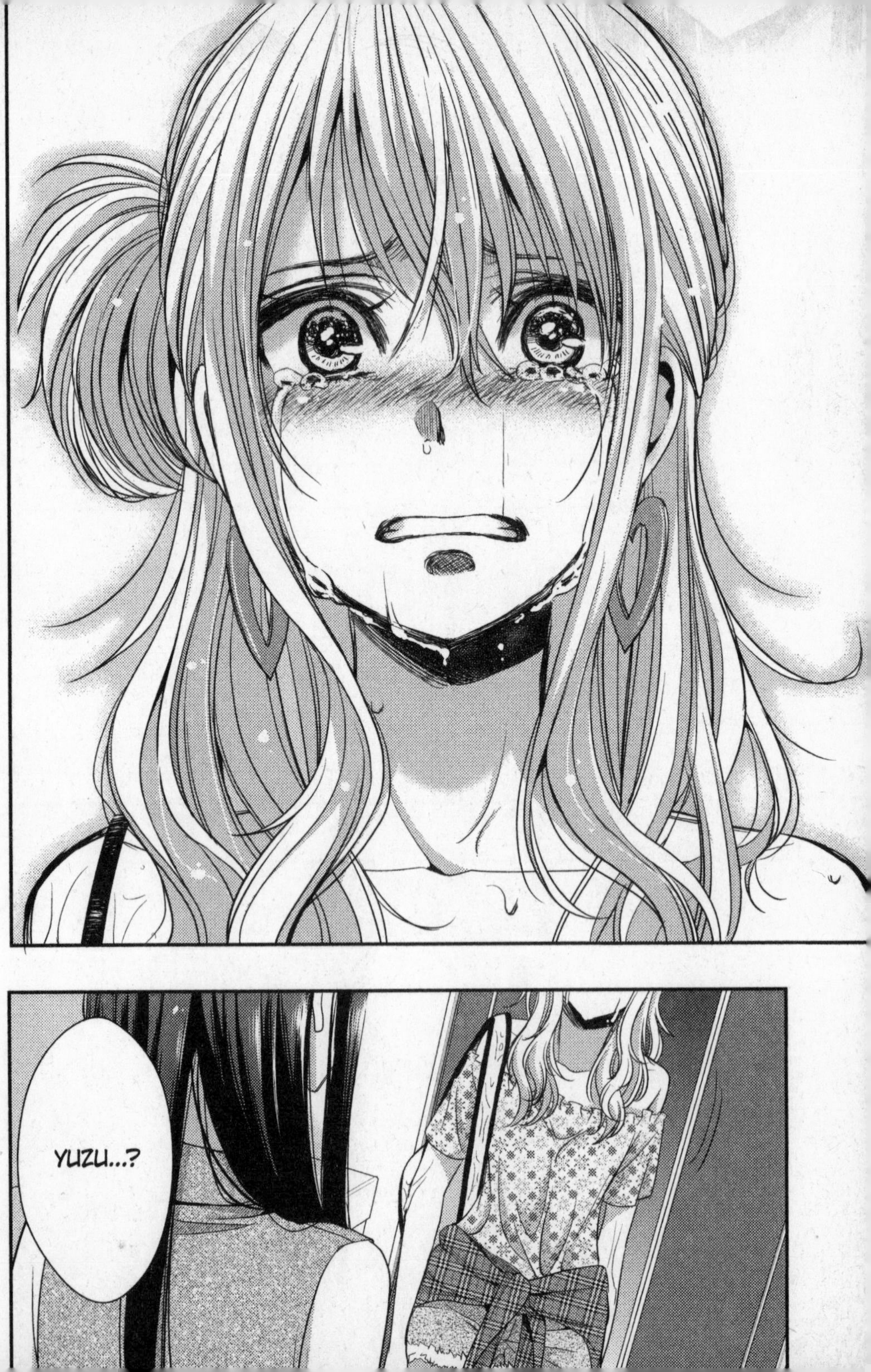
YUZU...?

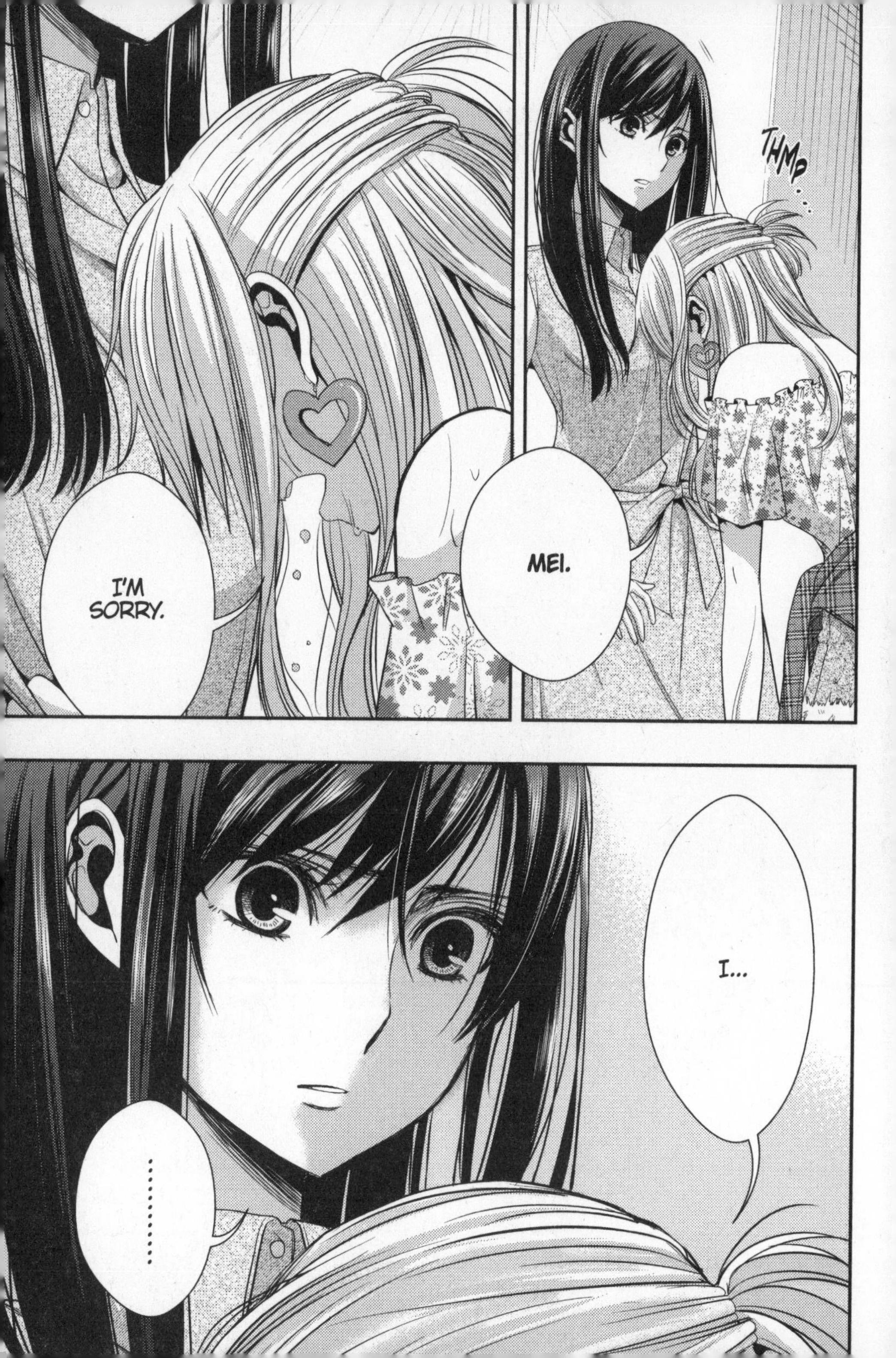
THMP...
MEI.
I'M SORRY.
I...
......

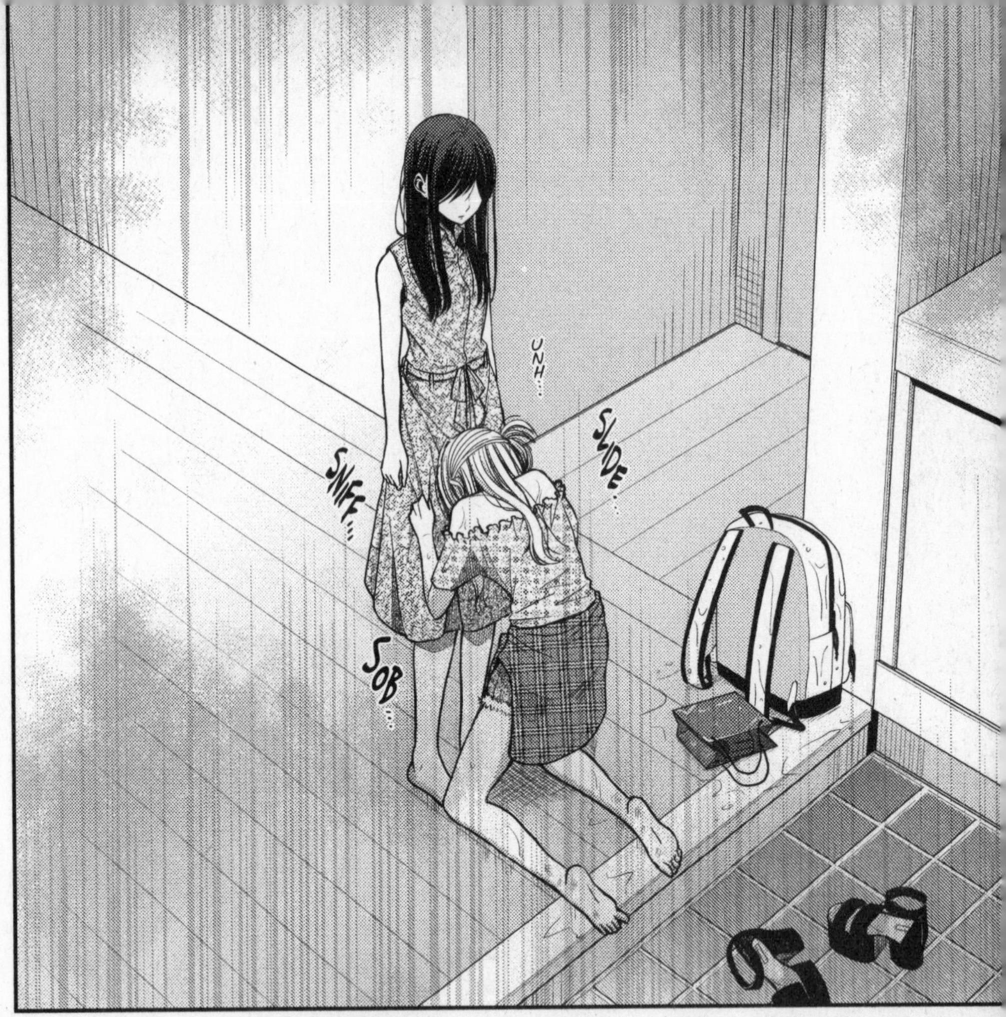
UNH...
SLIDE...
SNIFF...
SOB...
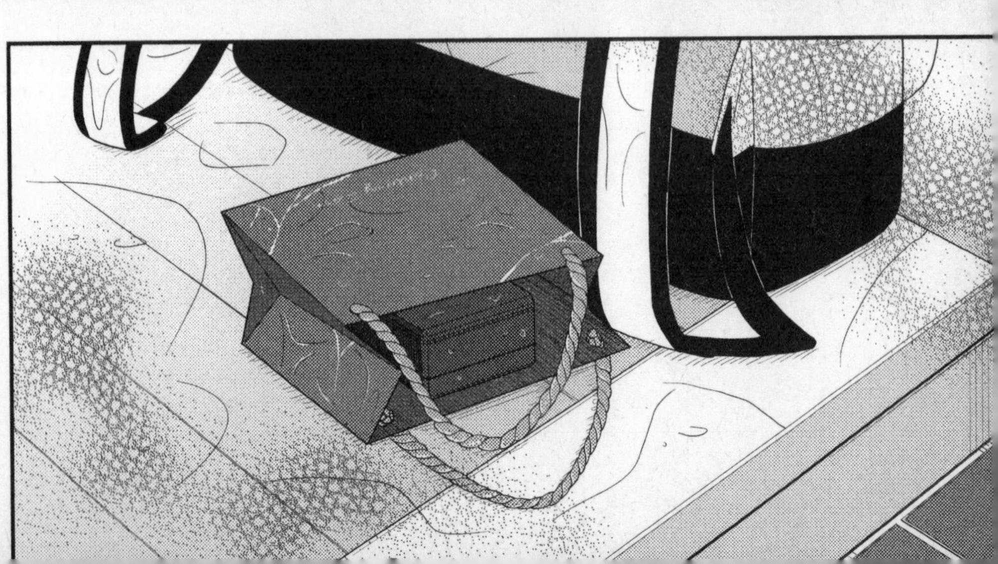

citrus
【シトラス】

SECRET LOVE AFFAIR WITH SISTER

citrus

SABUROUTA PRESENTS SECRET LOVE AFFAIR WITH SISTER

6

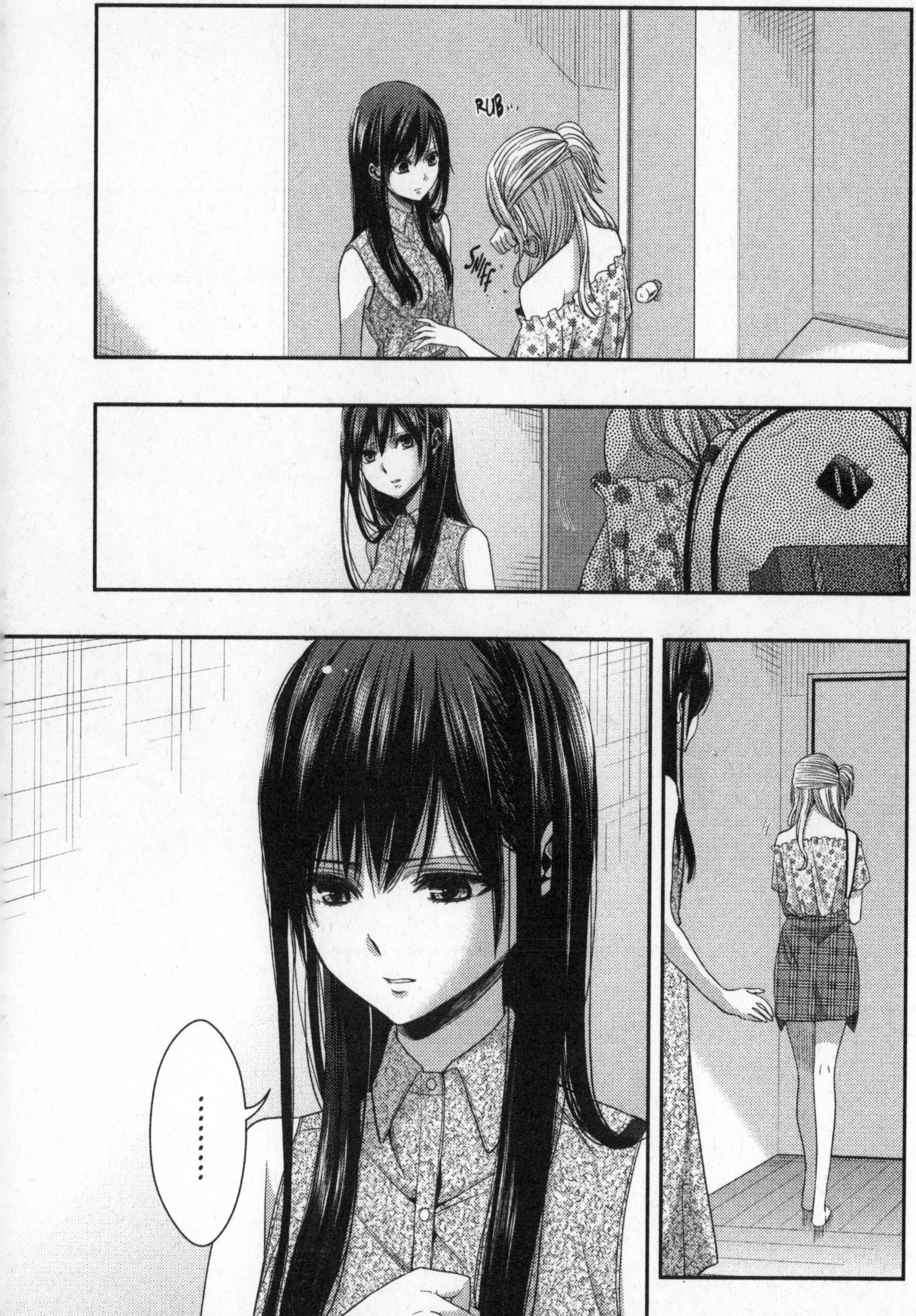
RUB...
SNIFF
......

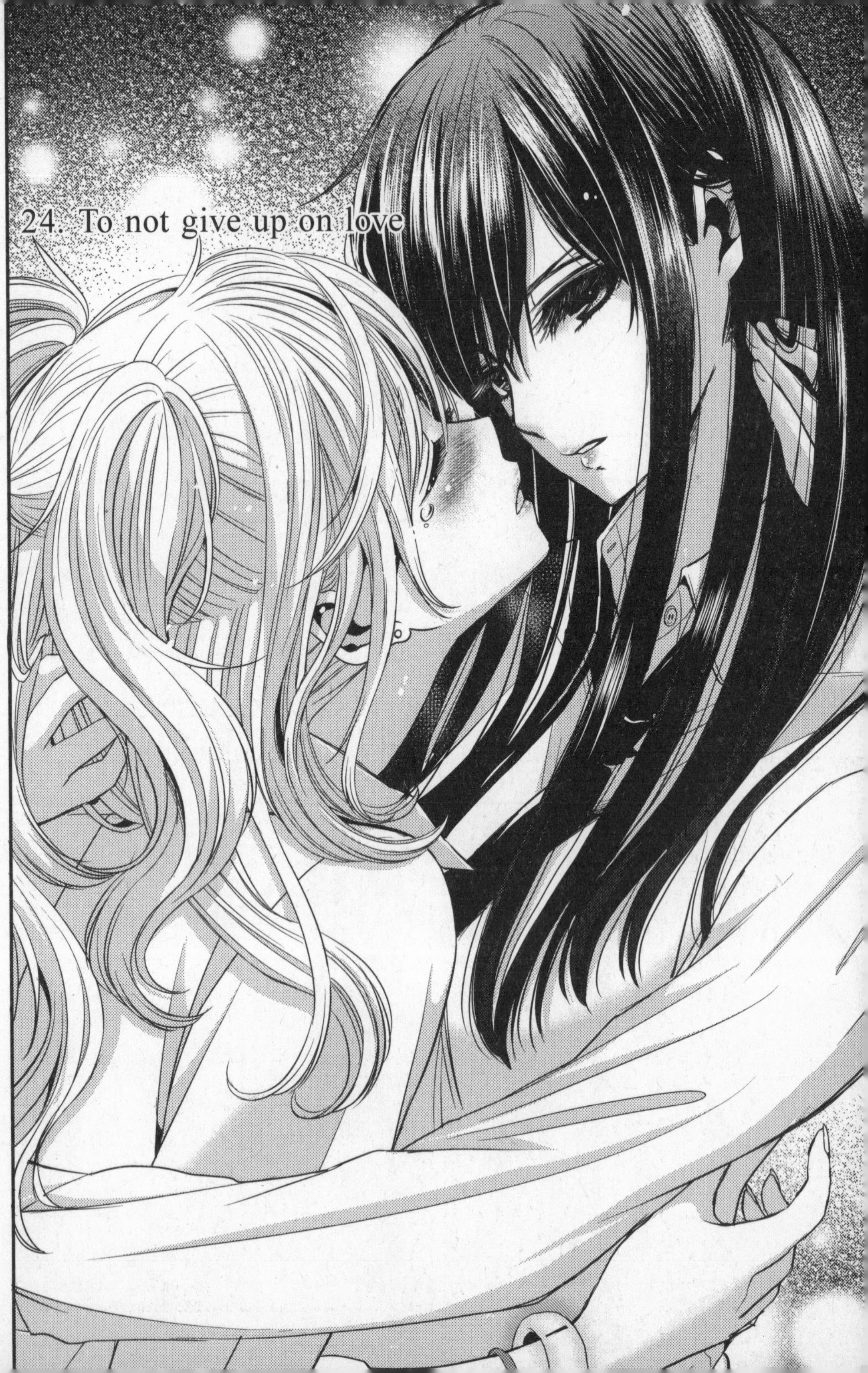

24. To not give up on love

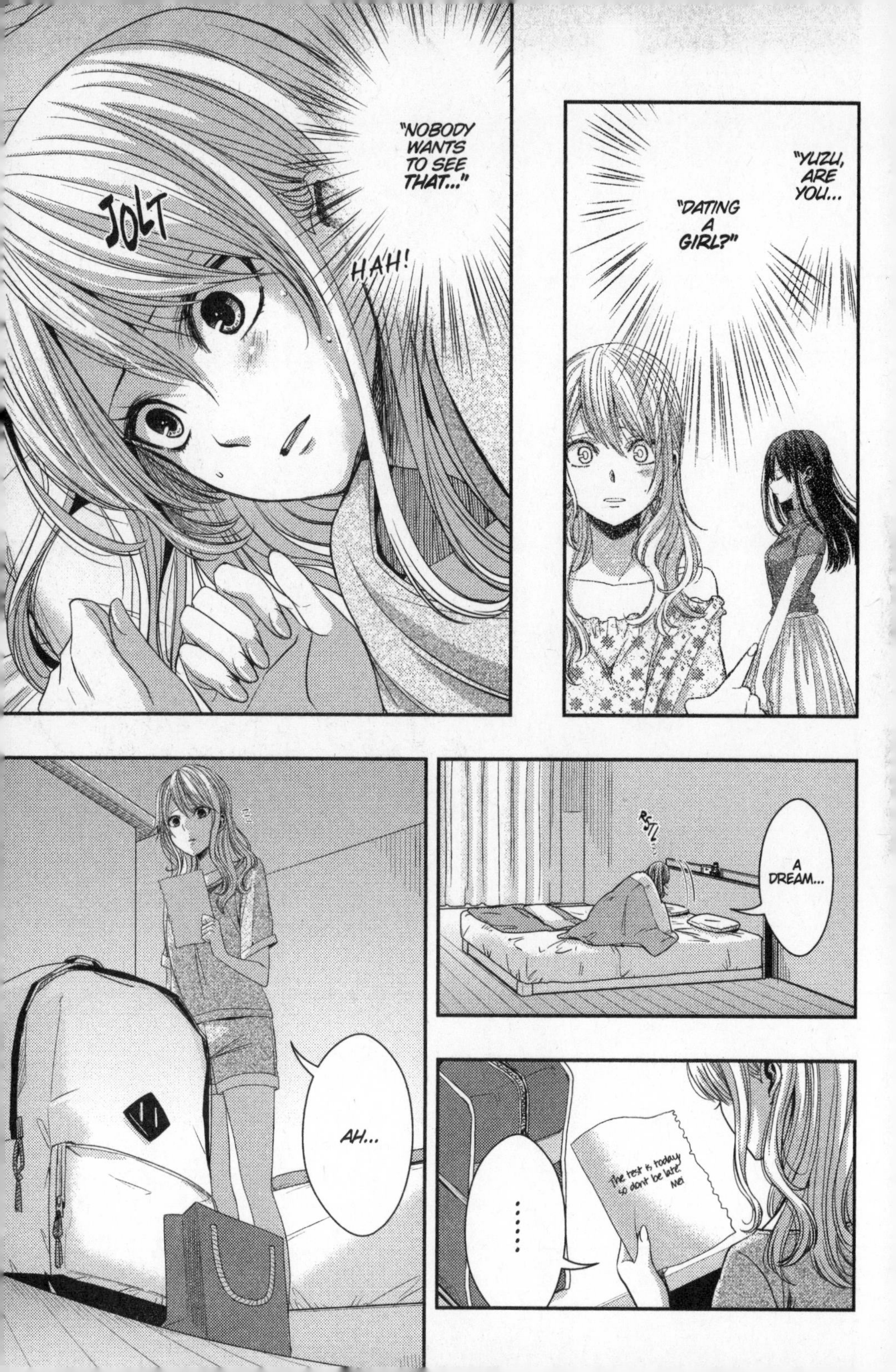
"YUZU, ARE YOU...
"DATING A GIRL?"
"NOBODY WANTS TO SEE THAT..."
JOLT
HAH!
RSTL
A DREAM...
The test is today so don't be late! Mei
......
AH...

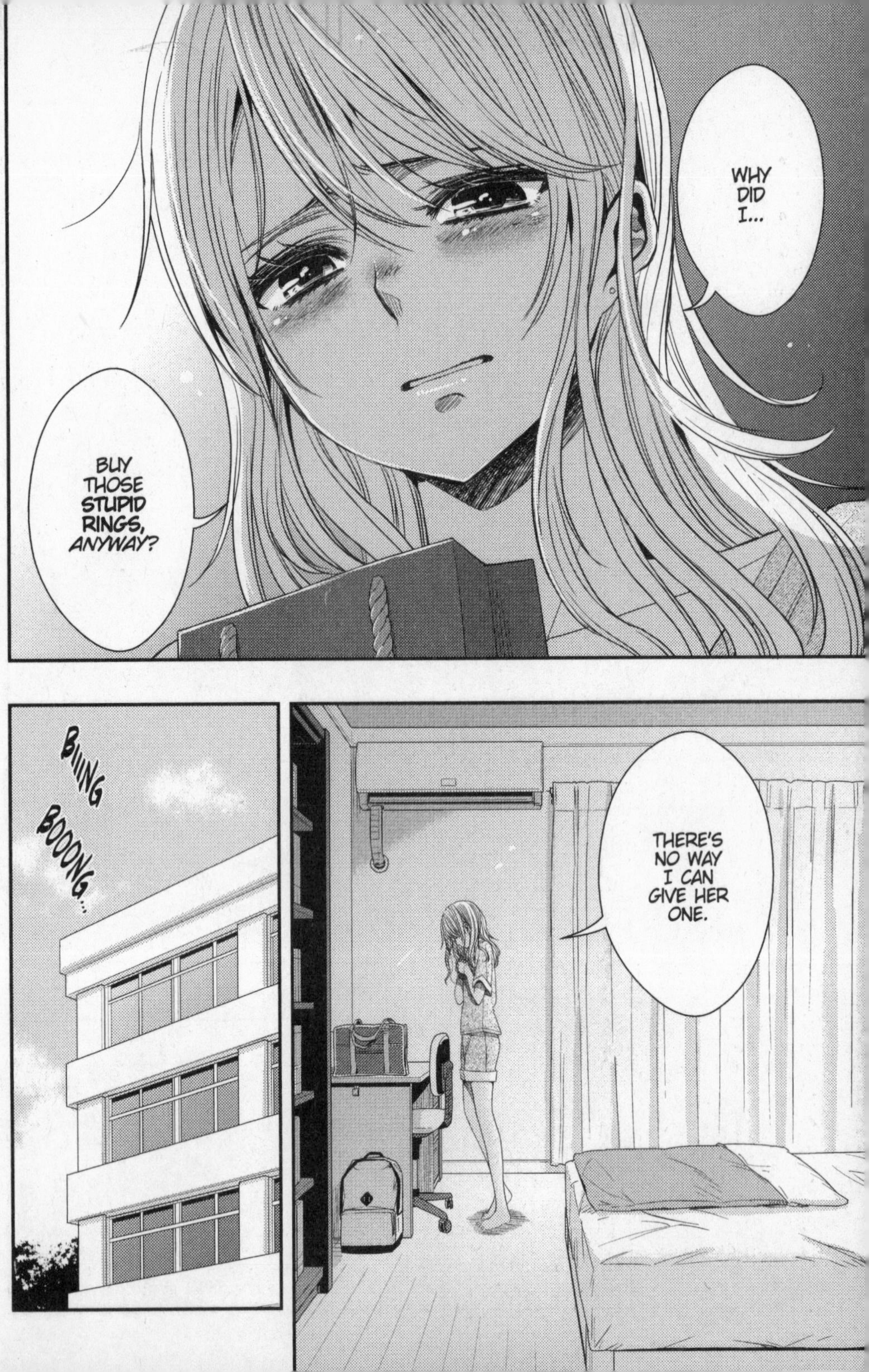
WHY DID I...
BUY THOSE STUPID RINGS, *ANYWAY?*
THERE'S NO WAY I CAN GIVE HER ONE.
BIIING BOOONG...

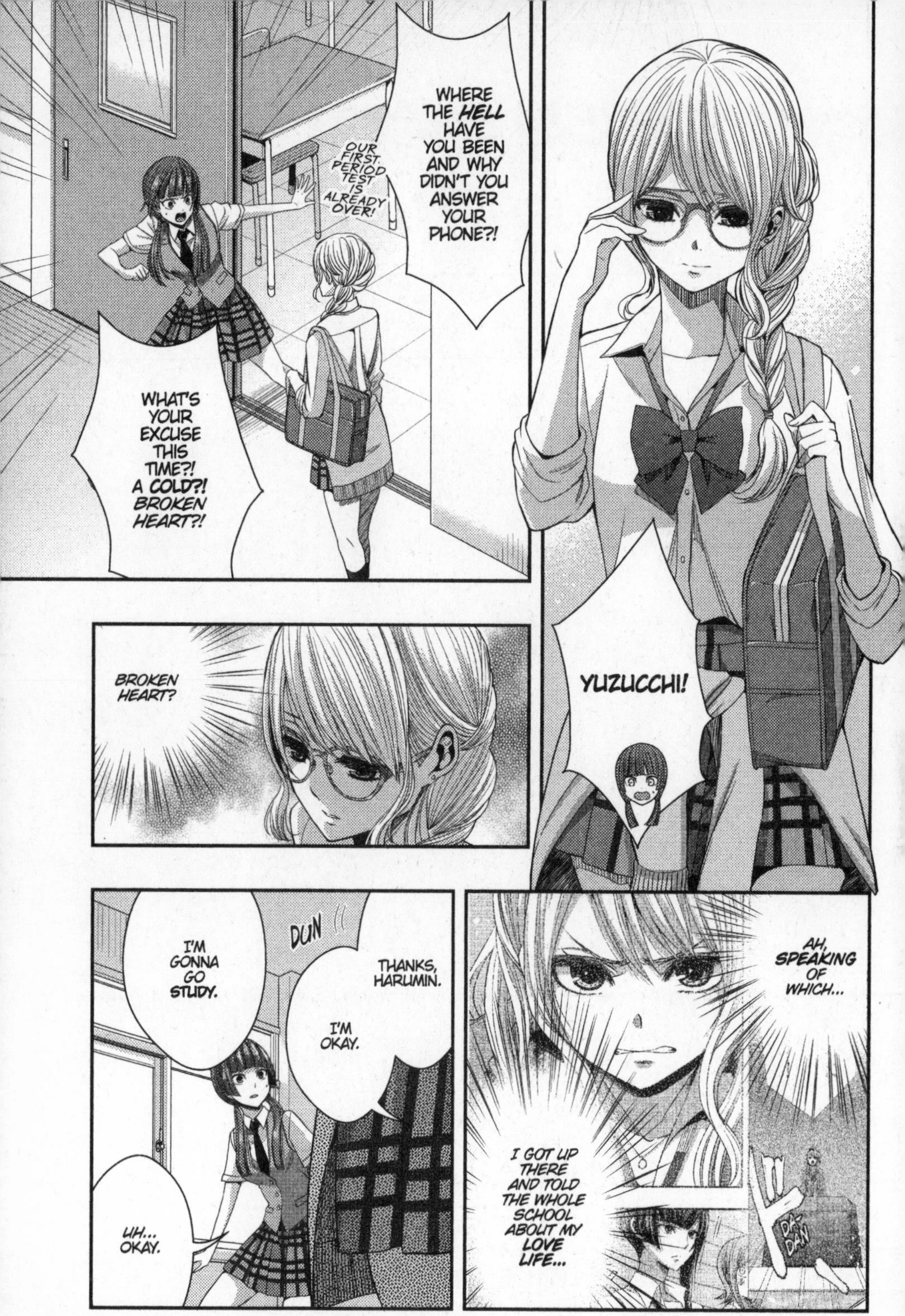
YUZUCCHI!
WHERE THE HELL HAVE YOU BEEN AND WHY DIDN'T YOU ANSWER YOUR PHONE?!
OUR FIRST PERIOD TEST IS ALREADY OVER!
WHAT'S YOUR EXCUSE THIS TIME?! A COLD?! BROKEN HEART?!
BROKEN HEART?
AH, SPEAKING OF WHICH...
I GOT UP THERE AND TOLD THE WHOLE SCHOOL ABOUT MY LOVE LIFE...
DA-DAN
THANKS, HARUMIN.
I'M OKAY.
DUN
I'M GONNA GO STUDY.
UH... OKAY.

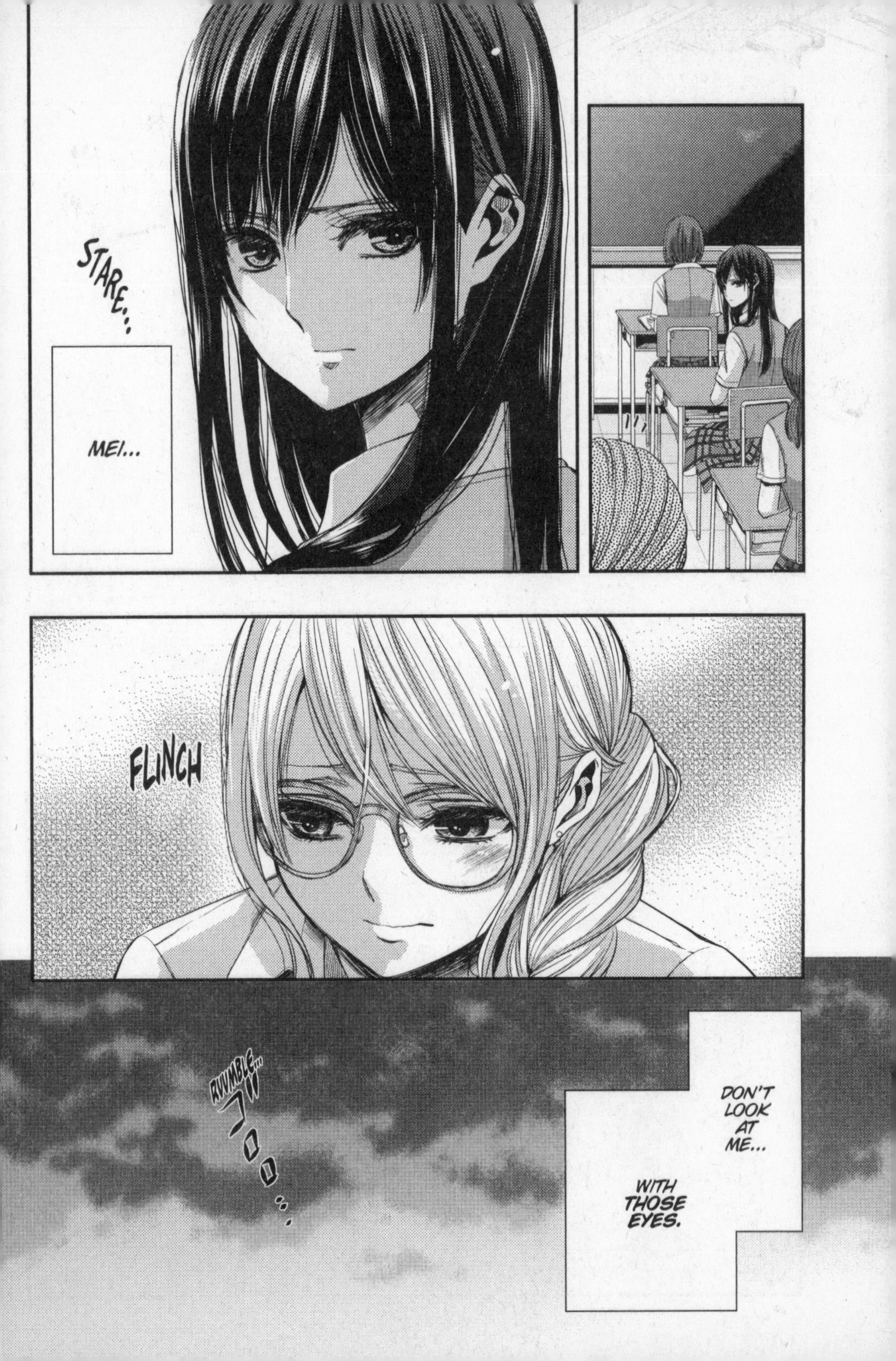
STARE...
MEI...
FLINCH
DON'T LOOK AT ME...
WITH THOSE EYES.
RUMBLE...

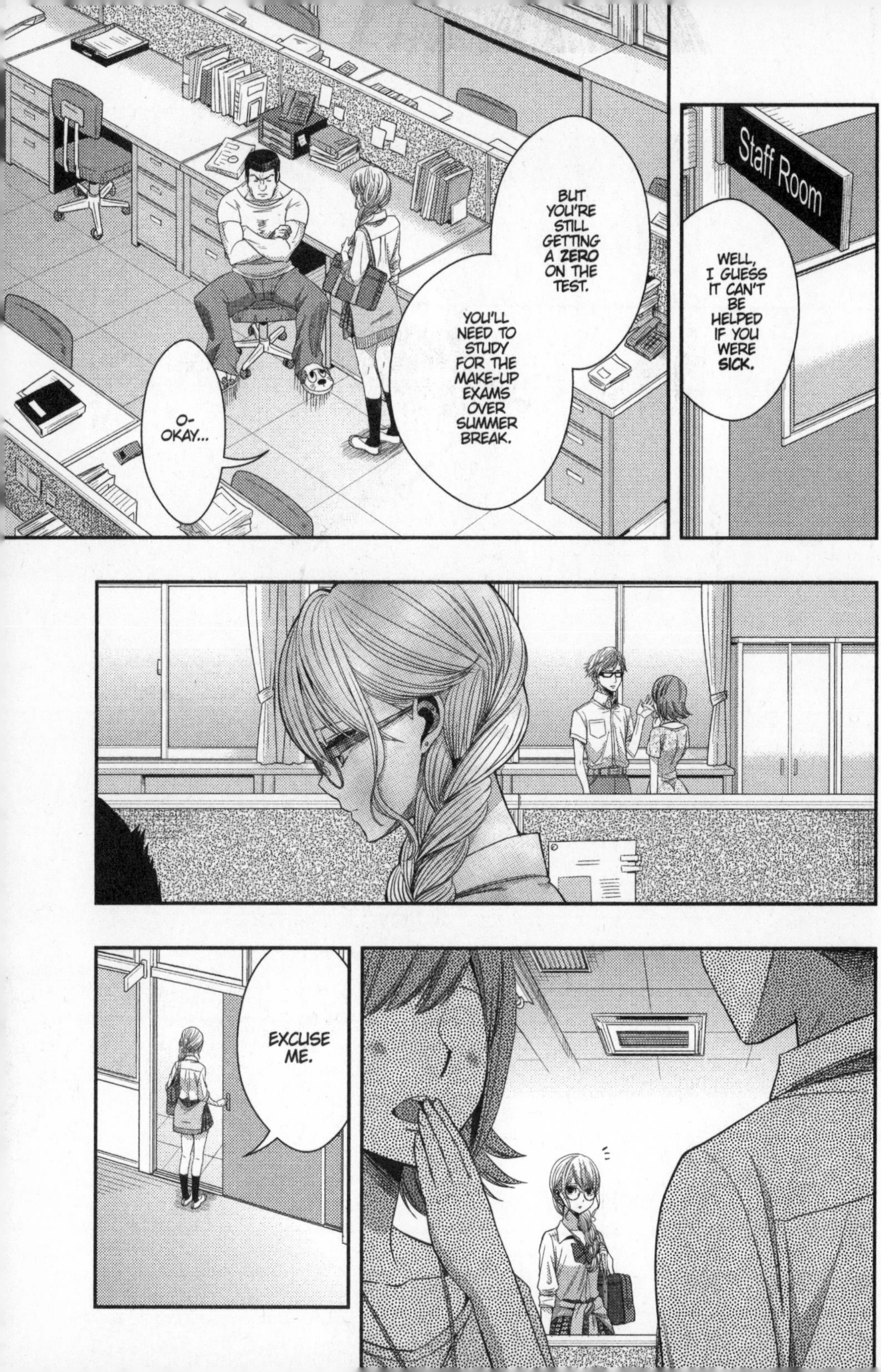
Staff Room
WELL, I GUESS IT CAN'T BE HELPED IF YOU WERE SICK.
BUT YOU'RE STILL GETTING A ZERO ON THE TEST.
YOU'LL NEED TO STUDY FOR THE MAKE-UP EXAMS OVER SUMMER BREAK.
O-OKAY...
EXCUSE ME.

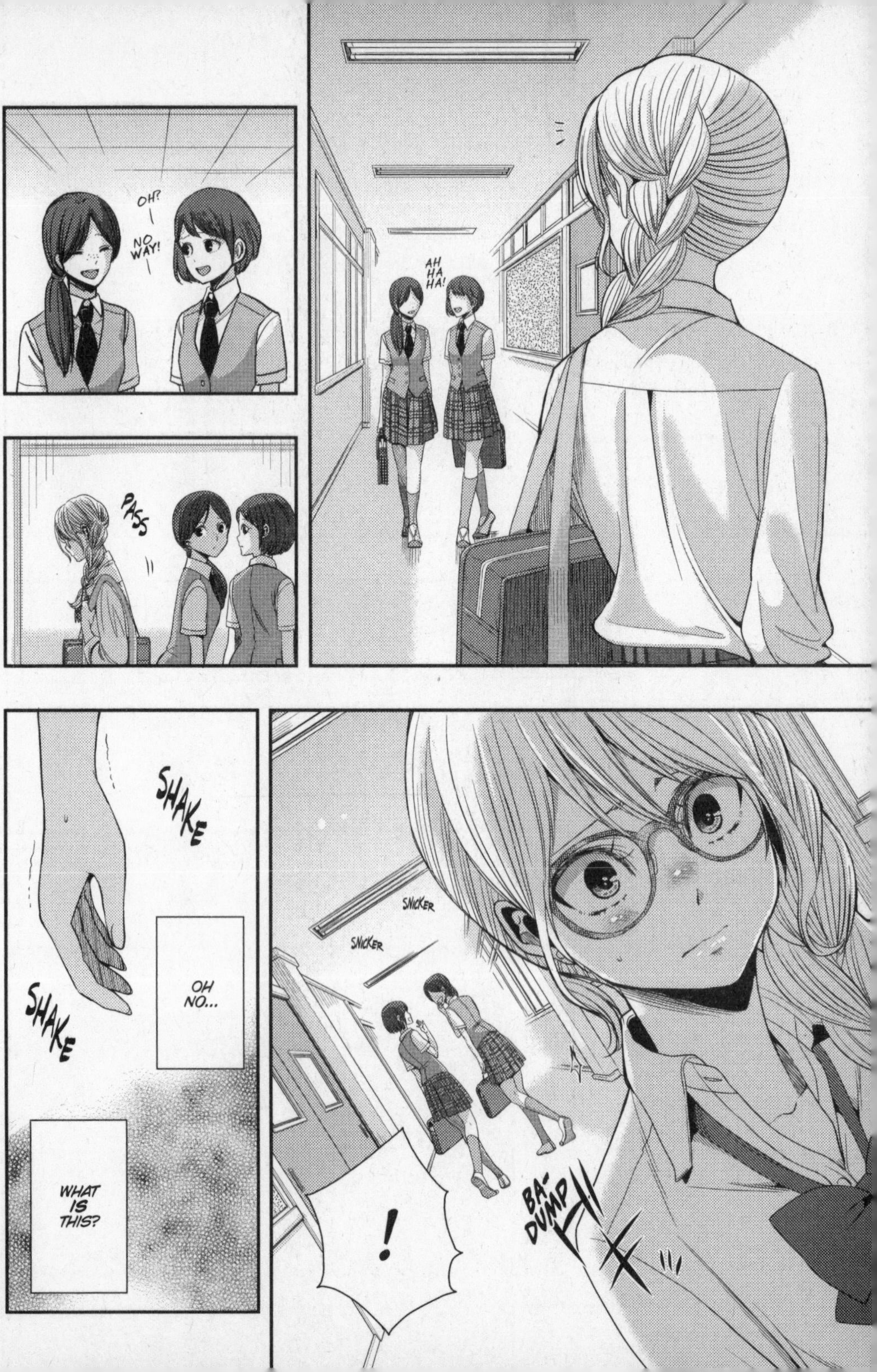
AH HA HA!
OH?
NO WAY!
PASS
SNICKER
SNICKER
BA-DUMP
!
SHAKE
SHAKE
OH NO...
WHAT IS THIS?

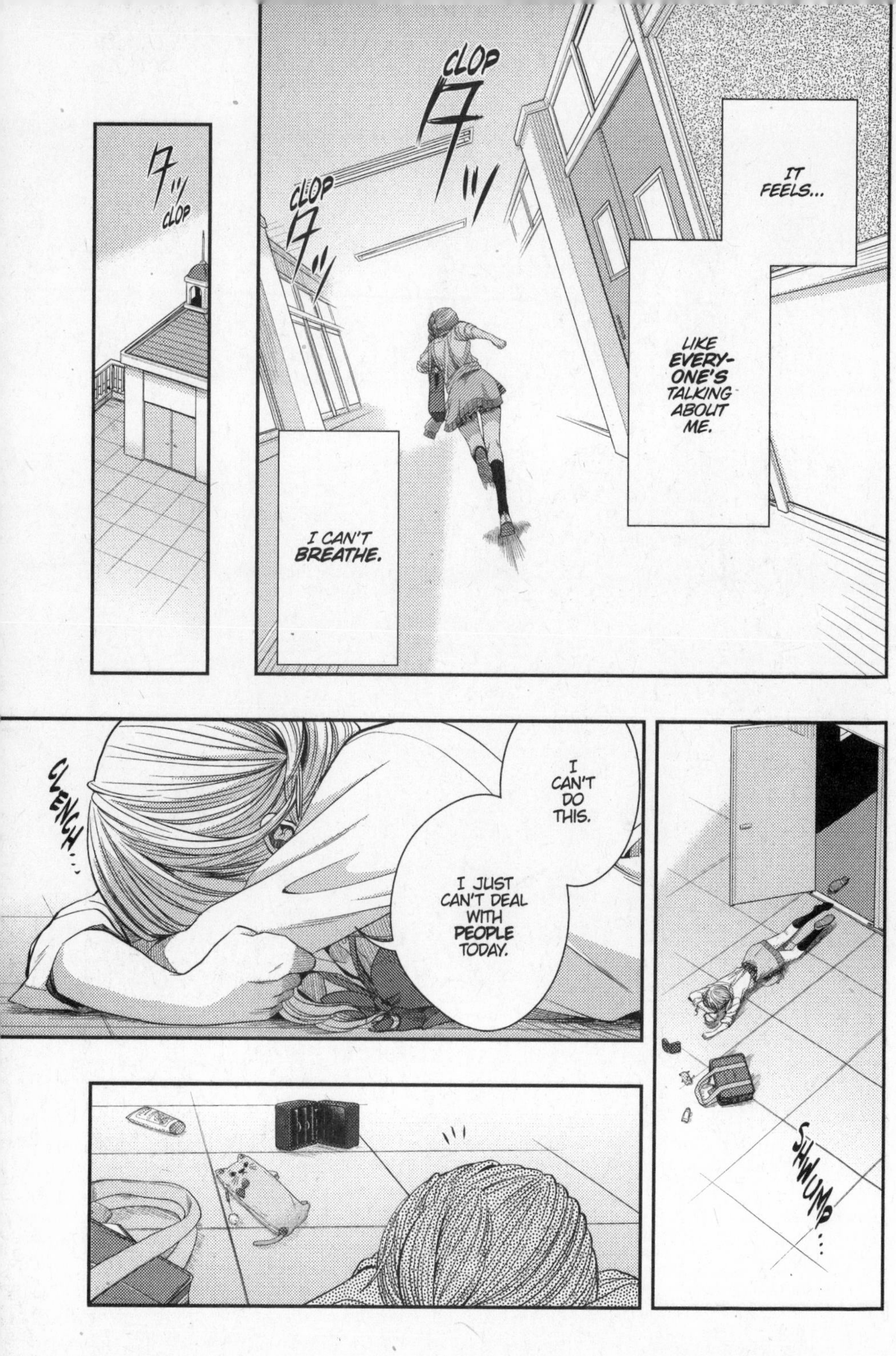

CLOP
タッ
IT FEELS...
LIKE EVERYONE'S TALKING ABOUT ME.
CLOP
タッ
I CAN'T BREATHE.
タッ
CLOP
SHWUMP...
CLENCH...
I CAN'T DO THIS.
I JUST CAN'T DEAL WITH PEOPLE TODAY.

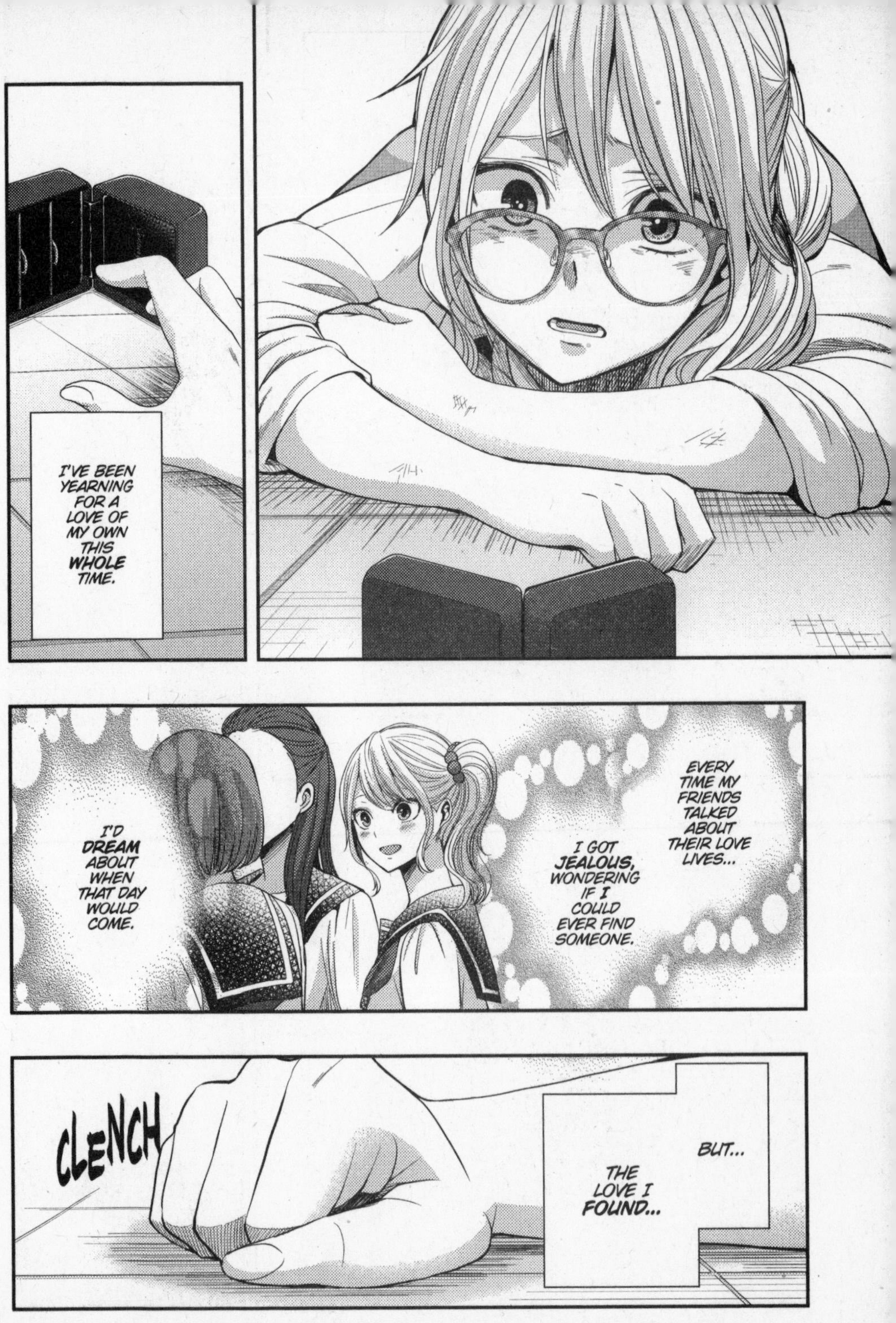
I'VE BEEN YEARNING FOR A LOVE OF MY OWN THIS WHOLE TIME.
EVERY TIME MY FRIENDS TALKED ABOUT THEIR LOVE LIVES...
I GOT JEALOUS, WONDERING IF I COULD EVER FIND SOMEONE.
I'D DREAM ABOUT WHEN THAT DAY WOULD COME.
BUT...
THE LOVE I FOUND...
CLENCH

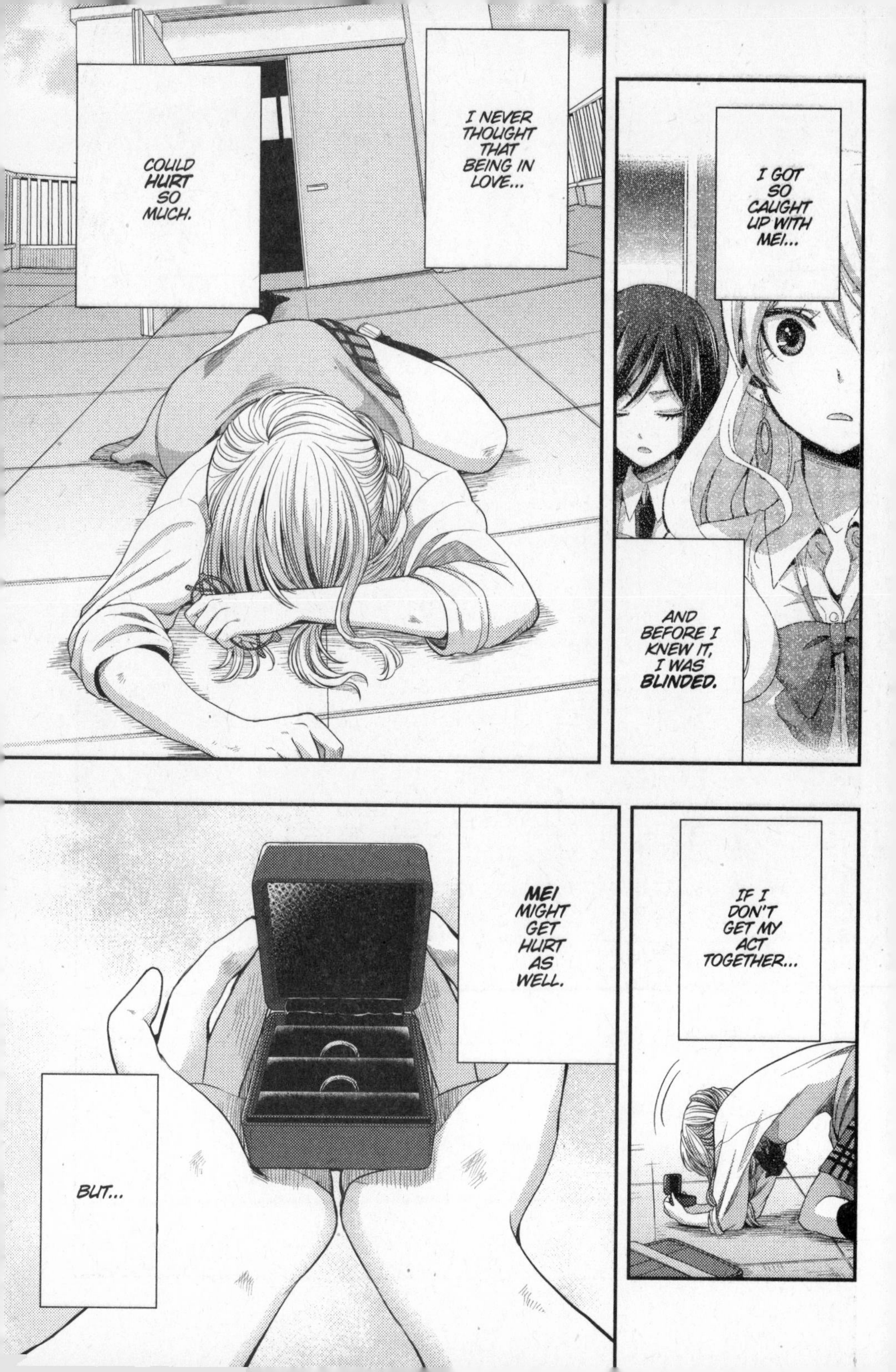
I GOT SO CAUGHT UP WITH MEI...
AND BEFORE I KNEW IT, I WAS BLINDED.
I NEVER THOUGHT THAT BEING IN LOVE...
COULD HURT SO MUCH.
IF I DON'T GET MY ACT TOGETHER...
MEI MIGHT GET HURT AS WELL.
BUT...

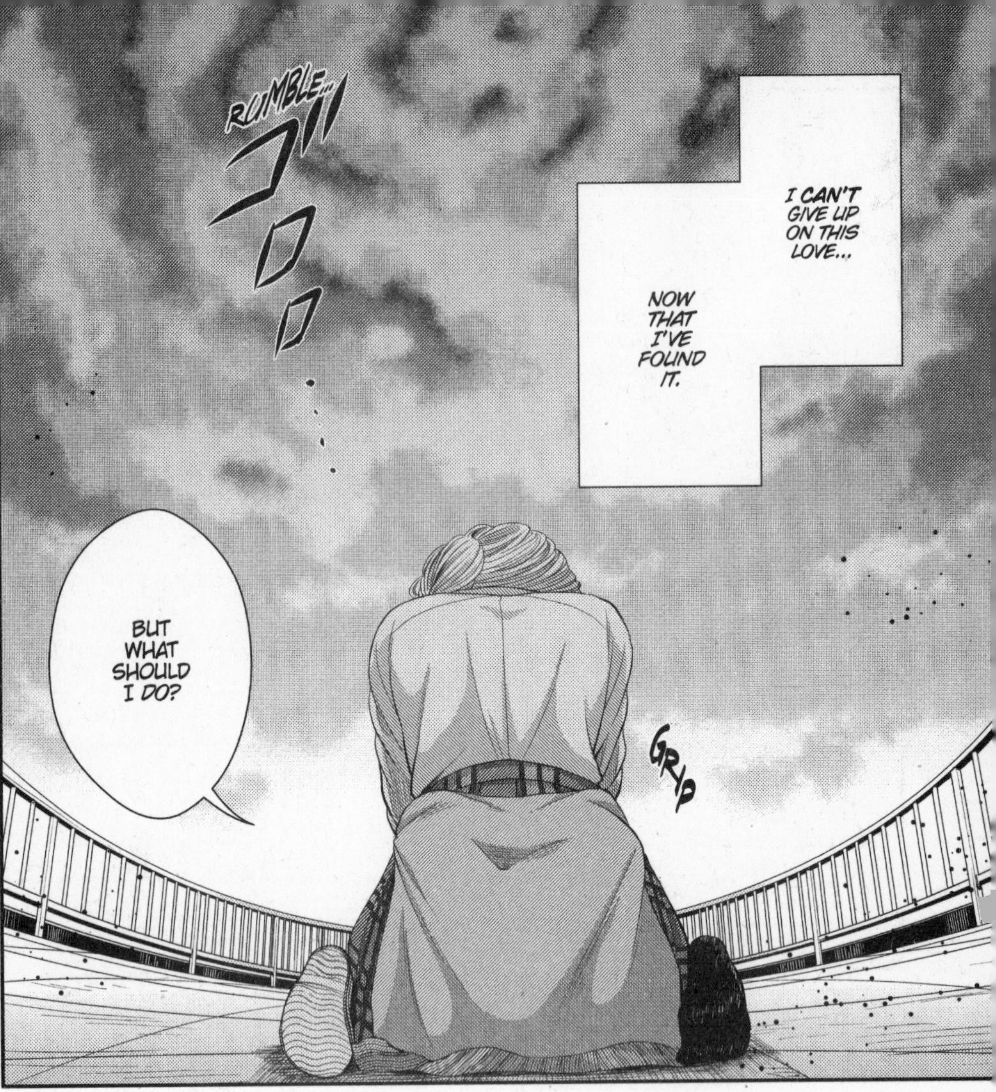
I CAN'T GIVE UP ON THIS LOVE...
NOW THAT I'VE FOUND IT.
RUMBLE...
BUT WHAT SHOULD I DO?
GRIP

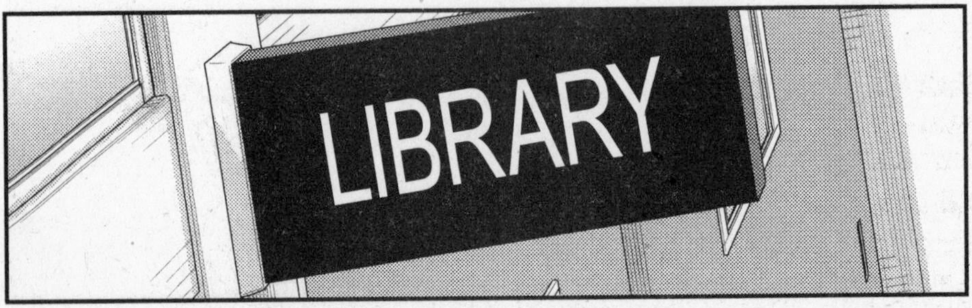
LIBRARY

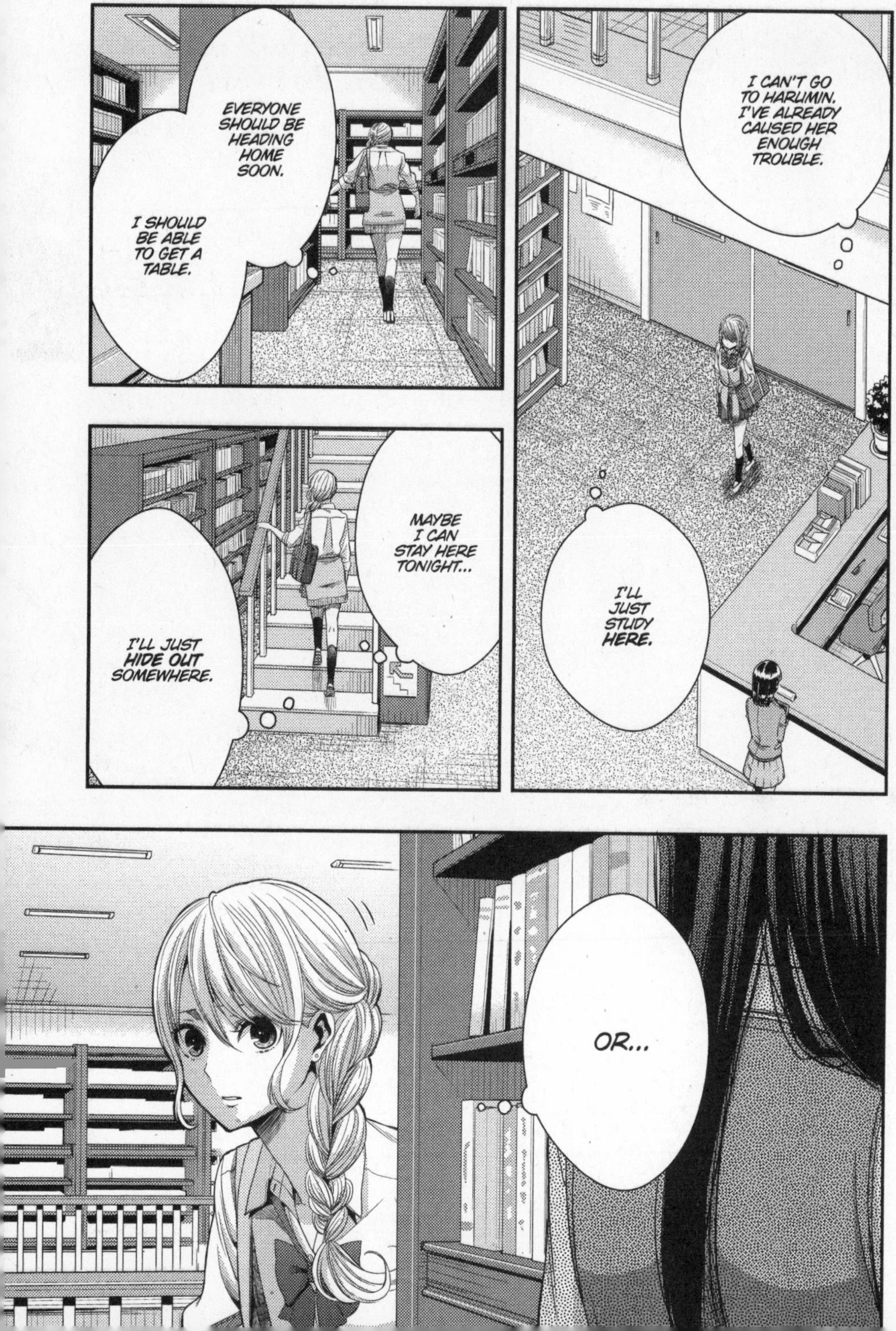
I CAN'T GO TO HARUMIN. I'VE ALREADY CAUSED HER ENOUGH TROUBLE.
I'LL JUST STUDY HERE.
EVERYONE SHOULD BE HEADING HOME SOON.
I SHOULD BE ABLE TO GET A TABLE.
MAYBE I CAN STAY HERE TONIGHT...
I'LL JUST HIDE OUT SOMEWHERE.
OR...

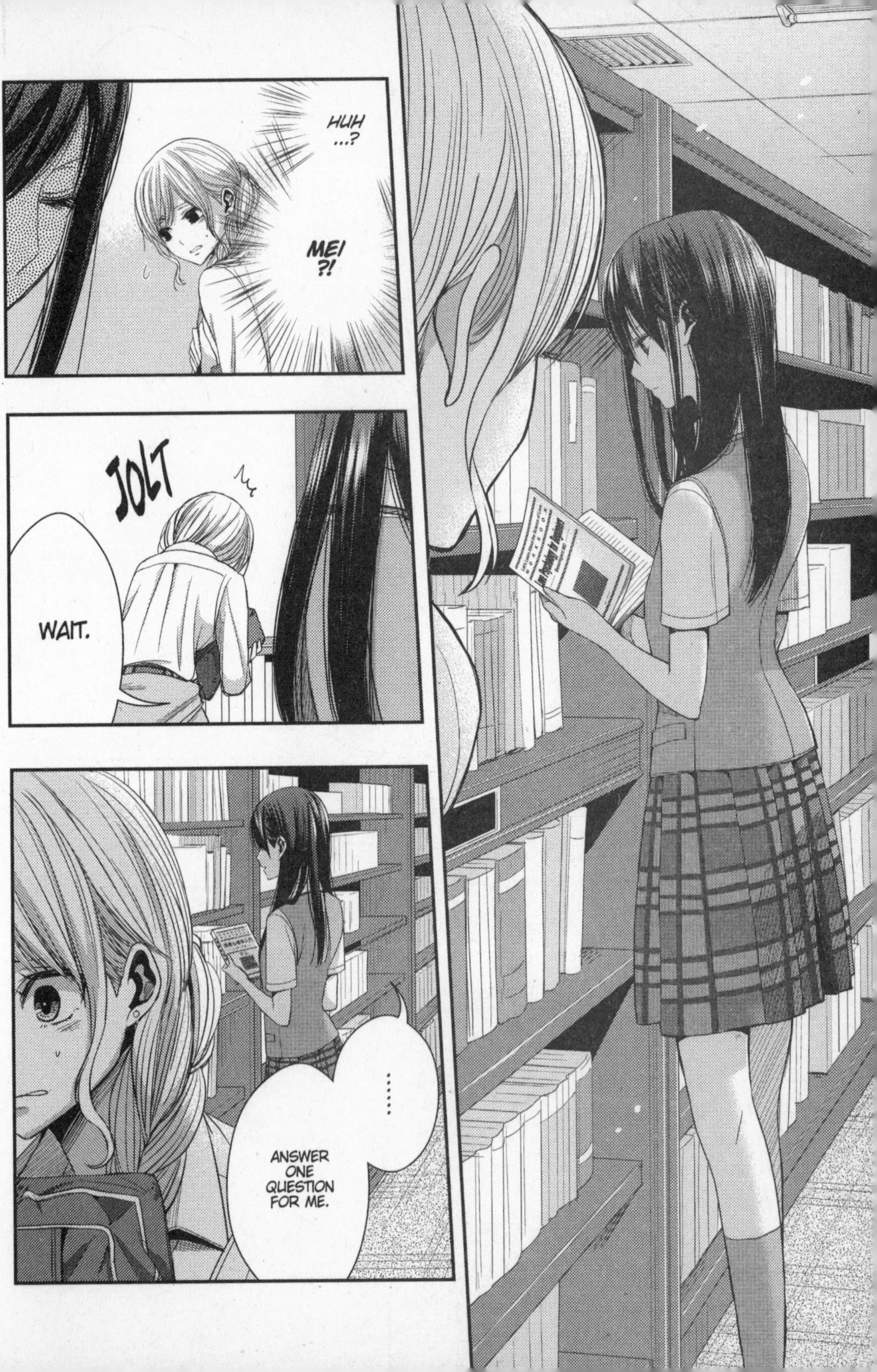
HUH ...?
MEI ?!
JOLT
WAIT.
......
ANSWER ONE QUESTION FOR ME.

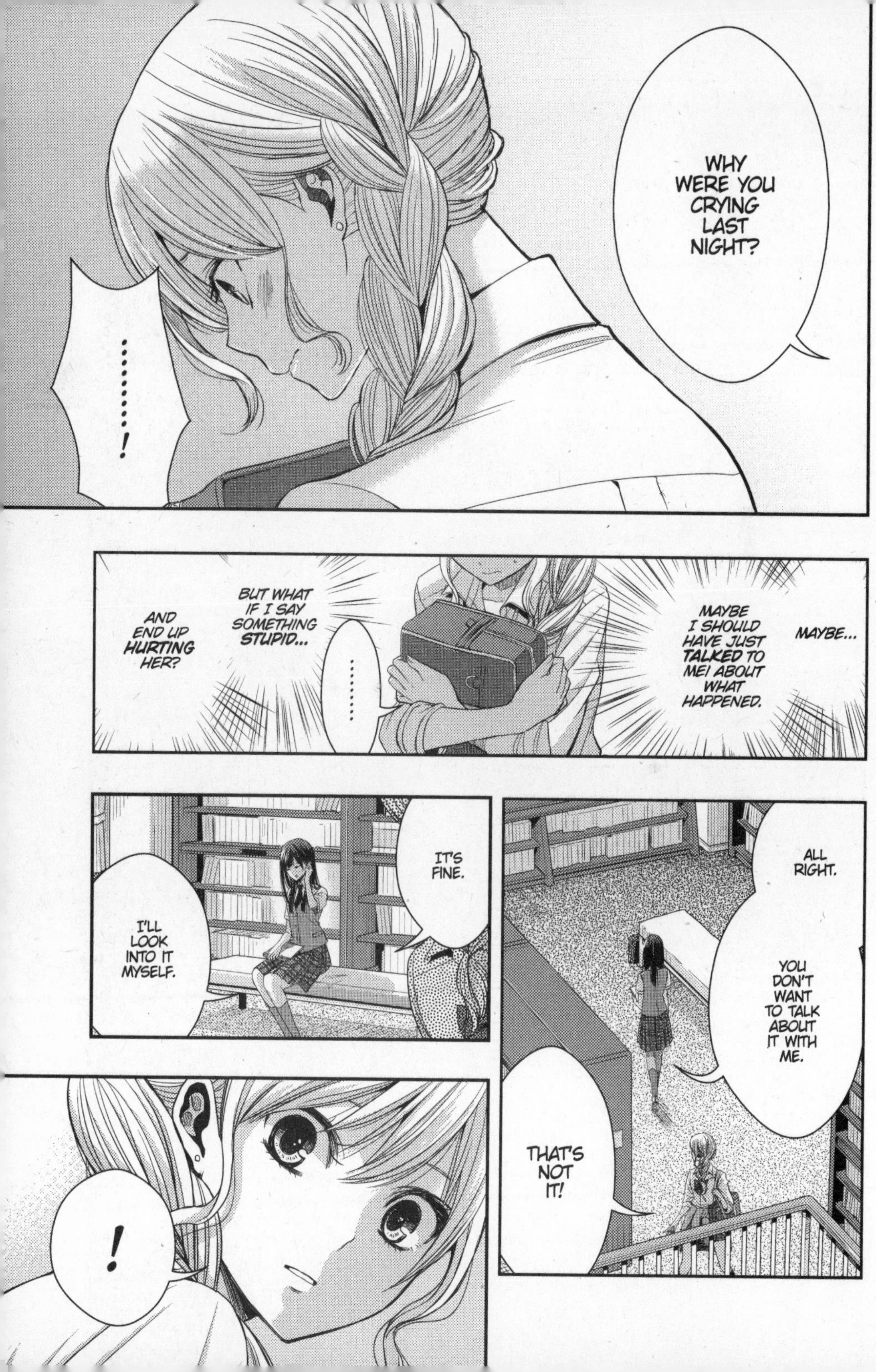
WHY WERE YOU CRYING LAST NIGHT?
......!
MAYBE...
MAYBE I SHOULD HAVE JUST TALKED TO MEI ABOUT WHAT HAPPENED.
......
BUT WHAT IF I SAY SOMETHING STUPID...
AND END UP HURTING HER?
ALL RIGHT.
YOU DON'T WANT TO TALK ABOUT IT WITH ME.
THAT'S NOT IT!
IT'S FINE.
I'LL LOOK INTO IT MYSELF.
!

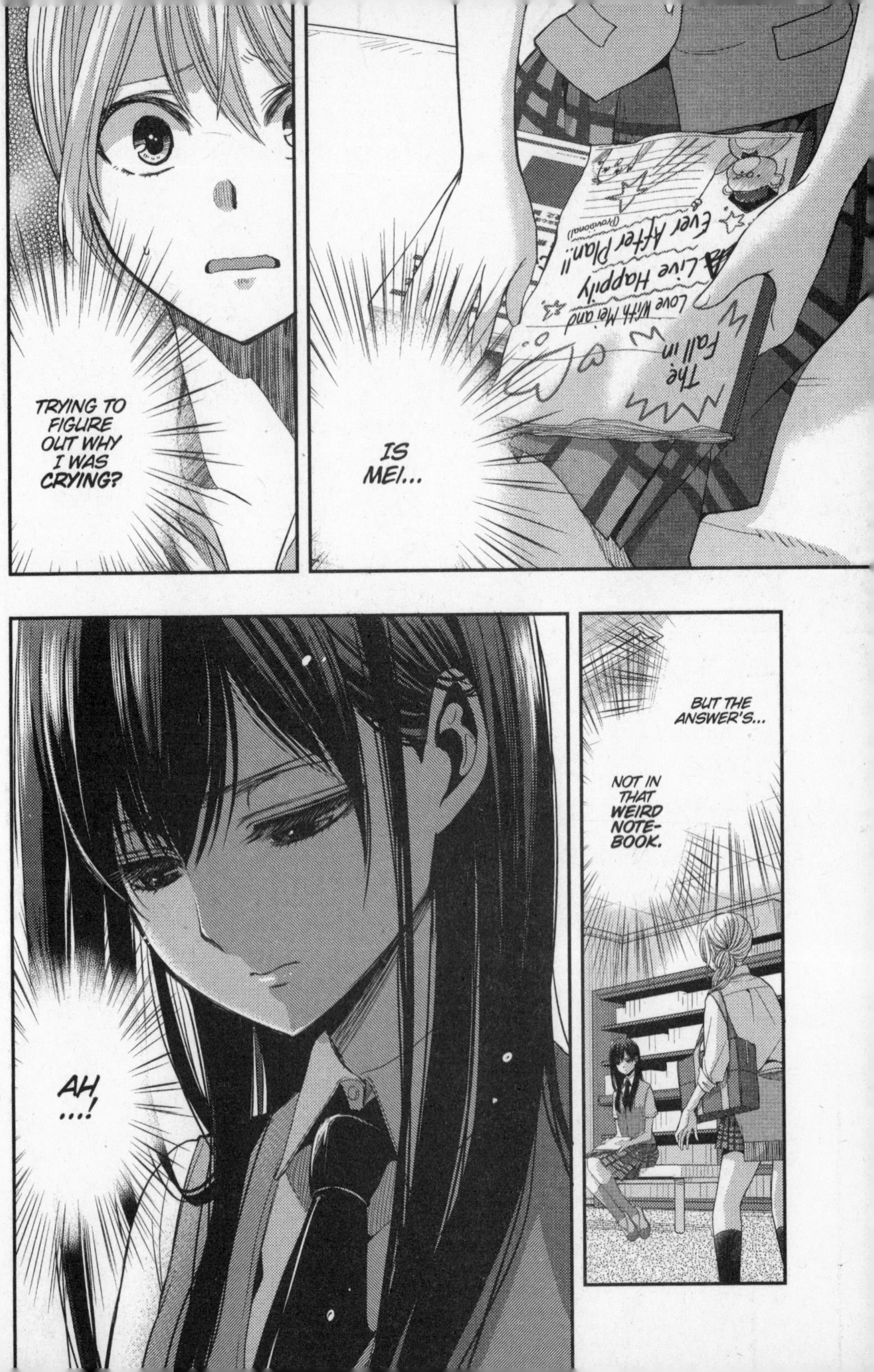
The Fall in Love With Mei and Live Happily Ever After Plan!! (Provisional)
IS MEI...
TRYING TO FIGURE OUT WHY I WAS CRYING?
BUT THE ANSWER'S...
NOT IN THAT WEIRD NOTE-BOOK.
AH ...!

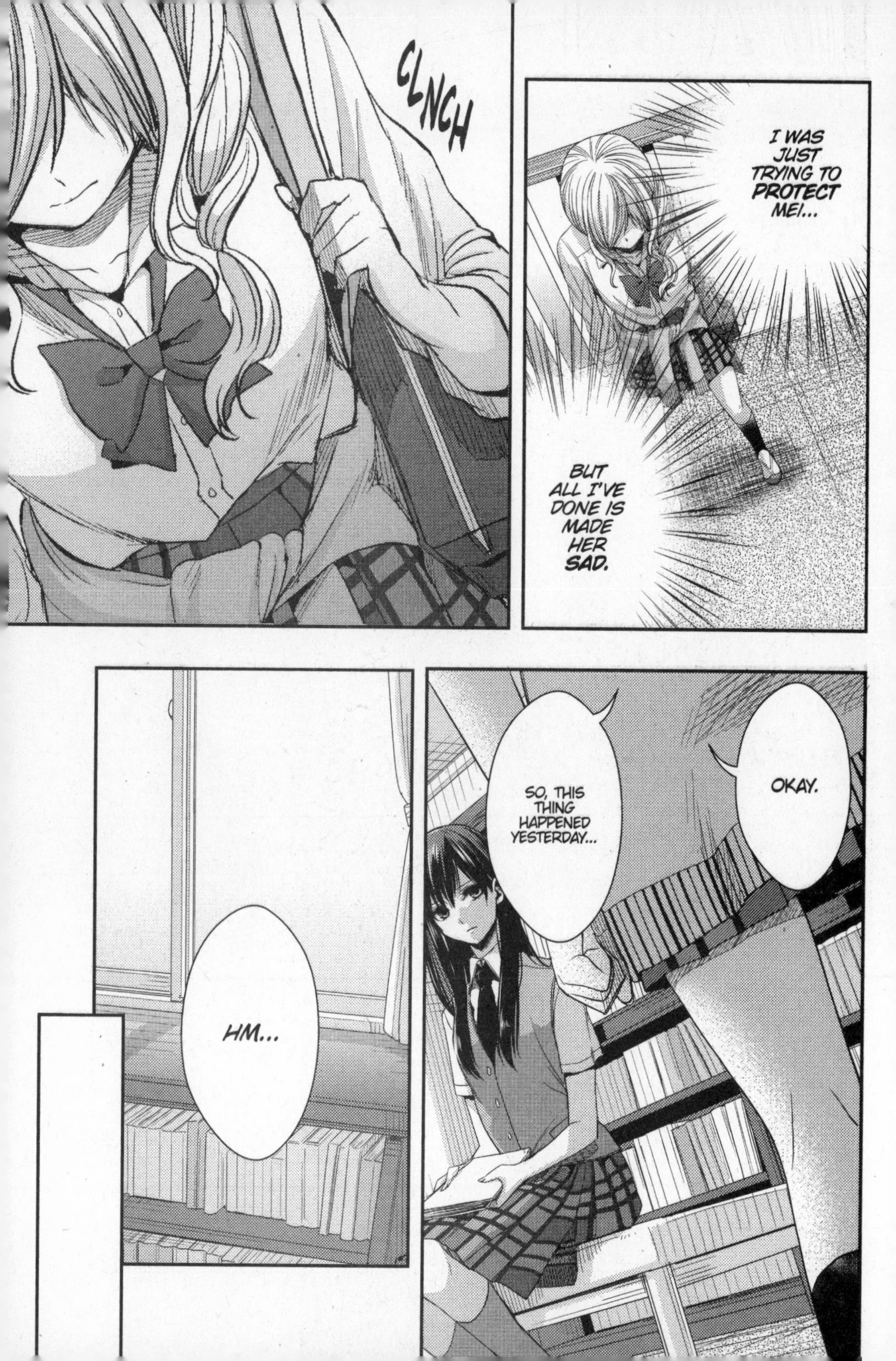
I WAS JUST TRYING TO PROTECT MEI...
BUT ALL I'VE DONE IS MADE HER SAD.
CLNCH
OKAY.
SO, THIS THING HAPPENED YESTERDAY...
HM...

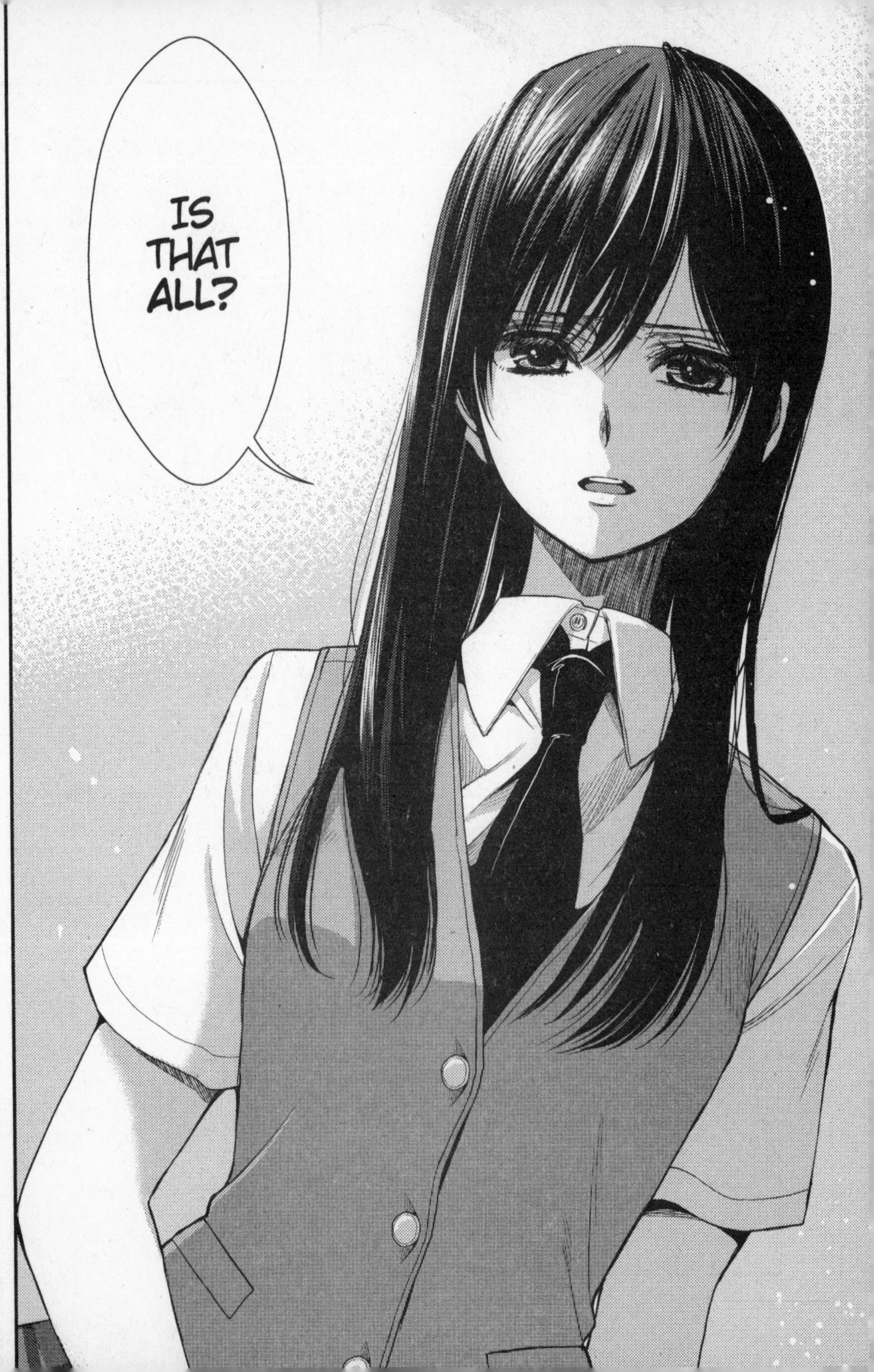
IS THAT ALL?

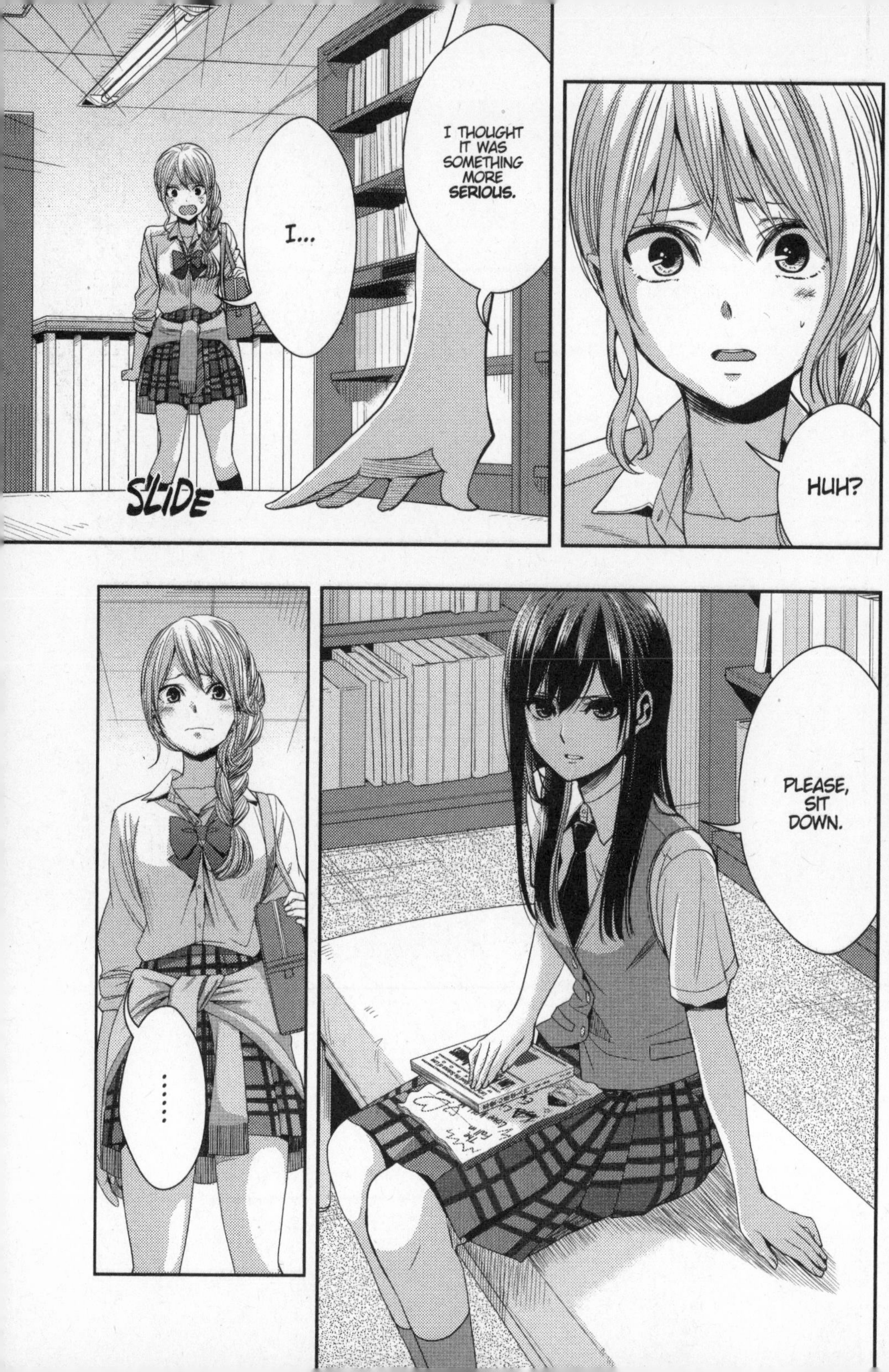
HUH?
I THOUGHT IT WAS SOMETHING MORE SERIOUS.
I...
SLIDE
PLEASE, SIT DOWN.
......

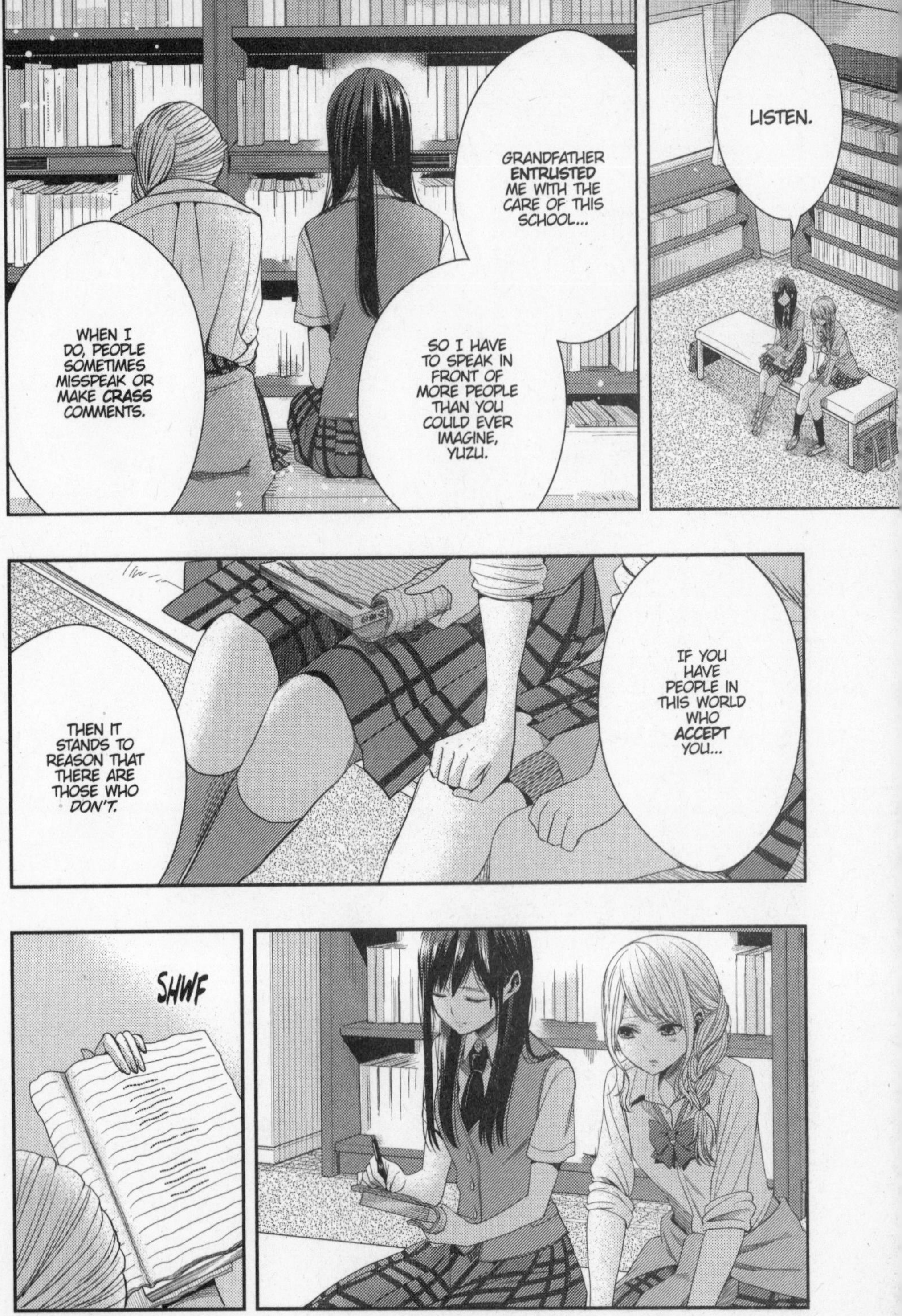
LISTEN.
GRANDFATHER ENTRUSTED ME WITH THE CARE OF THIS SCHOOL...
SO I HAVE TO SPEAK IN FRONT OF MORE PEOPLE THAN YOU COULD EVER IMAGINE, YUZU.
WHEN I DO, PEOPLE SOMETIMES MISSPEAK OR MAKE CRASS COMMENTS.
IF YOU HAVE PEOPLE IN THIS WORLD WHO ACCEPT YOU...
THEN IT STANDS TO REASON THAT THERE ARE THOSE WHO DON'T.
SHWF

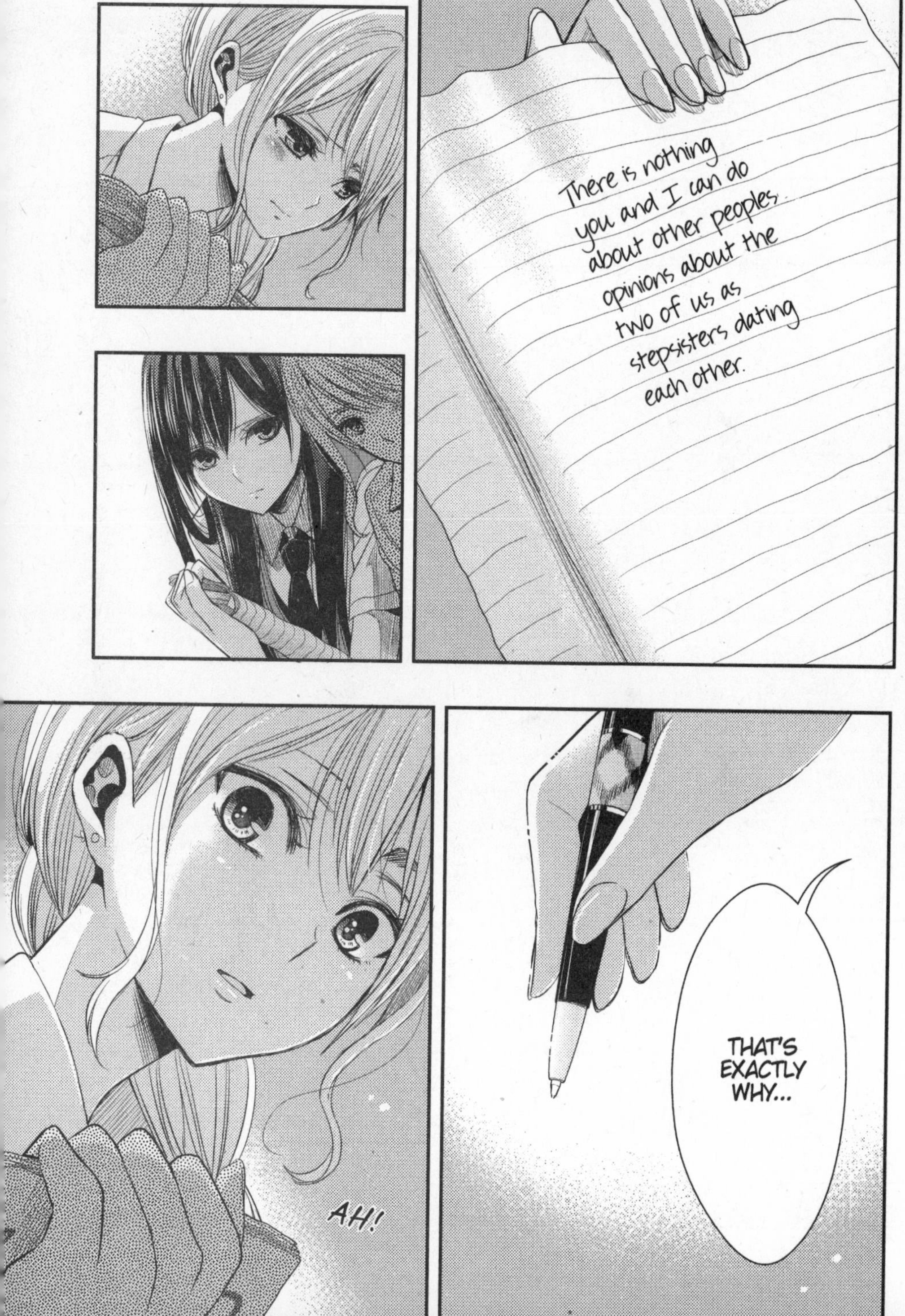
There is nothing you and I can do about other peoples opinions about the two of us as stepsisters dating each other.
THAT'S EXACTLY WHY...
AH!

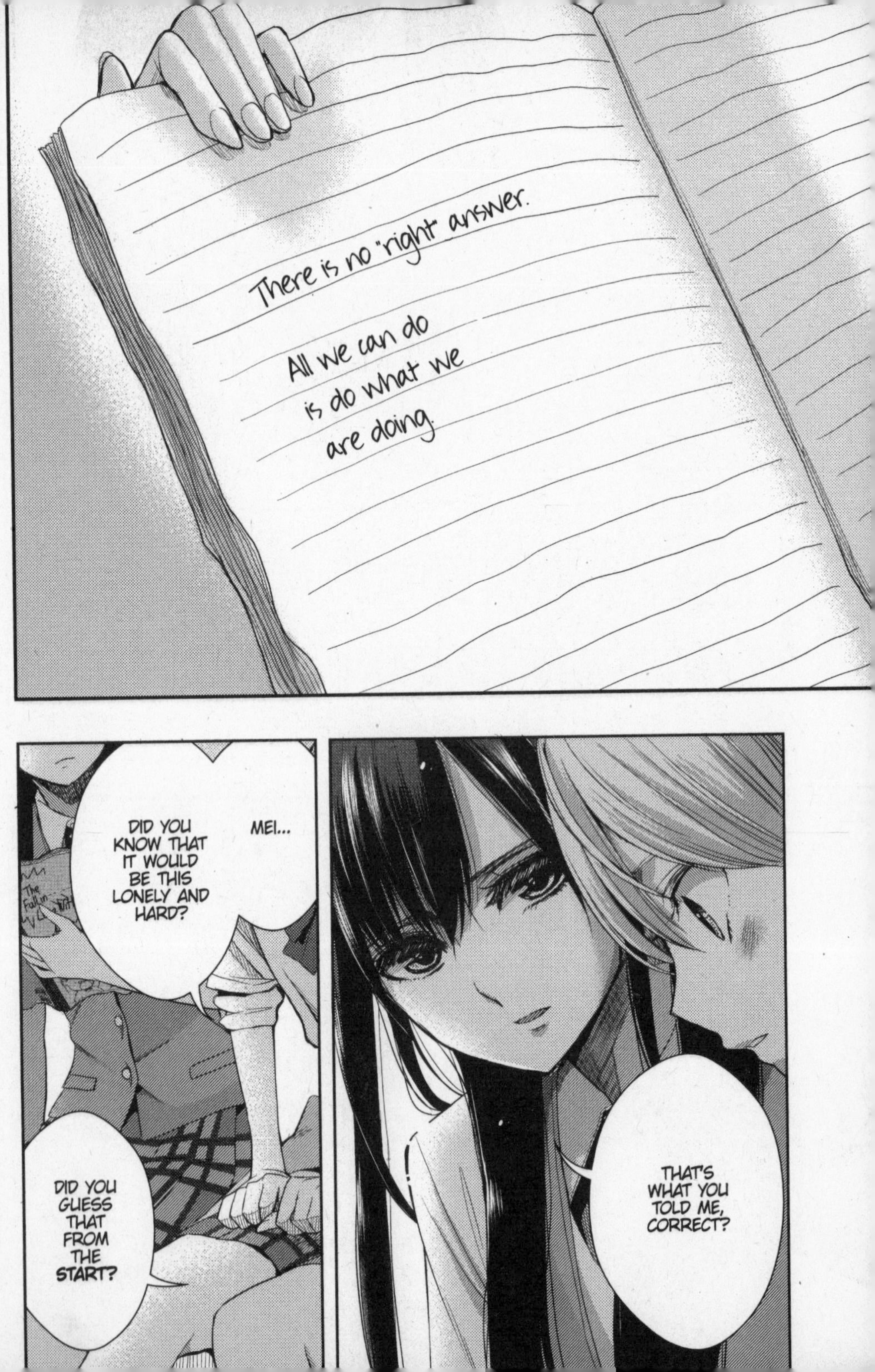
There is no "right" answer.
All we can do is do what we are doing.
THAT'S WHAT YOU TOLD ME, CORRECT?
MEI...
DID YOU KNOW THAT IT WOULD BE THIS LONELY AND HARD?
DID YOU GUESS THAT FROM THE START?

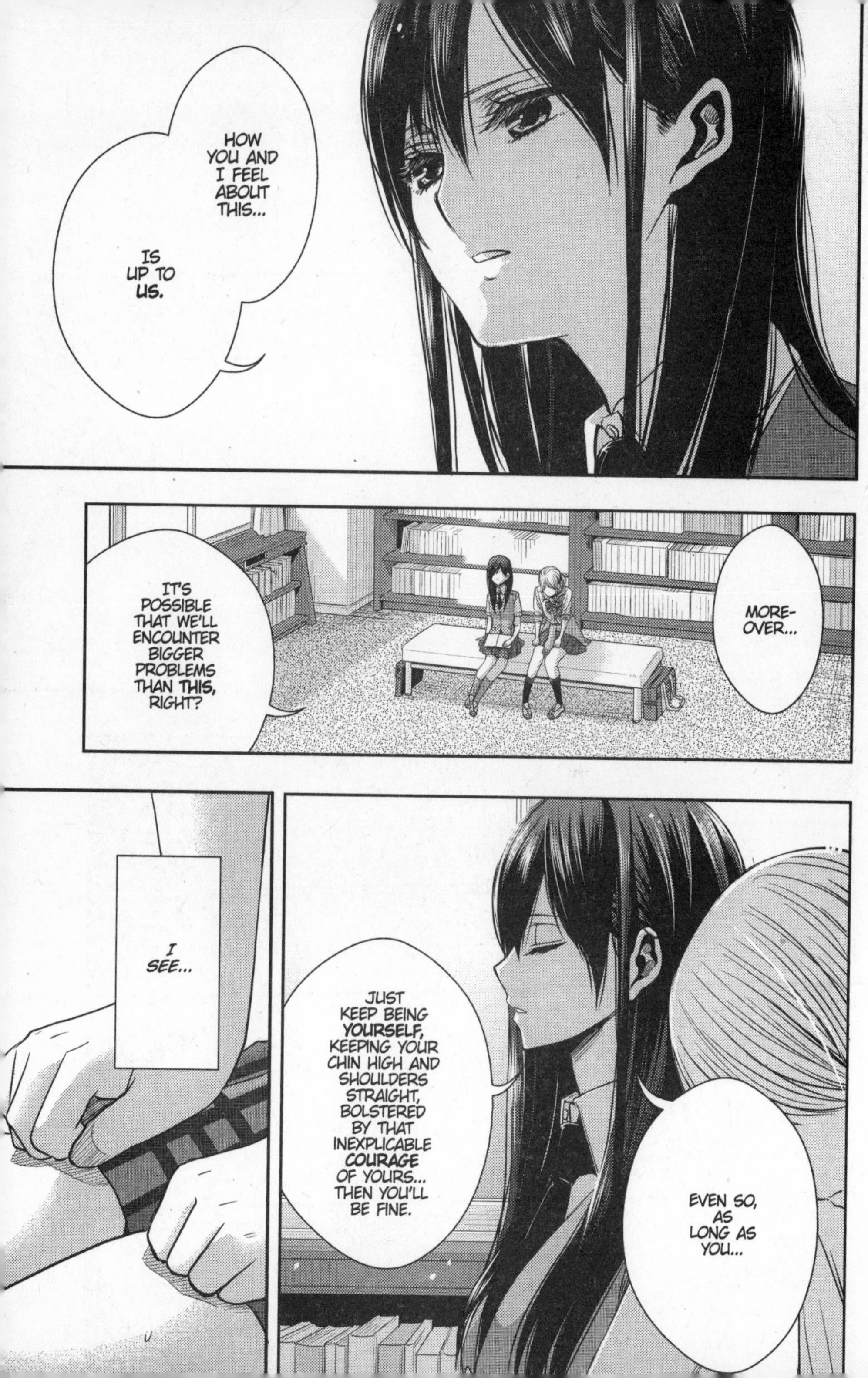
HOW YOU AND I FEEL ABOUT THIS...
IS UP TO **US.**
MORE-OVER...
IT'S POSSIBLE THAT WE'LL ENCOUNTER BIGGER PROBLEMS THAN **THIS,** RIGHT?
EVEN SO, AS LONG AS YOU...
JUST KEEP BEING **YOURSELF,** KEEPING YOUR CHIN HIGH AND SHOULDERS STRAIGHT, BOLSTERED BY THAT INEXPLICABLE **COURAGE** OF YOURS... THEN YOU'LL BE FINE.
I SEE...

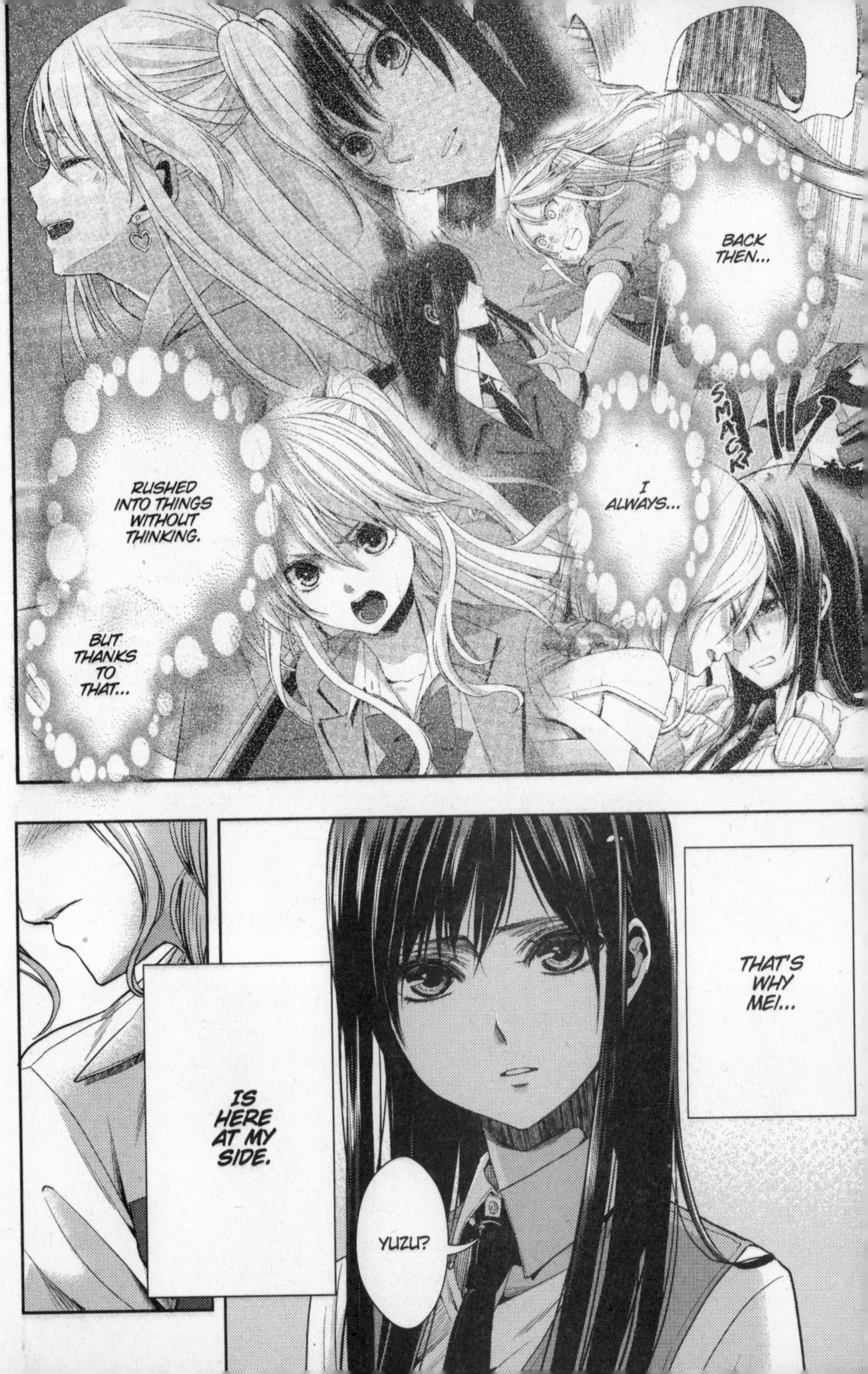
BACK THEN...
SMACK
I ALWAYS...
RUSHED INTO THINGS WITHOUT THINKING.
BUT THANKS TO THAT...
THAT'S WHY MEI...
IS HERE AT MY SIDE.
YUZU?

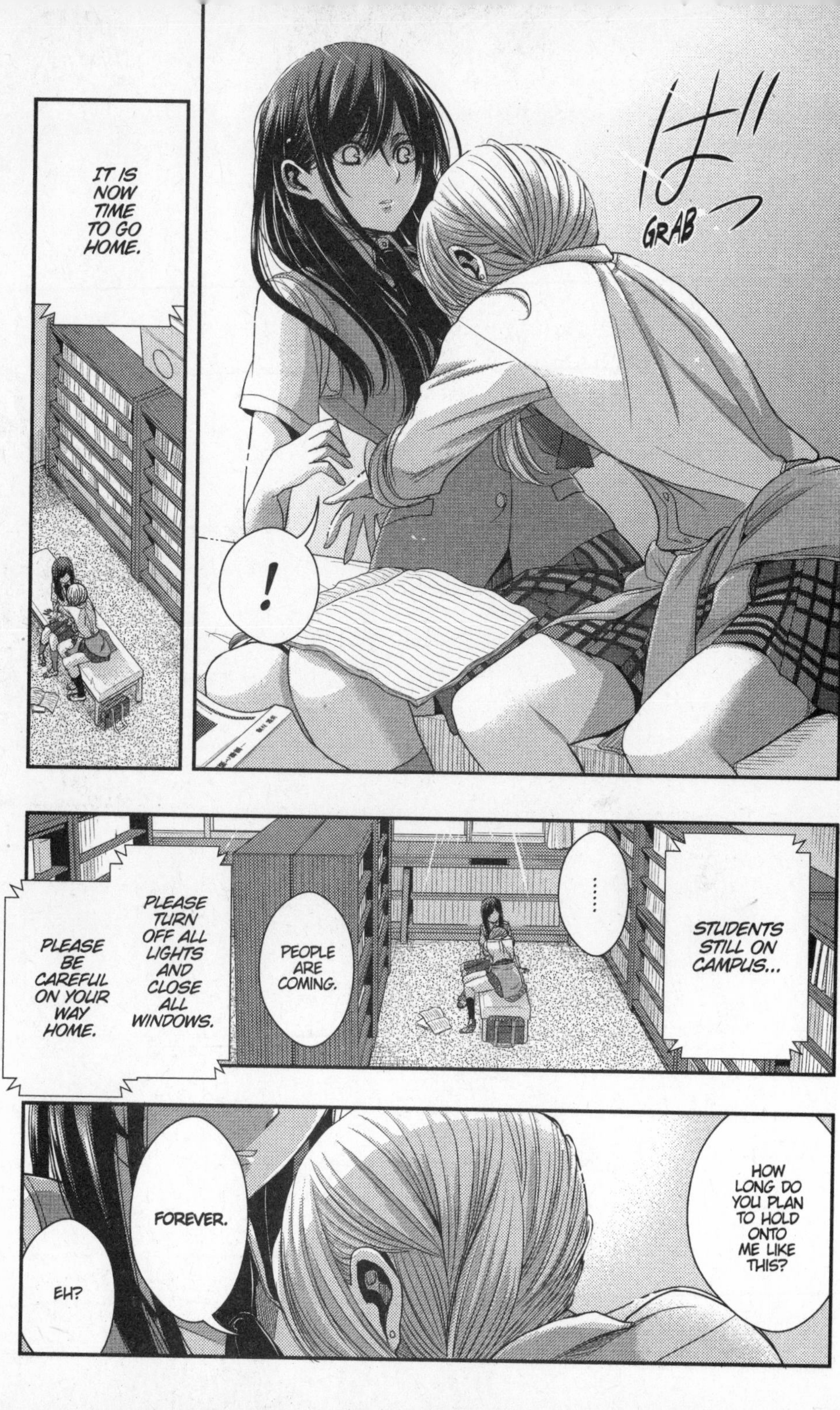
ばっ
GRAB
!
IT IS NOW TIME TO GO HOME.
STUDENTS STILL ON CAMPUS...
......
PEOPLE ARE COMING.
PLEASE TURN OFF ALL LIGHTS AND CLOSE ALL WINDOWS.
PLEASE BE CAREFUL ON YOUR WAY HOME.
HOW LONG DO YOU PLAN TO HOLD ONTO ME LIKE THIS?
FOREVER.
EH?

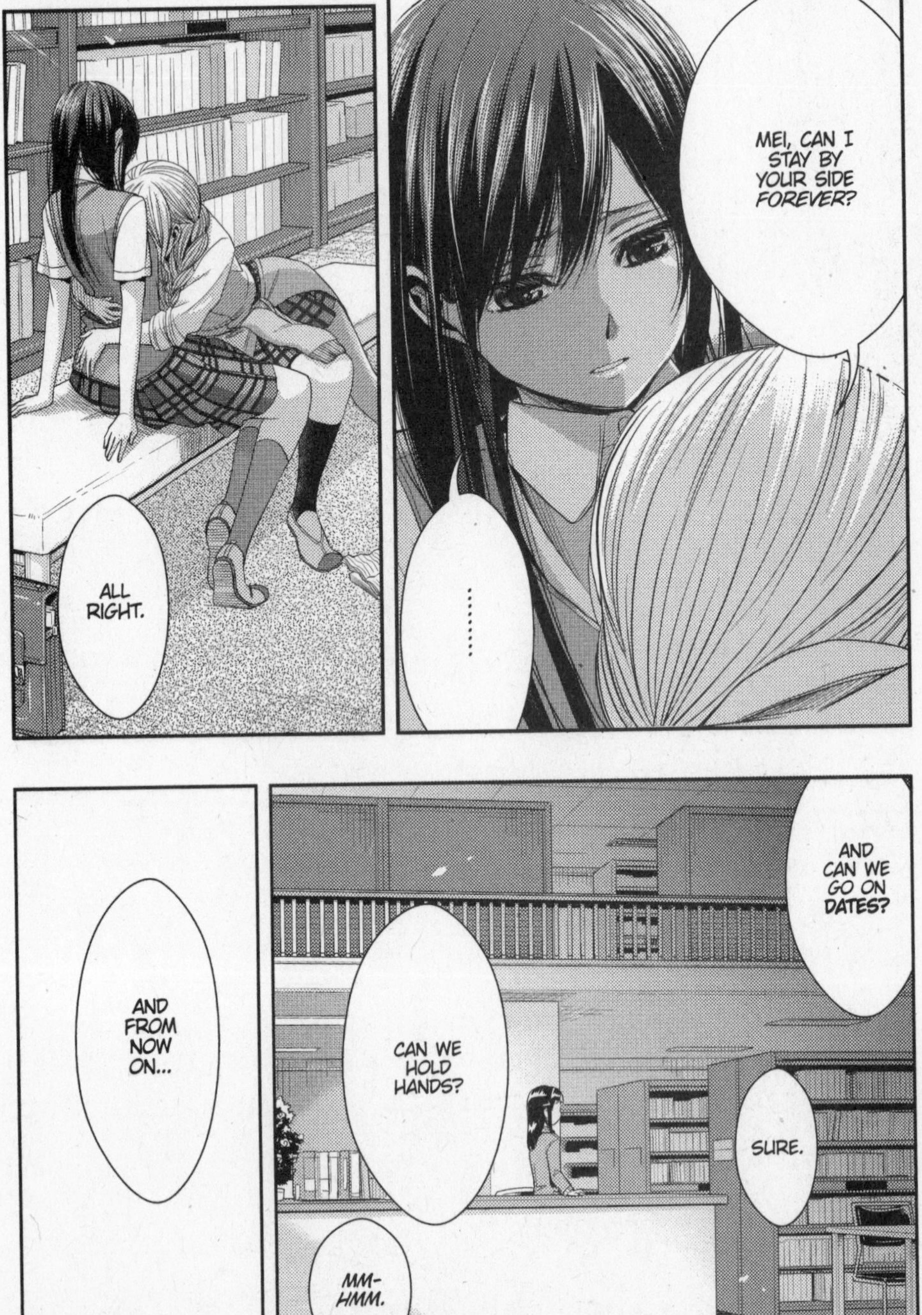
MEI, CAN I STAY BY YOUR SIDE FOREVER?
......
ALL RIGHT.
AND CAN WE GO ON DATES?
SURE.
CAN WE HOLD HANDS?
MM-HMM.
AND FROM NOW ON...

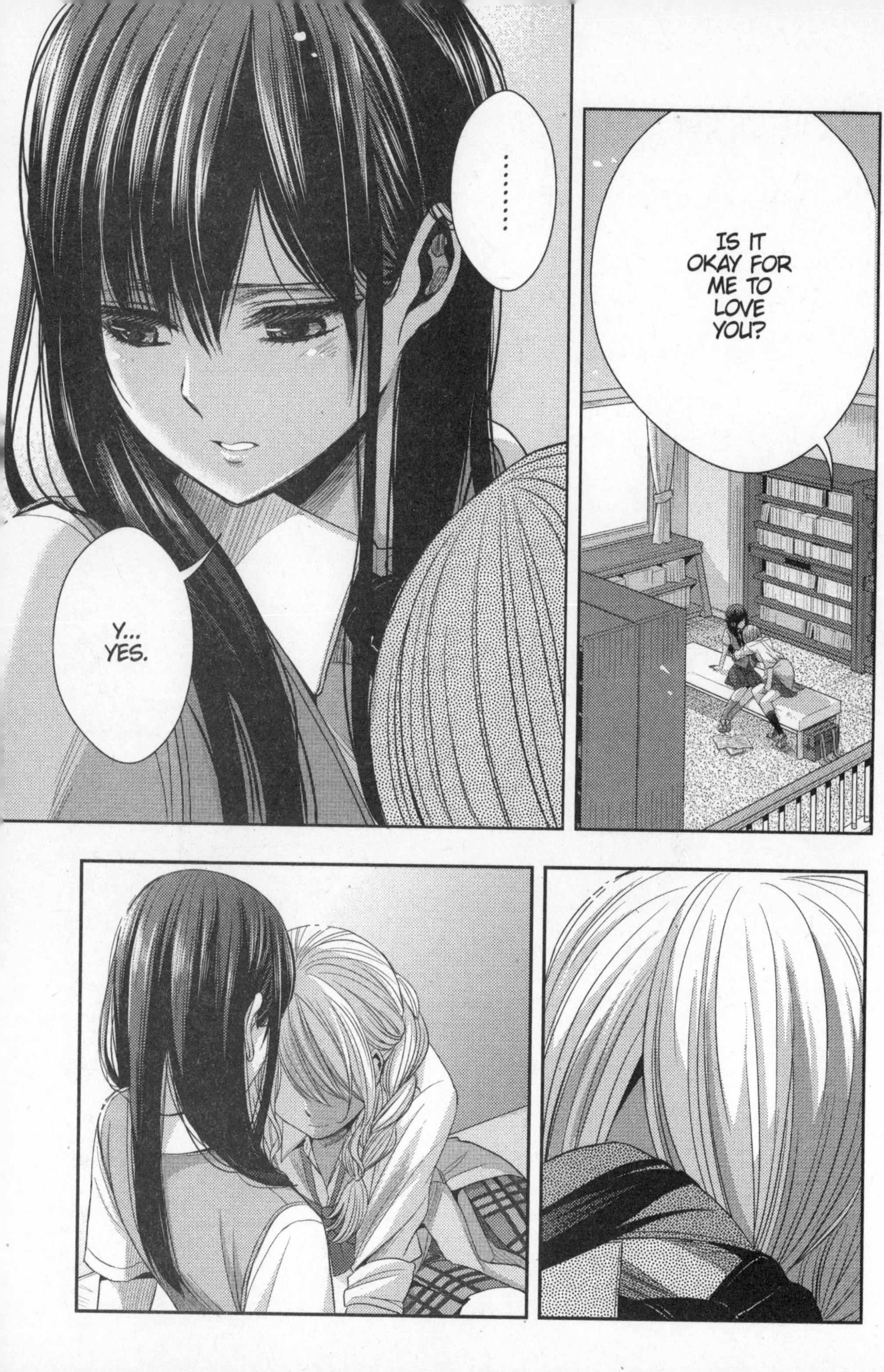
IS IT OKAY FOR ME TO LOVE YOU?
......
Y... YES.

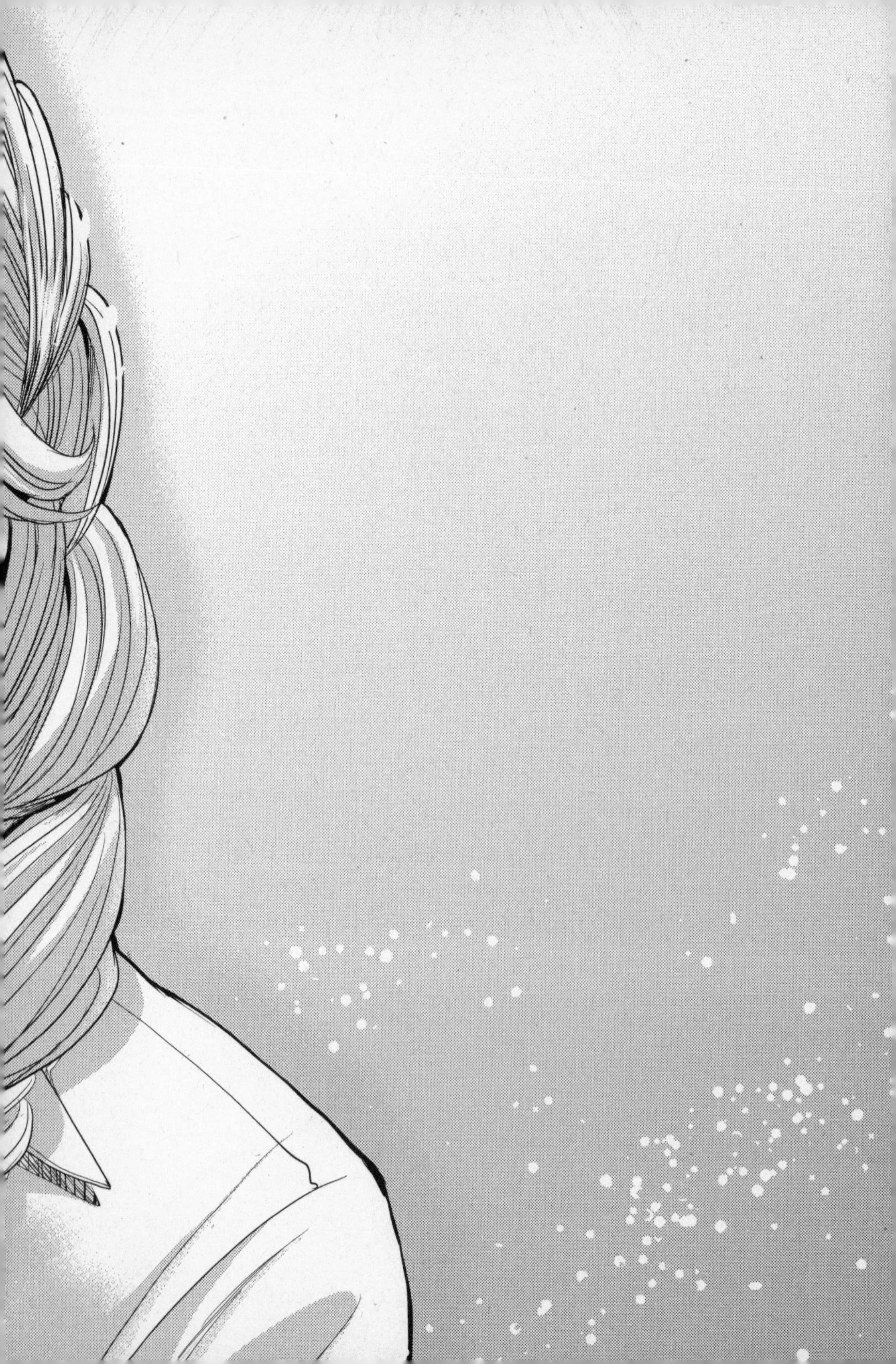

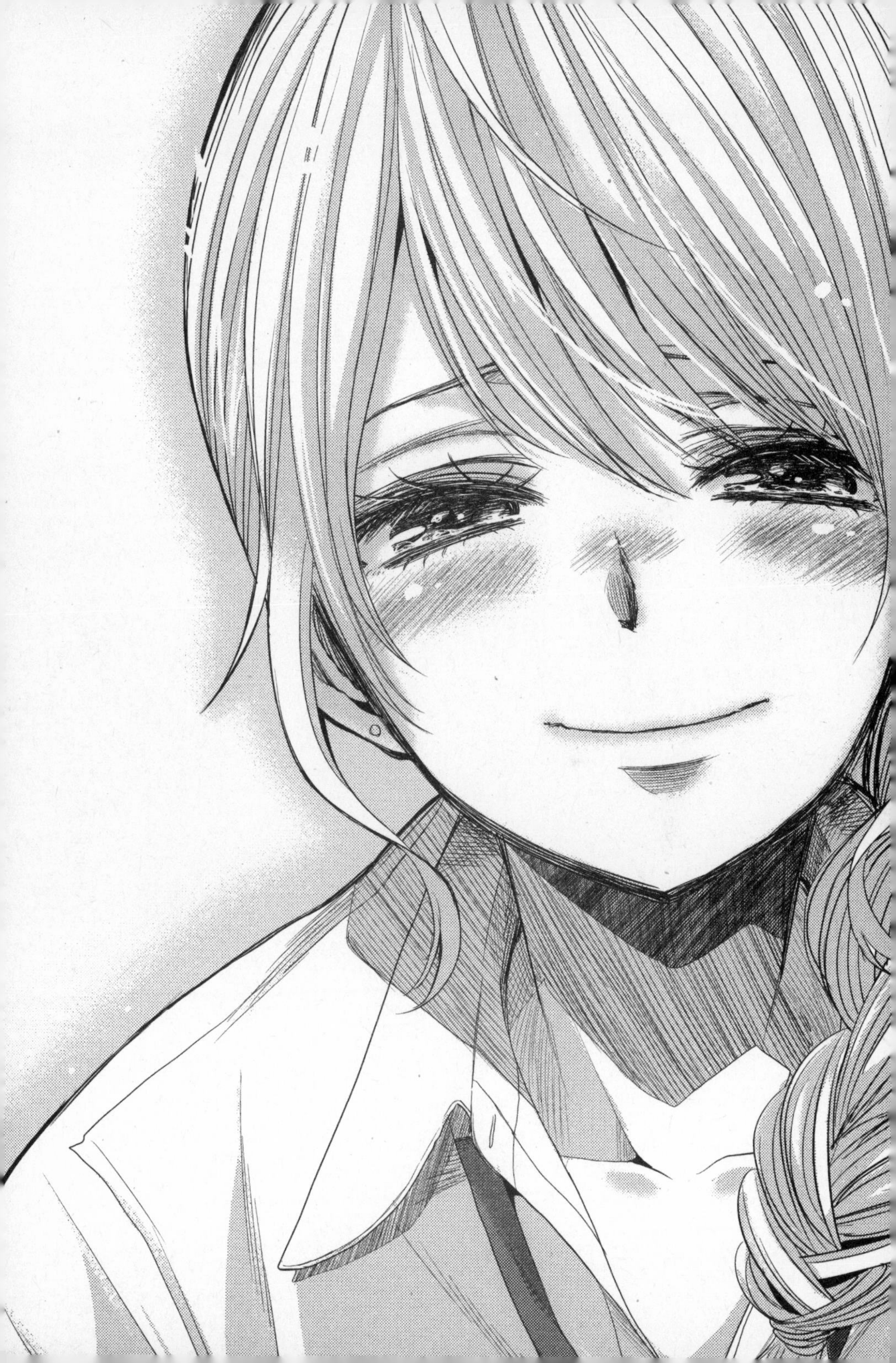

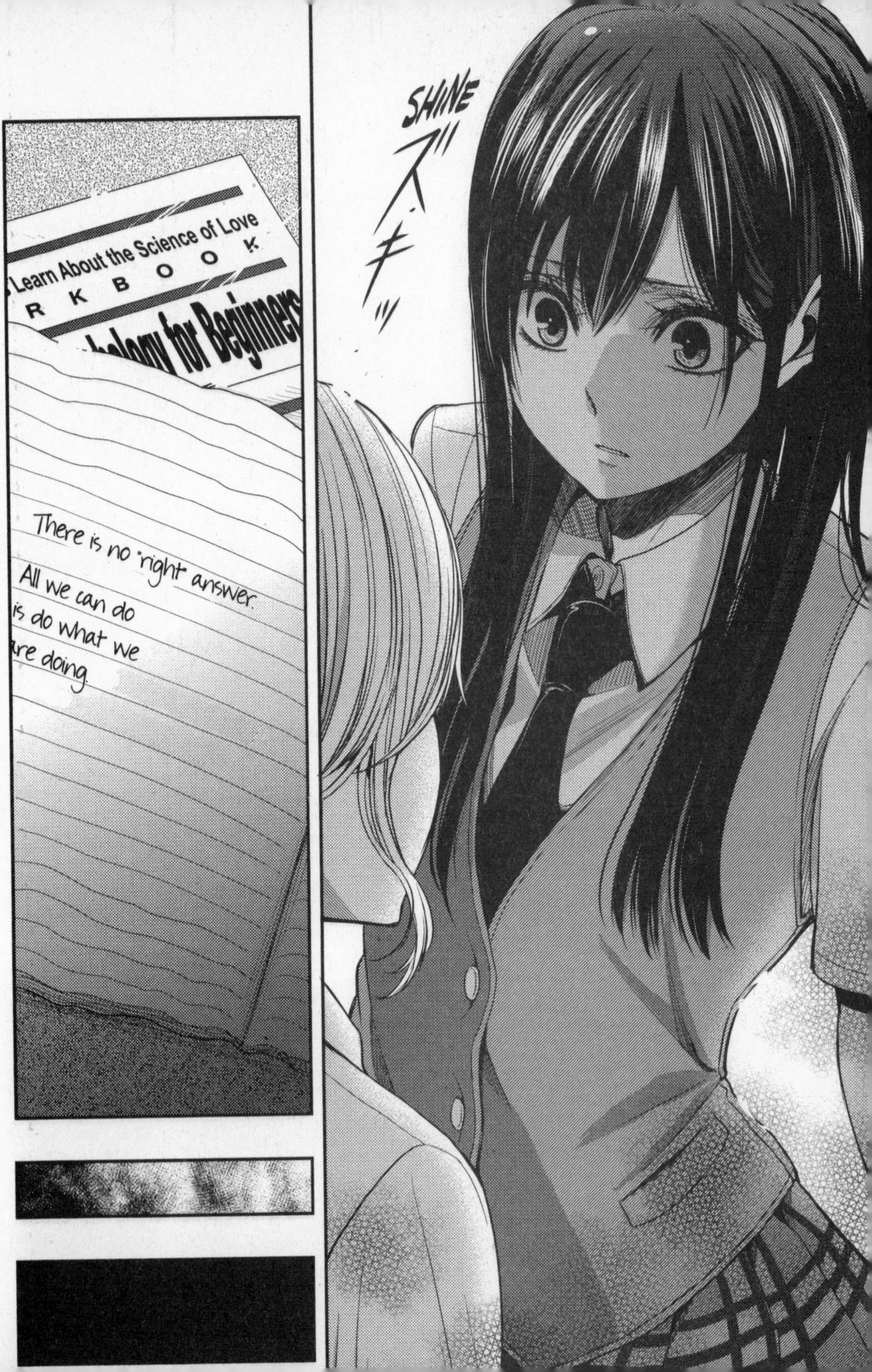
SHINE
Learn About the Science of Love
RKBOOK
hology for Beginners
There is no "right" answer.
All we can do
is do what we
re doing.

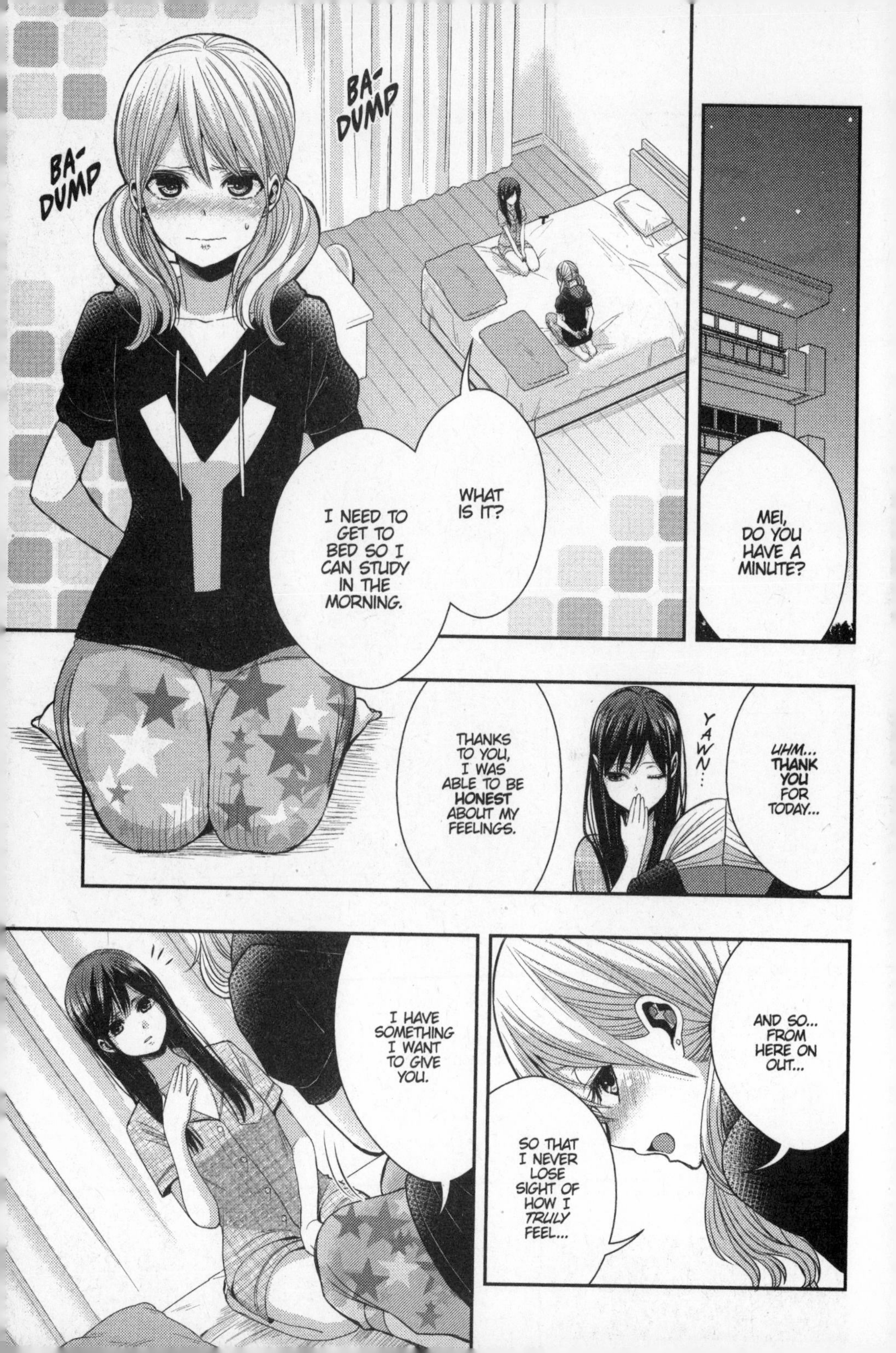
MEI, DO YOU HAVE A MINUTE?
WHAT IS IT?
I NEED TO GET TO BED SO I CAN STUDY IN THE MORNING.
UHM... THANK YOU FOR TODAY...
YAWN...
THANKS TO YOU, I WAS ABLE TO BE **HONEST** ABOUT MY FEELINGS.
BA-DUMP
BA-DUMP
AND SO... FROM HERE ON OUT...
SO THAT I NEVER LOSE SIGHT OF HOW I *TRULY* FEEL...
I HAVE SOMETHING I WANT TO GIVE YOU.

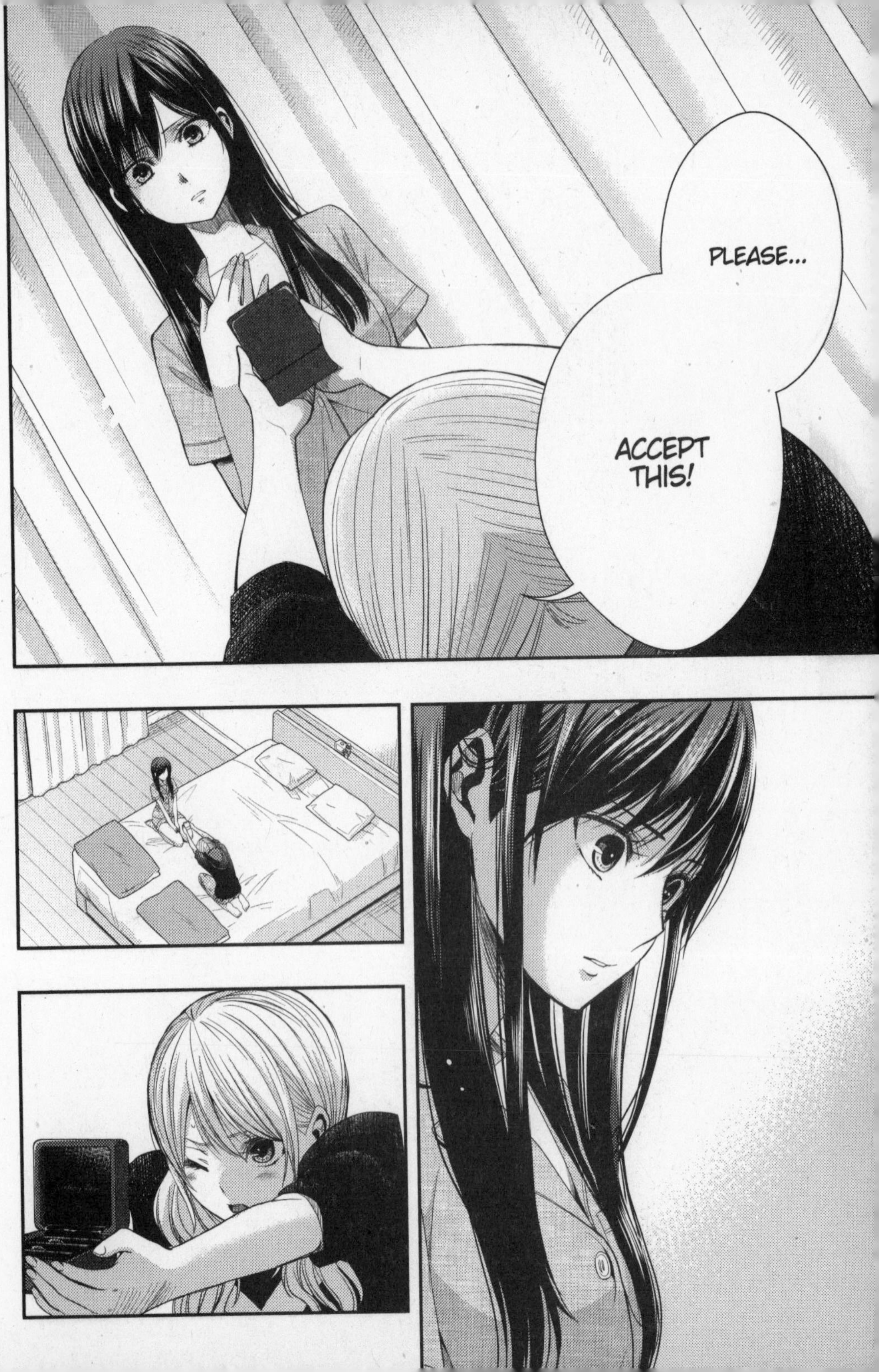
PLEASE...
ACCEPT THIS!

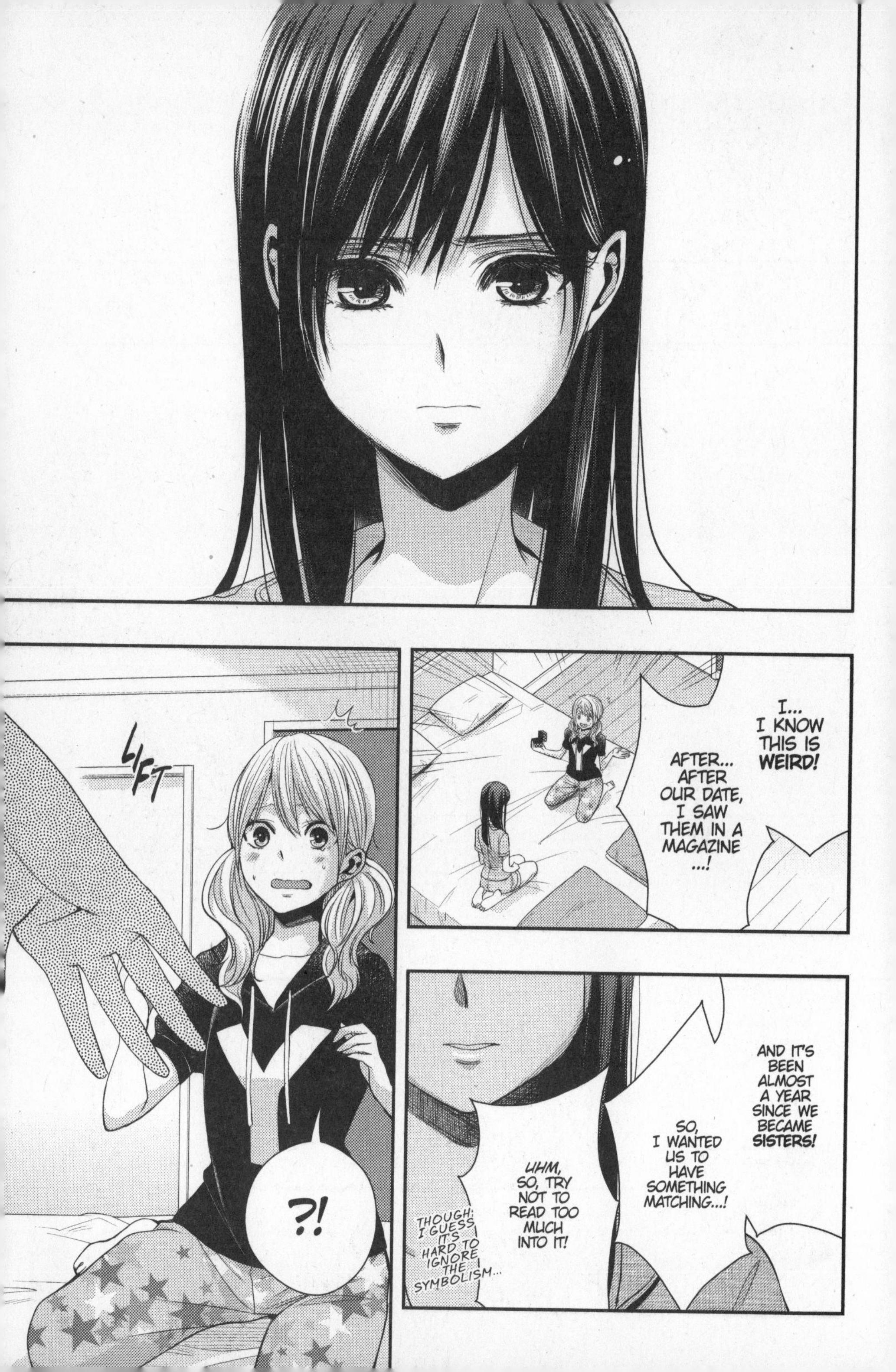
I... I KNOW THIS IS WEIRD!
AFTER... AFTER OUR DATE, I SAW THEM IN A MAGAZINE ...!
AND IT'S BEEN ALMOST A YEAR SINCE WE BECAME SISTERS!
SO, I WANTED US TO HAVE SOMETHING MATCHING...!
UHM, SO, TRY NOT TO READ TOO MUCH INTO IT!
THOUGH I GUESS IT'S HARD TO IGNORE THE SYMBOLISM...
LIFT
?!

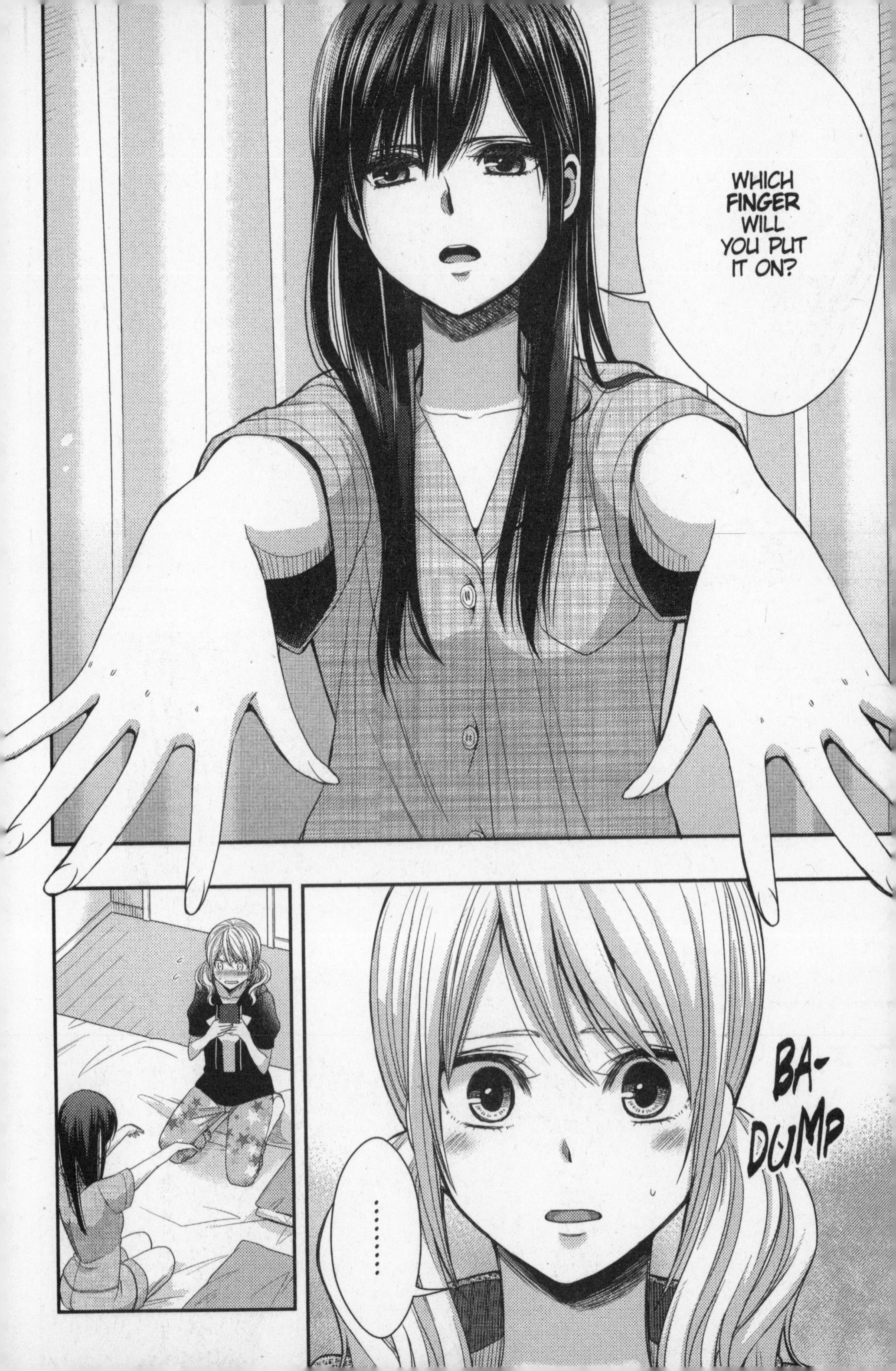
WHICH FINGER WILL YOU PUT IT ON?
BA-DUMP
......

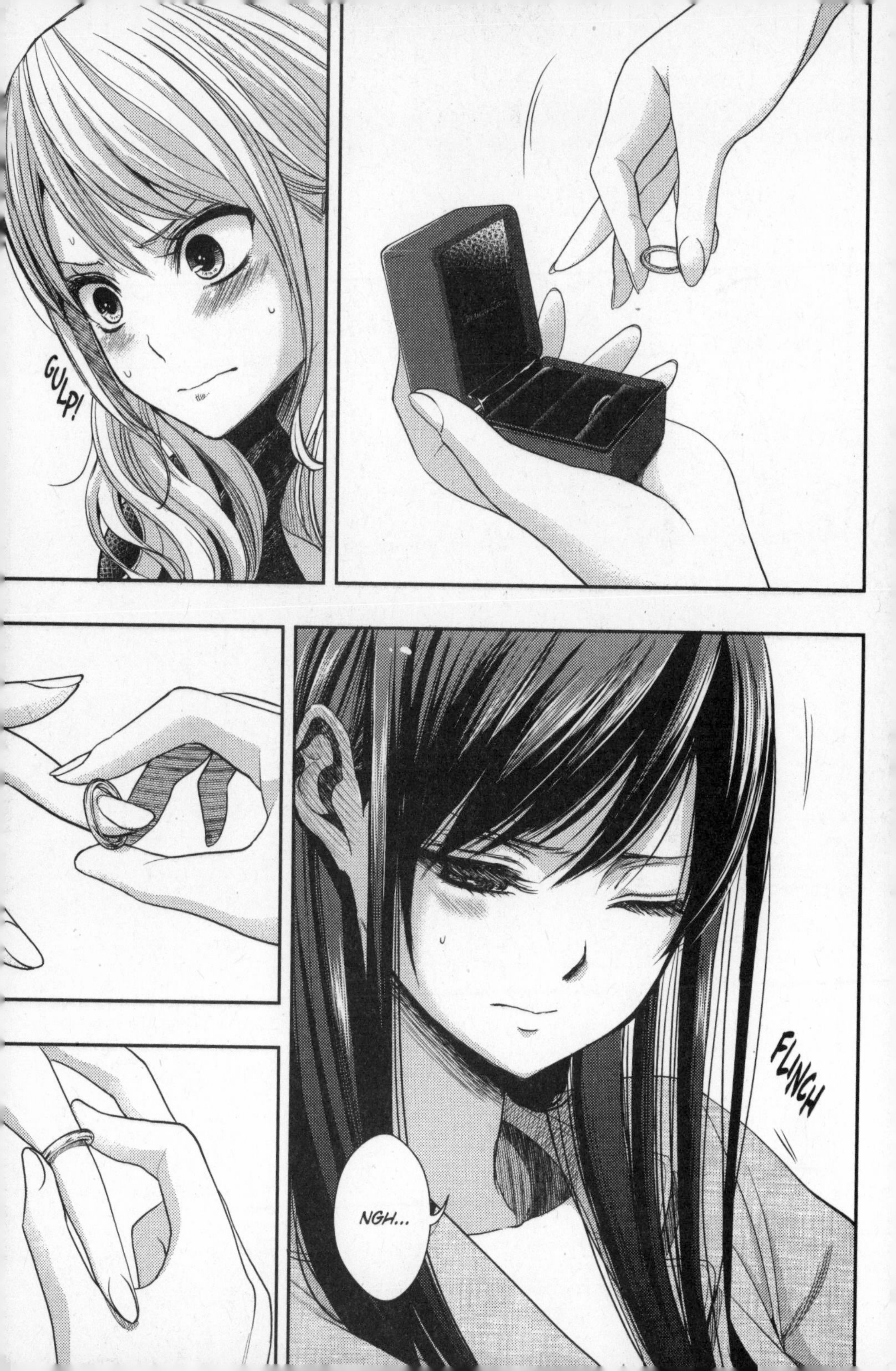
GULP!
FLINCH
NGH...

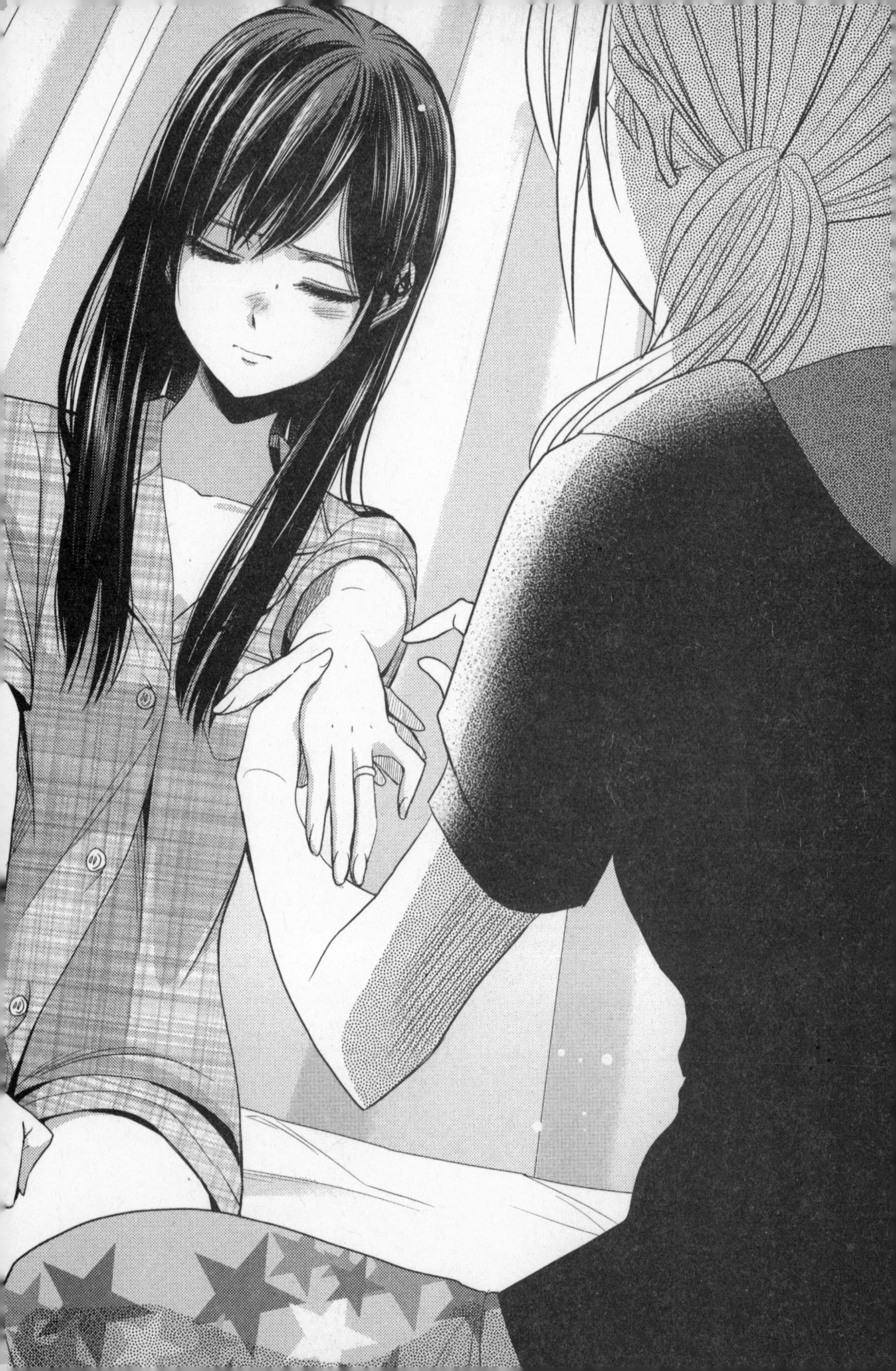

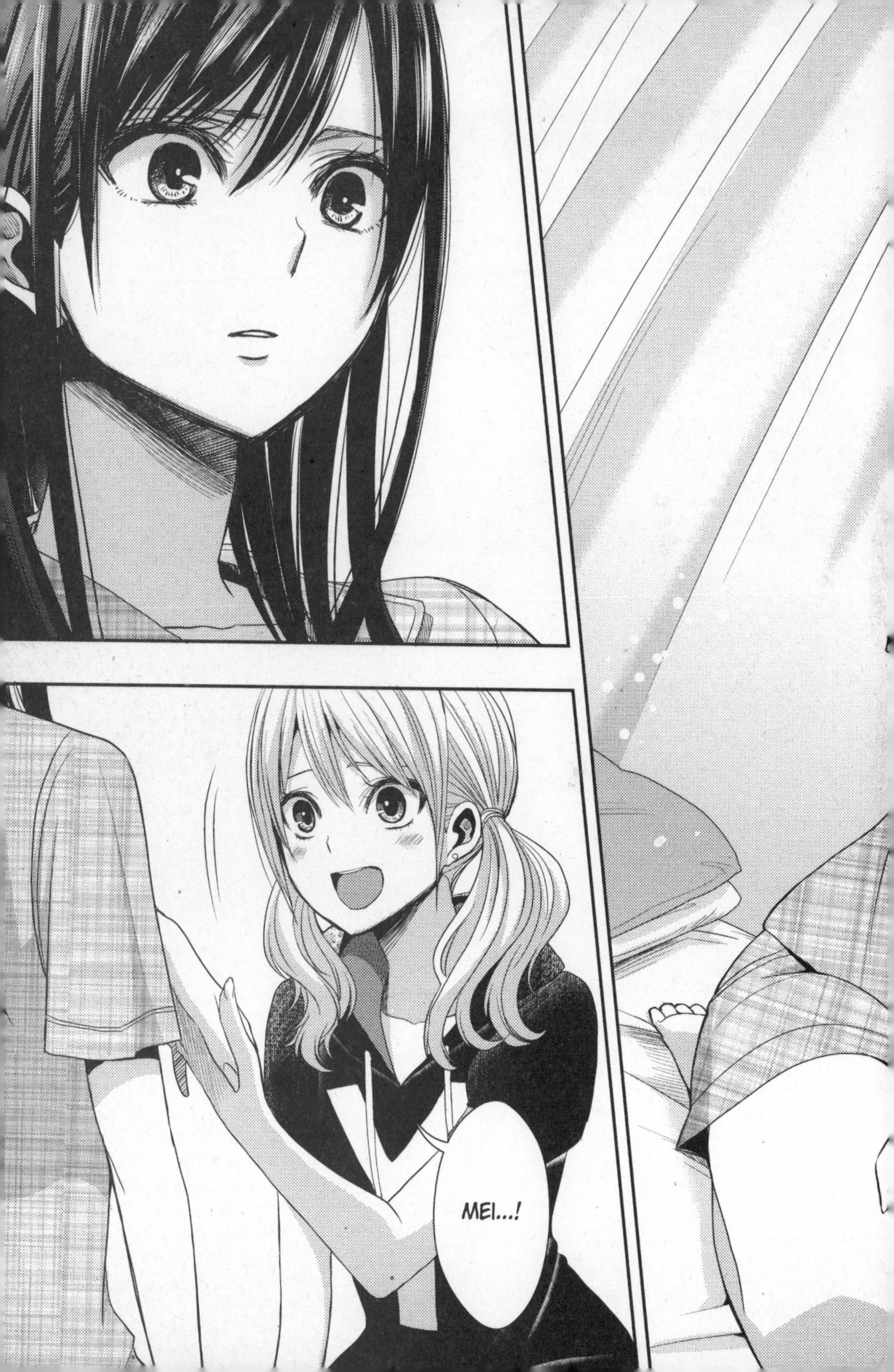
MEI...!

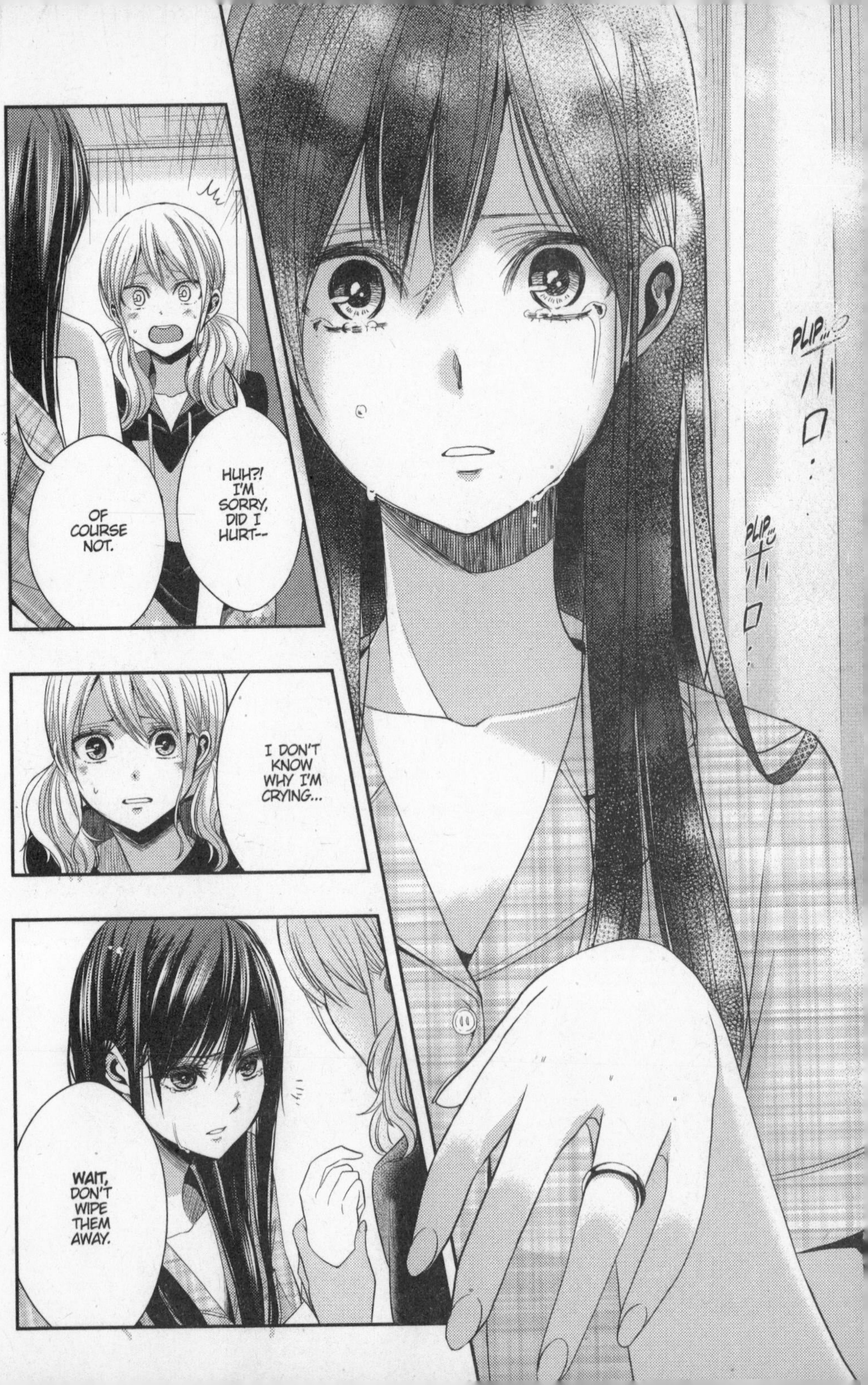
PLIP...
PLIP...
HUH?! I'M SORRY, DID I HURT--
OF COURSE NOT.
I DON'T KNOW WHY I'M CRYING...
WAIT, DON'T WIPE THEM AWAY.

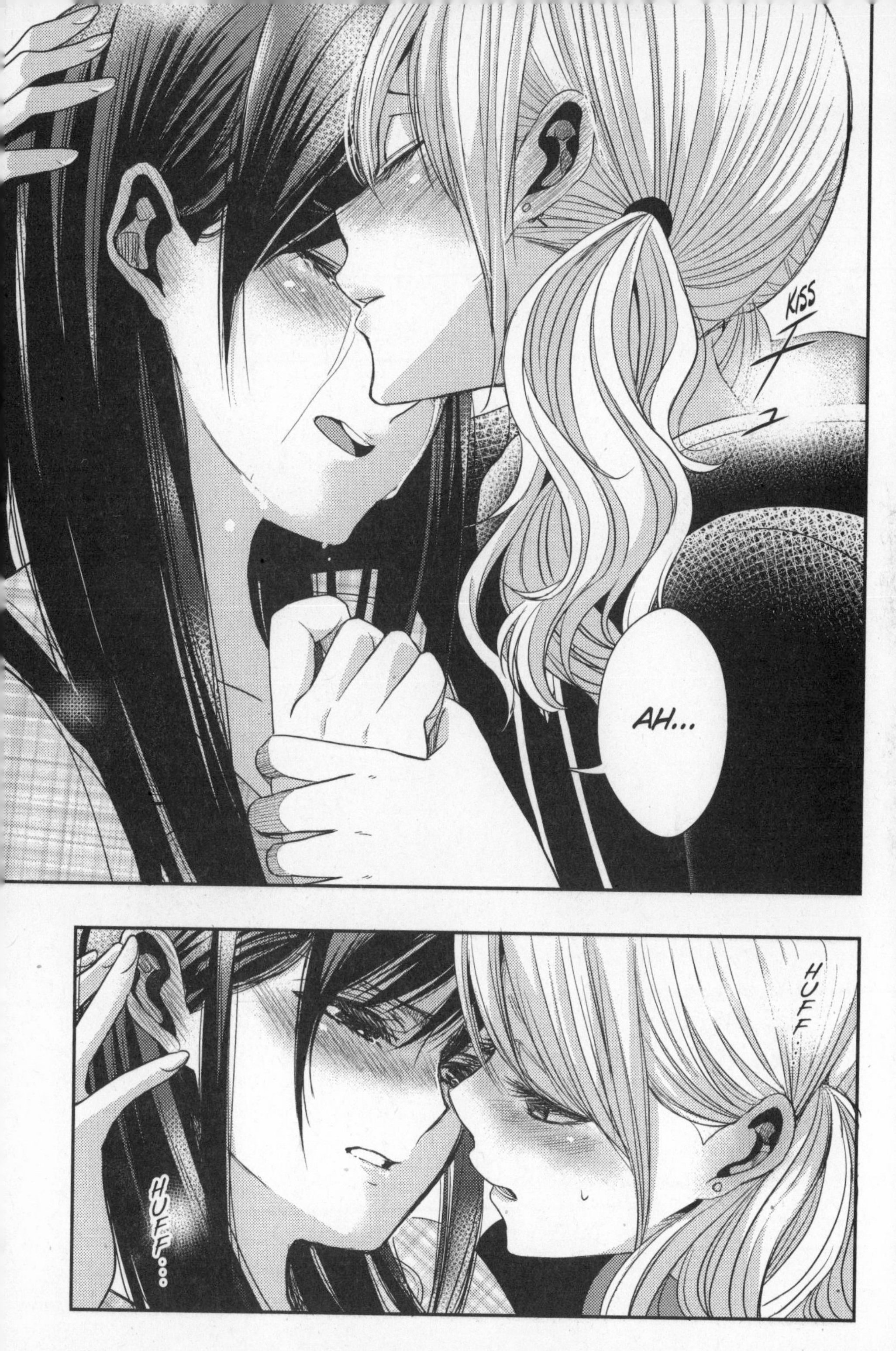
KISS
AH...
HUFF...
HUFF...

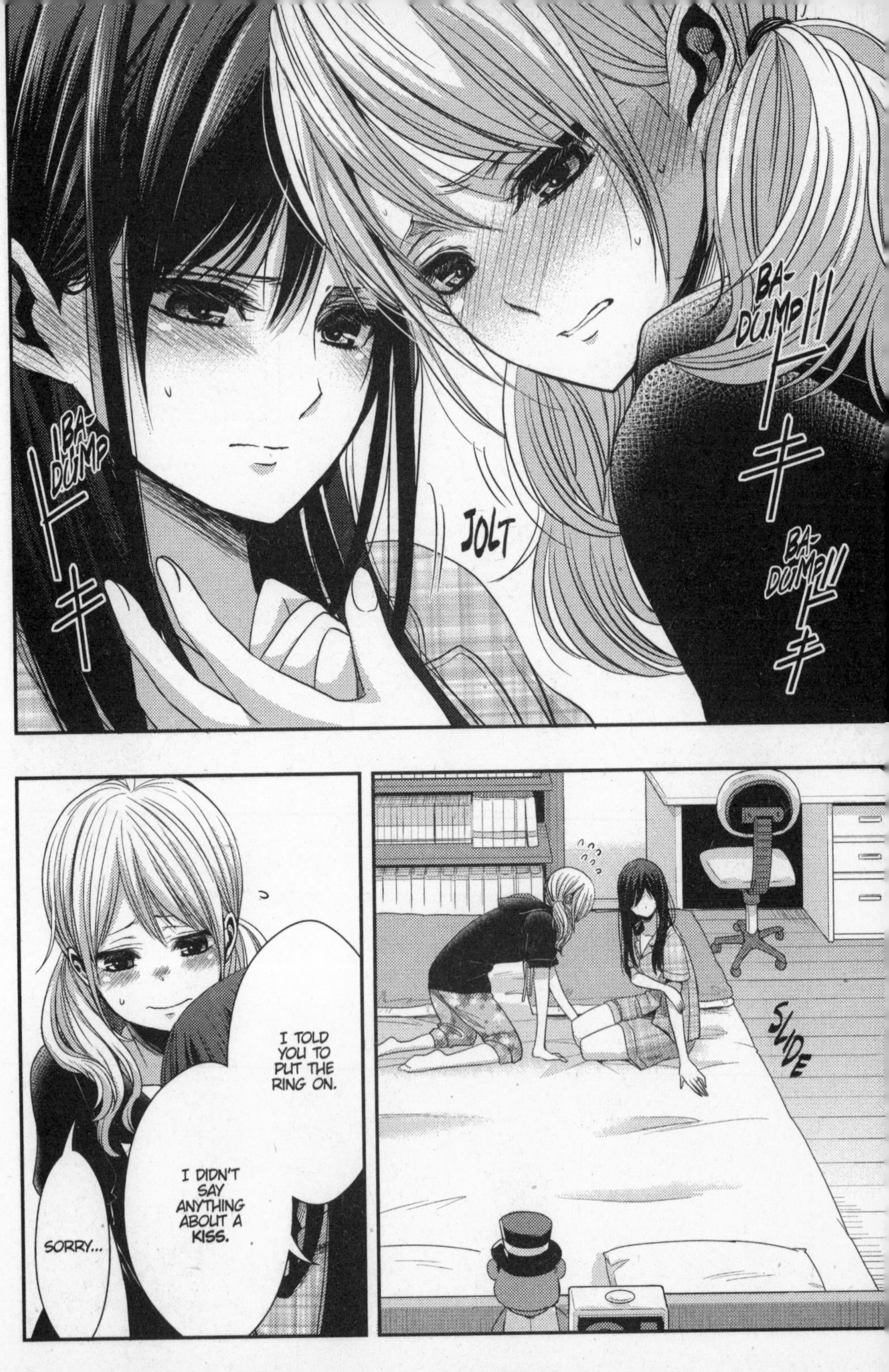
BA-DUMP
BA-DUMP
JOLT
BA-DUMP
SLIDE
I TOLD YOU TO PUT THE RING ON.
I DIDN'T SAY ANYTHING ABOUT A KISS.
SORRY...

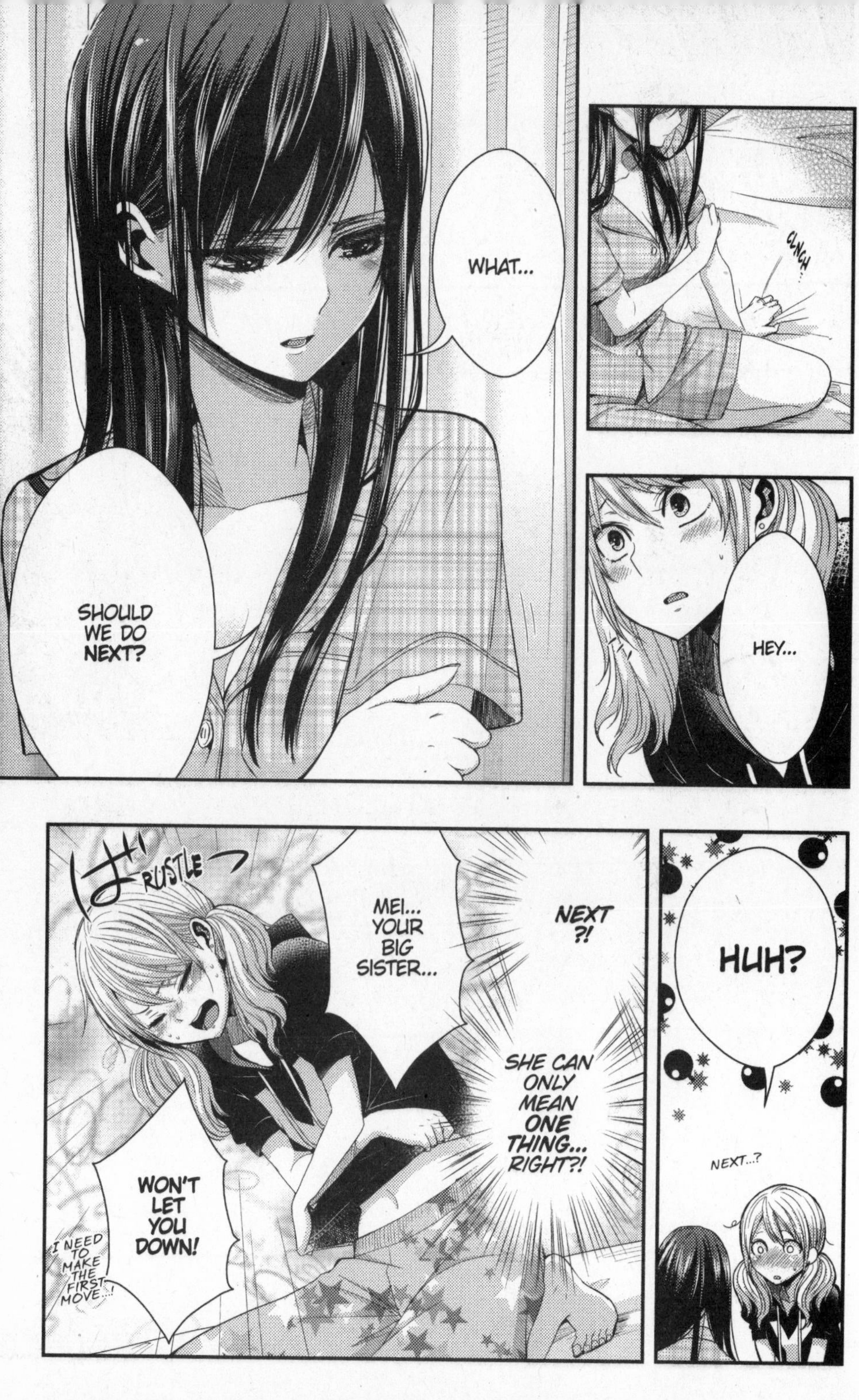
CLNCH...
HEY...
WHAT...
SHOULD WE DO NEXT?
HUH?
NEXT...?
NEXT ?!
SHE CAN ONLY MEAN ONE THING... RIGHT?!
MEI... YOUR BIG SISTER...
RUSTLE
WON'T LET YOU DOWN!
I NEED TO MAKE THE FIRST MOVE...!

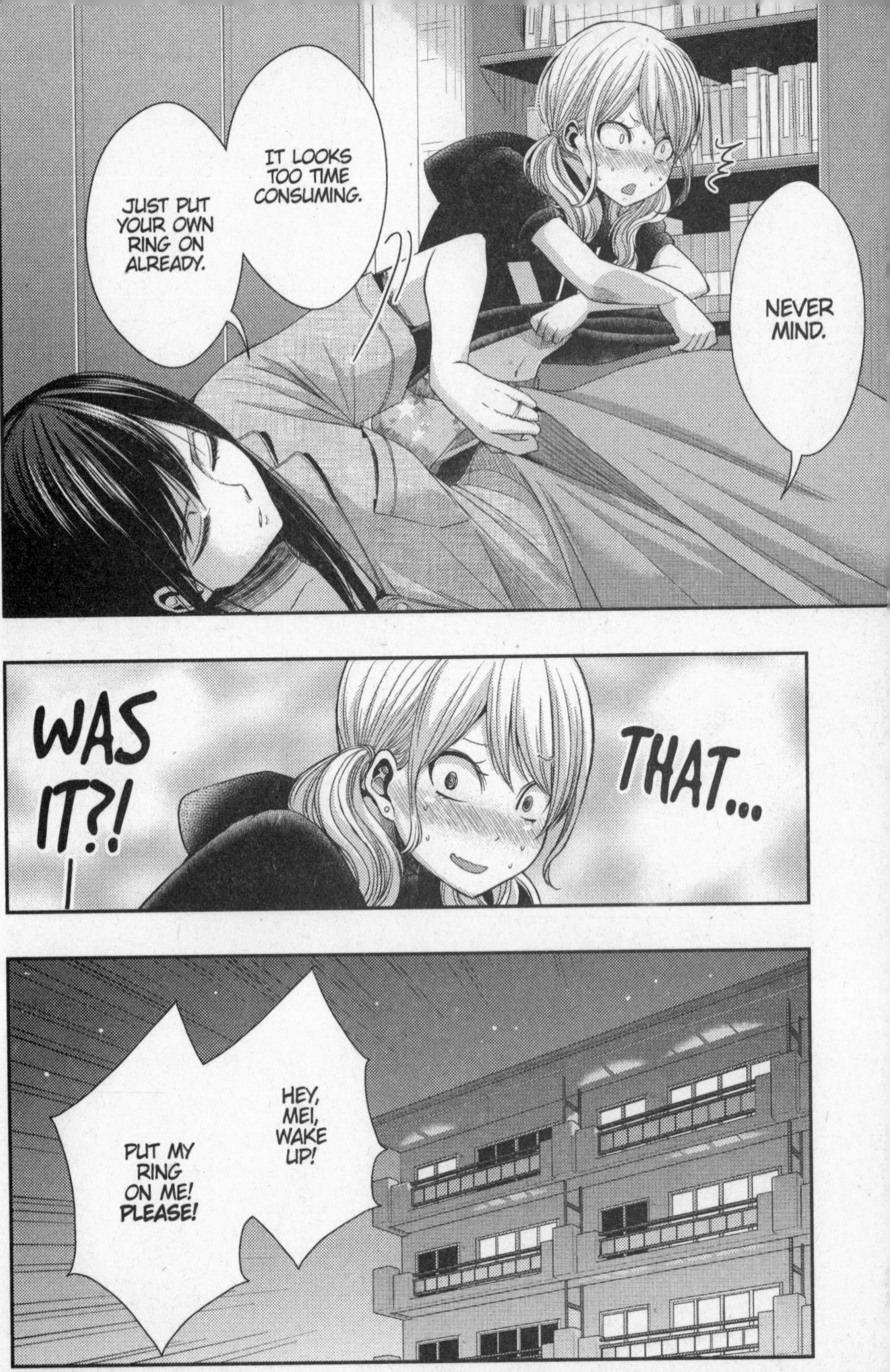
NEVER MIND.
IT LOOKS TOO TIME CONSUMING.
JUST PUT YOUR OWN RING ON ALREADY.
THAT...
WAS IT?!
HEY, MEI, WAKE UP!
PUT MY RING ON ME! PLEASE!

To be continued.

citrus

SABUROUTA PRESENTS SECRET LOVE AFFAIR WITH SISTER

6

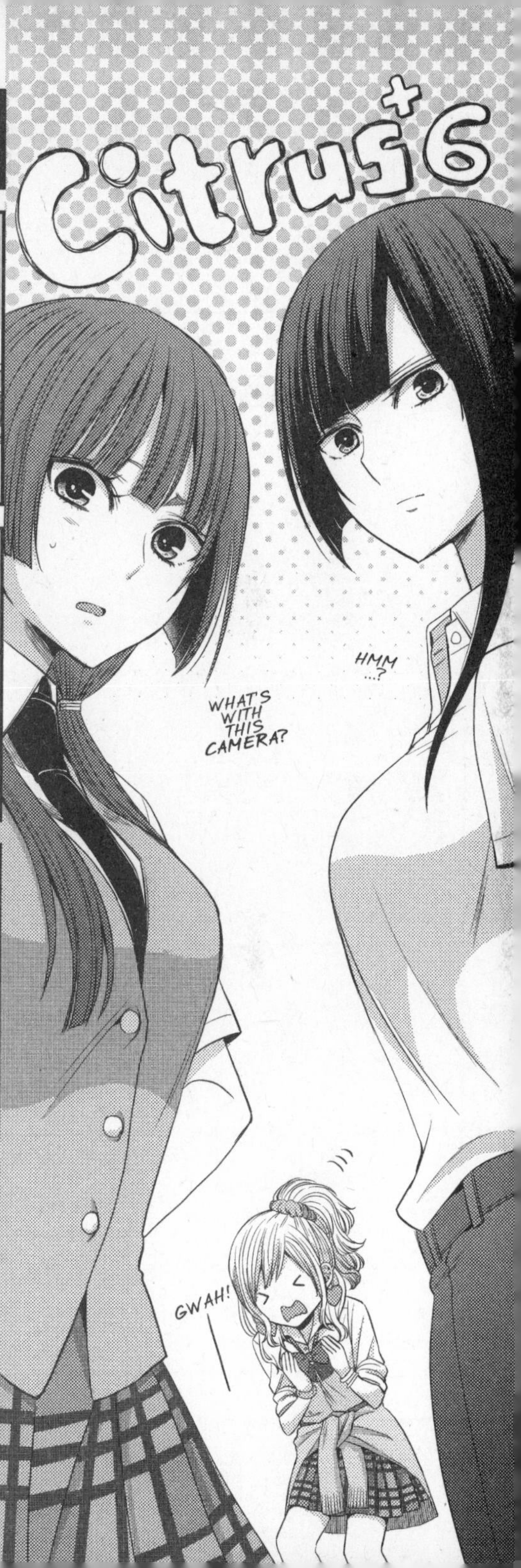
Citrus+6
HMM ...?
WHAT'S WITH THIS CAMERA?
GWAH!

OMEN

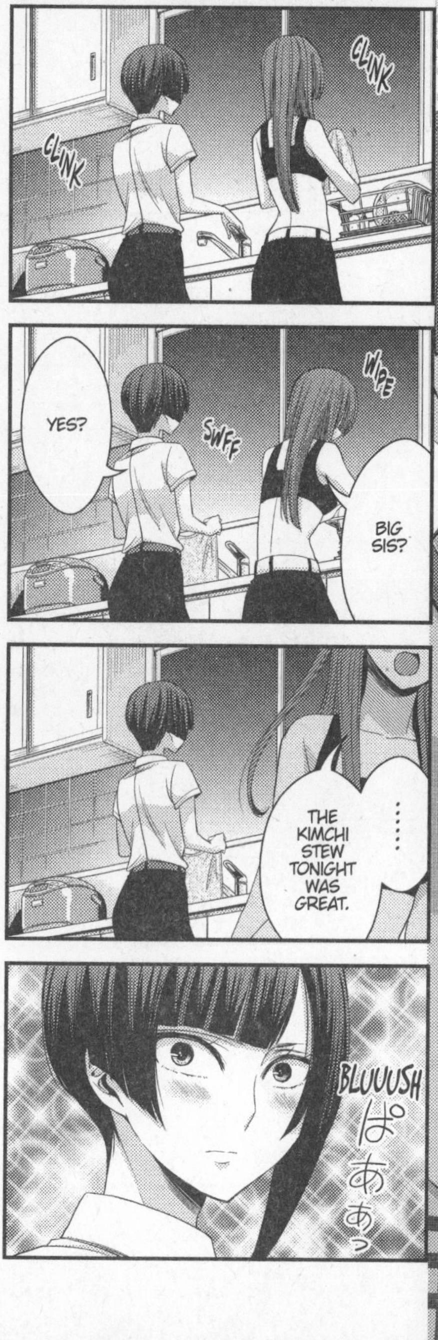
CLINK
CLINK
WIPE
SWFF
BIG SIS?
YES?
......
THE KIMCHI STEW TONIGHT WAS GREAT.
BLUUUSH
ぱあっ

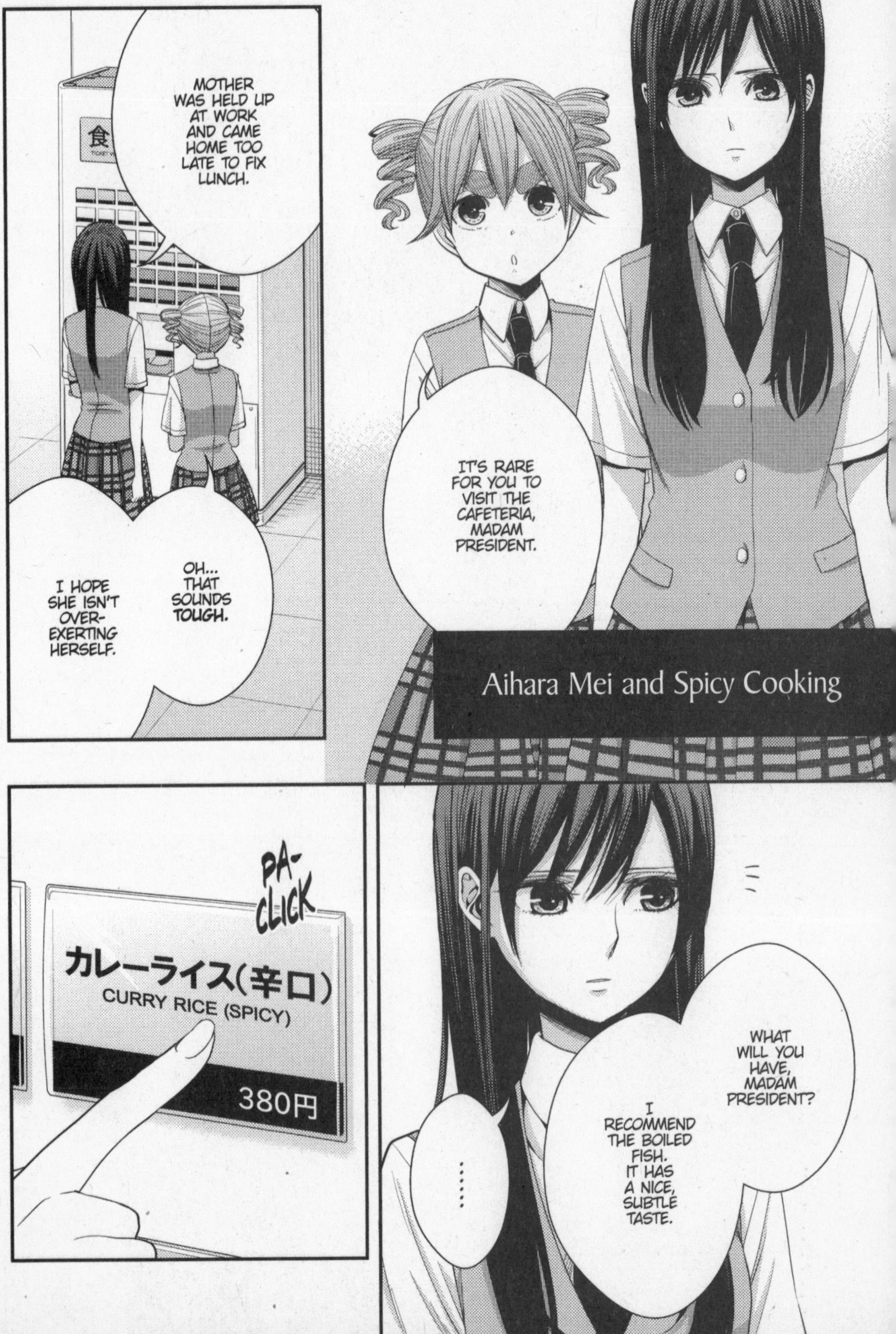
IT'S RARE FOR YOU TO VISIT THE CAFETERIA, MADAM PRESIDENT.
Aihara Mei and Spicy Cooking
MOTHER WAS HELD UP AT WORK AND CAME HOME TOO LATE TO FIX LUNCH.
OH... THAT SOUNDS TOUGH.
I HOPE SHE ISN'T OVER-EXERTING HERSELF.
WHAT WILL YOU HAVE, MADAM PRESIDENT?
I RECOMMEND THE BOILED FISH. IT HAS A NICE, SUBTLE TASTE.
......
PA-CLICK
カレーライス(辛口)
CURRY RICE (SPICY)
380円

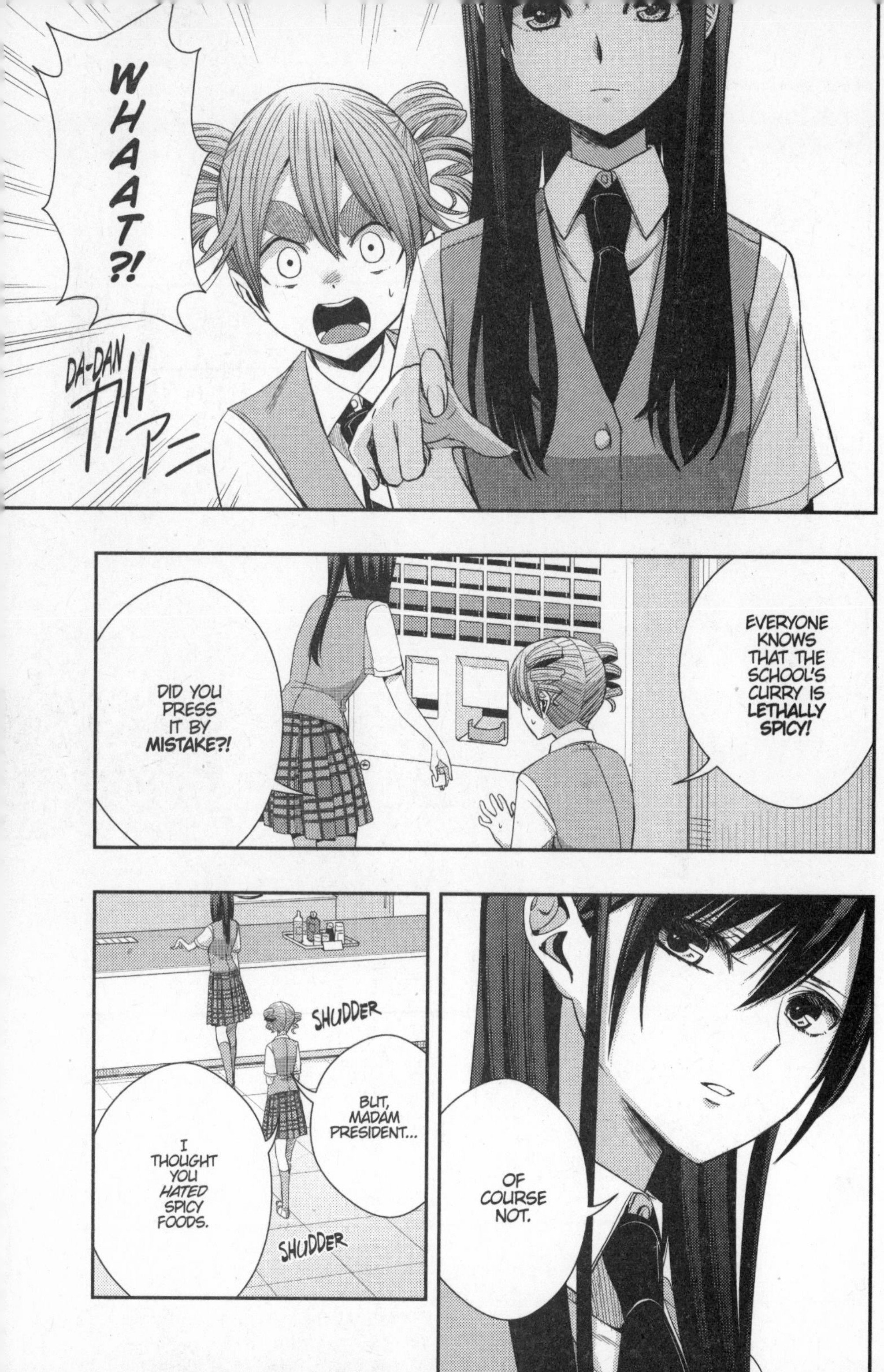
WHAAAT?!
DA-DAN
EVERYONE KNOWS THAT THE SCHOOL'S CURRY IS **LETHALLY SPICY!**
DID YOU PRESS IT BY **MISTAKE?!**
OF COURSE NOT.
SHUDDER
BUT, MADAM PRESIDENT...
I THOUGHT YOU *HATED* SPICY FOODS.
SHUDDER

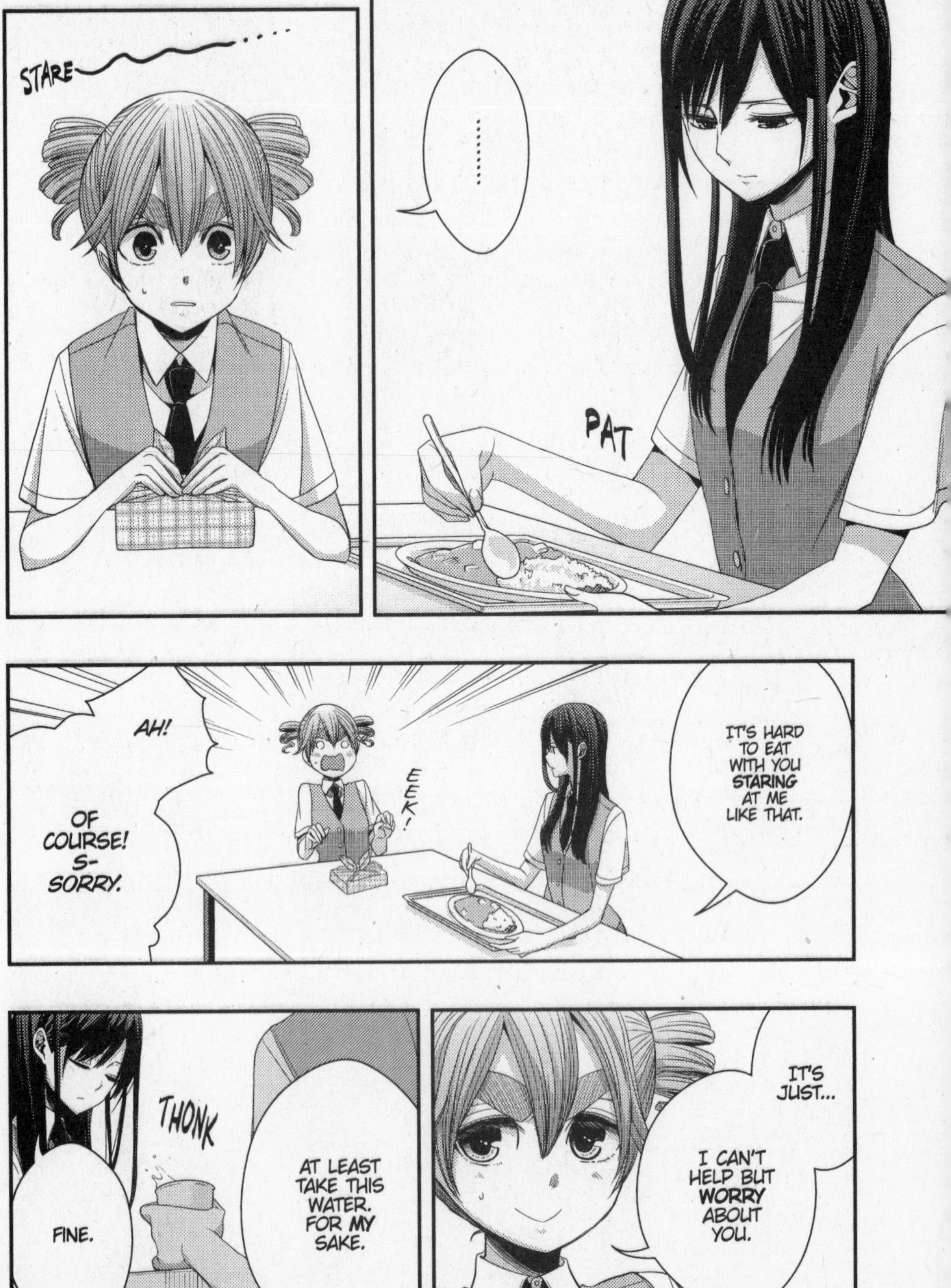
……
PAT
STARE……
IT'S HARD TO EAT WITH YOU STARING AT ME LIKE THAT.
EEK!
AH!
OF COURSE! S-SORRY.
IT'S JUST...
I CAN'T HELP BUT WORRY ABOUT YOU.
AT LEAST TAKE THIS WATER. FOR MY SAKE.
THONK
FINE.

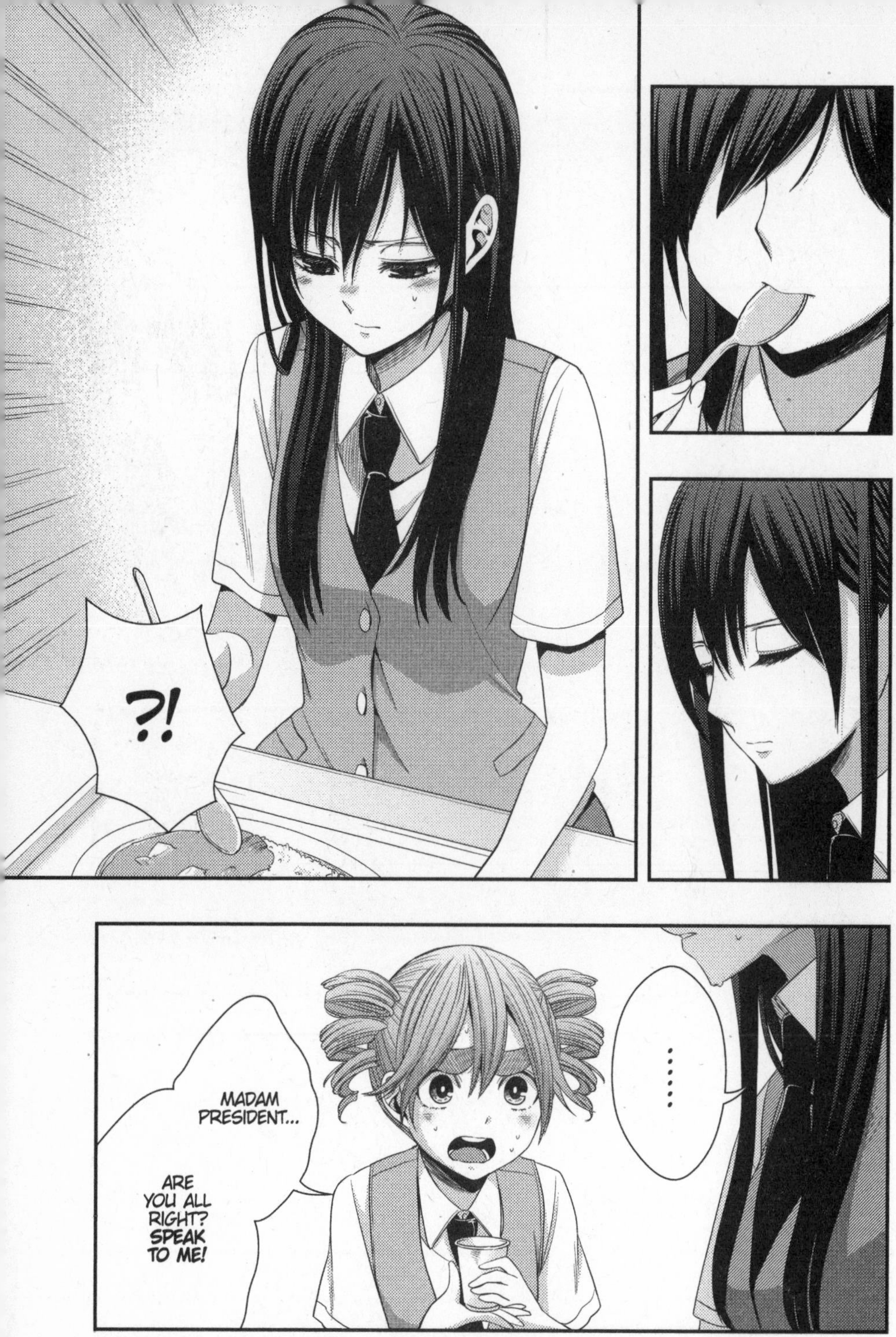
?!
......
MADAM PRESIDENT...
ARE YOU ALL RIGHT? SPEAK TO ME!

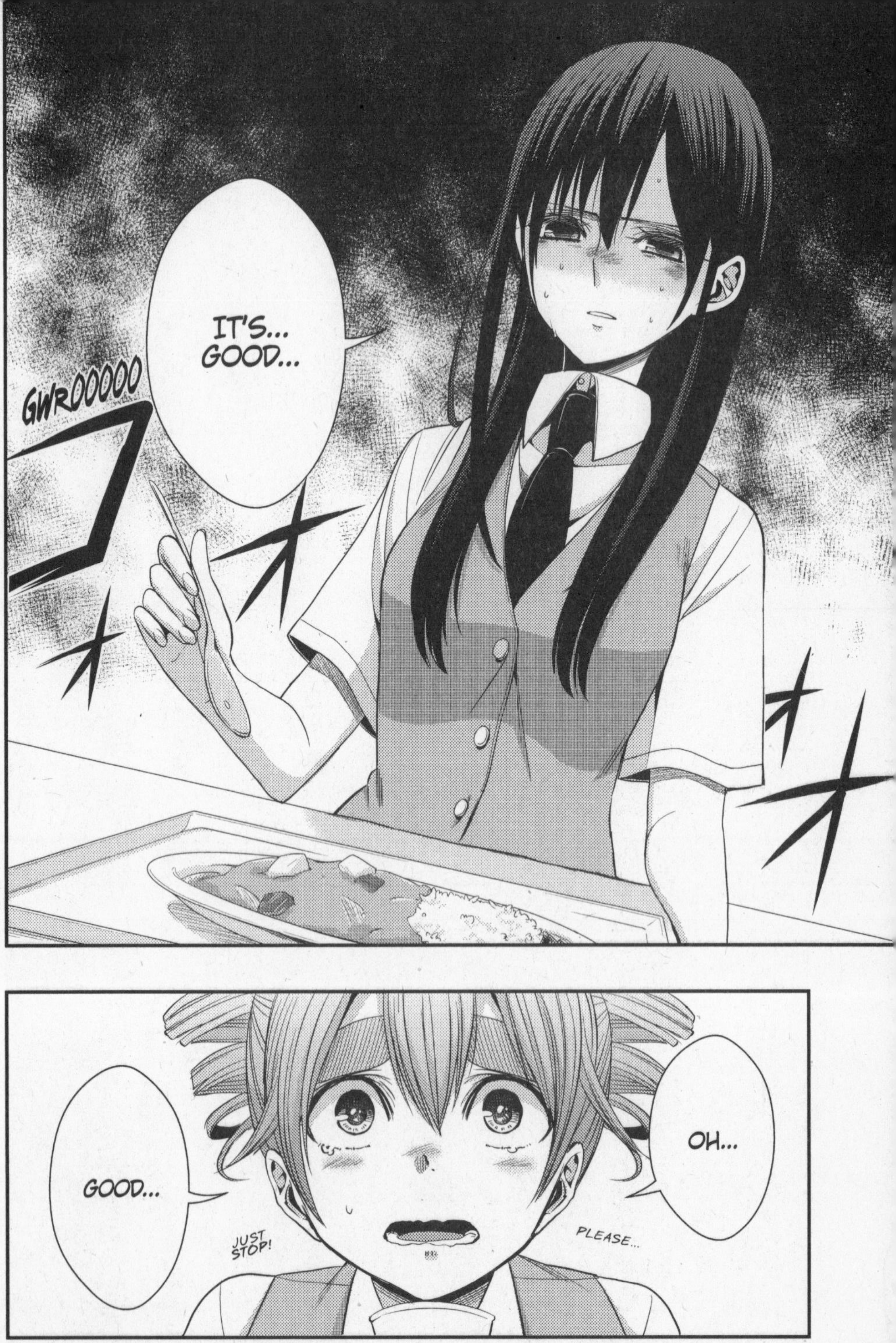
IT'S... GOOD...
GWROOOOO
OH...
PLEASE...
GOOD...
JUST STOP!

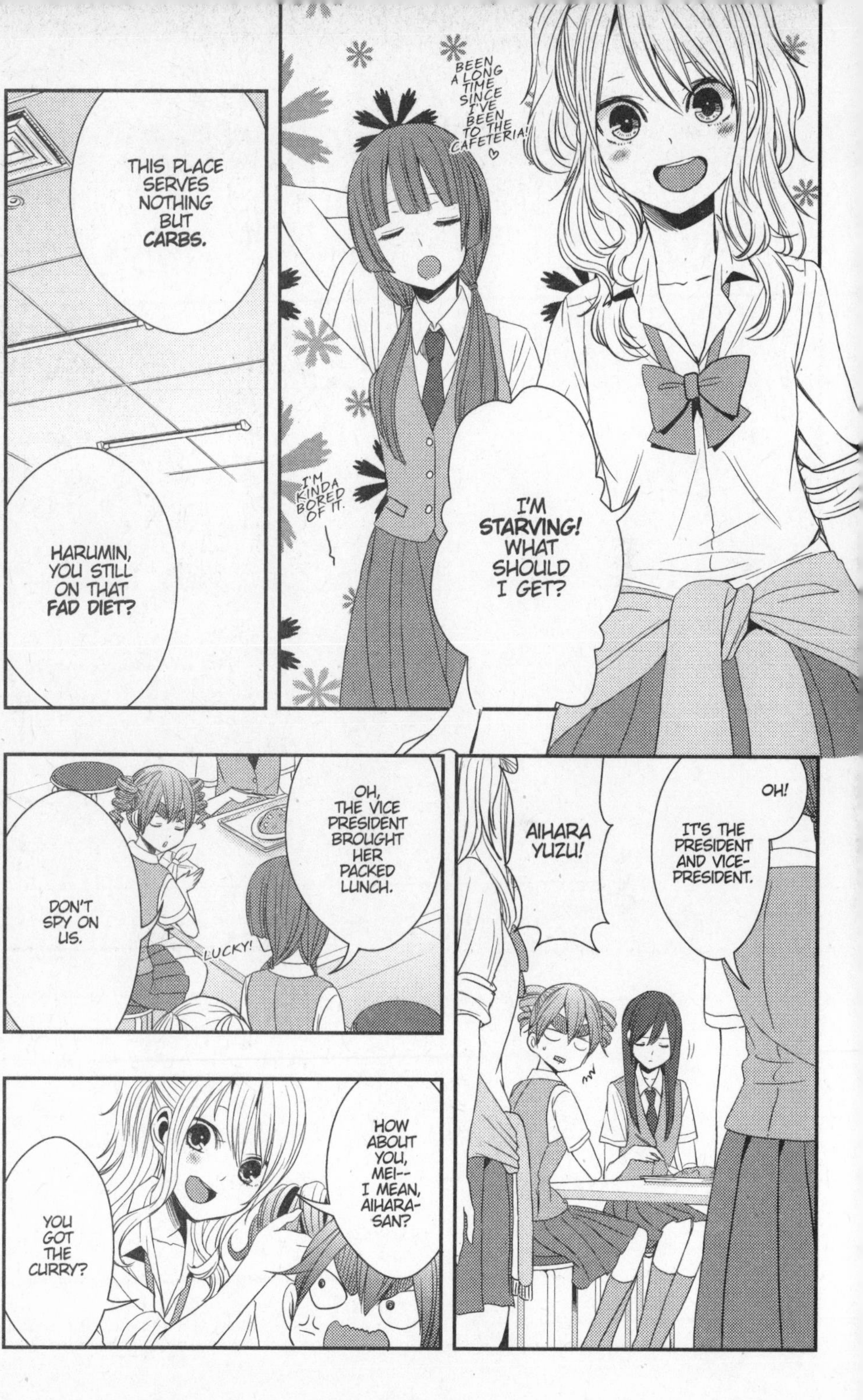
BEEN A LONG TIME SINCE I'VE BEEN TO THE CAFETERIA! ♥
I'M STARVING! WHAT SHOULD I GET?
I'M KINDA BORED OF IT.
THIS PLACE SERVES NOTHING BUT CARBS.
HARUMIN, YOU STILL ON THAT FAD DIET?
OH!
IT'S THE PRESIDENT AND VICE-PRESIDENT.
AIHARA YUZU!
OH, THE VICE PRESIDENT BROUGHT HER PACKED LUNCH.
LUCKY!
DON'T SPY ON US.
HOW ABOUT YOU, MEI-- I MEAN, AIHARA-SAN?
YOU GOT THE CURRY?

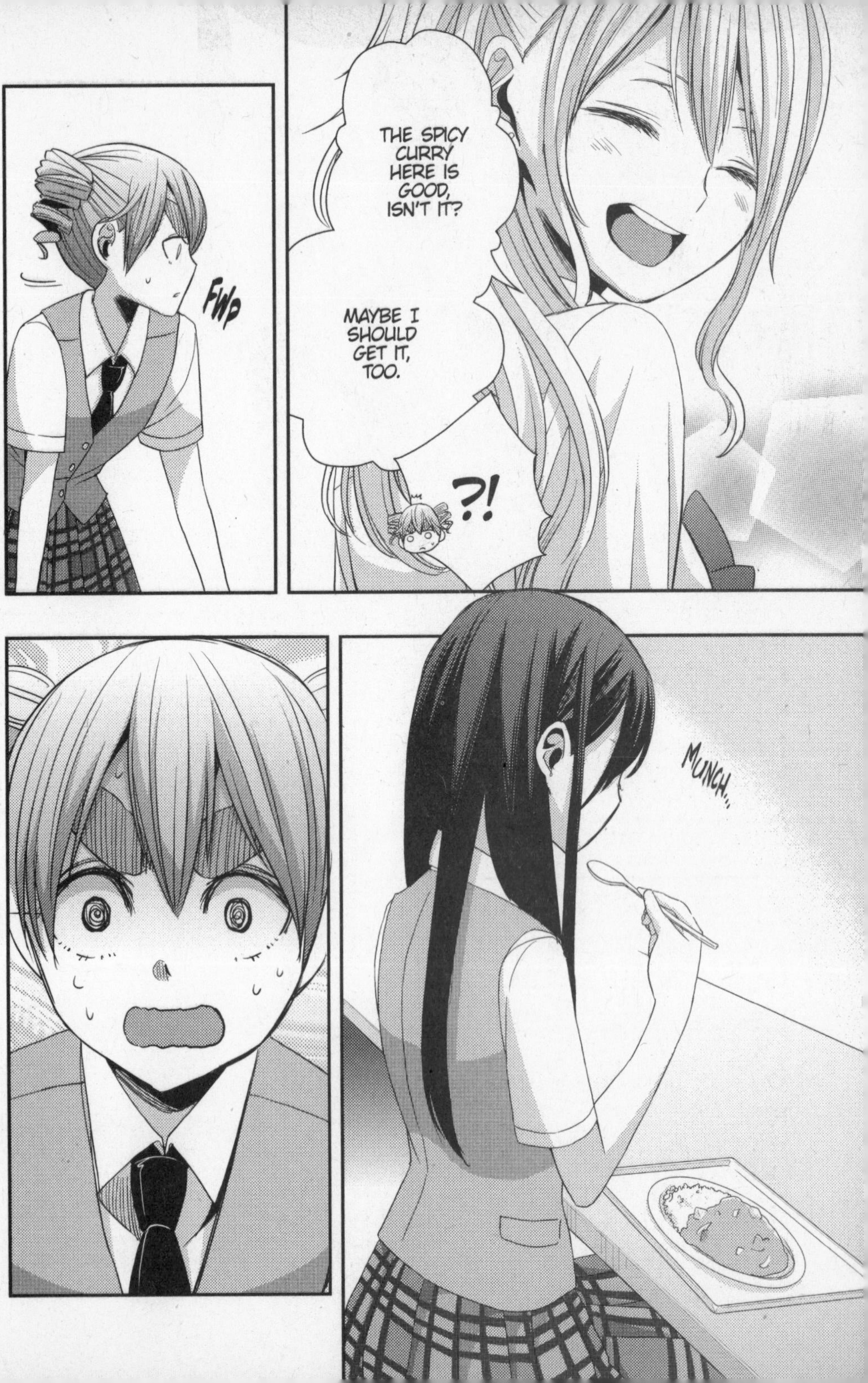
THE SPICY CURRY HERE IS GOOD, ISN'T IT?
MAYBE I SHOULD GET IT, TOO.
?!
FWP
MUNCH..

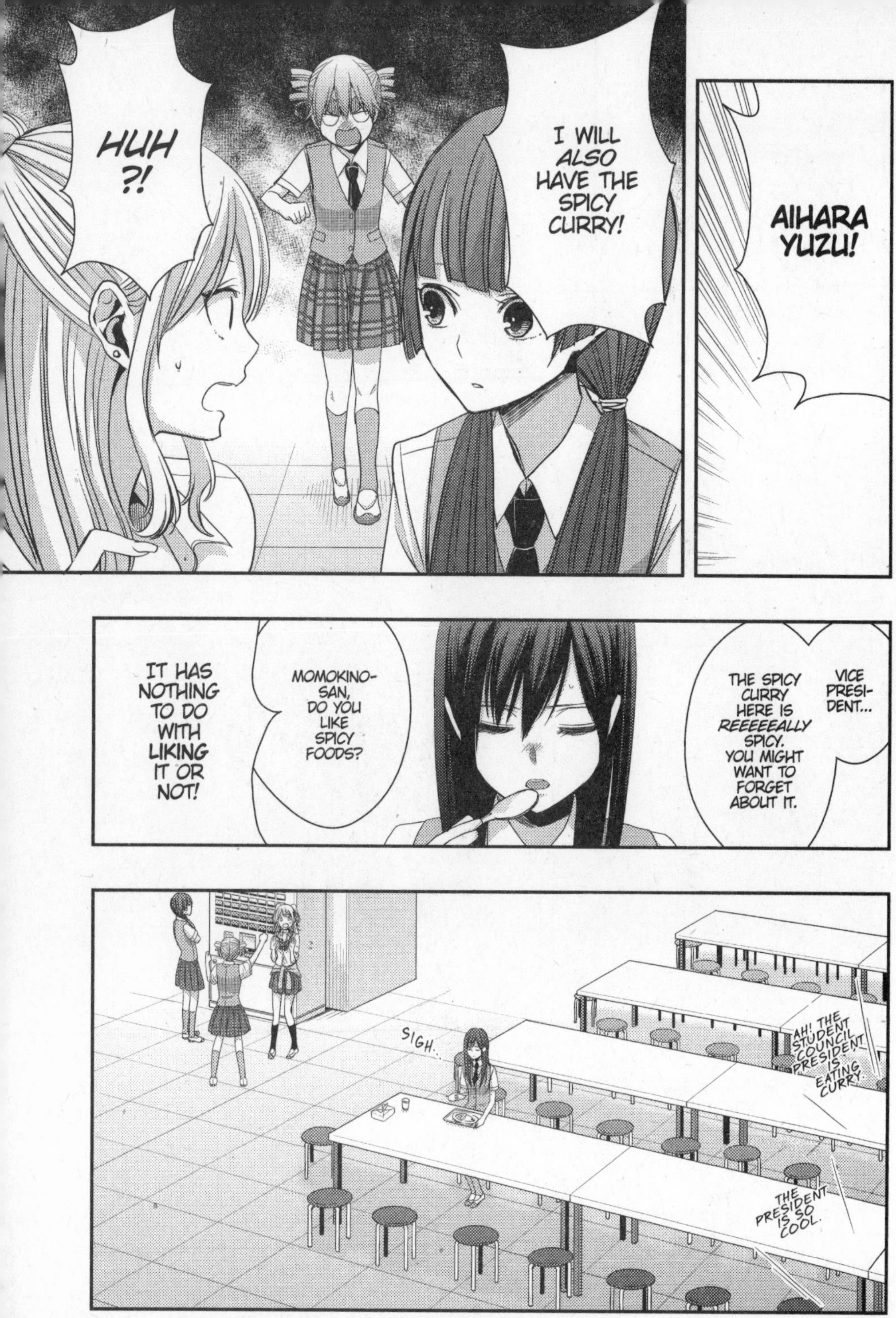
AIHARA YUZU!
I WILL ALSO HAVE THE SPICY CURRY!
HUH ?!
VICE PRESIDENT...
THE SPICY CURRY HERE IS REEEEEALLY SPICY. YOU MIGHT WANT TO FORGET ABOUT IT.
MOMOKINO-SAN, DO YOU LIKE SPICY FOODS?
IT HAS NOTHING TO DO WITH LIKING IT OR NOT!
AH! THE STUDENT COUNCIL PRESIDENT IS EATING CURRY.
THE PRESIDENT IS SO COOL.
SIGH...

THANK YOU FOR READING CITRUS VOLUME 6!!

HELLO! I'M SABUROUTA. THANK YOU VERY MUCH FOR PICKING UP VOLUME 6 OF CITRUS!

I HAVE A VERY IMPORTANT ANNOUNCEMENT... YUZU AND MEI ARE TYING THE KNOT... *COUGH COUGH* I MEAN, AN ANIME VERSION IS IN THE WORKS!! DU-DUN-DUN!

AAAH, AMAZING...! SO IT SEEMS THAT YUZU AND MEI WILL MOVE AND TALK AND KISS. WOW! (*SHAKING*) THIS IS THANKS TO EVERYONE WHO HAS SUPPORTED CITRUS AND ME. ;w; THANK YOU SO MUCH~!

YUZU AND MEI HAVE ALREADY MET SO MANY PEOPLE--AND NOW, IN THE HANDS OF SO MANY MORE, THEY WILL MOVE FORWARD, LAUGHING AND CRYING AS THEY GO. I'VE NEVER BEEN SO HAPPY.

IT'S BEEN A LONG JOURNEY, BUT FROM HERE ON, PLEASE CONTINUE TO WATCH OVER THESE TWO. [X]

WELL THEN, UNTIL NEXT TIME... HERE'S TO THEIR HAPPY FUTURE!

サブロウタ

2016.12.17

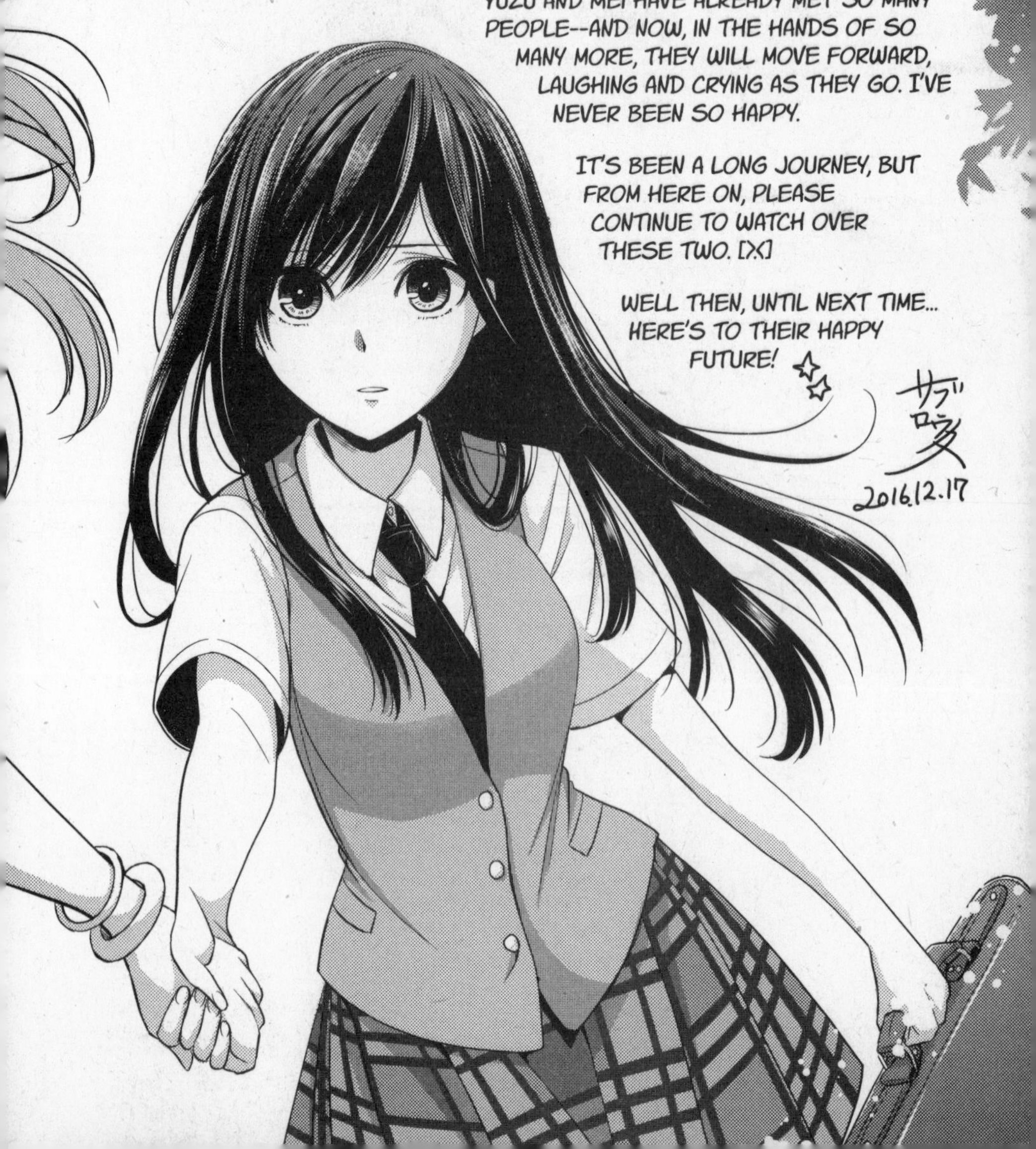

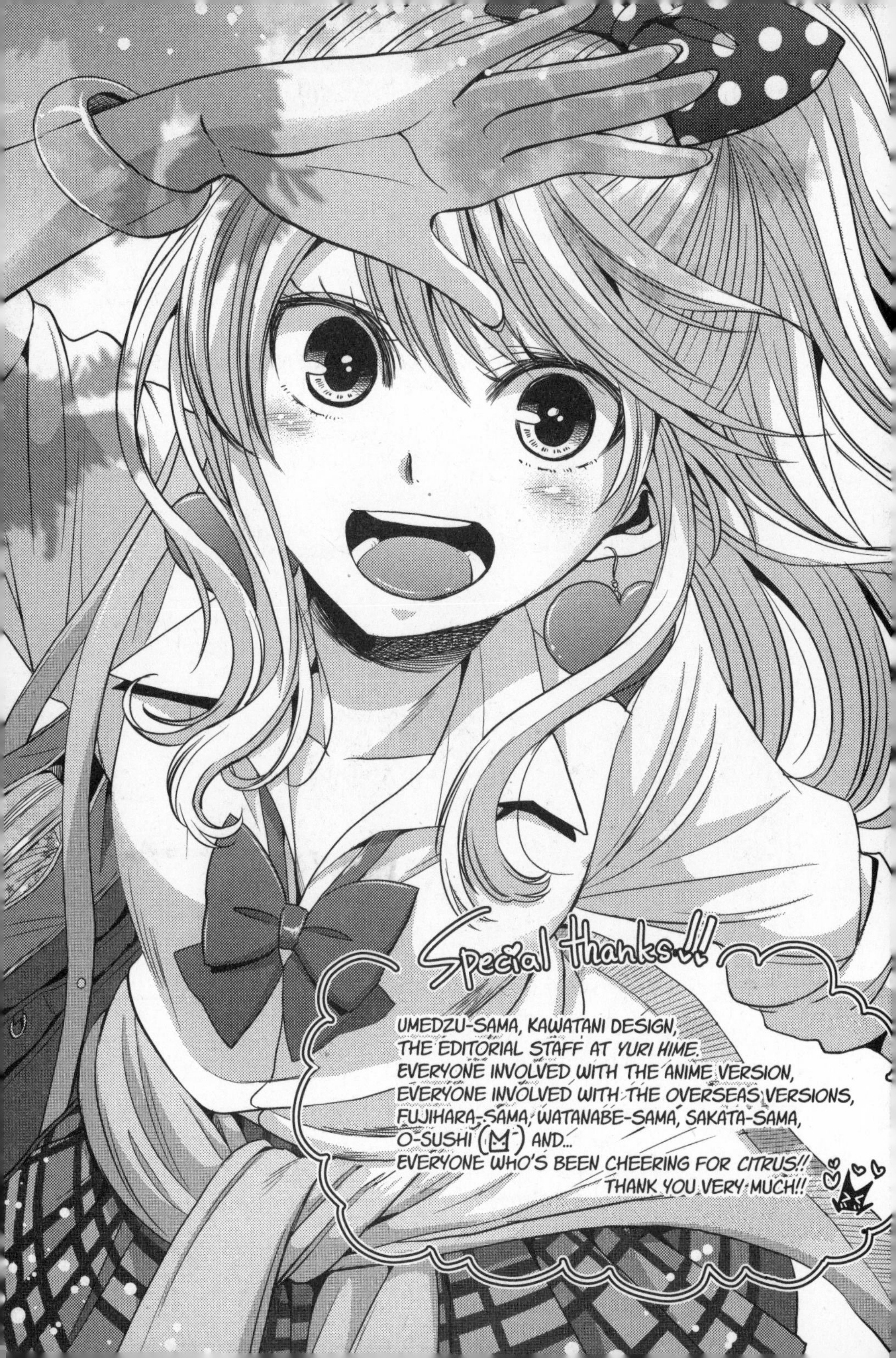
Special thanks!!
UMEDZU-SAMA, KAWATANI DESIGN,
THE EDITORIAL STAFF AT YURI HIME.
EVERYONE INVOLVED WITH THE ANIME VERSION,
EVERYONE INVOLVED WITH THE OVERSEAS VERSIONS,
FUJIHARA-SAMA, WATANABE-SAMA, SAKATA-SAMA,
O-SUSHI (M) AND...
EVERYONE WHO'S BEEN CHEERING FOR CITRUS!!
THANK YOU VERY MUCH!!

NOV 2 1 2017

citrus

story & art by **SABUROUTA**   VOLUME 6

FORTY-SEVEN

TRANSLATION **Amber Tamosaitis**	CITRUS VOLUME 6 © SABUROUTA 2017 First published in Japan in 2017 by ICHIJINSHA Inc., Tokyo. English translation rights arranged with ICHIJINSHA Inc., Tokyo, Japan.
ADAPTATION **Shannon Fay**	
LETTERING AND RETOUCH **Roland Amago** **Bambi Eloriaga-Amago**	No portion of this book may be reproduced or transmitted in any form without written permission from the copyright holders. This is a work of fiction. Names, characters, places, and incidents are the products of the author's imagination or are used fictitiously. Any resemblance to actual events, locales, or persons, living or dead, is entirely coincidental.
COVER DESIGN **Nicky Lim**	
PROOFREADER **Shanti Whitesides**	Seven Seas books may be purchased in bulk for educational, business, or promotional use. For information on bulk purchases, please contact Macmillan Corporate & Premium Sales Department at 1-800-221-7945 (ext 5442) or write specialmarkets@macmillan.com.
ASSISTANT EDITOR **Jenn Grunigen**	
PRODUCTION ASSISTANT **CK Russell**	Seven Seas and the Seven Seas logo are trademarks of Seven Seas Entertainment, LLC. All rights reserved.
PRODUCTION MANAGER **Lissa Pattillo**	ISBN: 978-1-626925-12-0
EDITOR-IN-CHIEF **Adam Arnold**	Printed in Canada First Printing: August 2017
PUBLISHER **Jason DeAngelis**	10 9 8 7 6 5 4 3 2 1

FOLLOW US ONLINE: www.gomanga.com

READING DIRECTIONS

This book reads from *right to left*, Japanese style. If this is your first time reading manga, you start reading from the top right panel on each page and take it from there. If you get lost, just follow the numbered diagram here. It may seem backwards at first, but you'll get the hang of it! Have fun!!

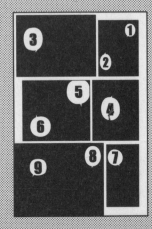